The Fate of Earthly Things

The Fate of Earthly Things
Aztec Gods and God-Bodies

>>> **Molly H. Bassett**

UNIVERSITY OF TEXAS PRESS ⌁ AUSTIN

RECOVERING
LANGUAGES & LITERACIES
OF THE AMERICAS

This book is a part of the Recovering Languages and Literacies
of the Americas publication initiative, funded by a grant from the
Andrew W. Mellon Foundation.

First edition, 2015
First paperback edition, 2015

Requests for permission to reproduce material from
this work should be sent to:
    Permissions
    University of Texas Press
    P.O. Box 7819
    Austin, TX 78713-7819
    http://utpress.utexas.edu/index.php/rp-form

∞ The paper used in this book meets the minimum
requirements of ANSI/NISO Z39.48-1992 (R1997) (Permanence of Paper).

Library of Congress Cataloging-in-Publication Data
    Bassett, Molly H., 1980– author.
    The fate of earthly things : Aztec gods and god-bodies / Molly H. Bassett.
        pages   cm. — (Recovering languages and literacies of the Americas)
    Includes bibliographical references and index.
    ISBN 978-0-292-76088-2 (cl. : alk. paper)
        1. Aztecs—Relgion. 2. Aztec gods. 3. Aztecs—Rites and ceremonies. I. Title.
F1219.76.R45B375   2015
299.7'8452—dc23   2014018627

ISBN 978-1-4773-0986-5 (pbk.)
doi:10.7560/760882

For Mike

>>>

People came to Tenochtitlan and moved through its ritual topography in part to see the processions, mock battles, and human sacrifices; to see the images of gods and deity impersonators; to gaze at the sacred places where they were consecrated; to see humans changed into gods; and to see other human beings seeing the divine in ceremonies and visions.
David Carrasco, *City of Sacrifice*

>>>

In Mexico, idolatry had attained to its full barbaric development. As in the Aztec mind the world swarmed with spiritual deities, so their material representatives, the idols, stood in the houses at the corners of the streets, on every hill and rock, to receive from passers-by some little offering—a nosegay, a whiff of incense, a drop or two of blood; while in the temples more huge and elaborate images enjoyed the dances and processions in their honour, were fed by the bloody sacrifice of men and beasts, and received the tribute and reverence paid to the great national gods.... [But] there is a general want of express statement how far the idols of America remained mere symbols or portraits, or how far they had come to be considered the animated bodies of the gods.
Edward B. Tylor, *Primitive Culture,* Vol. 2

>>>

The criticism of idolatry on the grounds that idols are not "alive" as human beings are (biologically) alive, or that idols are not realistic automata, but only statues, misses the point on both counts. The idol is worshipped because it is neither a person, nor a miraculous machine, but a god.

Alfred Gell, *Art and Agency*

CONTENTS

ACKNOWLEDGMENTS

Thank you:

. . . to the Instituto de Docencia e Investigación Etnológica de Zacatecas (IDIEZ) and my colleagues there, John Sullivan, Delfina de la Cruz, Manuel de la Cruz, Victoriano de la Cruz, Abelardo de la Cruz, Catalina de la Cruz, Sabina de la Cruz, and Ofelia Morales. No podría pedir mejores compañeros. Tlazcamati miyac.

. . . to the parents of Delfina and Manuel, for welcoming me into your community during Chicomexochitl, and to my host family for opening your home and kitchen to me in the hot Huastecan summer. A los padres de Delfina y Manuel, y a mi familia anfitriona, tlazcamati.

. . . to Joe Campbell for so generously sharing your Florentine Codex.

. . . to Rudy Busto for working through many lists and multiple drafts with me and for showing me how to be a scholar and a teacher.

. . . to Jeanette Peterson for your collegiality, collaboration, and friendship.

. . . to Davíd Carrasco for sending me on to Santa Barbara and keeping me in the Archive circle.

. . . to David White for incisive conversations and encouragement early on.

. . . to Kathryn McClymond, who read and offered feedback on portions of the book; Isaac Weiner, who helped me problem-solve along the way; Vincent Lloyd, whose marked-flesh project motivated me to think differently about flayed skins; and Kent Brintnall, who helped me think through the introduction.

. . . to colleagues who have read drafts, shared wisdom, and offered inspiration and insight: Kelly McDonough, María Ramos, Charles H. Long, Victoriano de la Cruz, Julia Madajczak, JoDavid Sales, Gene Gallagher, Gerardo Aldana, Barbara Holdrege, León García Garagarza, Randy Garr, Apostolos Athanassakis, Katrina Kimport, Deborah Spivak, Colleen Windham-Hughes, Annalise Glauz-Todrank, Ali Bjerke, Megan Sijapati, and Jared Cain.

. . . to my family: the Harbours, the Bassetts, and the Burrs.

. . . to the members of my department, a good-spirited group of colleagues, and to our supportive staff.

. . . to the librarians at Georgia State University, the University of California Santa Barbara, and Harvard's Tozzer Library.

. . . to Mary Grace Dupree, Natalie Barber, Kathryn Yates, Nick Newell, and Suzanne Tryon, my graduate student assistants.

. . . to Theresa May, Molly Frisinger, Nancy Warrington, and the University of Texas Press editorial staff, who have been gracious and patient while working with me.

. . . to the Press's anonymous readers for offering thoughtful and constructive criticisms. (Any errors that remain are my own.)

. . . to *Material Religion* and *History of Religions* for their permission to use my published materials.

. . . to the institutions that have supported my research and writing: the Department of Education's Foreign Language Area Studies Grant, the University of California's Chancelor's Fellowship, the University of California Institute for Mexico and the United States Dissertation Grant, UCSB Department of Religious Studies summer grants, Georgia State University's Cleon C. Arrington Research Initiation Grant, a PAG Grant from Georgia State's Center for Latin American and Latino Studies, a Wabash Fellowship, and the Mellon Foundation's Recovering Languages and Literacies of the Americas Initiative.

And one singular thank-you:

. . . to Mike, who moved across the country twice; who encouraged me in this and other outlandish pursuits; and whose generosity, good sense of humor, and affection are animating and sustaining.

God-Bodies, Talk-Makers

Deity Embodiments in Nahua Religions

The Mexicas walked out of their place of origin many years before they finally stepped into the Central Valley.[1] During their long and winding peregrination, the people frequently begged their patron god Huitzilopochtli to settle, but he forced them to press on again and again. When the Mexicas finally arrived in the Central Valley, the Colhuas, an established polity, allowed them to live at Tizaapan, an area believed to be uninhabitable because of an epic scorpion and snake infestation. Against these odds, the Mexicas thrived in Tizaapan, a feat that launched their reputation as fierce and fearless. Seeing that his people were prepared—yet again—to settle permanently, Huitzilopochtli called his priests and officials. The following events took place near the end of their migration; seventeenth-century Nahua historian Chimalpahin dates it to "the year Thirteen Reed, 1323."[2]

After gathering his senior officials, Huitzilopochtli asked them to travel to nearby Colhuacan and invite Achitometl, the local ruler, to send his daughter to Tizaapan. Huitzilopochtli told the priests, "oc ce tlacatl y neciz. ytoca yaocihuatl. ca nocitzin." (My fathers, another personage is to appear. Her name is Yaocihuatl; she is my grandmother. And we are to acquire her.)[3] Diego Durán explains that Huitzilopochtli planned to marry her, and both sources attest that Huitzilopochtli wanted the young woman to become Yaocihuatl (Enemy Woman) and be venerated as Toci, Tonantzin (Our mother, our grandmother).[4] She would motivate the Mexicas to leave Tizaapan and move on to founding their own city.

And so the priests went to Colhuacan and asked Achitometl for his daughter's hand in marriage:

> nopiltzitzine tlacatle tlahtohuanie. ca timitztotlatlauhtilia yn timocolhuan yn timomacehualhuan yhua yn ixquichtin yn Mexica. ca ticmomacahuiliz ca titechmomaquiliz. yn mocozqui yn moquetzal yn mochpochtzin yn toxhuiuhtzin yn cihuapilli ca ompa motlapiellitiez. y noncan yn tepetitlan tiçaapan.

(My nobleman, lord, ruler, we beg you, we who are your grandfathers, we who are your subjects, and all the Mexica, to concede, to give us your necklace, your precious quetzal feather, your daughter, the noblewoman our granddaughter. She will be watched over there among the mountains in [Tizaapan].)[5]

Achitometl "was enthralled by the idea that she should reign and be a living goddess, so he surrendered her to the Aztecs."[6] When she arrived in Tizaapan, the priests followed Huitzilopochtli's instructions:

[They] took the young princess of Colhuacan, heiress to that kingdom, and killed her, sacrificing her to their god. They then flayed her and dressed one of the principal youths in her skin, as their deity had willed. Then they went to the sovereign of Colhuacan and invited him to come adore his own daughter and offer sacrifices to her as a goddess, since Huitzilopochtli had proclaimed her his bride and his mother.[7]

Or:

auh niman ye quimictia. yn quixipehua yn cihuapilli. yn oconxipeuhque yn iyehuayo nima ye conaquia. yn ce tlacatl tlamacazqui. Auh niman oquihto yn Huitzilopochtli. notlahuane tla xicnotzati yn achitometl.

(And then they killed and flayed the noblewoman. When they had flayed her, they then dressed a certain offering priest in her skin. And then Huitzilopochtli said: My fathers, summon Achitometl.)[8]

Achitometl accepted the Aztecs' invitation to attend his daughter's wedding and see the goddess, and when he arrived with rubber, copal, tobacco, flowers, and quail, Huitzilopochtli's priests led him inside the dark temple:

nima ye conana yn holli. yn copalli. yn xochitl. yn iyetl yn tlacatlaqualli. ye quitlamamaca yxpan quitequillia yn çan tlapic yteouh. in yehuatl yn oquixipeuhque. auh in yehuatl yn achitometl. niman ye yc yxpan quin-quechcotona yn çoçoltin, yn iteouh.

(Then he took up the rubber, the copal incense, the flowers, the tobacco, and the abstinence foods. He distributed, he laid them out before his pretended god, her whom they had flayed.)[9]

When Achitometl lit his brazier of incense, he was (understandably) shocked and horrified to see a priest enfleshed in his daughter's skin: "yn achitometl. cenca omomauhti." (Achitometl was exceedingly terrified.)[10] He declared war upon the Mexicas, saying, "They have killed my daughter, they have flayed her and dressed a youth in her skin and have made me worship him!"[11]

This vignette established the mythohistorical paradigm for the ritual process through which the Aztecs manufactured localized embodiments of their gods. The young Colhua woman's sacrifice brought about the apotheosis of Toci, Tonantzin in the person who wore the flayed skin. By virtue of wearing the skin, the ritual actor *became the goddess*. In this example, a human body became a god-body, but *teteo* (gods) and their *teixiptlahuan* (localized embodiments) took many forms in Aztec religion, including effigies made of natural materials and *tlaquimilolli* (sacred bundles) that contained precious objects. What might be surprising is that the manufacture of god-bodies has persisted well past Contact. Hernando Ruiz de Alarcón (1574–1646) describes ritual specialists engaging in deity embodiment, and today speakers of modern Nahuatl preserve *costumbres* (traditions) that incorporate *totiotzin* (gods) made from paper into their daily lives.

While it would be misguided and misleading to claim that either Alarcón's contemporaries or my own preserve "Aztec religion," the idea that ritual activity—and most notably the intentional creation of deity embodiments—can affect nature and culture remains current among Nahuatl speakers. Narratives shared by Nahuatl speakers past and present provide the primary frame of reference for my examination of *teotl* (god), *teixiptla* (localized embodiment), and *tlaquimilolli* (sacred bundle). These three Nahuatl terms lie at the foundation of Aztec religion and find their best expression in the stories about them. Accounts like the one above and those that follow situate these terms in scenarios where the actions of the gods and their embodiments have a direct and often immediate effect on the lives of their devotees. In the instance above, the Mexica patron deity guides his devotees toward their homeland, and in the process, they establish ritual models for practices the Aztecs continued into the early sixteenth century.

Myth, History, and Mythohistory: Studying the Gods of Nahua Religions

In the following, I will explore the questions of what *teotl* (god) meant in Aztec religion and how *teteo* (gods) came to be present in *teixiptlahuan* (localized embodiments). My work involves analyzing the terms' etymology, investigating their construction and functions, and exploring how they might prompt a reexamination of existing theories of animacy, agency, and embodiment—all with an awareness of the concepts' histories of interpretation. Throughout, I insist on the importance of understanding the terms and their visual and physical manifestations in context: in the context of Nahuatl or of the codex in which they appear or of the ritual stage upon which they acted. Interpreting *teotl* or *teixiptla* from only one vantage point—that of linguistics *or* iconography *or* t(h)eology—would impede appreciating the relationship between *teteo* and their *teixiptlahuan*, let alone the ways in which devotees interacted with them. Understanding Nahua gods as mere names, as lifeless representations, or as supernatural essences separable from the bodies they inhabited fails to appreciate the fullness of their animacy and the intricacies of these religions.

One of the challenges of studying Nahua religions, especially that of the Aztecs, centers squarely on the kind, origin, and number of sources available to scholars. In this study of Aztec religion, I draw principally on alphabetic texts and codices, pictorial texts made in pre-Contact styles. The relative paucity of pre-Contact sources makes archaeological data and material culture essential to the work of interpreting Aztec culture. The lack of pre-Contact sources, a wealth of (variously biased) colonial sources, and the scholarly and cultural contributions of the modern descendants of Mesoamerican peoples simultaneously enrich and complicate reconstructions of pre-Contact Mesoamerica.

To further complicate matters, some of the best alphabetic sources are also the most problematic sources. For example, sixteenth-century friars' descriptions of pre-Contact and early colonial Nahua culture offer unparalleled insight into their subjects, but they tend to see the New World through Old World eyes. After alphabetizing Nahuatl, which prior to Contact had been a spoken language represented by ideograms, friars produced numerous texts that served the religious and secular needs of the colonial project in New Spain. Their texts are indispensable tools in understanding pre-Contact and post-Contact religiosity, but the stories they tell are embedded in layers of conflicting motivations and cross purposes. Intentionally or not, they occlude as much as they reveal.

My interpretations of these sources, their form and contents, depend both on understanding the cultures that produced them as well as on my awareness of the methods of study I bring to them. Modern critical theories' potential to clarify the relationship between deities and their embodiments, for instance, depends on one's willingness to engage in "reading" sources that rarely distinguish between categories taken for granted in the modern West: history and myth, natural and supernatural, or profane and sacred. Finding a way through history and myth is both a first step and a model for how I will interpret Aztec religion.

The extent to which accounts of Mesoamerica's past are "history" or "myth" has been contested by Mesoamericanists at least since the time of German anthropologist Eduard Seler (1849–1922). (Seler came down squarely in favor of myth's preponderance.) In a recent reprisal of this contestation, Federico Navarrete Linares argues that as long as we understand "myth" and "history" as mutually exclusive categories, neither can do justice to the rich stories codices, colonial texts, and contemporary voices tell about Mesoamerica.[12] Thinking of myths as fictitious accounts embedded with symbols that need analysis and of history as a straightforward narration of events as they actually proceeded leads to continually misunderstanding both what might have happened *and* the importance of how Mesoamericans and colonial Mexicans narrated what they said happened.[13] Michel-Rolph Trouillot underscores the importance of remembering that histories are produced by historical agents/ narrators: "In vernacular use, history means both the facts of the matter and a narrative of those facts, both 'what happened' and 'that which is said to have happened.' The first meaning places the emphasis on the sociohistorical process, the second on our knowledge of that process or on a story about that process."[14] In Mesoamerica and many indigenous Mexican communities today, the symbolic potential of myths and the powerful claims of history function as complementary (rather than as competing) means of communicating about and engaging in the world.

Throughout this text, I read mythohistory as a version of historiography and Mesoamerican historiography as largely a product of the contact perspective that emerged during the Encounter. In *The History of a Myth*, Gary Urton uses the word "mythohistory" to signal the "potentially equal and simultaneous, and thus fully ambiguous, mythical and historical status of the accounts contained in [the Spanish chronicles]."[15] I adopt this term in order to gesture to the shortcomings of both "history" and "myth" with respect to the texts produced in pre-Contact (oral and pictographic) and post-Contact (alphabetic and pictorial/pictographic) Nahuatl.[16] Thinking of "historiography"—the writings produced about Mesoamerican religions—as mythohistory facilitates my examination of the ideological frameworks through which writers from the early colonial period until today have interpreted *teotl*, *teixiptla*, and *tlaquimilolli*.

In his introduction to *Letters from Mexico*, Anthony Pagden characterizes Cortés's letters to Charles V as histories: "The two surviving manuscript copies of the letters, one in Vienna, the other in Madrid, are both compiled as if they constituted a history of the conquest, which in a sense they do."[17] In these letters, Cortés described his experiences in New Spain and intimated his expectations for the future, and he did this not just for the benefit of the king but also for a public readership. Pagden makes the case that, for Cortés, the letters constituted a public relations campaign. To the extent that he included historical elements in the *cartas*, they served his own immediate needs, and with the help of his father, Cortés worked to ensure that each letter arrived in Spain as soon as possible and was immediately published.

Cortés was "acutely aware of the importance of arguing his case before posterity. If his *fama et gloria* which, as he knew, were the nobleman's most precious, and most precarious, possessions were to survive, they had to be preserved for later generations in his own words, and in print."[18] Cortés's letters were not a history of the distant past nor were they intended to be a history for readers of the distant future. Neither were the letters, chronicles, and accounts of many other Contact-era writers. To the extent that some of them did provide accounts of the pre-Contact past, such as Durán in his *History of the Indies of New Spain* (ca. 1581), confining their texts to the genre of "history" would conceal other aspects of the stories they were telling, including those moments in which the religious imagination—whether of the author or his subjects—emerges.

The Work of Storytelling and Translation

The simultaneity and ambiguity that characterize Contact-era chronicles and modern Nahua accounts of the (super)natural world remind us of the tangled relationships between happening, experience, and storytelling. These were and are worlds in which devotees fashioned mountain-shaped deity embodiments and venerated mountains as god-bodies. Neither the fabricated nature of these enchanted *teixiptlahuan* (localized embodiments) nor the stories told about them detract from their lively participation in their communities; quite the opposite. In *Other Peoples' Myths*, a study of the stories told about stories, Wendy Doniger emphasizes the compelling action of myth, a characteristic we could extend to mythohistory:

> The myth is persuasive to us because the *action* itself is persuasive. Even when what happens in the myth is not physically possible in this world (as when, for instance, a man turns into a fish), when the event is described in detail, as something that happened, we can *see* it happening, and so it enlarges our sense of what might be possible. Only a story can do this. Myth, then, is a story, or a narrative. How, then, is it different from other narratives, from the narratives of history or the narratives of legend? . . . Let me merely say that the stories that I want to talk

about as myths (and that I wish to distinguish from, for example, stories about George Washington or Paul Bunyan) are about the sorts of questions that religions ask, stories about such things as life after death, divine intervention in human lives, transformations, the creation of the world and of human nature and culture—and, basically, about meaning itself.[19]

The action of myth—what a myth does—concerns Doniger more than the definition of "myth." What she calls the myth's action is like effective speech. J. L. Austin called effective speech "performative utterances," meaning the kind of talk that does what it says.[20] The example of a groom's "I do" wedding him to his betrothed demonstrates that the spoken word's effective activity is not confined to myth or mythohistory. In bringing about what it says, effective speech powerfully fuses the worlds of thought, speech, and action. Effective speech explodes in the space of storytelling, where the suspension of disbelief opens hearers, who become Doniger's "seers," to the (im)possibilities of fantasy, mystery, violence, and the miraculous.

To draw an analogy, Native American literature reproduces storytelling spaces in which effective speech acts in the world. In *Ceremony*, for example, Laguna Pueblo author Leslie Marmon Silko (re)tells a story that illustrates myth's action, story's affective ability, and speech's effective quality. In the novel's account of the creation of white people, one witch outdoes all the others through storytelling. Instead of mixing foul brews, this one bewitches the rest with an account of *"white skin people like the belly of a fish covered with hair"* who travel across the ocean and bring with them evils that upend the world. In this myth, the storyteller's words shape the (meaning of) the world:

. . . They see no life
When they look
they see only objects.
The world is a dead thing for them
the trees and rivers are not alive
the mountains and stones are not alive.
The deer and bear are objects
They see no life.

They fear
They fear the world.
They destroy what they fear.

They fear themselves.

. . .

They will bring terrible diseases
the people have never known.
Entire tribes will die out

. . .

Set in motion now
set in motion by our witchery
set in motion
to work for us.

They will take this world from ocean to ocean
they will turn on each other
they will destroy each other

. . .

Set in motion now
set in motion
To destroy
To kill
Objects to work for us
objects to act for us
performing the witchery

. . .

whirling
set into motion now
set into motion.

So the other witches said
"Okay you win; you take the prize,
 but what you said just now—
it isn't so funny
It doesn't sound so good.
We are doing okay without it
we can get along without that kind of thing.
Take it back.
Call that story back."

But the witch just shook its head
at the others in their stinking animal skins, fur and feathers.

It's already turned loose.
It's already coming.
It can't be called back.[21]

The witch speaks the future into being by using the imperative mood to "set in motion" and "whirl" events into action. Or at least he or she seems to. As the novel's reader, I know, however, that Silko has written this cosmogony and that she wrote it in the post-Contact, postcolonial world. Nonetheless, my knowledge of this neither changes the effective quality of the story within the novel nor does it dilute the meaning-making work of the myth. What the witch intends—to bring the world into being in a specific manner—works on me when I glimpse the story world as the witch describes it, if only for a moment. The witch describes a world I can envision, a world I can recognize: one in which Old World diseases decimated Native American populations. In Doniger's words, "We can *see* it happening."[22] We can see it happening because it has happened, but we can also see it happening as the witch tells the story. The telling of the story brings about what (in the novel's timeline) has yet to happen, but what we know will/did happen. Silko takes advantage of the effective quality of speech and the magic of storytelling to take her reader back to a time when a witch spoke the world into being the way it came to be. In *Ceremony*, she binds together the past and the present in ritual storytelling; she produces a mythohistorical account of the Encounter.

This foray into *Ceremony*, an experience and analysis of the effective quality of storytelling, brings into focus the significance of narratives as contexts and sources for understanding the Aztec cosmovision.[23] After all, "setting aside the claims of authorship made by most sacred scriptures, we have no stories composed *by* gods. . . . But stories—myths—are one of our only sources of knowledge about the gods. And stories told by other peoples are one of our best sources of knowledge about them."[24] In order to understand better what the Aztecs meant by *teotl*, I look to the stories they told about their gods and about the stuff, people, and places they inhabited. Rather than translate the stories and their terms into more familiar ones—be they other traditions' myths or the scholarly language used to describe other polytheistic systems— my aim is to work toward understanding what the Aztecs meant when they said, "*teotl*."

Insofar as this book tells a story of Aztec gods, it does so by moving toward a clearer sense of *teotl*'s meaning. In the long run, this work leads to a more satisfactory understanding of human religiosity and the religious imagination, which are impossible to explain, "not because religiousness is inherently mystifying, but because it responds to mystery, and because its data are always proliferating and changing the landscape of what can be known and hence interpreted."[25] My analysis of *teotl*, *teixiptla*, and *tlaquimilolli* adds one more data point to conversations about what and who (the) G/god(s) are in Meso-american religions and the world's religions. But understanding these Nahua concepts depends on meaning and context and not just translation.

Instead of simply glossing *teotl* as "god," and assuming that my readers and I share a common sense of what a G/god is, in the following I outline some central qualities that *teotl* denoted and connoted in older Nahuatl. Rather than "translate" *teotl*, *teixiptla*, and *tlaquimilolli*, my intention is to hear their Nahuatl resonances when they are glossed as "god," "localized embodiment," or "sacred bundle." What no one—not even a native speaker of modern Na-huatl—can do is be in direct contact with those words spoken in their native contexts. Richard Andrews addresses the complexities inherent in translation and the difficulties of negotiating the "translational mirage"—the illusion that reading a work in translation places the reader in contact with the original text.[26] Andrews provides the following as a concrete example of the challenges scholars confront when they try to convey the meanings of Nahuatl words in another language:

> While it is true that all human languages are mutually translatable and that every utterance in one has an analogue in another . . . the qual-ity of meaning that the original utterance has for a native speaker of the source language is necessarily lost [in translation]. At times a trans-lation is obvious because of the clarity of the analogue; for example, "I have become a widower" easily *translates* the Nahuatl **onicihuamic**. But how does an Indo-European mind grasp the *meaning* of that ut-terance which "literally" says "already I woman-died." . . . The *mean-ing* of the English utterance "I have become a widower" . . . has nothing in common with the *meaning* of the Nahuatl utterance **onicihuamic** beyond the lowest common denominator of the analogous event. The particularity of the culturally controlled native-speaker experience as encapsulated in the linguistic expression is discarded and ignored. Nu-ances, connotations, implications, and suppositions—unconsciously understood and felt dimensions of the source texts (the entire range of the "unsaid" that every speaker of any language unwittingly employs in producing/interpreting the "said")—are unavoidably replaced by other, different ones. Translational mirage hides all of this from a reader of a translation.[27]

I do not work under the illusion that I can capture what Andrews describes as "the particularity of the culturally controlled native-speaker experience." But I can do more than translate *teotl* as "god" and assume that because I have some vague notion of what "god" means, I have a decent sense of what *teotl* meant.

The difference between translating *teotl* and understanding its meaning is like the difference between translating a foreign text into one's own language (adapting a foreign concept in terms of the familiar) and acquiring fluency in a foreign language (adapting one's self in terms of the unfamiliar). In Andrews's estimation, language learning "should not be, as it almost always is, a mere pragmatic search for equivalences ('how does one say . . . ?'); it should be an anthropological quest for foreign meaning. That is, the goal should be meaning, not translation."[28] Focusing on meaning rather than translation requires me to attend to the contexts in which *teixiptlahuan* (localized embodiments) became *teteo* (gods), work that has the potential to affect understanding Aztec religion (and not just *teotl*).

Speaking the Language of Today's *Totiotzin* (Gods)

In the summer of 2006, I began research on language and ritual animacy with Kelly McDonough and a group of modern Nahuatl-speaking colleagues, including Victoriano de la Cruz, Delfina de la Cruz, Catalina de la Cruz, and Sabina de la Cruz, at the Zacatecas Institute for Teaching and Research in Ethnology (IDIEZ). Several aspects of the research we have conducted since then have made distinct impressions on how I see Aztec and modern Nahua religions. Modern Nahuatl speakers experience the world as a powerfully and pervasively animate place, an observation that Arturo Gómez Martínez and others have made concerning Nahua perceptions of liveliness in the natural environment.[29] Native speakers from the Huasteca of Veracruz evaluate animacy along a spectrum, a form of folk taxonomy that maps the intersections of Nahuatl language and human observations of the natural and made world(s). Each speaker can locate every known object and entity along a spectrum of animacy. (Of course, not all speakers agree on the same assessment of every word.) They identify objects and entities as animate or inanimate based primarily on their ability to move, a sign of their liveliness. Depending on a noun's classification as animate or inanimate, it follows specific linguistic rules, including its affiliation with a particular "to be" verb and the composition of its plural form.

Nahuatl speakers recognize a wide spectrum of animate entities, and all nouns fall along a linguistic spectrum of animacy with respect to two char-

Spectrum of Animacy

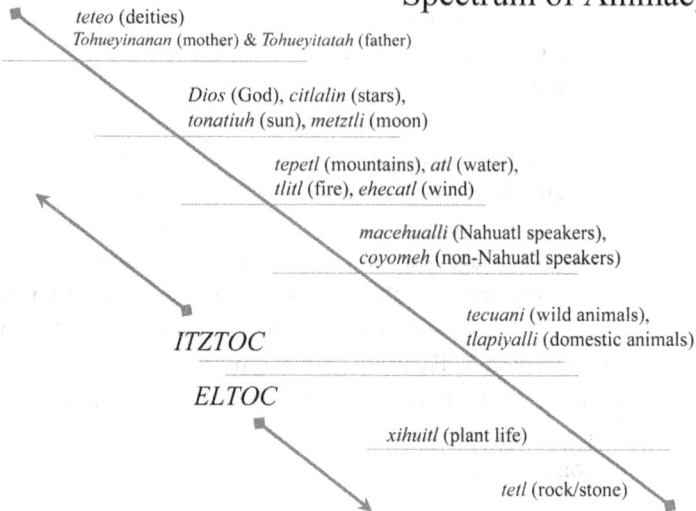

teteo (deities)
Tohueyinanan (mother) & *Tohueyitatah* (father)

Dios (God), *citlalin* (stars),
tonatiuh (sun), *metztli* (moon)

tepetl (mountains), *atl* (water),
tlitl (fire), *ehecatl* (wind)

macehualli (Nahuatl speakers),
coyomeh (non-Nahuatl speakers)

ITZTOC

tecuani (wild animals),
tlapiyalli (domestic animals)

ELTOC

xihuitl (plant life)

tetl (rock/stone)

I.1. Spectrum of animacy

acteristics: which "to be" verb they regularly acquire, and whether they can be made plural (Figure 1.1).[30] In the modern Nahuatl worldview, two "to be" verbs—*itztoc* and *eltoc*—indicate whether a noun is animate or inanimate.[31] *Itztoc*, from the verb *itta*, means "for a person or animal to be someplace or in some state" and functions with subjects that are animate.[32] *Eltoc*, "to be," functions with inanimate nouns. When asked whether a noun is animate or inanimate, a modern speaker may have an immediate answer because of the word's obvious nature; such was the case for the highly animate *totiotzin* or essentially inanimate *tetl* (rocks), for instance.

A classificatory system—including one that functions along a spectrum—may appear to make neat and tidy divisions among terms and concepts. However, most nouns fall somewhere between the extremes of high animacy and inanimacy, and native speakers are not always certain of how to classify a term or concept. For example, when we talked about *mixtli* (cloud/clouds), native speakers Catalina and Sabina debated whether clouds take *itztoc* or *eltoc* for several minutes. As they considered *mixtli*'s animacy, they thought about the characteristics of clouds, and they discussed the qualities of the word "cloud(s)." They considered the possible animacy of the thing—a cloud—based on their observations of it and also on how the noun *mixtli* functions in Nahuatl. Movement is important in determining the animacy of an object or entity, so one of the native speakers' tests was to ask if a cloud *nehnemi* (walks). They agreed that clouds move because the winds blow them, not because they go from place to place of their own volition or under their own power. They also noted that clouds could be classified in three of the major categories they identified along the spectrum: *totiotzin* (gods), *cuerpos celestiales* (heavenly bodies), or *inorgánicos* (inorganic material). *Mixtli*, they said, does not have a plural form, which would indicate that it is inanimate and takes *eltoc*. They found themselves caught between knowing that clouds move, an indication that they are animate, and feeling constrained by the fact that *mixtli* has no plural form, an indication that clouds are inanimate. This exercise in the exploration of Nahuatl's linguistic ideology illustrates the negotiations that take place when Nahuatl speakers examine the relationship between their language, the elements and entities of the perceptible world, and their cosmovision.[33] It also demonstrates that the spectrum is not a rigid system of immutable classifications, but rather one shaped by modern speakers' sense of Nahuatl and the world.

We repeated this exercise again and again over the course of a summer. Based on a series of conversations during which native speakers examined the animacy of more than seventy-five nouns, they determined that nouns that take *itztoc* fall within five identifiable categories.[34] At one end of the animacy spectrum, *totiotzin* (gods) have the most animacy, and Tohueyinanan (divine personage: our great mother) and Tohueyitatah (divine personage: our great father)—the mother and father of the prototypical family—are the most animate gods.[35]

Moving in order of descending animacy, the second group collects luminous celestial bodies, including *citlalin* (stars), *tonatiuh* (sun), *metztli* (moon), and Dios (God). Curiously, these modern Nahuatl speakers locate Dios alongside celestial entities rather than with the *totiotzin*. The third classification includes features of the more immediate natural world, such as *tepetl* (mountain), *atl* (water), *tlalli* (earth), *tlitl* (fire), and *ehecatl* (wind). My colleagues labeled this category as "*tlen oncah*" (what exists) and explained that because all of these features of the natural world "*tienen dueño*" (have owners), they are also *totiotzin*. They were reluctant to rank these deities as "less important" than the parental pair, but on other occasions, they described the celestial bodies and earthly phenomena as having less animacy than the Tohueyinanan and Tohueyitatah.[36]

Modern speakers recognize two categories of human beings, *macehualmeh* (Nahuatl speakers) and *coyomeh* (nonspeakers), both of which belong to the fourth group of animate entities. *Tecuanimeh* (wild animals) and *tlapiyalmeh* (domestic animals) compose the next category. Finally, some modern speakers class *xihuitl* (grass, plant life) as animate because it exhibits movement in the form of growth. All of these entities take the animate "to be" verb *itztoc*.

Most modern speakers identify two groups of inanimate nouns that use the second "to be" verb, *eltoc*. *Eltoc* means "to be (inanimate subjects)."[37] For speakers who do not recognize plant life as animate, the first *eltoc* group includes *xihuitl* (grass, plant life), and *tetl* (rocks) compose the second. By contrast to nouns that take *itztoc*, words in these groups usually have identical singular and plural forms, like the English word "moose." In certain contexts, particularly that of ritual manufacture, some inanimate materials become highly animate *teteo* and acquire a plural form, although they would not ordinarily do so. I will explore this transformation shortly.

As an all-encompassing taxonomy, the spectrum of animacy organizes every animate and inanimate entity in the modern Nahuatl world. Despite the order it imposes on (or observes in) modern Nahuatl and native speakers' cosmovision, the spectrum is not static. It reveals Nahuatl speakers' cosmological and linguistic capacities to integrate foreign entities, like Dios, into the existing taxonomic structure. Further, it definitively demonstrates that Nahuatl speakers have ways of visualizing and organizing their cosmos and its inhabitants that differ from—and sometimes defy—Western modes of classification.

The organization of inanimate materials and animate beings along the spectrum is neither fixed nor static. Because the qualities of objects and entities change depending on their environmental, ontological, and linguistic contexts, the question of animacy remains relative and relevant: relative to the social agency a speaker perceives in or attributes to an object or entity and relevant to the dynamics of language in the lifeworld. Thus, the spectrum of animacy provides an analytical framework for understanding some of the ontological changes brought about in rituals like Chicomexochitl (7 Flower), an annual rite of agricultural renewal and petition for rain and beneficence. One such transformation involves the ritual manufacture of highly animate and beloved *totiotzin* (gods) from everyday paper.

Chicomexochitl (7 Flower) and the *Totiotzin*

In communities where modern Nahuatl speakers maintain *costumbres* (traditional practices), ritual manufacture in ceremonies like Chicomexochitl (7 Flower) brings about ontological transformations in ordinary materials that become highly animate entities. In the summers of 2006 and 2010, I attended a celebration of Chicomexochitl in the Huasteca of Veracruz as a guest of the sponsoring family and acted as a participant observer. My experiences of the ceremony and the interviews I conducted with participants in 2010 indicate that they perceive the transformations these entities experience through their change in shape, their treatment by ritual participants, and the way *macehualmeh* (Nahuatl speakers) talk about the beings.

Watching the manufacture and animation of *totiotzin* impressed upon me modern Nahuatl speakers' perception of the world as fundamentally and pervasively animate. The rules of modern Nahuatl state that inanimate materials and objects take a specific verb and cannot be made plural. However, many modern Nahuatl speakers participate in ceremonies during which materials with no (or relatively low) animacy become highly animate *totiotzin* through their ritual manufacture, and the adults who sponsor these ceremonies adopt the *totiotzin* into their families as their children. Modern Nahuatl expresses the world's animacy by categorizing every object and entity as either animate or inanimate, and Nahuatl speakers use ritual to transform inanimate materials into venerable animate entities.

During this (roughly) annual celebration, participants manufacture a family of six *totiotzin*, and in the process, the inanimate objects ceremonially transform into animate entities, a ritual act that effects change along the spectrum of animacy. The most obvious shift in animacy takes place within the Chicomexochitl, the six *totiotzin* at the center of the ritual. Over a period of a few days, the *tepahtihquetl* (ritual officiant) cuts ordinary store-bought *amatl* (paper) into *tlatecmeh* (paper figures of natural deities used in ceremonies) that come to embody the highly animate Chicomexochitl, Tohueyinanan (mother), Tohueyitatah (father), and their four children, whom the participants venerate throughout the year.[38]

During Chicomexochitl, ritual participants manufacture an extravagant assortment of offerings, including thousands of paper cutouts and hundreds of bundled reeds. A group of (mostly) female participants prepare bundles of palm fronds and other floral arrangements. If there is not other work to be done, some men assist in making the reed bundles. Meanwhile, other women prepare elaborate meals and clothing for the six colorful paper effigies that represent the Chicomexochitl family, the ceremony's focus (see Figure I.4). Men clear brush from the path up the *altepetl* (water mountain; community) to the ceremony's altars. During this time, the *tepahtihquetl* and a few male assistants create thousands of paper cutouts representing elements of the natural world, including beans, chilies, and corn, and the family of six Chicomexochitl figures.

Depending on the *tepahtihquetl*'s stamina, Chicomexochitl preparations last about four days. Dancing punctuates ongoing ritual activities. Each eve-

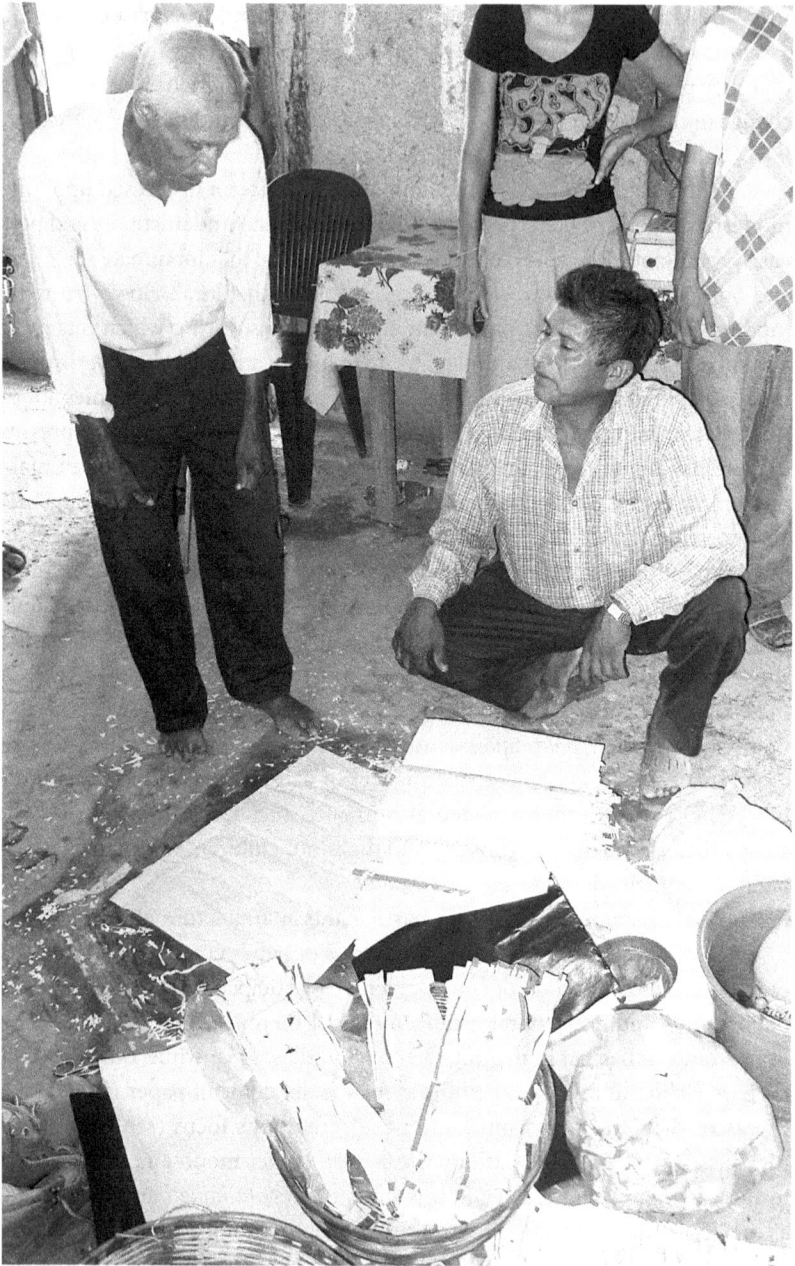

I.2. The *tepahtihquetl* and his assistant stand behind the Chicomexochitl and *totiotzin*. Photograph by author.

I.3. One bundle of twenty palm fronds, each of which holds a *cempaxochitl* (marigold). Photograph by author.

ning (and throughout the day), the ritual participants gather in the home of the family sponsoring Chicomexochitl and dance in a circle around the *te-pahtihquetl*, who continues cutting the *tlatecmeh*. They take turns censing the Chicomexochitl activities and offerings with copal while a band of three men, playing a guitar, a classical guitar, and a violin, play atonal songs that invite the presence of nature spirits into the ritual.[39] One afternoon near the end of the ritual's preparations, the participants gather to dance while the women dress the Chicomexochitl figures. They dress the figures in hand-sewn clothes and store-bought accessories. Each member of the Chicomexochitl family has a distinct look (Figure I.4).

On the final day, all of the participants and the offerings undergo a *limpia* (cleansing) before going up the *altepetl*. The community identifies the *alte-petl's* summit with Xochicalco (Flower House), the home of the Chicomexo-

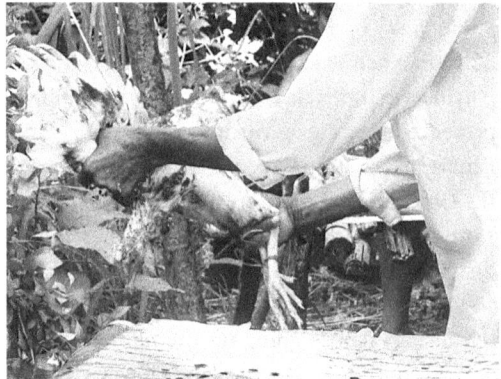

I.4. (above) Ritual participants dress members of the Chicomexochitl family. Photograph by author.
I.5. (left) The *tepahtihquetl* sprinkles blood on the altar following an avian sacrifice. Photograph by author.

chitl. Once the group arrives on the *altepetl*'s summit, the *tepahtihquetl* hangs the bag containing the Chicomexochitl effigies above the center of the summit's principal altar.[40] From there, the Chicomexochitl family observes the decoration of a series of altars and the arrangement of offerings. Participants cover the largest altar table with sheets of paper cutouts representing beans, corn, and chilies. Members of the sponsoring family hold two chickens and a turkey while the *tepahtihquetl* feeds them sips of soda and beer. After "intoxicating" the birds with these luxury beverages, the *tepahtihquetl* uses scissors

I.6. The completed *altepetl* altar. Photograph by author.

I.7. *Voladores* on the *altepetl* summit. Photograph by author.

to cut their necks, and the three family members pass the birds over the altar and beneath it. The birds' blood soaks into the paper cutouts and the earth. The *tepahtihquetl* then pours libations on and beneath the altar. The participants complete the offering by arranging food, beverages, and bundles on the altar.

In addition to the altar above which the Chicomexochitl family hangs, a second altar features a hole dug into the ground in which participants place a living chicken. They complete this avian offering to the earth by covering the hole with papers tacked to the ground over which they place reeds and other offerings.[41] They arrange a third altar/offering of baby chick *voladores* (fliers) atop a stand from which they string four colored ribbons in the four directions (Figure 1.7).

Walking from the community up the mountain, arranging the altars and offerings, offering a series of prayers (for good crops, good relationships, and a good year), completing a second *limpia* for anyone suffering from illness or injury, and walking back down the *altepetl* takes the better part of a day. As the ceremony draws to a close, one of the participants carries the Chicomexochitl figures back down the mountain, and they reside on the home altar of the family that sponsored the ceremony for the next year. Before the group feasts, they accompany the *tepahtihquetl* to the *pozo* (well), where they make a final series of offerings and petition rain. The day culminates in a meal of pork tamales made from a hog that the men slaughter for the occasion. The community performs Chicomexochitl primarily to invoke rain, and they consider it to have been successful if rain comes within four days of the festival's close.

Making a Modern God

During the course of Chicomexochitl, the paper figures transform from inanimate/*eltoc amatl* (paper) into animate/*itztoc tlatecmeh* (paper figures of natural deities). By the ceremony's end, the sponsors recognize the Chicomexochitl effigies as living beings and family members. The parents of the sponsoring family refer to the Chicomexochitl figures as their children, and throughout the year, they feed them, change their clothes, and talk to them. After witnessing the ceremony in 2006 and learning about the spectrum of animacy, I became interested in how this transformation occurs. Specifically, I wondered how ordinary sheets of paper become *totiotzin*. When I returned to the community in 2010 to participate in Chicomexochitl, I conducted a series of short interviews focused on the nature of the ceremony and the participants' perception of the Chicomexochitl deities. I interviewed three women and three men, including the *tepahtihquetl*.[42] In these conversations, I learned more about how participants perceive Chicomexochitl. For example, they explained that the *altepetl*'s summit is Xochicalco, the home of the Chicomexochitl, and that by contrast to the gods, whom they envision as adults, the Chicomexochitl are seen to be children: "zohuapiltzitzin huan oquichpipiltzitzin yanopa" (these, yes they are small girls and boys).[43] The women described the foods they prepared and contributed to the altars as both coming from and sustaining the gods.[44]

The people I interviewed affirmed that animacy pervades the Nahua life-world. *Altepemeh* (mountains) occupy a singularly important position in the Nahua cosmovision. In his study of contemporary Nahua cosmovisions, An-drés Medina Hernández begins his explanation of sacred geography by de-scribing the centrality of water and mountains:

> El agua y los cerros son dos referentes fundamentales en la percepción del paisaje para los campesinos nahuas. Los cerros son entidades vivas a las que se atribuyen relaciones amorosas y conflictivas entre sí; entre ellos se establece una jerarquía de acuerdo con su altura; esto remite a su condición de ejes cósmicos que relacionan a los tres niveles espacia-les, el cielo, la tierra y el inframundo; es a través de los cerros como se puede entrar en comunicación con las entidades que los habitan y que inciden poderosamente en la existencia humana.

> The water and the mountains are two fundamental referents in Nahua farmers' perception of the landscape. The mountains are living enti-ties to which are attributed loving and contentious relationships; their heights establish a hierarchy among them; this explains their condition as cosmic axes that connect three spatial levels, the sky, the earth, and the underworld; it is through the hills that one may enter into commu-nication with the entities that inhabit them and that powerfully affect human existence.[45]

When Victoriano de la Cruz, my colleague and research assistant, and I asked one of the women with whom we spoke if she considered the *altepetl* adjacent to her community to be alive, she began her response with reference to the hill's water: "Quena, ne yoltoc. Ne yoltoc. Pampa tlan titlehcozceh huetziqui atl huan tlan axcanah quitlacualtihqueh axcanah huetziqui atl. Quemman tlatomoni tlananquilia. Quemman axcanah tlanquilia porque axtlananquilia porque axquitlacualtihtoqueh." (Yes, it's alive. It's alive. Because if we go up to the waterfall and don't take food, the water won't fall. When there is thunder, they [the mountains] answer. When they don't answer, when there is no an-swer, it's because we haven't fed them.)[46] She went on to explain that the moun-tains' need for food demonstrates their animacy, as do the conversations the mountains have with one another: "Quemman tlatomoniz ne piltepetzin no como tlanquilia. No tlatomoni quehuac. Ne quennopa ne piltepetzin." (When it thunders, it is as if this hill also answers. It also responds. That's the way the hill is.)[47] In other words, she explained, when we hear thunder and its echo, what we are hearing is one hill speaking and another replying.

The mountains, thunder-talkers and homes to the gods, participate in both the natural world and the manufactured world. They are, in Bruno Latour's words, fetishes: "As a noun, it means form, figure, configuration, but as an adjective, artificial, fabricated, factitious and finally, enchanted . . . Yes, the fetish is a 'talk-maker.'"[48] These mountains traverse the (super)natural because their community forms them and is formed by them, fabricates them and is made by them, and enchants them and, yes, is enchanted by them. These thunderous entities are, quite literally, "talk-makers." They talk, and they are the subject of talk.

Modern Nahuas—like their Aztec ancestors—perceive the mountains as features of the natural landscape that interact with proximate elements and entities. Rather than demarcate the animate god living on or in the mountain from the inanimate mountain, for instance, they describe the *totiotzin* as the mountain, the mountain as the *totiotzin*, the mountain as a mountain, and the mountain-talk as echoing thunder. Their designation of these entities' animacy derives from their observation of the ways in which they relate (socially) and communicate. By virtue of talking and being talked about—aspects of their manufacture and (super)natural state—*altepemeh* occupy a relational, if not social, location in the modern Nahua cosmovision; the mountain is a mountain, and it is also more than a mountain because modern Nahuas have *made* it so. After all, "in all our activities, what we fabricate goes beyond us."[49] (That said, it is worth observing, as have Christopher Pinney and Webb Keane, that "we must consider the ways in which material things work independently of, or in contradiction to, their discursive surround. Otherwise we risk treating humans as if their capacity to endow the world with meaning had no limits, and, I [Keane] would add, as if the world could hold no further surprises for them."[50])

To return for a moment to a specific instance of manufacture, the *tepahtihquetl's* explanation of how the paper Chicomexochitl figures acquired animacy underscores the autonomy generated in the ritual manufacture of deity embodiments. In the process of manufacturing *tlatecmeh*, the inanimate *amatl* (paper) comes to embody highly animate deities, *totiotzin* and Chicomexochitl, a transformation that registers linguistically and ontologically.[51] By contrast to *amatl*, which takes the verb *eltoc*, *totiotzin* and Chicomexochitl acquire the animate "to be" verb *itztoc*. When I asked the *tepahtihquetl* what brought about this change and when it happened, he acknowledged that the *tlatecmeh* started out as "*puro papel*" (only paper), and in response to my question of whether there is a moment in the ritual when they take on life, he replied, "nopa nopa yanopa mismo yanopa eltocca ne testigoh mochihuahya como vivos por eso tiquintlalanahya ma mopresentarocan es en el momento de la invocación pero también en la vestimentah ajá." (Now, right now and with this witness, they are made as if they were alive, and because of this we lift them up so that they are presented in the moment of the invocation. But also right when they are dressed.)[52] The *tepahtihquetl* acknowledged that because they are "made as if they are alive"—that is, they have physical bodies and sensory capabilities—the community recognized them as the *totiotzin*. He went on to explain that even though they may have been born in a far-away place—in Xalapa, in the north, from near the sea—"huallazceh tlananu-atianih . . . huallaz mopresentaroqui nican . . . eso sí, le hemos dado un vestigo, una medalla, un arete." (The powers that be will come . . . they will come and present themselves here . . . this yes, we have given a little vest, a medal, an earring.)[53] In both descriptions, he emphasized the importance of the gods' clothing and insignia. Then in the rhythmic cadence of a secret-keeping sto-ryteller, he reminded me that he was 70 years old, that his teacher had been 125 years old when he died, and that it had been years since he himself had had training. In that time, he had forgotten many of the names of "*los cortes*" (the cuts, cutouts), but each *tlatectli* (cutout) had its own name.[54] During the rit-ual, he explained, the Chicomexochitl acquire animacy when they are raised up, offered an invocation, and dressed.

These deities' presence extends far beyond their linguistic attributes and ritual animation into the daily lives of those who care for them, and the total incorporation of these highly animate gods into an ordinary family represents the quintessence of modern Nahua cosmology. The modern Nahuatl spec-trum of animacy reflects the linguistic transformation of ritually animated en-tities, and while it is possible to discuss the two—language and ritual—sepa-rately, they act in cosmological concert. Animacy functions along a spectrum, and the spectrum encompasses everything in the world—even those entities outsiders might assume dwell beyond the limits of this world.

Like modern-day Nahuatl speakers, the Aztecs understood life and be-ing as existing along a continuum that did not (and still does not) draw hard-and-fast distinctions between the (in)animate, the (super)natural, or the (super)human. Rather, they evaluated life, liveliness, and godlikeness according to a folk taxonomy that collected qualitative clusters. As seems reasonable, Aztec devotees expected the *teixiptla* (localized embodiment) of a *teotl* (god) to be recognizable, and the qualities that clustered around particular *teteo* (gods) both defined their personae and rendered them identifiable. Inasmuch as this book is about grasping how the Aztecs conceived of and produced their *teteo, teixiptlahuan,* and *tlaquimilolli,* it is also an opportunity to examine how scholars perceive and represent religions like those of the Nahuas: religions whose proliferating pantheons challenge modes of and models for G/god(s), religions whose attribution of life to things made by human hands confounds common conceptions of immanence and transcendence, belief and the believable.

>>> And many of the Mexicans also came to see the men—so new, so famous—and surprised by their beards, clothing, weapons, horses and gunshots, they said, "These are gods."

>>> Y también venían muchos de aquellos mexicanos a ver hombres tan nuevos, tan afamados; y sorprendidos de las barbas, vestidos, armas, caballos y tiros, decían: "Éstos son dioses."
Francisco López de Gómara, 1552[1]

>>> Marina was called Malintzin by the natives and held as a goddess in the highest degree.

>>> Marina que por los naturales fué llamada Malintzin y tenida por diosa en grado superlativo.
Diego Muñoz Camargo, 1576[2]

>>> When he heard it, he quickly sent out a party. He thought and believed that it was Topiltzin Quetzalcoatl who had landed. For they were of the opinion that he would return, that he would appear, that he would come back to his seat of authority, because he had gone in that direction [eastward] when he left. And [Moteucçoma] sent five [people] to go to meet him and give him things. The leader had the official title of Teohua [custodian of the god] and the personal name of Yohualli ichan. The second was Tepoztecatl, the third Tiçhua, the fourth Huehuetecatl, and the fifth Hueicamecatl eca.

>>> in oquicac, niman iciuhca tlaioa, in iuh quima, in iuh moma, ca iehoatl in topiltzin Quet-zalcoatl in oquiçaco: ca iuh catca iniollo in çan oallaz, in çan quiçaquiuh, quioalmatiz in ipetl, in icpal: ipampa ca vmiztia, in iquac ia. Auh in quimiloã macuiltin, in quinamiquitivi, in quitlama-macativi: in teiacantia Teuoa, in itecutoca, in ipiltoca Ioalli ichan. Inic vme Tepuztecatl. Inic ei, tiçaoa. Inic navi vevetecatl. Inic macuilli Veicamecatl heca.
Bernardino de Sahagún, 1580[3]

>>> The Mexica stopped to observe their dress and the appearance of their faces, noting their beards and long hair. . . . They were even more frightened to see people on horseback in full armor, and, fearing their artillery, said, "These are gods." Others said that they were sons of the sun, believing them immortal and other things which they could not comprehend.

>>> Estauanse los Mexicanos de ber el traje y de la menera (*sic*) de sus rostros y de que te-nian varbas, y largos cauellos . . . y mas se espantauan en ber Gente de a cauallo, y bien ar-mados de hierro, y de los tiros con que se espantauan, y dezian ellos estos son Dioses, y otros dezian que eran Hijos del Sol que los tenian por ynmortales y otras cosas que a estos no se les alcanzaua.
Chimalpahin, 1593-1620[4]

CHAPTER 1

Meeting the Gods

These four episodes of apotheosis from the Encounter underscore the roles of religion, material culture, and embodiment in early exchanges between Mesoamericans and Europeans. According to these accounts (all redacted by Europeans), the Aztecs identified Hernán Cortés and his companions as *teteo* (deities) and *teixiptlahuan*, their localized embodiments: first, in Francisco López de Gómara's account, "the Mexicans"—a gathering of Amecamecan locals—associate the Spaniards with gods; second, the Tlaxcalans describe Cortés's translator Marina/Malintzin as a goddess; third, the *tlahtoani* (speaker; ruler) Moteuczoma Xocoyotl (Lord Angry, Younger) identifies Cortés with Quetzalcoatl (Quetzal Feather Serpent); and fourth, Chimalpahin's annotation reiterates and elaborates upon the Spaniards' divine characterization established by López de Gómara.[5] In addition to being identified as *teteo* in alphabetic texts, visual records substantiate the claim that Moteuczoma received Cortés with gifts befitting a god. The idea that Central Mexicans identified the Spaniards, Cortés, and Marina/Malintzin as gods held particular appeal for Europeans. Among the many fantastical accounts of the Americas that traveled to Europe, these circulated widely. In particular, the account of Cortés's recognition by the Aztecs as one of their own deities became the prototype for other sixteenth- to eighteenth-century encounters.[6]

I begin with these accounts because they represent the incommensurability of Aztec cosmology and the European worldview. Rather than searching for the "true" history, an ambiguous enterprise in itself, I am exploring the substance of histories, the narratives about that which is said to have happened. Such stories are never divorced from the real and become in themselves historical agents.

Contact-period narratives, including Cortés's letters and accounts compiled by López de Gómara, Sahagún, and others, present Mesoamericans in the context of confusing encounters, partial translations, and the ensuing establishment of colonial order. These narratives have a decidedly "*contact perspective*," one that "emphasizes how subjects are constituted in and by their

relations to each other. It treats the relations among colonizers and colonized
. . . in terms of copresence, interaction, interlocking understandings and practices, often within radically asymmetrical relations of power."[7] Interpreting
these texts as mythohistories with contact perspectives complicates—or perhaps clarifies—their reading by acknowledging that they both betray Mesoamericans and belie Europeans. In other words, those places where the texts
seem most manipulated by the European worldview—such as the apotheosis
episodes—or crucial to the colonial project—such as the exchange between
Moteuczoma and Cortés—may be the precise points through which a clearer
vision of the Mesoamerican perspective is possible.

In this chapter, I examine the implications of naming, translating, and re-
vising mythohistories through alphabetic and visual records of the exchange
that took place between Marina/Malintzin, Moteuczoma, and Cortés. First,
I explore the *Codex Mexicanus*'s visual record of the gifts exchanged in comparison with Aztec practices of state gift giving. Then I address the question
of Cortés's apotheosis. I suggest that in this gift exchange and its aftermath,
contact between the Mesoamerican cosmovision and European worldview facilitated two related transformations: first, Aztec observers perceived Cortés
as a potential deity *teixiptla* (localized embodiment), and second, Europeans
saw Cortés being seen as a *teotl* (god). For the Europeans, Cortés's apotheosis
in the New World confirmed their suspicion of the natives' misguided religiosity and created a powerful political advantage for the conquistador(s). For
the Aztecs, the possibility that Cortés might become a *teotl*'s embodiment by
wearing Moteuczoma's *teotlatquitl* (deity belongings) and thereby initiate a
ritual scenario through which he could be a sacrificial victim proved irresistible. More emphatically, were Cortés to have become the localized embodiment of a *teotl*, he would have presented Moteuczoma and the Aztecs with
real-world possibilities of mythic proportions.

Gifts Fit for a God: Transferring Materials and Negotiating Meaning

The gift exchange between Cortés and Moteuczoma marks the initial clash of
the conquistador's European understanding of myth and history (or rather,
their distinction) and the Mexica *tlahtoani*'s cosmovision. According to some
accounts, Moteuczoma perceived Cortés's landing at Veracruz in 1519 as the
fated return of the Mesoamerican god Quetzalcoatl, who had fled to the East
and was prophesied to return to rule his homeland again. For Cortés, the Mesoamerican belief that he was their returning god was purely fortuitous; perceived as a god, Cortés could play the role to his advantage. However, for the

Aztecs and for Moteuczoma in particular, Cortés's return signified the end of an era of rule and, ultimately, the end of their cosmovision. For us, the myth of Quetzalcoatl's return complicates the process of understanding the implications of both the Encounter and the exchange.

The most complete alphabetic account of Cortés's perception as Quetzalcoatl by Moteuczoma appears in *Book 12: The Conquest* of the *Florentine Codex: General History of the Things of New Spain*, a text compiled by Bernardino de Sahagún in the 1560s, nearly two generations after Contact. As I note above, scholars disagree about whether the myth is a pre- or post-Contact narrative.[8] Camilla Townsend asserts that in *The Aztec Kings*, Susan Gillespie "has proven that the story as we know it did not exist until Sahagún edited the Florentine Codex in the 1560s."[9] Why, then, entertain the question of Cortés's reception as a god? First, historically (and still today) some scholars identify Cortés and the gifts he received with Quetzalcoatl; second, whether or not Cortés was thought to be Quetzalcoatl, Mesoamericans initially referred to him and his men as *teteo* (gods); and third, even if the Mexicas never thought of Cortés as Quetzalcoatl or any other deity proper, this association became part of the larger contact perspective circulating in the mid- to late sixteenth century.

Furthermore, the precise meaning of *teotl* (god) complicates our understanding of how the Aztecs received Cortés and company. For sixteenth-century Nahuatl speakers, *teotl* was "a well-defined indigenous concept" in the "special vocabulary" of Aztec religion.[10] And so to read *teotl* and hear "g/God" with associations other than those of sixteenth-century Nahuatl speakers misconstrues Moteuczoma's response to the Spaniards' appearance if, indeed, "when he learned that the 'gods' wished to see him face to face, his heart shrank within him and he was filled with anguish."[11] (In fact, differing emphases in the translation of this very passage illustrate how crucial Nahuatl concepts are in understanding Aztec religion. In this translation of the *Florentine Codex*'s Nahuatl text, León-Portilla emphasizes the identification of the Spaniards as gods through scare quotes; by contrast, Anderson and Dibble do not accentuate the word "gods": "And when Moctezuma had thus heard that he was much enquired about, that he was much sought, [that] the gods wished to look upon his face, it was as if his heart was afflicted; he was afflicted. He would flee . . . he wished to take refuge from the gods."[12] Whereas León-Portilla's translation suggests that the Aztecs did not really and truly think of the Spaniards as gods, Anderson and Dibble leave the question open for their readers' interpretation.) In much of the literature surrounding the question of Cortés as Quetzalcoatl, the connotations scholars attribute to *teotl* vis-à-vis their personal or comparative understandings of "G/god" cloud the issues involved in identifying Cortés as a *teotl*. As we shall see, *teteo* were marvelous and valuable entities with their own possessions, calendric associations, and exclusive occupations. Associating these qualities with *teteo* will aid us in understanding why Moteuczoma and other Nahuatl speakers identified Cortés and company as "gods."

In the following pages, however, I am less concerned with weighing in on the question of whether the myth of Quetzalcoatl's return is of pre- or post-Contact vintage than with examining the stakes that underpin the question. Regardless of whether the myth existed pre-Contact, its appearance in the *Florentine Codex* documents its post-Contact importance. I am more concerned with the specific nature of Moteuczoma's gifts, for, as I shall argue, a close examination of these gifts' roles in an Aztec ritual of exchange highlights the decidedly symbolic nature of Moteuczoma's religious obligations as *tlahtoani*. Specifically, Moteuczoma gives Cortés gifts appropriate for the *teixiptla* of a *teotl*, a ritual action with implications that exceed a simple welcome. This gift exchange thus offers a window into the historic moment in which both leaders' visions were confirmed, for better and worse, and it reveals some of the gaps between Aztec and European epistemologies.

The Archive of Exchange

Although several accounts of the leaders' (and their emissaries') meetings exist, two sources, the *Codex Mexicanus* and the *Florentine Codex*, offer outstanding depictions of the gifts they exchanged. The *Florentine Codex* provides extraordinarily detailed descriptions of the *teotlatquitl* (god's belongings) in two languages, and the *Codex Mexicanus* is the only extant visual record of the items exchanged by both leaders.

The *Florentine Codex* contains the most elaborate description of the gifts Moteuczoma gave Cortés, and the richest accounts of the *teotlatquitl* appear in the Spanish text. In marked contrast to the majority of the *Florentine Codex*, the Spanish descriptions of the deity attire include much more detail than those in Nahuatl, and they provide the reader with a truly exceptional sense of how each *teotl*'s attire would have been worn. For example, the scribes explain that a turquoise mask with serpents twisting along the bridge of the nose "was set in a large high crown full of very beautiful, long, rich plumes, so that when one put the crown on one's head one also put the mask on one's face."[13] Details like these give the reader the impression that Sahagún, his informants, or scribes had access to a source—whether material, pictorial, oral, or alphabetic

1.1. Gifts given by Moteuczoma to Cortés (below the row of day signs) and those received from Cortés by Moteuczoma (above the row of day signs). *Codex Mexicanus*, 76–77. Courtesy of the Bibliothèque nationale de France.

—from which they drew rich descriptions of the elaborately worked masks, capes, shields, and headdresses.[14] Although it may be impossible to determine the source of these descriptions, they describe the exclusive attire of specific *teteo*, including Quetzalcoatl, Tezcatlipoca (Smoking Mirror), and Tlalocan Teuctli (the Lord of Tlalocan), among the gifts given Cortés. By contrast, the *Codex Mexicanus* presents a more complete picture of the exchange. Though it lacks the *Florentine Codex*'s level of detail, the *Codex Mexicanus* provides a visual context for the exchange.

The *Codex Mexicanus* (1571–1590), a pictorial manuscript painted on bark paper bound like a European book, contains the only images of the gifts exchanged by both Moteuczoma and Cortés (Figure 1.1). Above a row of date signs, Cortés sits in a European-style folding chair facing one of Moteuczoma's ambassadors, who wears a *tilmahtli* (cloak). Cortés hands his gifts for Moteuczoma to the Aztec intermediary: a beaded necklace, European shoes, and a steel-tipped lance (Figure 1.2). Moteuczoma's gifts for Cortés appear below the sequence of date signs and include "a beaded cape, two feather headdresses, two feather cloaks, five disks of turquoise mosaic, a tunic and two shields (Figure 1.3)."[15] Likely drawing on the *Florentine Codex*'s description of numerous gifts, Elizabeth Boone identifies the vestments of the god Quetzalcoatl among Moteuczoma's gifts.[16]

1.2. (top) Detail of gifts given by Cortés. *Codex Mexicanus*, 76–77. Courtesy of the Bibliothèque nationale de France.
1.3. (bottom) Detail of gifts given by Moteuczoma. *Codex Mexicanus*, 76–77. Courtesy of the Bibliothèque nationale de France.

Based on the extensive descriptions of the gifts in the *Florentine Codex*, however, it seems probable that the *Codex Mexicanus* depicts select or representative items from the *teotlatquitl* Moteuczoma gave Cortés. In fact, the *Codex Mexicanus* may focus on gifts decorated in greenstone or quetzal feathers, perhaps because their blue-green color reflected their high value. Taken together, these contact perspective texts document the luxurious *teotlatquitl*, literally the belongings of the *teteo*, that Cortés received from Moteuczoma.

Aztec rites of hospitality required that Moteuczoma provide the Spaniards with an appropriate greeting. In his exchange with Cortés, Moteuczoma employed a traditional understanding of relationships between rulers and of the ritual production of *teixiptlahuan* in order to welcome a potential ruler *cum*-god. Furthermore, the images suggest that both the *tlahtoani's* ceremonial gifts and the conquistador's reciprocation held the possibility of double meanings.

Gifts Fit for a God: Precedents and Implications

Rituals of exchange and bodily adornment emphasized the powerful relationships forged between the Mexicas and peripheral rulers. Various occasions, including the declaration of war, petitions for peace, state burials, and accessions, all required gift exchanges. As Diego Durán reports, "When the Indians go to welcome someone or to visit a person it is not their custom to go empty-handed because this would be considered offensive. This is customary with the hosts as well as with the guests."[17] While gifts exchanged between rulers were always reciprocal, they were rarely equivalent. A survey of ethnohistorical instances of gift exchanges recorded in Durán's *History of the Indies of New Spain* and Hernando de Alvarado Tezozómoc's *Crónica mexicana* identifies the materials involved in exchanges commemorating accession and death and denoting war and peace. Reconstructing the mythohistorical relationships expressed by gifts exchanged and occasions for exchange provides us with cultural precedents for the exchange between Moteuczoma and Cortés. Furthermore, it prepares us to speculate about the symbolic implications of Moteuczoma's gifts.

Among the many diplomatic interactions described in the histories of pre-Contact Central Mexico, colonial authors record declarations of war, battles, and victories in particular detail. Both Alvarado Tezozómoc and Durán describe an extraordinary gift exchange between the Mexica *tlahtoani* Itzcoatl and the ruler of Azcapotzalco that marked a new era of Mexica military exploit.[18] Following a period of political instability in the early decades of the fifteenth century, Itzcoatl sent an emissary to Azcapotzalco to inquire about the ruler's intentions toward the ascendant Tenochtitlan. Itzcoatl instructed his messenger Tlacaelel, "If he answers that there is no remedy, that he must annihilate us, then take this pitch with which we anoint the dead and smear it upon his body. Feather his head as we do to our dead and give him the shield, sword, and gilded arrows, which are the insignia of a sovereign; warn him that I say he must be on his guard."[19] The following day, the ruler of Azcapotzalco told Tlacaelel that against his own wishes, his people had decided to declare war on the people of Tenochtitlan. Understanding the Mexica pitch as an extraordinary sign, "the king allowed himself to be anointed and armed by Tlacaelel, and after he had donned the warrior's insignia he requested him to thank King Itzcoatl for his message."[20] In addition to demonstrating the symbolic power accrued in culturally charged situations by otherwise quotidian objects, the gift exchange between Itzcoatl and the ruler of Azcapotzalco became paradigmatic for declarations of war.

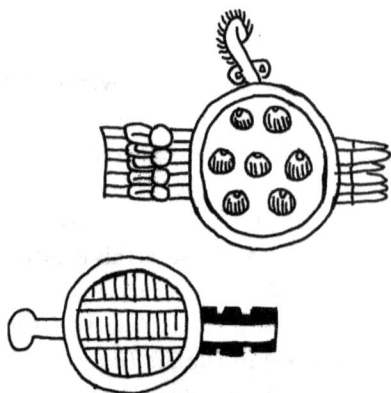

1.4. Shields as ideograms. Line drawings by author.

Itzcoatl sent the ruler of Azcapotzalco a set of extraordinary symbols, and by accepting and then wearing the warrior's insignia, ceremonial weaponry, and mortuary preparations, the ruler marked himself as a warrior to be sacrificed in battle. According to Durán, "These [gifts] were like insignia of a challenge, of perpetual enmity."[21] Durán's presentation of the gifts of war as signs recalls Boone's definition of ideograms as "single images [that] convey larger or unportrayable ideas, concepts or things."[22] Like ideograms in codices, gifts given in diplomatic exchanges functioned as signs conveying more information than they might outside the context of exchange. For example, the ideogram depicting a shield with arrows or a club represents the declaration of war like the gift of a warrior's insignia did in exchanges (Figure 1.4). In declarations of war, the warrior's insignia and funeral or priestly paraphernalia were sent to the enemy ruler as signs of war and impending death—concepts much grander than the gifts themselves.

In contrast to such exchanges, those signifying peace or commemorating death or accession were of many kinds. These types of exchanges involved lavish sets of jewelry, featherwork, ornamental armor, ceremonial weapons, and fine cloths and clothing. Durán describes the display of gifts given by foreign rulers to Tizoc at the time of his accession: "The Tezcoco king took a diadem set with green stones and placed it upon the head of the young monarch. He pierced the cartilage of his nose and inserted a nose plug of green emerald . . . on his legs were placed two anklets with golden bells hanging from them."[23] Each foreign ruler, in turn, presented Tizoc with gifts like these, though Durán does note that "some [were] more magnificent than others."[24] Likewise, similar gifts were given as inducements for peace. For example, during the reign of Moteuczoma Ilhuicamina, the Texcocoan ruler Nezahualcoyotl sent gifts of "gold jewelry, precious stones, ear ornaments, lip plugs, exquisite featherwork, shields, weapons, mantles and beautifully worked breechcloths" along with his request for peace.[25]

Finally, gifts given to the dead at the time of their burial included many of the same finely wrought artisanal crafts and weaponry exchanged at accessions and peace accords. At the funeral of the ninth *tlahtoani* Axayacatl, Tizoc paid his respects with "four slaves, two men and two women, a labret, ear pendants, a nose pendant, and a diadem, all of gold . . ."[26] Compared to gifts declaring war, gifts at peace accords, accessions, and burials showcased luxury goods, occasionally including ceremonial weaponry and even retainers; they signified wealth and power rather than war and death.

In the cultural context of Aztec gift exchanges, the gifts Moteuczoma gave Cortés responded to the demands of a god's appearance, while simultaneously intimating death in war. Moteuczoma's *teotlatquitl*, which according to the *Codex Mexicanus* included a beaded cape, two feather headdresses, two feather cloaks, five disks of turquoise mosaic, a tunic, and two shields, simultaneously symbolized war and peace and sacrificial death and apotheosis (see Figure 1.3). Pictorial histories of the gift exchange vary in the quantity of goods they illustrate, but they consistently represent luxury gifts and occasionally feature the addition of ceremonial weaponry and priestly vestments. In the *Codex Vaticanus A*, Durán's *History of the Indies*, and Sahagún's *Florentine Codex*, the necklace functions synecdochically as the ideogram representing all of Moteuczoma's gifts (Figures 1.5 and 1.6).

In these texts and elsewhere, a necklace serves as the conventional sign of declarations of peace. For instance, necklaces number among the gifts described in Sahagún's *Florentine Codex*, and López de Gómara and Chimalpahin report the two leaders exchanging necklaces. After describing the necklace exchange, Chimalpahin (but not López de Gómara) lists the luxury items Moteuczoma displayed for Cortés, including "many round feather shields of many colors and designs . . . many bracelets, feather ornaments, and other insignia . . . [and] beautiful mats . . ."[27] In the tradition of Mesoamerican gift exchanges and their depiction, Moteuczoma gave Cortés multiple sets of *teotlatquitl*, the luxury goods of the gods. Moteuczoma's gifts may have proffered peace, but they also gave occasion for Cortés to dress (or be dressed) as a *teotl*'s embodiment.

Iconographers, including Boone, have introduced the question of how Quetzalcoatl's return relates to the representations of gift exchange by identifying the *teotlatquitl* with specific *teteo*. Boone identifies the gifts as "part of

1.5. (left) Necklace given to Cortés in gift exchange. *Historia de las Indias de Nueva España*, 208v. Courtesy of the Biblioteca Nacional de España.
1.6. (right) Necklace given to Cortés in gift exchange. *Florentine Codex*, 3:415v. Courtesy of the Biblioteca Medicea Laurenziana.

the costume of the deity Quetzalcoatl . . . gifts that Cortés donned when Aztec ambassadors boarded his ship off the Veracruz coast."[28] The illustrations accompanying Sahagún's text depict Cortés receiving a mantle and two necklaces, and his inventory of the gifts includes two Quetzalcoatl costumes along with one of Tezcatlipoca and another of Tlalocan Teuctli (see Figure 1.6). The other items Cortés wears—the *quechquemitl*, necklaces, bell anklets, and feathers—figure prominently in the ceremonial dress of deity embodiments.

The *Florentine Codex* depicts Cortés wearing *teotlatquitl*, though not those of a single identifiable deity. The mantle Cortés wears appears to be a *quechquemitl*, a garment made by joining two rectangular pieces of fabric in such a way that the piece hangs from the shoulders in a triangular shape. Thought to have originated in the Gulf Coast region, by the time of Contact, the *quechquemitl* was a women's garment found throughout Mesoamerica, but its uses differed among cultural groups. In her "Analysis of the Aztec

Quechquemitl," Patricia Anawalt explains that "all evidence indicates that the Aztec quechquemitl was used solely in religious contexts."[29] Its appearance on Cortés, then, may indicate that the text's illustrators dressed him in ritual garments without understanding their specific associations, that they intentionally and perhaps mockingly dressed him in this women's garment, or that they imagined this man—like the priest who wore the Colhua princess's skin—wearing the garments of a goddess.

More importantly, the next illustration in the *Florentine Codex*'s sequence depicts Cortés wearing the necklaces and mantle along with two adornments not pictured in the preceding image: feathers in his hat and two anklets with bells. Both necklaces and bell anklets number among the *teotlatquitl* Moteuczoma gave Tezcatlipoca's embodiment during Toxcatl, and in the list of deities in the *Primeros memoriales*, Quetzalcoatl appears with what are described as "yteucuitlaacuechcuzqui . . . ocelotzitzili yn icxic contlaliticac." (His necklace of gold shells. . . He has placed bands of jaguar skin with bells on his legs.)[30] As Quetzalcoatl's name—Quetzal Feather Serpent—indicates, he had direct and distinct associations with feathers.

In fact, the "Anales de Cuauhtitlan" describes how Quetzalcoatl received his feathers, a story that has direct bearing on our interpretation of the feathers Cortés wears in his hat. According to the "Anales," a group of sorcerers grew tired of Quetzalcoatl, who, as ruler of Tula, refused to perform human sacrifices, and the sorcerer named Tezcatlipoca tricked Quetzalcoatl into looking at his appearance—"his flesh"—in a mirror.[31] After seeing himself, Quetzalcoatl was too embarrassed to appear in public. To increase his misery, the sorcerers agreed to "dress [him] up."[32] And so they contacted Coyotlinahual (Coyote Sorcerer), patron deity of the *amanteca* (featherworkers). Coyotlinahual made Quetzalcoatl a greenstone mask and feathered beard: "First he made Quetzalcoatl's head fan. Then he fashioned his turquoise mask, taking yellow to make the front, red to color the bill. Then he gave him his serpent teeth and made him his beard, covering him below with cotinga and roseate spoonbill feathers."[33] Quetzalcoatl looked at his reflection again and was pleased, but at the sorcerers' urging, Quetzalcoatl soon became drunk and disgraced himself. Deeply ashamed, Quetzalcoatl left Tula in the year 1 Reed. Quetzalcoatl arrived at the coast, put on his feathery attire, and sacrificed himself:

> And they say as he burned, his ashes arose. And what appeared and what they saw were all the precious birds, rising into the sky. They saw roseate spoonbills, cotingas, trogons, herons, green parrots, scarlet macaws, white fronted parrots, and all the other precious birds. And as

soon as his ashes had been consumed, they saw the heart of a quetzal rising upward. And so they knew he had gone to the sky, had entered the sky. The old people said he was changed into the star that appears at dawn. Therefore they say it came forth when Quetzalcoatl died, and they called him Lord of the Dawn . . . So it was after eight days that the morning star came out, which they said was Quetzalcoatl. It was then that he became lord, they said.[34]

A series of fiery and feathery transformations took Quetzalcoatl through a sequence of ontological states. In Alessandra Russo's words, feathers and flame brought about the "metamorphosis of the divinity," as the leader of Tula became the Lord of the Dawn.[35] Although the *Codex Mexicanus* and the *Florentine Codex* depict different sets of *teotlatquitl*, both sources document the presence—even abundance—of Aztec featherwork among the gifts presented to Cortés.

In her compelling study of feathers and sacrifice, Russo argues that feathers join the humans sacrificed as deities with the vital presence of deities in those sacrificial victims: "Feathers are not the sole property of any one specific deity, but rather a kind of *common denominator* for the entire Mexica pantheon of deities."[36] According to Russo, feathers, which Durán describes as the property solely of Aztec nobles, brought about transformations in both sacrificial victims and deities.[37] Drawing on the association of feathers with deified sacrificial victims, as well as feathers' transformative properties, Russo suggests that the featherwork banner held by one of the Aztec messengers during the gift exchange may indicate that some of these same principles are at play in the illustration (see Figure 1.6). She explains:

> It's important to note how this historical encounter was reelaborated on the narrative level: works of art—particularly, featherwork images—serve to introduce and aestheticize novelty, and in some sense, to make it visible. Just as the hideous serpent Quetzalcoatl is transformed through the emotive force of featherworks, Cortés also attains supernatural status through art.[38]

The featherwork gifts depicted in the *Codex Mexicanus* substantiate Russo's point and support my claim that in these contact perspective images and accounts, Cortés was imagined—and, from a contact perspective, "documented"—as having worn the *teotlatquitl*. (Notably, the contact perspective also "documents" local rulers wearing Cortés's *teotlatquitl*: "On several occasions, Cortés's presents to the caciques involved dressing them in Castilian clothes, and once the Conquistador even offers several items from his own wardrobe."[39]) In Russo's words, "Cortés is transformed by the works he receives as gifts and will be reborn in Mexico with the proper *tonalli* transferred to him by the Sun through feathers and precious stones."[40] Russo interprets the second illustration—the one in which Cortés wears feathers in his European-style hat—as signaling his transformation. Cortés, she argues, "has implicitly become a future conqueror"; alternatively—an alternative Russo does not explore—he became a sacrificial victim.[41]

Even though the *Florentine Codex*'s illustrations were typically done after the text had been completed, these images, like Chimalpahin's text, document the post-Contact circulation of a story in which Cortés, as was the custom, wore the luxurious gifts given him by Moteuczoma.[42] If, as in other codices, the necklaces function as ideograms, they depict Cortés donning the signs and symbols of a deity in the manner of a *teixiptla* (localized embodiment). The *Florentine Codex* and the *Codex Mexicanus* record the ambiguous situation in which Moteuczoma gave appropriately lavish gifts to Cortés, who is represented as having accepted and worn the gifts without knowing their full significance.

These images and their accompanying texts present a contact perspective, one that forefronts the interdependent constitution of colonial actors, including Moteuczoma, Cortés, and some of their contemporaries, while also incorporating the views of chroniclers, scribes, and artists working decades after the leaders' exchanges occurred. Insofar as they are the products of the colonial project, we could deem these texts (and perhaps especially the *Florentine Codex*'s Book 12) untrustworthy or contaminated. But to see them as such would undercut their capacity to help us interpret diverse contact perspectives. In other words, if we see *Book 12* only as a product of the Church's extirpation program, then we miss opportunities to unpack the competing claims embedded in its text and images, including the claim that the Aztecs recognized—in word and gift—Cortés and his company as *teteo*.[43] Additionally, *Book 12* and the other texts that describe or depict the exchange introduce the question of how the exchange's history—pictorial and textual—relates to the stories of Quetzalcoatl's return.

Prophetic Vision: The Reappearance of Quetzalcoatl's *Ixiptla*

By characterizing the texts that depict the gift exchange between Moteuczoma and Cortés as having a contact perspective, I am suggesting that in certain cases, times, and cultures, of which the Encounter is one example, there is little possibility of excavating or even documenting an empirical, objective, and unitary historical "truth." Gary Urton's ascription of the term "mythohisto-ry" to texts like these captures the ambiguity embedded in accounts in which myths, stories about the "sorts of questions that religions ask," modify histo-ries, or when we find "what happened" and "what is said to have happened" complicated by what only the (religious) imagination can make happen.[44] This is not, however, to claim that there are simply competing mythohistories: one Spanish and the other Aztec. Drawing principally on Cortés's "Second Letter" and the accounts by Sahagún and Durán, we turn now to texts that helped construct (or at least support) the Contact-era prophecy of Quetzal-coatl's return and consider the exchange's outcome in light of the roles Mo-teuczoma and Cortés adopted.

The myth of Quetzalcoatl's return appears in three colonial documents: the *Florentine Codex*'s *Book 12: The Conquest*, Durán's *History of the Indies*, and—perhaps originally—Hernán Cortés's "Second Letter." Cortés's "Second Let-ter," written to Charles V on October 30, 1520, contains two speeches attrib-uted to Moteuczoma. In the second speech, Moteuczoma greets Cortés with a divine welcome:

> For a long time we have known from the writings of our ancestors that neither I, nor any of those who dwell in this land, are natives of it, but foreigners who came from very distant parts; and likewise we know that a chieftain, of whom they were all vassals, brought our people to this region. And he returned to his native land and after many years came again, by which time all those who had remained were married to na-tive women and had built villages and raised children. And when he wished to lead them away again they would not go nor even admit him as their chief; and so he departed. And we have always held that those who descended from him would come and conquer this land and take us as their vassals . . . Thus as you [Cortés] are in your own country and your own house, rest now from the hardships of your journey and the battles which you have fought.[45]

Judged by Henry B. Nicholson to be "the most significant account" relating the return of Quetzalcoatl, the "Second Letter" speech declares Cortés a re-turned Aztec leader, if not a deity.[46] As the primary text of a contact per-spective myth, Cortés's letter raises obvious problems regarding its accuracy and author's motivations.[47] If Cortés embellished the kernel of a Mesoameri-can myth to suggest his own apotheosis, later elaborations on the narrative of Quetzalcoatl's return demonstrate that whatever the mythohistory's origin, it (re)entered the Mesoamerican corpus during the Encounter.

Sixteenth-century accounts, including *Book 12* of Sahagún's *Florentine Codex* and Durán's *History of the Indies*, attest to the narrative's vitality in the early colonial mythohistorical imagination. Moteuczoma's speeches in Durán and Sahagún largely accord with the one recounted by Cortés, especially with regard to the ruler having guarded Quetzalcoatl's people and property in his absence. In Durán's account, Moteuczoma orders his artisans to make Cortés's gifts in secret and then instructs his messenger, "I want you to find out who their commander is, since he is the one to whom you must give all these presents. You must discover with absolute certainty if he is the one our ancestors called Topiltzin or Quetzalcoatl."[48] In Sahagún's account, Moteuczoma's messengers greet Cortés as Quetzalcoatl even before he disembarks: "When the Indians drew alongside the flagship, those on it asked them where they were from, who they were, and what they wanted. To this they replied that they were Mexicans, that they came from Mexico in search of their lord and king, Quetzalcoatl . . ."[49] In *Book 12*, Sahagún reports that when Moteuczoma first heard of the ships' sighting, "He quickly sent out a party. He thought and believed that it was Topiltzin Quetzalcoatl who had landed. For they were of the opinion that he would return, that he would appear, that he would come back to his seat of authority, because he had gone in that direction [eastward] when he left."[50] These passages demonstrate one of the ways in which Sahagún or a group of his Aztec informants or scribes (re)imagined and mythohistoricized Contact.

Appropriately, scholars debate the relative authority of late-sixteenth-century accounts of Contact and find woven within them various political, economic, and theological agendas. In "Meeting the Enemy," Louise Burkhart explains that the *Florentine Codex*'s account of the conversation between Moteuczoma and Cortés, "is better seen as a Nahuatlized version of the Cortés-based tradition and a reflection of prevailing anti-Moteuczoma sentiments than an accurate transcription passed through Nahua tradition."[51] Scholars also criticize *Book 12*'s account of the omens. Townsend speculates that they were an attempt on the part of Sahagún's informants to salvage the memories of their families, elites who would have been responsible for foreseeing and ensuring the safety of Tlatelolco and Tenochtitlan.[52] Recently, Diana Magaloni Kerpel has argued that Catholicism heavily influenced the omens' depiction. The "eight omens of the Conquest," she explains, "relate how Christ became the new sun in Mesoamerica" by infusing native divinatory structures with Christian content.[53] (Notably, Kevin Terraciano observes that by contrast to López de Gómara's chronicle or Cortés's letters, "the Nahuatl-language text [of *Book 12*] makes no mention of Christianity whatsoever. Nor do the artists of Book XII present images of the crucifix or the Virgin Mary or any other Christian icon which might have signified a clear association between the war and the arrival of Christianity."[54]) Contact perspective accounts, like those that describe Cortés's apotheosis and the omens, incorporated both Mesoamerican and European modes of working through New World encounters.[55] The presence of competing *and* complementary interests sometimes makes the two modes difficult to parse; Aztec rituals and divination coincided and collided with European expectations of the exotic, extraordinary, and divine (providence).

Prophetic Vision: The Divinatory Mode of Mythohistory

We are left now to return to the question of who benefits from the myth of Quetzalcoatl's return if it is—as it seems to have been—a post-Contact invention. Without a way to positively identify the myth's origin, we can examine it in both pre- and post-Contact Mesoamerican and European mythic (or narrative) traditions. On the one hand, European explorers are known for their imaginative descriptions of the New World. Consider Antonio Pigafetta's sighting along the coast of South America of "a misbegotten creature with the head and ears of a mule, a camel's body, the legs of a deer and the whinny of a horse."[56] Although Cortés's reports to Charles V are not as phantasmagoric, his political desires motivated him to recount the myth and Moteuczoma's recognition of him as a returned leader. More importantly, the speeches he recorded in the "Second Letter" took on a life of their own in Europe. As Gananath Obeyesekere observes, we know that "the event [of Cortés's apotheosis] itself was treated as a true occurrence by Europeans. Thus, the very beginnings of the voyages of discovery carried with them the tradition of the apotheosis of redoubtable European navigators who were also the harbingers of civilization."[57] For Europeans, Cortés's apotheosis became the founding narrative for other explorers' apotheoses.

In the wake of Contact's devastation, the Aztecs and Spaniards incorporated the myth of Quetzalcoatl's return into their shared mythohistory. For the Aztecs, "history" was already an integrative system of many histories subject to revision, rather than an exclusionary search for a univocal history. Aztec concepts of "history" incorporated ahistorical modes of meaning making, including divinatory and oneiric practices. Although the Aztecs maintained both divinatory and historical manuscripts and used them for different purposes, the two systems—one prophetic and the other archival—acted in concert on occasions that called for the diviner to interpret historic circumstances, including the arrival of the Spaniards and the ensuing Encounter:

Divination was not a simple act of reading but was fundamentally a work of judgment and interpretation, where the diviner mediated between the spirit world and the concerns of the individual who sought guidance. The ever-present forces were revealed in the divinatory book, but it was the responsibility of the calendar priest to draw out and shape them into a sound prognosis.[58]

Diviners mediated between a measured tradition inscribed in texts and reinscribed through ritual and an ongoing unfolding present. No diviner could foresee the future with precision, but ritual and mythohistory provided practical and narrative frameworks through which events became comprehensible and coherent. The natures of divination and what we are calling mythohistory, symbiotic systems that integrated new information according to an age-old story structure, prevent us from consistently being able to distill the pre-Contact from the post-Contact as López de Gómara, Muñoz Camargo, Sahagún, Durán, and Chimalpahin remember them. Regardless of the Quetzalcoatl myth's pre- or post-Contact origin, post-Contact mythohistories document the myth's life and liveliness in the years following the Encounter.

Most significantly, when Cortés accepted the gifts and (if he) wore them, Aztec witnesses could have identified him as a *teixiptla*, someone who assumed the identity of a god. Whether or not he actually wore the gifts, the *Florentine Codex*'s illustrators provided at least one picture of that possibility (Figure 1.6). This image of Cortés's dress performance affirmed the possibility that he could have been revered or sacrificed or both. To put it simply, Cortés as a *teixiptla*/sacrificial victim certainly seems to have been a topic of Contact conversation.

For Cortés, Moteuczoma's gifts represented the enormous wealth the Spaniard sought; he accepted the luxurious gifts in order to advance himself and likely without knowing their possible consequences. From the contact perspective, when Cortés wore the *teotlatquitl*, he became a *teixiptla*, perhaps even Quetzalcoatl, and entered into a ceremonial game in which he could be conqueror or sacrificial victim. By accepting the gifts, Cortés unwittingly played on the idea of being a god, and in his play, he, in turn, was played on by the Aztecs—in the stories that developed in contact perspective accounts, if not historically. As Paul Ricoeur observes, "The player is metamorphosed 'in the true'; in playful representation, 'what is emerges'. But 'what is' is no longer what we call everyday reality; or rather, reality truly becomes reality . . . something to fear or to hope for, something unsettled."[59] Indeed, elements of fantastic play enter into both Cortés's letter to Charles V, which casts him (in

Moteuczoma's speech) as a leader expected to return, and in texts that "document" his acceptance and wearing of *teotlatquitl*. Regardless of these events' historicity (i.e., that which happened), they became significant elements of that which was said to have happened. Cortés as a deity's *teixiptla* initiated a reality that Europeans considered mythic but Mesoamericans considered real. Cortés was greeted as a god's embodiment; he survived to tell the story that was retold on both sides of the Atlantic. However, had the game gone in favor of the Aztecs instead of the Spaniards, the myth could have ended in Cortés's sacrifice as a *teixiptla* instead of (what he perceived as) his apotheosis.

Either way, the issue of why the Mexicas and their neighbors called Cortés and his retinue "*teteo*" is clearly more complicated than a case of mistaken identity or some confusion surrounding the Spaniards' ontologies. From a contact perspective, Cortés was (or at least could have been) a deity's localized embodiment: the *teixiptla* of a *teotl*. Certainly, the Aztecs needed a name for the strangers who landed on the coast of Veracruz in 1519, but they also already had ritual means of incorporating foreign threats and strange gods into their own sacrificial ceremonies and pantheon. As we will see, the Aztecs ritually manufactured god-bodies from a variety of materials, including humans and human body parts. Indeed, the *teotlatquitl* that the Aztecs gave Cortés provided him with the cluster of divine qualities that could have facilitated his transformation into a god-body through a process similar to that of the Colhua princess/Toci, Tonantzin. Before we can understand the ways in which the Aztecs made gods, we must first explore the meanings of *teotl* (god) and *teixiptla* (localized embodiment).

CHAPTER 2

Ethnolinguistic Encounters
Teotl and *Teixiptla* in Nahuatl Scholarship

Understanding "the gods" concerned both the Aztecs and the Spaniards from the earliest moments of Contact. As the Aztecs observed the Spaniards, apprehension about the gods' presence and absence plagued Moteuczoma and his priests. Accounts of the Encounter leave us with a mythohistorical mix of (re)actions ascribed to the *tlahtoani* (speaker; leader): in the days leading up to the Spaniards' arrival, Moteuczoma desperately attempted to read a series of eight omens; he sent messengers disguised as merchants to spy on the strangers; he gave Cortés deity costumes as an enticement to leave; he stopped eating and suffered from insomnia; and as a final resort, he sent enchanters and sorcerers to captivate (or capture) the Spaniards. Meanwhile, the Spaniards marched through Mesoamerican *altepemeh* (water mountains; communities) as they moved from the coast of Veracruz inland to Tenochtitlan. At each village, town, and city, they demolished temples, destroyed "idols," "converted" locals, and erected crosses and Marian images. Those who did not convert (and likely many who did) maintained the names, rituals, and beliefs associated with pre-Contact deities. Archaeological records from the colonial period document the persistence of indigenous ritual and religious life, and today many indigenous communities in Mexico practice ceremonies that bear striking resemblance to those Sahagún and his contemporaries described.[1]

Vivid accounts of Aztec ceremonies and the ingenious hybridities that emerged from the Encounter have attracted scholars' attention for centuries. My exploration of the gift exchange demonstrates, however, that Mesoamericanists are still struggling to understand what *teotl* means and what constitutes a *teixiptla*. Indeed, a nagging doubt that the Mexicas and their neighbors would actually have mistaken Cortés or other Spaniards for *teteo* persists in the study of Aztec religion. In "Burying the White Gods," Camilla Townsend urges us to consider whether the story of the Spaniards as gods persists because scholars have been unwilling to concede that the technological disparity between Mesoamericans and their invaders led to the Spaniards' victory. Our refusal to admit that printing presses, ships, ammunition, and diseases gave

Spaniards an overwhelming advantage over Mesoamericans has led us, she argues, to perpetuate the incredible notion that the Aztecs stood "wide-eyed" in awe of the white gods.[2] In Townsend's estimation, the Aztecs had to call the Spaniards *something*, and until they could place their adversaries, *teotl* functioned as an identifier and little more.[3] Townsend's lucid and convincing explanation of *why* the Aztecs called the Spaniards *teteo* stops short of exploring exactly *what teotl* meant to the Aztecs. Historian Kevin Terraciano also wonders what about *teotl*'s meaning made the Aztecs associate it with Spaniards:

> Did these Nahuas really think of the Spaniards in such terms? It is difficult to believe that these references, attested in other contemporary native-language sources such as the Annals of Tlatelolco, were later invented by people who had witnessed the conquest. A more salient question concerns the meaning of the Nahuatl term "*teotl.*" Lockhart put it best that "we are still far from a full understanding of the semantic range of the Nahuatl word *teotl.*" Despite our inability to understand the range of meaning inherent in this word, however, it is clear that "*teotl*" did convey some sense of the sacred and venerable.[4]

The gift exchange highlights the significance of the term *teotl* and calls our attention to the importance of a *teixiptla* looking like the *teotl* he/she embodies, but Terraciano's question, which is also our initial question, remains: What does *teotl* mean? Further, what is a *teotl*? And finally, how does a *teotl* relate to a *teixiptla*?

I am not the first to wonder about the meanings and functions of *teteo* and *teixiptlahuan*. Identifying recurrent trends in the study of these terms is crucial to my project, because they evoke larger concerns about what has been considered normative in the study of Mesoamerican religions. We will see that sixteenth-century friar-scholars, including lexicographers, struggled to understand Aztec religion both in its terms and in their own. Like his contemporary Alonso de Molina, Sahagún considered himself a linguist, and he intended for students of Nahuatl to use the *Florentine Codex* as a linguistic reference as much as an illustrated encyclopedia of the Aztec world. Along with Molina's *Vocabulario* (1571) and Sahagún's *Florentine Codex* (1570–1585), lexicons by Horacio Carochi (1645) and Rémi Siméon (1885) compose the foundational sources of older Nahuatl studies.[5] Serious inquiries into the meanings of *teotl* and *teixiptla* began again with the publication of Arild Hvidtfeldt's 1956 dissertation, which examines *teotl* and *teixiptla* in the context of *Book 2: The Ceremonies* of the *Florentine Codex*. In this comparative study, Hvidtfeldt likened *teotl* to the Polynesian concept *mana*, and for decades after its publication in 1958, his work stood as the most comprehensive exploration of *teotl* and *teixiptla*. That scholars began citing Hvidtfeldt's definitions immediately—and have continued to do so—testifies to the impact of his research. Art historian Richard Townsend—to take just one example—summarized and popularized Hvidtfeldt's definition of *teotl* in his *State and Cosmos in the Art of Tenochtitlan*:

> *Teotl* was universally translated by the Spanish as 'god,' 'saint,' or sometimes 'demon,' but its actual meaning more closely corresponds with that of the Polynesian term *mana*, signifying a numinous, impersonal force diffused throughout the universe. . . . *Teotl* expresses the notion of sacred quality, but with the idea that it could be physically manifested in some specific presence—a rainstorm, a mirage, a lake, or a majestic mountain. It is as if the world was perceived as being magically charged, inherently alive in greater or lesser degree with this vital force. Everything in the world was potentially a hierophany: things, animals, people, transitory phenomena had the capacity to manifest some aspect of the sacred. And for ritual purposes, of course, a *teixiptla* especially acted as a talismanic token of the sacred.[6]

The understanding of *teotl* Hvidtfeldt and Townsend popularized idealizes indigenous religions as close to the pantheistic spirit world and—at least in Townsend's case—adds a touch of the universal-perennial. In this example, we see that *teotl* became more intelligible as it began to sound like and be associated with other familiar terms of religion, like *mana* and "hierophany." Hvidtfeldt and Townsend made *teotl* more accessible by translating it into the idiom of religious studies, and prominent researchers, including Elizabeth H. Boone, John M. D. Pohl, and Rebecca Stone, have drawn upon these translations in their studies on Mesoamerican and Andean religions.[7]

Since the publication of Hvidtfeldt's dissertation, two major modes of analysis have characterized studies of *teotl* and *teixiptla*: linguistic analysis and the hermeneutics of comparison.[8] The interdisciplinary nature of Mesoamerican studies makes distinguishing lexicographers from art historians from scholars of religions rather artificial, as their best work often occurs in consultation and concert. For the sake of clarity, though, I will examine the lexicographers apart from the comparativists and delineate two lineages among the comparativists. The first originates in Alfredo López Austin's foundational studies of Aztec religion, myth, and the human body, which address *teotl*, *teixiptla*, and *hombre-dios* (human-god), a related category López Austin established. We shall see that both Davíd Carrasco and Inga Clendinnen draw on López Austin's work in their own interpretations of Aztec religion. The second genealogy begins with Jorge Klor de Alva's *Spiritual Warfare in Mexico: Christianity and the Aztecs* (1980), which examines *teotl* in the context of Aztec religion's post-Contact survival. Kay Read develops Klor de Alva's interpretation of *teotl* in relation to the transformative power of sacrifice, and philosopher James Maffie elaborates on some of his themes. Additionally, in 2006, Read and Nahuat-l listserv subscribers informally discussed their interpretations of *teotl* and *teixiptla* in an online exchange.[9] For centuries, *teotl* and *teixiptla* have evaded easy transcription. My intention in what follows is to summarize and critique the major approaches scholars have taken in the study of these concepts. I will survey the moments of clarity and confusion that surround these terms before I offer an interpretation of them.

Sahagún's *Florentine Codex*: A Cultural Lexicon

Sahagún began collecting accounts of the pre-Contact world from informants in Tlatelolco and Texcoco in the 1540s. His notes took a more formal shape after 1558 when he received an official commission to compile a document that would assist friars in converting the people of New Spain. At the convent of San Francisco of Mexico in Tepeapulco, Sahagún worked with a team of trilingual scribes from the Colegio de Santa Cruz in Tlatelolco. Together they transcribed interviews of local informants and organized the material into the "Manuscript of 1569." Several years later, Sahagún returned to his manuscript at the urging of Fray Rodrigo de Sequera, Commissary General of the Franciscans, and in the late 1570s, Sahagún prepared two copies of the *General History of the Things of New Spain*, both of which featured parallel Nahuatl and Spanish columns. Sequera delivered one copy to Philip II in 1580, but the second copy's fate remains unknown. Today, the Laurentian Library in Florence, Italy, houses the *General History*, which, because of its location, is known as the *Florentine Codex*.

Inevitably, Sahagún's Franciscan training and his order's desire for an aid to the conversion of native Mexicans shaped the final form, language, and images of the *Florentine Codex*. Scholars debate the extent to which Sahagún sympathized with his order's interest in extirpating indigenous religion. Some argue that the *Florentine Codex* "represented an extraordinary attempt at Christianising by means of cultural understanding rather than force."[10] Sahagún recognized as one of his objectives "to write in the Mexican language that which seemed to me useful for the indoctrination, the propagation and perpetuation of the Christianization of these natives of this New Spain."[11] However, he repeatedly expresses a cautious interest in preserving the Nahuatl language as well as describing pre-Contact cultures, concepts, and religion:

> This work is like a dragnet to bring to light all the words of this language with their exact and metaphorical meanings, and all their ways of speaking, and most of their ancient practices, the good and evil. It will be a source of great satisfaction, because, with much less effort than it costs me here, those who may so desire will be able to know many of the ancient practices and all the language of this Mexican people in a brief time.[12]

Although he seems to have been intrigued by many aspects of Aztec culture, Sahagún's interest in creating and preserving Nahuatl competes only with the extraordinary comprehensiveness of his work as its most striking feature.

As a linguist, Sahagún held himself to the high standards established by grammarians and linguists in Spain. Efforts to standardize Castilian Spanish began in the thirteenth-century court of King Alfonso X, who assembled scribes to author texts on the arts, law, and sciences. In his reflections on writing dictionaries, Sahagún refers to Ambrogio Calepino's *Cornucopiæ* (1502), the first bilingual (Castilian-Latin) dictionary, and along with a handful of grammars, including Elio Antonio de Nebrija's *Gramática de la lengua castellana* (1492), Sahagún had the Calepino in mind as a model for his own work. Some attribute a copy of Nebrija's text with Nahuatl annotations to Sahagún, a notion dismissed by Mary Clayton.[13]

According to Sahagún's own commentary, writing a Nahuatl dictionary was one of his unfulfilled wishes, even though Mendieta claims Sahagún was well prepared to do the work: ". . . aprendió en breve la lengua mexicana, y súpola tan bien, que ninguno otro hasta hoy se le ha igualado en alcanzar los secretos de ella, y ninguno tanto se ha ocupado en escrebir en ella." (. . . he learned the Mexican language quickly, and he knew it so well that no one else to date has equaled him in achieving the secrets of it, and no one else has been so busy writing in it.)[14] Indeed, many of his colleagues assumed he was following in the footsteps of Calepino and Nebrija:

> When this work began, it began to be said by those who knew of it, that a dictionary was being made. And, even now, many keep on asking me: "How does the dictionary progress?" Certainly it would be very benefi-

cial to produce so useful a work for those who desire to learn this Mexican language, just as Ambrosio Calepino prepared one for those who desire to learn the Latin language and the meaning of words.[15]

Sahagún knew that pre-Contact Nahuatl speakers had no alphabetized language and that the overwhelming majority of their pictorial texts had been destroyed during the Encounter. He lamented the lack of available Nahuatl texts, as he thought of them as necessary references for writing a dictionary:

> And, so, it was impossible for me to prepare a dictionary. But I have laid the groundwork in order that whosoever may desire can prepare it with ease, for, through my efforts twelve Books have been written in an idiom characteristic and typical of this Mexican language, where, in addition to its being a very pleasing and profitable writing, also are found therein all the manners of speech and all the words this language uses, as well verified and certain as that which Virgil, Cicero, and other authors wrote in the Latin language.[16]

Indeed, Sahagún's work—though not a dictionary like those of his contemporaries—incorporates many features common to European reference works.

Sahagún and his trilingual collaborators began gathering and compiling information from Nahuatl speakers in the 1550s that they would eventually include in the *Florentine Codex*.[17] The scribes' Franciscan educations had familiarized them with European languages and artistic conventions, and their native knowledge of Nahuatl facilitated their editorial and illustrational work. Indeed, the *Florentine Codex*'s hybridity stems from its multicultural influences, and its organization—and, to some extent, its contents—reflects European models for cataloguing the natural world and human cultures. Scholars have identified in it the imprint of Aristotle's *History of Animals* (350 BCE), Pliny the Elder's *Natural History* (ca. 77–79 CE), Isidore de Seville's *Etymologies* (ca. 630 CE), Jacob Meydenbach's *Hortus Sanitatis* (1491 CE), and Bartholomaeus Anglicus's *On the Properties of Things* (ca. 1240 CE). In the Colegio's library and Sahagún's study, European models and theories met with indigenous language and concepts to produce a nearly comprehensive record of Aztec culture and classical Nahuatl organized along Old World paradigms.

For example, the form and structure of the *Florentine Codex* demonstrates Sahagún's familiarity with medieval "encyclopedias," such as Isidore de Seville's *Etymologies*, written in the seventh century and published in the fifteenth, or Bartholomaeus Anglicus's *De Proprietatibus Rerum*, as well as herbals (or her-

baria).[18] Originally specimen books, herbals collected, preserved, and cata-
logued plant specimens. Over time, illustrations replaced the specimens in
herbals, and the texts expanded to include not only plants but also animals,
rocks, minerals, and imaginal creatures. With the advent of printing in the
early fifteenth century, the popularity of illustrated herbals increased, and Sahagún probably had access to herbals in the library at Tlatelolco. Given the
similarity of their structures and illustrations, it seems likely that he patterned
portions of the *Florentine Codex* after texts like the *Hortus Sanitatis* (1491), a
possibility I discuss in more detail below. Additionally, he integrated features
common in other types of reference works, such as glossaries, in both the
Primeros memoriales (1561) and the *Florentine Codex*. For example, in a section of *Book 10: The People* dedicated to the human body, Sahagún lists more
than three hundred physiological features along with their descriptions:

> ehuatl, teehuatl, topanehuayo, iztac, tlatlactli, chichiltic, chichilpahtic,
> tlatlacpahtic, yayactic, yayauhqui . . .

> Skin, our skin, our outer skin, white, ruddy, chili-red, very chili-red,
> very ruddy, dark, darkish . . .[19]

In the process of reaching his own goal for the *Florentine Codex*—that of creating a linguistic reference—and of carrying out the mission of his order, Sahagún drew upon existing European reference works to convey the richness
he encountered in his informants' descriptions of Aztec culture and cosmovision. In so doing, he provided his brothers and later readers with a nearly encyclopedic (though not exhaustive) overview of Aztec life.

Looking back, the comprehensive and descriptive nature of the *Florentine
Codex* makes it seem as though Sahagún exceeded his own goal of writing a
dictionary. The *Florentine Codex* remains an invaluable resource precisely because it is not constrained by the format of a dictionary or lexicon. By contrast to the methodical definitions provided in dictionaries, the expository
style of his text amplifies words' denotations and connotations rather than
restricts them. Whereas early bilingual lexicons limit a word's meaning to a
list of (translated) synonyms or a brief description, *teotl* and *teixiptla* occur
throughout the *Florentine Codex* and sometimes in unexpected contexts. Sahagún's older Nahuatl text serves as the primary ethnolinguistic source for
my analysis because it provides multiple attestations of *teotl* and *teixiptla* in
passages describing extraordinary rituals *and* everyday objects and occasions.
In fact, contexts that are not explicitly religious generate some of the richest

insights into the meaning of *teotl*, which, as the following demonstrates, linguists have almost always translated as "god."

Early Lexicons and Grammars

According to Karttunen, "the most important reference works about Nahuatl in existence" include those of Fray Alonso de Molina (1571), Horacio Carochi (1645), and Rémi Siméon (1885).[20] The lexicons compiled by these three grammarians are essential for the study and translation of older Nahuatl in part because they reveal the difficult work of defining foreign terms that describe a new world's perspective.

Alonso de Molina learned Nahuatl as a child and compiled his first dictionary, *Aquí comienza un vocabulario en la lengua castellana y mexicana* (or *Vocabulario en la lengua castellana y mexicana*), in 1555. This first volume contained Spanish entries translated into Nahuatl, and it formed the basis of Molina's later *Vocabulario* (1571).[21] In his prologue, he explains, "Para la variedad y diferencia que hay en los vocablos, según diversas provincias, se tendra este aviso que al principio se pondran los que se usan aqui in Tetzcoco y en Mexico, que es donde mejor y mas curiosa se habla la lengua." (Because of the variety and difference that exists in the vocabularies, because of different provenances, be advised that initially [the words] are those used in Tetzcoco and in Mexico, which is where the language is spoken better and more interestingly.)[22] Molina worked alongside other friars, including Sahagún, compiling resources for the Church in New Spain. In fact, by the time he published the second *Vocabulario*, Molina and Sahagún had worked together to translate other manuscripts, most notably *Sumario de las indulgencias concedidas a los cofrades del santísimo Sacramento, traduzido en lengua mexicana* (1568–1572). To a significant extent, Molina's lexicon is a product of his collaboration with Sahagún, and it seems likely that an ongoing working relationship existed between the two friar-scholars:

> Fray Bernardino, with his Tlatelolcan students, had collected multiple texts in Nahuatl and continued busily preparing what they called "their Calepino." As many idiomatic words and expressions had to be collected in it as it was possible to have. . . . It should not be thought odd that, when after these years, [Molina] was giving the finishing touches to his new and richest lexicon, he sought the advice and help of his wise brother of the cloth. In this sense, it is possible to think that, although

the *Vocabulario* of 1571 was basically Molina's work, in some sense, Sahagún's influence was felt in it.[23]

As members of the same religious order, instructors in the same Colegio, and linguists with common interests, Molina and Sahagún—and the texts each authored—shared a profound intimacy. Their collaboration inevitably enhanced their ability to define Nahuatl concepts. Working in the mid- to late sixteenth century, Sahagún and Molina produced independent and comprehensive sources in and on Nahuatl, and together their contemporaneous texts provide both standard meanings and numerous contextual uses of Nahuatl words.

Many of the approximately 23,600 entries in Molina's *Vocabulario* (1571) duplicate one another, because he lists multiple forms of words rather than single canonical forms.[24] While Molina's inclusion of multiple entries sometimes causes confusion, the variants elucidate semantic nuances, as well. For example, Molina defines *teotl* as simply, "*dios*," but this basic entry falls among nearly three hundred entries that begin with the prefix *teo-*.[25] By comparison, he lists several variants of *teixiptla*, including both substantive and verbal forms.[26] His translations of *teixiptla*'s substantive forms emphasize images, substitutes, and representatives, as well as representations and substitutions (see Table 2.1).

Table 2.1. *Teixiptla* Variants in Molina's *Vocabulario*: Substantive Forms

Nahuatl Word Form	Spanish Translation	English Translation
teixiptla	imagen de alguno, sustituto, o delegado	image of someone, substitute or delegate
teixiptla	copinaloni, molde de imagen de vazia dizo	(a copinaloni is an instrument for making copies), mold for a cast image
teixiptlatini	representador de persona en farza	representative of a person in a comedy
teixiptlatiliztli	representación de aqueste (persona en farza)	representation of this one (the person in the comedy)
tlaixiptlayotl	imagen pintada	painted image
tlaixiptlayotilli	cosa restituida en otra especie, o cosa que se da en lugar de otra	a thing restored in another kind, or a thing that is given in the place of another[a]

[a] Molina, *Vocabulario*, 46v and 123v.

Table 2.2. *Teixiptla* Variants in Molina's *Vocabulario*: Verbal Forms

Nahuatl Word Form	Spanish Translation	English Translation
ixiptlayoua	recompensarse o satisfazarse algo	to recompense or satisfy something
ixiptlayotia (nicn.)	hazer algo a su imagen y semejanza. pre. onicnixiptlayoti.	to make something in one's image or likeness
ixiptlayotia (nin.)	delegar, o sostituir a otro en su lugar. pre. oninixiptlayoti.	to delegate; to substitute in its place
ixiptlati (nite.)	asistir en lugar de otro, o representar persona en farsa. preterito. oniteixiptlatic.	to attend in the place of another or to represent a person in a farce[a]

[a] Molina, *Vocabulario*, 45v. These definitions and forms, along with those of Clavijero and Siméon, also appear in Appendix A

In addition to these substantive forms, Molina also includes four verbal variants of *ixiptla*: *ixiptlayoua, ixiptlayotia* (nicn.), *ixiptlayotia* (nin.), and *ixiptlati* (nite.).[27] He defines these as shown in Table 2.2. Like his definitions of the substantive forms, Molina's glosses of the verbal variants reflect three primary meanings: substitution for something, representation (physical resemblance), and representation (by proxy). These variations raise the question of *teixiptla*'s original referent and whether it was an action or an entity.[28]

The *Reglas de la lengua mexicana con un vocabulario* (1731–1787) by eighteenth-century grammarian Francisco Xavier Clavijero and the *Dictionnaire de la langue nahuatl ou mexicaine* (1885) by nineteenth-century lexicographer Rémi Siméon give us insight into the stability of *teixiptla* and *teotl* over time. Clavijero glosses *teotl* as "*dios*" and provides three succinct entries for *teixiptla* variants, which can be seen in Table 2.3. Clavijero's emphasis on a sense of portraiture in two of his three *teixiptla* entries may reflect an eighteenth-century interest in portraying the peoples, wealth, and natural beauty of New Spain.[29] In contrast to the relatively brief definitions given by Molina and Clavijero, Siméon incorporates contextual details into his entries. We also know that Siméon's definitions draw directly from his work translating Andrés de Olmos's grammar in 1875 and Sahagún's *Florentine Codex* in 1880, as well as from his knowledge of other sixteenth- and seventeenth-century

Table 2.3. *Teixiptla* Variants in Clavijero's *Reglas*

Nahuatl Word Form	Spanish Translation	English Translation
ixiptlayotl	imagen, retrato	image, portrait
ixiptlatia (nite.)	retratar, representar	to paint a portrait, to represent
ixiptlayohua (ni.)	quedar pagada o satisfecha la deuda	to be paid or to satisfy a debt[a]

[a] Clavijero, *Reglas de la lengua mexicana*, 95.

Table 2.4. *Teixiptla* Variants in in Siméon's *Dictionnaire*

Nahuatl Word Form	Spanish Translation	English Translation
ixiptlayoua	ser sustituido, hablando de un objeto	to be substituted, speaking of an object
ixiptlati	sustituir a alguien, representar un papel, a un personaje	to substitute as someone, to represent a role, by a person
ixiptlatia	entregar su cargo a alguien; sustituir a alguien	to hand over one's post to someone; to substitute for someone
ixiptlatl	representante, delegado	representative, delegate[a]

[a] Siméon includes the following examples of *ixiptlatl*'s use: "En comp.: nixiptla (por no-ixiptla), mi Delgado; pl. nixiptlauan, mis representantes (my representatives); nixiptla niqu-iua, delego a alguien (someone's delegate); *ititlan, ixiptla ipatillo in sancto Padre, enviado, delegado, nuncio papel (emissary, delegate, papal ambassador); *Obispo ixiptla, represent-ante del Obispo (the Bishop's representative); *teixiptla*, delegado de alguien (someone's delegate). Rev. ixiptlatzin: cuix ticmahuiztili in ixiptlatzin in totecuiyo Jesu Christo yhuan in imixiptlahuan sanctome? (J. B.), ¿Has adorado la imagen de Nuestro Señor Jesucristo y las imágenes de los santos? (Have you venerated the image of Our Lord Jesus Christ and the images of the saints?)" Siméon, *Dictionnaire*, 218.

Nahuatl texts.[30] He includes one entry for *teotl*, "*dios, diosa*," and four related to *teixiptla*.[31] Siméon's definitions of *teixiptla* express its representative function with an emphasis on substitution (see Table 2.4).

In general, Siméon's definitions of *teixiptla*'s verbal forms emphasize one person representing, substituting, or standing in for another person. He does not define *teixiptla* in relation to images or portraits. Unlike Molina and Clavijero, Siméon directly addresses the issue of *teotl*'s meaning in compounds by explaining that "combined with other words, *teotl* signifies sacred, marvelous, strange, surprising, terrible."[32] Siméon opens *teotl* to translations other than "god," at least in compounds, which prompts us to wonder if these glosses reflect changes in the word's meaning or observations he made during his work as a translator. In later interpretations, especially those by scholars of religion and anthropology, the notion of *teotl* as "the sacred" takes on even greater prominence. Molina, Clavijero, and Siméon clearly share an understanding of *teotl* as "*dios*/god," but they emphasize different aspects of *teixiptla*.[33]

A significant distinction between *teixiptla* as representative, substitute, or delegate and *teixiptla* as representation or image surfaces through the comparison of these definitions. This difference may reflect what are actually two canonical forms of *teixiptla*: *ixiptlatl* (representative, impersonator, substitute) and *ixiptlayotl* (representation, image, likeness). Modern lexicographers, principally Karttunen, formalize the canonical forms of many older Nahuatl words, but as the examples above demonstrate, differences in meanings emerge in the works of early linguists, as well. Drawing on these sources and others, later interpretations of *teotl* and *teixiptla* emphasize *teotl*'s connotation of the sacred and *teixiptla*'s relationship to rituals.

Arild Hvidtfeldt's *Teotl*

Arild Hvidtfeldt (1915–1999) was the first scholar of religion to examine *teotl* and *teixiptla* together, and Mesoamericanists have relied upon his interpretations of these foundational terms for more than fifty years. Hvidtfeldt's definitions have appealed not simply because they were the first—and for many years the only—attempts to understand the terms, but also because of the comparative style of his study. His dissertation, *Teotl and *Ixiptlatli: Some Central Conceptions in Ancient Mexican Religion, with a General Introduction on Cult and Myth* (1958), principally concerns the relationship of myth to ritual. He argues that the Polynesian concept *mana* functions as a "way of conception" that by comparison to *teotl* and *teixiptla* illustrates the primacy of ritual over myth.[34] In actuality, Hvidtfeldt undertook two comparisons: within his examination of *teotl* and *teixiptla* he embedded a comparative study of *teotl* and *mana*, a concept indigenous to the Pacific Islands.

In many ways, some of which we shall explore below, Hvidtfeldt had the right idea. The word *mana* appears in languages throughout the Pacific Islands, and it is commonly thought of as "a generic Polynesian term for self-effacing or self-transcending efficacy ('power') that is at once personal and impersonal, sacred and secular, contained and containing."[35] A close comparison of *teotl* to its analogues in other cultures might help us better understand the Aztec concept, and it would be difficult, indeed, to gain a sense of *teotl* in isolation from *teixiptla*.[36] However, Hvidtfeldt's reliance on *mana* as the comparative term in his interpretation of *teotl* and *teixiptla* both strengthens and weakens his study. His comparison of *teotl* to *mana* strengthens his analysis by highlighting the terms' complexity and prompting us to consider the comparative method's utility. But the converse is true, as well. Comparing *teotl* to *mana* reminds us of the terms' complexity, including their adoption, adaptation, and (mis)construal by well-intentioned anthropologists and scholars of religions. Ultimately, the interpretation of *mana* Hvidtfeldt inherited from earlier scholars and his insistence on *mana's* presence in Aztec religion distracts him (and us) from clarifying what Nahuatl speakers, who knew nothing of *mana*, meant by *teotl* and *teixiptla*.

Mana became a popular term and comparative category in the anthropology of religions beginning in the late nineteenth century, and Hvidtfeldt derived his understanding of *mana* from three sources: Robert Henry Codrington's *The Melanesians* (1891); Edward Tregear's *The Maori Race* (1904); and Marcel Mauss's *The Gift* (1926).[37] Hvidtfeldt quotes Codrington in his description of *mana* as "a power or influence, not physical, and in a way supernatural."[38] Both Hvidtfeldt and Mauss drew upon Tregear, who defined *mana* broadly as "prestige . . . [or] influence derived from former achievements and from a confident expectation of future success" combined with "a spiritual influence, a kind of awe tinctured with fear of the supernatural power."[39] According to Tregear, *mana* may adhere to weapons, especially ones owned by historic personages; "great chiefs as part of their god-inheritance" have *mana*; ordinary men and slaves may acquire *mana* through feats on the battlefield; and geographic features and territories possess *mana*.[40] Given the foregoing definitions and examples, including Tregear's comparison of *mana* to "what we might vaguely call good luck, genius, reputation, etc.," we might expect Tregear and Codrington to translate *mana*. Both shy away from doing so, however.

In fact, Tregear admitted he thought translating *mana* to be impossible, because "the word *mana* itself has no English equivalent . . ."[41] The difficulty of translating *mana*, and other similar terms, made the concept more malleable in the hands of scholars interested in studying indigenous and otherwise "exotic" religions. Anthropologists working in the late nineteenth and early twentieth centuries began using *mana* alongside the Maori *tapu* (taboo), the Siouan *wakan*, and the Arabic *baraka*, as convenient comparative categories—convenient because their untranslatability made them pliable and their exotic sound lent them an air of authenticity. A notable example of this occurs in Durkheim's *Elementary Forms of Religious Life*; he introduces *mana* as one "impersonal religious force" among many, including the Siouan *wakan*. Quoting J. N. B. Hewitt's study of the Iroquois concept *orenda*, Durkheim, who attributes his understanding of *mana* to Codrington, writes:

This power is "regarded by the undeveloped intellect of man as the efficient cause of all the phenomena and of all the activities that are occurring around him." . . . *The same idea* is found among the Shoshone, with the name *pokunt*; among the Algonquins, *manitou*; *mauala* among the Kwakiutl; *yek* among the Tlingit; and *sgâna* among the Haida. But it is not peculiar to the Indians of America; it was first studied in Melanesia. . . . We find among these peoples, under the name "mana," *a notion that is exactly equivalent to* the wakan of the Sioux and the orenda of the Iroquois.[42]

Durkheim's equation of concepts from different cultures exemplifies the mode of comparison that characterized discussions of *mana* for decades.[43] In addition to discussing its relative translatability, Durkheim and his contemporaries debated whether *mana* was a noun, verb, or adjective, and their confusion over the concept's grammatical classification facilitated its reification and semantic reinscription. Roger Keesing explains that at first scholars like Codrington and Tregear thought of *mana* as a noun, that is to say, as something akin to a spiritual energy, but that "for subsequent generations of anthropologists, *mana* has been a 'thing'; a substantive if not quite a substance, something manifest in objects, something people had more of or less of."[44] As he began translating *teotl* and *teixiptla* in the mid-twentieth century, Hvidtfeldt had in mind these conceptions of *mana*.

In the first half of *Teotl and *Ixiptlatli*, Hvidtfeldt expounds on theories of *mana* and its importance in Aztec cult practices. For Hvidtfeldt, *mana*, "power," provided the missing link in understanding the concept *teotl*, because, *mana* "has been adopted by research as a technical term; for after attention had been called to the phenomenon, it was soon discovered that similar conceptions occurred in many other places."[45] In fact, he posits that the Nahuatl concept *teotl* derived from "*mana*," or something like it. Initially, Hvidtfeldt suggests that "it is presumably possible in a number of compounds to establish the occurrence of traces of a meaning of 'mana', but some of the compounds are so peculiar that rather comprehensive unravelments would be required. We shall therefore provisionally content ourselves with leaving it as a possibility."[46] Hvidtfeldt's comparison of *teotl* with *mana* is more than provisional. Because it prevents him from understanding *teotl* on its own terms, this comparison becomes a determinative hermeneutic in his analysis.

Hvidtfeldt acknowledges that he finds no linguistic connection between *teixiptla* and *mana* in the *Florentine Codex*, and yet he concludes, "from the factual point of view we have established usages which must be supposed to be based on concepts of 'mana', and in such a way that the word *teotl* itself must be assumed still to have—or at least to have had—a meaning which corresponds to the meaning 'mana.'"[47] Hvidtfeldt repeatedly asserts *teotl's mana*-like meaning, but his perception of the words' likeness comes from reading what he knows of *mana* into *teotl* rather than by carefully considering the terms' similarities and differences. For instance, he points to the compounds *cinteotl* (maize god) and *malteotl* (captive god) as demonstrating the "extraordinarily concrete and material semantic contents" of *mana* in *teotl*, and his exploration of these words in relation to *mana* gives us a sense of how his comparative method helps and hinders his analysis.

Mana provided Hvidtfeldt with a basis for understanding descriptions of complex Aztec ritual actions and language. His discussion of *cinteotl's* relationship to *mana* during Huei Tozoztli, a festival that featured Cinteotl (Maize God) and Chicomecoatl (7 Serpent), reveals the sense of confusion he felt regarding the variety of names and forms the Aztecs gave their *teteo*. Hvidtfeldt explains, "On general religio-historical assumptions it seems evident that the acts described [rituals involving planting maize] are based on concepts of 'mana.'"[48] Because he understood *mana* as "a supernatural power or influence" like the "growing power" present in plant life, Hvidtfeldt interpreted *cinteotl* as storing *mana* in its seeds. In his mind, the seeds' *mana* produced green, life-sustaining maize plants. From his perspective, the description of priestesses planting *cinteotl* during Huei Tozoztli demonstrated that the Aztecs had not yet passed from thinking of *teotl* as *mana* to thinking of *teotl* as "god." In other words, if *teotl* originally meant *mana*, as Hvidtfeldt thought it did, then the descriptions of *cinteotl* as corn, at times, and as a human form, at others, indicated to him that the Aztecs had not distinguished between *teotl* as *mana* and *teotl* as god. The irony of the situation is, of course, that Hvidtfeldt's insistence upon the presence of *mana* (or something like it) in the meaning, form, and function of *teotl* and upon a hard-and-fast distinction between *mana* and "god" introduced the very confusion that he attributed to the Aztecs. (He does not, for example, seem to have considered that the Aztecs may have conceived of *teotl* as inclusive of characteristics he would have attributed to both *mana* and "god.") Nonetheless, Hvidtfeldt interprets the perceived confusion as evidence that the Aztecs thought of the *teotl* inside Cinteotl as *mana*-like.[49]

He also discusses the term *malteotl* (captive god), which referred to the thigh bone of a sacrificial victim kept by the captive's captor as a symbol of his success in war. Hvidtfeldt, who understood the bone as containing some form of potency, again elides *teotl* with *mana*. In his commentary on the *Florentine Codex*'s description of Tozoztontli, he writes, "On a general religio-historical assumption it seems evident that the treatment described [the thigh bone's adornment and display] is based on concepts of 'mana'. It seems that *malteotl* originally must have meant 'captive's mana'."[50] Rather than investigating the meaning of *teotl* in Nahuatl, Hvidtfeldt argues that the captive's bone contained *mana*. Once again, Hvidtfeldt is on the right track, as some scholars of Aztec religion will eventually equate the potential of seeds to the potency of bones.[51] However, he employs a faulty method to arrive at this feasible conclusion. Hvidtfeldt's focus on *teotl* as *mana* leads him—and, later, other scholars—further away from defining *teotl* in a culturally specific manner and closer toward associating it with other exotic signifiers emptied of their original meanings and reinscribed as "the sacred."[52]

Arild Hvidtfeldt's *Teixiptla*

Hvidtfeldt values the primacy of ritual or cult activity, and this propensity causes him to emphasize the role of masking in his interpretation of *teixiptla*. The issue of how the meanings of *teotl* and *teixiptla* related to the ways in which the *Florentine Codex* describes their forms (as "idols," humans, plants, etc.) clearly troubled Hvidtfeldt. Early in his discussion of *teixiptla*, he professes that because of the word's significance and its unambiguous meaning, it could function (like *mana*?) as a "religio-historical technical term."[53] An interest in the question of the primacy of myth or ritual in religions brought Hvidtfeldt to the Mexican material, and he follows Robertson Smith in arguing that rituals should take priority over myth.[54] This focus on rituals leads him to investigate the relationship of *teixiptlahuan* to ritual activity and eventually to conclude that *teixiptla* means "image," rather than "representative."

Hvidtfeldt acknowledges the use of *teixiptla* as "deputy, representative" in Molina, but he argues that these translations are not essential to the term's meaning.[55] Instead, he insists that *teixiptla* as "'image' be coloured by the meaning 'mask, masked raiment', for it seems everywhere to be the dressing, painting, and adornment which constitutes a given *teixiptla*, respectively a given 'god'."[56] His emphasis on masking comes from his reading of passages that describe the use of masks in the creation of *teixiptlahuan* during ceremonies like Izcalli: "quitlaliaya, ixiptla, zan colotli, in quichioaya, quixaiacatiaya, in ixayac chalchiuhitl in tlachihualli, xihuitl inic ixtlan tlatlaan, cenca mahuizoticatca, cenca pepetlaca iuhquin cuecueioca, cenca mihiyotia." (They set up his image; it was only a framework [of wood] which they made. They gave it a mask. His mask was made of green stone horizontally striped with turquoise. It was very awesome; much did it gleam; it was as if it shone; it cast much brilliance.)[57] Many *teixiptlahuan* wore masks, and Hvidtfeldt's insistence on the importance of a *teixiptla*'s appearance rings true. Indeed, many would agree with his conclusion that "physically a *teixiptla* can be a number of things; its name is determined by raiment, painting, and other adornment."[58] However, we should remember that *teixiptla* has no etymological connection to *xayacatl* (face; mask). By insisting on reading image as mask, Hvidtfeldt risks overlooking the importance of *teixiptla*'s etymology while he overemphasizes one aspect of the term.

Hvidtfeldt's work makes three significant contributions to the study of *teotl* and *teixiptla*: first, he recognizes the importance of studying the two concepts together; second, he introduces a comparison between *teotl* and *mana* that may prove fruitful if more carefully drawn; and third, he emphasizes the constructed nature of *teixiptla*, a point to which I shall return. *Mana*'s predominance in Hvidtfeldt's comparison forces us to consider the comparative method's risks, especially that of reading sameness into the terms of comparison without attending to their differences. Indeed, it is difficult, if not impossible, to arrive at how something *is* (versus how something is conceived of) using a comparative method.[59] The tension between Hvidtfeldt's approach and his desire to understand his terms confounds his analysis. Although his definitions of *teotl* and *teixiptla* distance the concepts from their indigenous contexts, his comparative approach and focus on key terms—elements of his dissertation that earned Paul Kirchhoff's praise—distinguish his work from the scholarship that preceded it. He established a model for subsequent engagements with the concepts of Aztec religion.[60] Later scholarship, including much of what I discuss below and my own, bears out Hvidtfeldt's influence. By contrast to early lexicographers' definitions of *teotl* and *teixiptla*, Hvidtfeldt's interest in how context affects semantics takes us into the pages of the *Florentine Codex*, where we begin investigating not just the meanings of these words but their meaning in Aztec religion.

Contemporary Comparative Studies of *Teotl* and *Teixiptla*

Broadly speaking, two interpretive lineages characterize Mesoamericanist scholarship on *teotl* and *teixiptla* since Hvidtfeldt. We can trace one to the work of historian Alfredo López Austin and the other to that of historian and anthropologist J. Jorge Klor de Alva. Because of Hvidtfeldt's work, scholars feel comfortable comparing these terms both to related Nahuatl concepts and to ideas from other religions. A second trend concerns translations of *teotl*. Extrapolating from Hvidtfeldt, both López Austin and Klor de Alva prefer translating *teotl* as "force" or "power," and maintain a distance from equating it with "god." This trend reflects a genuine interest in understanding indigenous religions in their own right, but it may also be indicative of their desire to avoid using terms that constrain the concept or risk correlation with the terms of other, namely Western, religions. For instance, both Clendinnen and Read raise questions about the relationship of *teotl* to *teixiptla* with reference to Cinteotl (Maize God). Given that the god appeared in green and dried corn and also in the shape of human *teixiptlahuan*, they wonder how form and substance shape or dictate embodiment. Ultimately, many scholars have some provisional idea(s) about what *teotl* and *teixiptla* do or do not mean, and an even greater number of us rely on the work of Hvidtfeldt, López Austin, and Klor de Alva—with or without realizing we are. Rather than say there seems to be little consensus about *teotl* and *teixiptla*, a more accurate sense of the terms' histories seems to be that the two lineages we are about to investigate established interpretive paradigms that have rarely been challenged.

Despite the fact that the majority of López Austin's scholarship examines the Mesoamerican cosmovision and attends particularly to the body's role in it, he rarely employs the Nahuatl terms *teotl* and *teixiptla*. When he does, he quickly glosses the terms, observes the need for further study of them, and avoids additional elaboration. In *The Myths of the Opossum: Pathways of Mesoamerican Mythology* (1993), he devotes three chapters to "The Nature of the Gods," but provides only one brief (and relatively obscure) mention of *teotl*: "The Nahuatl word *teotl*, which means 'god,' also seems to signify 'blackness' in some compound words."[61] He then lists four terms, the names of three birds—*teotzinitzcan* (mountain trogon), *teoquechol* (or *tlauhquechol*, roseate spoonbill) and *teotzanatl* (boat-tailed grackle)—and one stone, *teotetl* (jet), as evidence that *teotl* signifies blackness.[62] Unfortunately, López Austin does not elaborate on the relationship he sees between blackness and *teteo*; instead he focuses on deities as "forces."[63] However, it is worth exploring why López Austin made a connection between *teotl* and *tliltic* (something black).

Of the four terms López Austin associates with blackness and divinity, the *Florentine Codex*'s descriptions of *teotzinitzcan* (mountain trogon) and *teotetl* (jet) provide the best sense of their relationship to *teotl*. Sahagún notes that *teotzinitzcan*'s name refers metaphorically to its preciousness, and he attributes *teotzanatl*'s name to its mythic origin: "It is named *teotzanatl* because it did not live here in Mexico in times of old. Later, in the time of the ruler Auitzotl, it appeared here in Mexico."[64] The corresponding Spanish gloss observes, "Llamanse teutzanatl que qujere dezir aue rara, o tzanatl preciosa." (It is called *teotzanatl* because it means that it was rare or precious *tzanatl*.)[65] We will return to the significance of black in relation to *teotl* and ritual in our examination of *teotetl*, but for the time being it seems that the *teotl* element of at least two of López Austin's examples relates more closely to their rarity or scarcity than to their black color.[66] (Of course, the Aztecs may have valued more than one of the qualities of these exceptional stones and birds.)

López Austin's sense of *teteo* as "forces" pervades his study of Aztec theology and deities. He closes his examination of the nature of the gods, their images, and essences by posing a series of questions characteristic of his musings on the subject:

> The forces—the gods—live in their images, their relics, etc. They are the forces that determine characteristics. Surely everything has characteristics. Can anything exist without having qualities? Must not the gods therefore inhabit everything that exists on earth? This being so, sacredness is really a question of intensity.[67]

López Austin's rhetorical tone exposes strong feelings he has about the relationships between the powers of intangible *teteo* and their incorporation in *teixiptlahuan*.[68] This passage also underscores the importance of materiality in his understanding of the Aztec cosmovision. As he frames *teteo* here, López Austin understands Aztec gods as forces that "live in their images," a perspective he introduced in *Hombre-Dios: Religión y política en el mundo náhuatl* (1973).

López Austin grounds the term *hombre-dios* (man-god) in the myths of emergence from Chicomoztoc based on a tenuous linguistic link and his identification of the seven mythic brothers (or ethnic progenitors) Quetzalcoatl, Tenuch, Ulmecatl, Xicalancatl, Otomitl, Mixtecatl, and Huemac as the *hombre-dios* prototypes.[69] López Austin begins his discussion of the nature of the *hombre-dios* by listing deities who had human origins, including Quetzalcoatl, Tezcatlipoca, Huitzilopochtli, and Huemac.[70] His basis for asserting that these gods had been men originates in his alternating treatment of early post-Contact sources as at times "historical" and at others "mythic." The ambiguity surrounding his vision of the sources replicates what is confounding about the texts themselves: that sometimes the gods are men (or were originally) and at other times the men (or sacred bundles or material instantiations) are gods. Nevertheless, taking a cue from Euhemerus (fourth century), he argues that several Aztec and Maya gods had human origins.

Neither the first nor the last scholar to interpret Aztec gods as having had human origins, López Austin encapsulates an innovative interpretation of the relationship between humans and gods in the *"hombre-dios."* Hombre-dios or *mujer-diosa*, literally man-god or woman-god, describes the (Aztec conception of the) human condition as López Austin understands it: "Se debe entender que el hombre-dios . . . es la semejanza del dios." (It should be understood that the *hombre-dios* . . . is the likeness of the god.)[71] He traces the origins of this relationship to Chicomoztoc, but more precisely, he ties *hombre* to *dios* through a series of excerpts from Chimalpahin's accounts of emergence. These texts describe people emerging from the seven caves as *"itech quinehuac,"* a verbal phrase glossed by Molina as *"endemoniado"* (possessed) and translated by Garibay K. as *"hechizado"* (enchanted).[72] López Austin feels strongly that Garibay K. conveys the verb's truest sense, despite the liberties he takes with Molina's gloss and the terms preferred by other translators.[73] With reference to Garibay K.'s translations of Chimalpahin, López Austin argues:

> El sentido más fiel de los cuatro textos enunciados es que en Chicomóztoc . . . los hombres recibieron dentro de su cuerpo "algo" divino que llegó a trastornarlos mentalmente, cuando menos en forma momentánea. "Algo" penetra en los hombres y los hace participar de la naturaleza de los dioses. Al parecer, este "algo" que todos reciben en el momento del parto es más intenso en los hombres-dioses, en su papel de intermediarios y depositarios.

> The most faithful sense of the four texts articulated is that in Chicomoztoc . . . people received inside their bodies "something" divine that became mentally upsetting, at least momentarily. "Something" penetrates into the people and causes them to participate in the nature of the gods. Apparently, this "something" that everyone receives at the moment of birth is more intense in the *hombres-dioses*, in their role as intermediaries and repositories.[74]

Despite the extraordinary quality of Chimalpahin's descriptions of emergence from Chicomoztoc, little evidence exists—at least, in recent translations—that the people experienced a transformation of the type López Austin describes. For example, apart from one aside describing Chicomoztoc as a "site of sacrifices, of demons, of gods," nothing in Anderson and Schroeder's translation indicates that the Aztecs who emerged from Chicomoztoc left the caves in an altered state.[75] (López Austin later mentions that people could acquire this "something" through contact with the *hombre-dios*'s relics or through psychotropics: "el vehículo de éxtasis fuse la droga."[76])

And yet, there does seem to have been something remarkable about the humans who became *teixiptlahuan*, a point López Austin observes, too. What Carrasco will later call "charisma," López Austin terms "force," and he sees it manifesting especially in the *hombre-dios*'s military prowess and miraculous activities. It is this force (or "something") that awakens the god in its representations, its *teixiptlahuan*. For López Austin, "*ixiptla*" means "imagen," "delgado," "reemplazo," "sustituto," "personaje" or "representante" (image, delegate, replacement, substitute, character, or representative).[77] He freely admits that the term may be more complex than his glosses indicate, but he resists the temptation to undertake his own study of *teixiptla*'s etymology. Indeed, in other discussions of the many types of images in Aztec religion, he reveals his position on the uselessness of attempts to distinguish one from another.[78] With regard to *teixiptla*'s etymology, then, López Austin rehearses established positions that pointed to the *xip** (flaying, peeling, shaving) element as indicating the importance of "*la cobertura*" (the cover).[79]

The cover, he argues, is the *nahual*. Drawing on colonial (and later) descriptions of *nahualli*, scholars have traditionally thought of a *nahualli* (sorcerer, one who uses spells and incantations) as the form an individual takes when transforming into an alter-state, such as that of an animal double. As the following indicates, López Austin views the *nahualli* as the cover of the divine force, and it is tempting to read *cobertura* as both material overlay and disguise:

> No hay, pues, identidad, ni encarnación del dios, ni consubstanciación después de la muerte, ni avatar. Hay, como afirma Piña Chan, una adquisición de su poder o la conversión del hombre en el nahual del dios, como dicen los textos mayas. El nahual en el sentido estricto—no quiero aquí generalizer—de receptor, de cobertura de la fuerza divina. Cobertura como lo son los ebrios de la energía enloquecedora de los cuatrocientos conejos.

> There is not, then, identity, nor incarnation of the god, nor consubstantiation after death, nor avatar. There is, as Piña Chan affirms, the acquisition of their power or the conversion of the person into the god, as the Maya texts explain. The *nahual* in the strict sense—I don't want to generalize here—of the receiver, of the cover of the divine force. Cover like that of those drunk from the maddening energy of the four hundred rabbits.[80]

López Austin rejects interpretations of *teixiptla* that equate it with a deity's incarnation or avatar in favor of asserting the centrality of the *nahualli*. His association of the two concepts may have as much to do with the confusing multiplicity of deity image types—an issue of which he is keenly aware—and with the persistent interpretation of *teixiptlahuan* as containers of divine essence as it does with the precise meanings of either *teixiptla* or *nahualli*. If, after all, *teixiptla* simply meant *nahualli*, it seems that more primary sources would use the words interchangeably or that lexicons would indicate their synonymity. As the work of Roberto Martínez González demonstrates, comparing *nahualli* and *teixiptla* produces useful insights about the two concepts, but replacing *teixiptla* with *nahualli* is less productive.

Martínez González notes important distinctions between *nahualli* and *teixiptla*: "Un hombre que representa a una divinidad puede ser considerada como su *nahualli* o su *ixiptla*; sin embargo, un cautivo sacrificial que representa a una divinidad con frequencia es mencionado como su *ixiptla* pero nunca como su *nahualli*. Una imagen religiosa es *ixiptla* del dios o la persona que representa y no su *nahualli*." (A man who represents a divinity could be considered his *nahualli* or his *ixiptla*; however, a sacrificial captive who represents a divinity is frequently mentioned as his *ixiptla*, but never as his *nahualli*. A religious image is an *ixiptla* of a god or the person that it represents, and never his *nahualli*.)[81] Martínez González goes on to say that *nahualli* always designates a metaphoric relationship, whereas *teixiptla* signals a relationship that is both metaphoric and metonymic. Furthermore, he explains that "*nahualli siempre sería un tipo de ixiptla*" (*nahualli would always be a type of ixiptla*).[82] By contrast to López Austin, Martínez González sees *nahualli* as one kind of *teixiptla*, not as the essence of deity embodiments.

However carefully they may be constructed, comparisons that focus exclusively on terms' sameness—like López Austin's comparison of *nahualli* and *teixiptla*—fall short of full explorations or explanations of complex words, their meanings, and contexts.[83] We may observe a similar (in)distinction in some of his later work on the human body's divine potential.

In a chapter entitled "The Body in the Universe," López Austin introduces the phrase "teteo imixiptlahuan" (images of the gods) as one of four categories of human sacrifice.[84] This typology synthesizes Mesoamerican human sacrifices and restricts "teteo imixiptlahuan" to human deity impersonators. "Teteo imixiptlahuan" has two defining elements: first, humans became gods, and second, humans became gods only temporarily. Gone, it seems, is the notion that all people contained within them "something" of the divine—or at least enough of that "something" to become a god; they were "not men who died, but gods—gods within a corporeal covering that made possible their ritual death on earth. . . . Men destined for sacrifice were temporarily converted into receptacles of divine fire, they were treated as gods, and they were made to live as the deity lived in legend."[85] López Austin leaves us wondering whether "teteo imixiptlahuan" were *hombres-dioses*. If so, were they the *hombres-dioses* who had received an intense enough dose of that "something" to qualify as "teteo imixiptlahuan?" López Austin's neologism enmeshes the two categories—*teotl* and *teixiptla*—so completely that they become indistinguishable, and further confusing the issue, he manages to blur the line between his own categories: *hombre-dios* and "teteo imixiptlahuan."

Perhaps not surprisingly, López Austin's most recent discussion of *hombre-dios* and "teteo imixiptlahuan" further collapses the two categories in favor of a typology that identifies four characteristics of Aztec deities.[86] In this typology, the essence of deity has four basic characteristics: divisibility, dispersion, restoration to an original form or location, and recombination into distinct divine forms.[87] These properties enable deities to appear simultaneously in multiple forms and at multiple temporal-spatial locations:

> For example, Quetzalcoatl occupied a place in the world of the gods; at the same time he was present in a great number of earthly individuals who shared his essence; and he was also present inside his images, including the living images who were human-gods; simultaneously his influence, that is, his substance, was sent to the world in the shape of time.[88]

Based on his earlier explanations of "teteo imixiptlahuan" and *hombre-dios*, one would expect the "great number of earthly individuals who shared [Quetzalcoatl's] essence" to be *hombres-dioses*. Rather than recognize distinct types—say the *hombre-dios* or "teteo imixiptlahuan"—in this passage, we find a summative statement that gathers together a deity's many and simultaneous manifestations.

These many manifestations raise the question of a *teixiptla*'s functions. For López Austin, cosmovision intimately relates to how humans sense and perceive their physical world, and his characterization of *ixiptla* as covers, receptacles, or vessels reflects his attempt to understand how the Aztecs reconciled the invisible and visible realms. In *The Myths of the Opossum*, he parses the words *ixiptla* and *toptli* (chest, container, wrapper) to explain his interpretation of *ixiptla* as vessels:

Images are vessels. The ancient Nahua used to refer to the images of the gods as *teixiptla* and *toptli*. *Teixiptla* derives from *xip*, meaning "skin, rind, or covering" (López Austin, [*Hombre-Dios*,] 119). *Toptli* means "covering or wrapping" (Molina, [*Vocabulario* (1944),] fol. 60v, 150r). The gods and their images recognize each other. Like naturally goes to like, so portions of divine forces are poured into their visible receptacles. In this way the gods fill natural formations as well, and humans detect the presence of the gods in the rocks that resemble them.[89]

López Austin derives his articulation of images as vessels from the "covering" connotation of *teixiptla* and *toptli*, and although a *toptli* (chest, container, wrapper) may be a receptacle, we will see later that *teixiptla* pertains to outer surfaces more than receptacles or inner essences. And yet, López Austin's interpretations of *teixiptla* have made a lasting impression in the study of Aztec religion.

For example, Serge Gruzinski integrates the comparisons drawn by Hvidtfeldt and the synthesis modeled by López Austin in his analysis of *teotl* and *teixiptla*. Drawing from the work of other scholars, he renders a composite image of how "the Nahua" articulated *teteo* with *teixiptlahuan*:

> The Mexican historian López Austin, according to others, categorically dismissed the familiar but anachronistic terms—in any case out of place here—of avatar, incarnation, or even identity. There would have been, on the one hand, the *teotl*—that is, the god halfway between the *mana*, the anonymous force, and the personalized divinity such as was known to Western antiquity. The *teotl* was the "heart of the pueblo," the dynamic motor unit of the group. On the other hand, there was the man-god— or better, the *ixiptla*, "the skin, bark, envelope" of the god, unless he appeared as his *nahualli*, a term that carried an analogous concept and a word, something penetrated the man, possessed him, transformed him into a faithful replica of a god, in that he partook of the divine force. Here one sees again the notions of sacred energy and celestial fire that informed the Nahua and even the Mesoamerican conception of power, of which the man-god appeared to represent the final term: he became divine. Once again, where we seek to dissect in order to understand, the Nahua perceived and conceived a whole, as if the contained transfigured the container. Where we would say that the man-god *possessed* the force *teotl*, the Nahua understood that the man-god *was teotl*, that he was the very authority he adored.[90]

Gruzinski constructs a seamless narrative at the expense of attention to etymological details and significant differences among the genealogies of terms he compares. Indeed, he extracts the terms—*teotl, teixiptla, mana, nahualli,* and even "Nahua"—from their linguistic, geographical, and historical locations in the service of understanding "Nahua powers" and the "man-gods." In so doing, he aims to reassemble a holistic sense of *teotl.* This treatment of *teotl* and *teixiptla* exemplifies the dangers of envisioning Aztec religion at a distance from its linguistic, visual, and material contexts. Extracted from their cultural context, *teteo* and *teixiptlahuan* quickly conjoin in the *hombre-dios/* man-god (or "teteo imixiptlahuan"). We end up with an idealized version of Aztec religion—one that is easier to understand because we have articulated it in our own invented or imported terms.

More productively, López Austin's work has strongly influenced historian of religions Davíd Carrasco, for whom the Aztec cosmovision and *teotl ixiptla* serve as the foundation for insightful interpretations of particular Aztec rituals. Carrasco defines *teotl ixiptla* as an "Aztec term meaning image of a god. These images were sometimes humans, usually destined for sacrifice in one of the major festivals of the Aztec calendar."[91] In both *Religions of Mesoamerica* (1990) and his later *City of Sacrifice* (1999), Carrasco emphasizes the living and divine qualities of a *teotl ixiptla.*[92] His most specific definition of a *teotl ixiptla* occurs in a discussion of human sacrifices at the Templo Mayor: "The major ritual participants were called *in ixiptla in teteo* (deity impersonators, or individuals or objects, whose essence had been cosmo-magically transformed into gods)."[93] For Carrasco, a *teotl ixiptla* is the "seminal image" in the politically and religiously potent ceremonies of the Xihuitl, the civil or solar calendar.[94]

Carrasco adopts López Austin's terminology and follows him in understanding *teixiptlahuan* as vessels. In his chapter on the Toxcatl ceremony, Carrasco emphasizes the importance of the *teixiptla*'s movement throughout the city, contrasting the *teixiptla* with Hindu and Catholic practices of "sacred sight seeing."[95] Later, addressing how the Aztecs envisioned their deity images, Carrasco cites López Austin's description of *teixiptlahuan* as "gods with a corporeal covering" and "vessels."[96] His inclusion of the lengthy physical description of the Tezcatlipoca *teixiptla* constructed during Toxcatl highlights the Aztec insistence on perfect *teteo* bodies in ceremonial contexts, and he interprets the body, life, and death of the *teixiptla* in Toxcatl as (re)presentations of Aztec ideals. As evidence he points to the ritual description's conclusion: "And this betokened our life on earth. For he who rejoiced, who possessed riches, who sought, who esteemed our lord's sweetness, his fragrance—richness, prosperity—thus ended in great misery. It was said: 'no one on earth went exhausting happiness, riches, wealth.'"[97] Although Carrasco mentions the stone *teixiptla* of Tezcatlipoca that was ceremonially dressed and revealed to the public during Toxcatl, neither he nor López Austin treat nonhuman *teixiptlahuan* in depth. Instead, both focus on *teixiptlahuan* as containers of divine force and on the physicality of human *teixiptlahuan*.

Anthropologist Inga Clendinnen also addresses *teixiptla* in *Aztecs* (1991), where she draws on López Austin's work and incorporates discussions of nonhuman *teixiptla*. For Clendinnen, *teixiptla* is "a marvelously elastic category."[98] She observes:

> Ixiptlas were everywhere, the sacred powers represented in what we would call multiple media in any particular festival—in a stone image, richly dressed and accoutred for the occasion; in elaborately constructed seed-dough figures; in the living body of the high priest in his divine regalia, and in the living god-image he would kill: human, vegetable and mineral ixiptla.[99]

Clendinnen expands upon the work of López Austin by incorporating nonhuman *teixiptla* into her discussion of deity images.

In reminding us of the fascinating relationship between Cinteotl (Maize God), what Clendinnen calls "Cinteotls (maize gods)," and Cinteotl's *teixiptlahuan*—one highlighted by Hvidtfeldt—Clendinnen extends the conversation about *teteo* and their representations in a new direction. "Maize," she writes, "presents a different case. On that same feast day [Huei Tozoztli] the sacred clusters of seven maize cobs, the selected seed maize specifically consecrated on that day, were simply called 'maize gods' (Centeotls), and I think were understood as 'being' the sacred substance, its very body, and therefore not 'representations.'"[100] Clendinnen raises a crucial issue—one we will take up again later: the significant difference between representation and being.

The *Florentine Codex* identifies human and material *teixiptlahuan*, including actual ears of corn, as Cinteotl. And given the long history of maize in Mesoamerica—Mesoamericans domesticated maize approximately 8,700 years before the present—Clendinnen's emphasis on the significance of maize in Mesoamerica and the substantial interdependence of Mesoamericans on maize deserves further attention.[101] During Huei Tozoztli, the dried ears of maize young girls carry to the temple of Chicomecoatl (7 Serpent) at Cinteopan, "*no cinteotl motocayotiaya*" (were also called Cinteotl), and elsewhere, young green maize is called Cinteotl.[102] Additionally, a Cinteotl *teixiptla* of unspecified material stood at Cinteopan, the temple where some human *teixi-*

ptlahuan of Cinteotl were sacrificed. Humans—both women and men—embodied Xilonen, from *xilotl* (tender ear of green maize before it solidifies), as well as the variously colored manifestations of Cinteotl during Huei Tecuilhuitl (Xilonen), Huei Tozoztli (Cinteotl), and Ochpaniztli (Cinteotl, male and female).[103] It seems, then, that the Aztecs recognized Cinteotl in/as young green maize, dried maize, human god-bodies, and perhaps other materials. Clendinnen finds this case intriguing because the manifestations of Cinteotl were the god rather than mere representations; in her own words, they "were 'maize gods', not ixiptlas."[104] Clendinnen's insistence that maize *was* the god rather than the god's *teixiptla* stems from her justifiable objection to the glosses "representation" and "image," neither of which accurately connotes the embodiment of a *teotl* by a *teixiptla*.

In response to the concerns Cinteotl raises about the relationship of *teotl* to *teixiptla*, Clendinnen works toward a more accurate rendering of *teixiptla* by suggesting that it has three primary characteristics: "An *ixiptla* was a made, constructed thing; it was formally 'named' for the particular sacred power, and adorned with some of its characteristic regalia; it was temporary, concocted for the occasion, made and unmade during the course of the action."[105] She also glosses *teixiptla* as "god-presenter" or "that which enables the god to present aspects of himself."[106] Although she experiments with other articulations of *teteo* and *teixiptla*, Clendinnen ultimately views *teixiptlahuan* as vessels constructed to contain "sacred forces." Her objection to equating a deity's presence in an embodiment with a representation or impersonator draws our attention to the importance of the *teotl*'s ontological relationship to her/his *teixiptla*. But her association of *teotl* with sacred force directs us away from a clear understanding of the term in Aztec religion.

The relationship of *teteo* to *teixiptlahuan*, an issue raised by López Austin, Carrasco, and Clendinnen, also preoccupies scholars who follow J. Jorge Klor de Alva's alternate interpretation. The second interpretive genealogy begins with Klor de Alva, who calls pre-Contact Nahua religion "teoyoism," which he derives from *teoyotl*, "the Nahuatl word with the closest semantic equivalent to 'religion.'"[107] He first explored this concept in his dissertation, *Spiritual Warfare in Mexico: Christianity and the Aztecs* (1980), an investigation of the ways in which pre-Contact religion survived (meta)physical conquest by Iberian Christianity. Klor de Alva's primary interests include teoyoism, Nahua spirituality, and "why and how the native religion in general survived the Spanish cataclysm."[108] Toward this end, he follows his teacher Miguel León-Portilla in suggesting that *teotl* derived from *tetl* (stone). In support of this position, he compares the qualities older Nahuatl speakers attributed to both *neltiliztli* (truth) and stone:

Considering the role of stone in Nahua civilization as the hardest, most enduring, and ubiquitous building material and physical element, and that among the Nahuas truth (*neltiliztli*) is based on what is well rooted, founded, or permanent and firm, it is not too much to suspect that the symbolic mode of expression for what was ultimately sacred (metaphysically most permanent) should have included the metaphor of stone.[109]

The connection Klor de Alva makes between the physical properties of *tetl* and the metaphysical properties of *teotl* is a new line of interpretation. Although he notes that "there is much literature to give credence to this conclusion," he neither incorporates nor cites that literature.[110] Instead, he turns from this thought-provoking point to his argument that *teotl* means more than "god."

Klor de Alva's openness to translations of *teotl* as "divine" or "sacred" stems from his desire to distinguish teoyoism from both Iberian Christianity and comparisons made between Aztec and Greco-Roman deities. In contrast to Christianity's theocentric focus, Klor de Alva describes teoyoism as a religion that derived its principles from natural cycles consisting primarily of apotropaic rituals, or those that avert evil influences and misfortunes.[111] As he explains, "The historical implications of this distinction are substantial: the elimination of the major gods in the Nahua pantheon did not necessarily spell the end of Nahua religiosity, nor, conversely, did the acceptance of a new god imply conversion."[112] Likewise, his identification of this distinction affects the direction of his argument as he traces the survival of Nahua religiosity through conquest and colonialism.

Klor de Alva ultimately derives his definition of *teotl* from Howard F. Cline's "Missing and Variant Prologues and Dedications in Sahagún's *Historia General*, Texts and English Translations." Cline intended his article as a supplement to the Spanish texts of the Sahaguntine corpus, many of which were incorrect, incomplete, or entirely unavailable. Klor de Alva draws on a portion of the Spanish prologue to *Book 11: Earthly Things*, which Cline translates as:

It would be opportune at this time, to give them to understand the value of the creatures, so that not attributed to them is [false] worth, because any creature whatsoever they see to be good or bad. They call it "teutl," which means "god," in such wise that they call the sun "teutl," because of its beauty, or at least because of its frightening disposition and fierceness. From this it can be inferred that this word "teutl" can be taken for a good quality or for a bad one. This is much better recognized when it is compounded in this name, "teupilzintli," "very pretty child," "teuhpiltontli," "very terrible or bad boy." Many other terms are compounded in this same way, from the meaning of which one can conjecture that this term "teutl" means a "thing extremely good or bad."[113]

Emphasizing the idea that "this term 'teutl' means a 'thing extremely good or bad,'" Klor de Alva builds a case for translating *teotl* as "sacred."[114] Working from a list of compound words drawn from secondary sources, Klor de Alva translates a list of *teotl* compounds that he believes convey the sense of "divine" or "sacred": *teopilzintli* (very pretty child), *teohpiltontli* (very terrible or bad boy), *teooctli* (divine wine, authentic wine, real wine, or wine of the gods), *teomiqui* (those who have died for the god), and Cihuateteo (Female-Deities).[115] Klor de Alva's work has inspired scholars drawn to an encompassing definition of *teotl*—one that distinguishes Aztec religion from Iberian Christianity by emphasizing its capacity to incorporate hierophanies.[116]

Like Klor de Alva, Read sees *teotl* and its compounds as meaning more than "god" or "divinity," and she supports her argument for a more ample translation of *teotl* by pointing to the variety of terms with which it combines and by comparing it to other Native American notions of animacy. She emphasizes "*teo-*" as the most basic semantic element of *teotl*, but acknowledges that her isolation of "*teo-*" is artificial. "The Nahua," she notes, "did not discuss *teotl* by itself, as we are doing here."[117] By this, she means that the Aztecs did not locate *teteo* outside or apart from the physical world or distinguish *teotl* from "power," which she associates with "*teyome*." Yet she explains,

> To indicate the importance of an object's potency, the prefix *teo-* was implanted in a Nahuatl word. Something with potency was called *teoyotl* (something with the quality of power), *teotl* meant god (something potent), the sea or blood was called *teoatl* (potent water), and a very bad little boy was called *teopiltontli* (powerfully small or insignificant child).[118]

These *teotl* compounds reflect Read's idea that "Nahuatl always includes powers in something else by using a prefix form that cannot stand alone (*teo-*)."[119] Interestingly, Read assigns a linguistic role to the *teo-* prefix that parallels the one she later attributes to ritual masks and costumes that identify a special potency in human deity images—all marking an otherwise quotidian entity as especially potent.

For Read, translating *teotl* as "god" or *teoyotl* as "divinity" limits the concepts' sense of animacy and potency. In her words, "Often translated simply as 'god,' *teotl* can be rendered with more depth if one includes some sense of animistic force or vitality."[120] She argues that like other Native American concepts of animacy, *teotl* manipulated the essence of the people, places, and things it modified. Read compares *teotl* to the Navajo concepts of inner forces and outer appearances described by Clara Sue Kidwell: "Every outer form or active physical phenomenon had its inner form that motivated it. All living and moving things, thus, had a spiritual sanction."[121] Read cites a deity impersonator as one example of how inner *teotl* affected outward appearances: "when a person donned a ritual costume to climb the mountain of Uixachtlan, that person became the god. It was no longer a person climbing the hill, but Quetzalcoatl or Tlaloc. Every mask, costume, effigy, and object embodied a particular force. To wear it meant to take on its *face* (*ixtli*), to become its identity."[122] Although comparing *ixtli* and *teixiptla* might have proved useful, Read does not elaborate on the relationship of the two or on other connections between *teo-* and deity identities. The omission of *teixiptla* from Read's discussion of *teotl* is striking, given her interest in animacy and potency, themes discussed at length by López Austin. Read cites López Austin at the conclusion of her list of the ways in which *teotl* shapes and affects various physical forms, but she avoids engaging him on the matter of *teixiptla*.

Read translates the dynamism of *teotl* into terms of potency and vitality, and in his work on *nepantla* (having to do with reciprocity and mutuality), philosopher James Maffie also conserves the concept's sense of movement and transformation. Maffie tantalizingly characterizes *nepantla* as "abundant middlingness," and argues that *teotl* exemplifies *nepantla* in cosmological action.[123] The two terms—*nepantla* and *teotl*—meet at the axis of acting and being. According to Maffie, *nepantla* describes actions or events "consisting of middling mutuality and balanced reciprocity," and *teotl* forms the conceptual heart of Nahua philosophy:

> The starting point of Nahua metaphysics is the ontological thesis that there exists a single, dynamic, vivifying, eternally self-generating and self-regenerating, sacred power or force. The Nahua referred to this power by the term *teotl*. *Teotl* is ultimate reality . . . *teotl* is not a deity, person, or subject who possesses power in the manner of a king or tyrant. Rather, *teotl* is power: an always active, actualized and actualizing, ever-flowing energy-in-motion.[124]

Teotl, Maffie explains, "is properly understood as neither being nor not-being but as becoming."[125] Maffie relates the becoming and movement of *teotl* to the instability of the Nahua world, in which cycles of creation-through-destruction prohibited prolonged stasis. Capturing *teotl*'s transformative sense is important in understanding the term, but subsuming *teotl* under "becoming" admits only a portion of the term's meaning, let alone its semantic range. Attestations throughout the *Florentine Codex* indicate, as we shall see, that the Aztecs used the term in reference to individual entities they conceived of nominally as *teotl.* To insist that each instance of the word connoted "becoming" or even that *teotl*'s essence was one of qualitative activity stemming from a singular sacred skews its range of signification.

Conversations about the meaning of *teotl* and *teixiptla* extend beyond published scholarship into online listservs dedicated to the study of Nahuatl. In December of 2006, scholars, students, and nonspecialists subscribed to Nahuat-l debated the meaning of *teotl.* (The thread may be accessed through the listserv's archive hosted on the website of The Foundation for the Advancement of Mesoamerican Studies.) Ramiro Medrano, who was a student at California State University, Monterey Bay, began the discussion by asking about *teotl*'s translation and its presence (or absence) in deity names.[126] Initial responses came from nonspecialists who suggested translating *teotl* as "supernatural," an idea Karttunen had proposed in an earlier thread.[127] Anthropologist Michael Swanton questioned the appropriateness of the term "supernatural" in Aztec religion, where the distinction between the natural world and the supernatural may not have existed.[128]

Read affirmed Swanton's response and cautioned list members against "tak[ing] a very old Western model of the cosmos and universaliz[ing] it to everyone, everywhere in the world."[129] She reiterated an argument made in *Time and Sacrifice in the Aztec Cosmos* (1998), and added, "Instead of this rather westernized (even medievalized) idea of nature and that which is beyond nature, I read all this stuff about -teo- as a very slim to no distinction between the natural and supernatural."[130] She also responded to a query about the difference between Cinteotl (Maize God) and maize by citing Kidwell and providing an example:

In the case of Cinteotl, how about this? Maize is the outer form that is filled with teo, making it Cinteotl, who is a being that can be depicted both as corn plants and as a "deity" with particular iconographic traits. Remember all the pictures of ears of corn being shown as little heads sticking out of the husks. Corn cobs themselves are beings, who sometimes appear as individual ears and other times appears as a kind of . . . overarching idea of corn-ness in the form of Cinteotl. But the form is naturally depicted as a human-like being with the powers of corn.[131]

With Cinteotl, Read raises a compelling example (and one Hvidtfeldt and Clendinnen considered). Although they lie outside the purview of this text, comparisons like the one Read makes between *teotl* and Navajo inner essences and outer forms have the potential—when carefully conceived—to provide incredible insight into religions native to the Americas.

A strong preference for translating *teotl* as "power" or "force" characterizes the work of Klor de Alva and Read. Even as Read notes other scholars' "Western" biases, her own desire to expand *teotl*'s definition beyond god or deity motivates her to generalize indigenous American thought. Klor de Alva and Read propose a definition of *teotl* that derives from a single passage in a Spanish prologue to one book in Sahagún's *Florentine Codex* and seems strongly influenced by their preference for translating *teotl* as "power." Given the increasing availability of digitized versions of older Nahuatl documents, important linguistic contributions being made by modern Nahuatl speakers, and ongoing excavations of Aztec archaeological zones, Mesoamericanists have ample opportunity to refine and redefine our understanding of Aztec culture and its attendant concepts.

Contemporary Linguistic Analyses of *Teotl* and *Teixiptla*

The studies I have surveyed raise certain questions, including What did the Aztecs mean by *teotl*? and What kinds of relationships existed between *teteo* and *teixiptlahuan*? To investigate these and related concerns, I draw on the work of scholars conducting linguistic analyses and those creating the tools for this work. In particular, publications by J. Richard Andrews, R. Joe Campbell, and Frances Karttunen have aimed to standardize Nahuatl orthography and spelling. Taken together, volumes by Andrews and Karttunen represent the most authoritative contemporary grammar and dictionary of older Nahuatl.

At the end of his *Introduction to Classical Nahuatl* (1975), Andrews includes a comprehensive vocabulary in which he cites both *teotl* and *teixiptla*. Unlike early lexicographers, Andrews acknowledges *ixiptlatl as a hypothetical reconstruction, and he notes that it appears only in a possessed form: "(*IXIP*-TLA)-TL > (*IXIP*-TLA)-Ø [for *(*IX*- IP -TLA)-TL] = *pos only*, representative, delegate, impersonator, image."[132] In addition to his primary entry for *teotl*, "god," Andrews lists several *teotl* compounds, and in some of these, he translates *teotl*, the modifier, as "divine" rather than as "god."[133] For example, he glosses *teoatl* as "divine water; ocean; blood"; *teonahuatilli*, as "a divine command"; and *teoyotl*, as "a thing characteristic of a god, i.e., divinity, godhead."[134] In addition to these compounds, Andrews notes that *teotl*'s stem sometimes has the variant *teoh-*, and he includes three compounds demonstrating this alternate form: *teohcihui*, "to be hungry"; *teohpohua*, "to cause s.o. ~ s.th. to suffer, to torment s.o. ~ s.th."; and *teohtlalli*, "plains, desert plains, desert region."[135] However, both Karttunen and Campbell identify *teotl* and *teoh-* as two distinct morphemes.[136]

Karttunen lists *teotl* and its canonical compounds alphabetically in *An Analytical Dictionary of Nahuatl* (1983). She provides the canonical form of *teotl*: "TEO-TL *pl:* TETEOH god / dios."[137] Karttunen lists the canonical form of *teixiptla* as "IXIPTLAYO-TL image, likeness, representation" and refers the reader to the stems IX-TLI, XIP-, and -YO.[138] She defines *ixtli* as "face, surface, eye"; *xip-* as "an element in numerous compounds and derivations [that] refers to peeling, flaying, shaving, etc."; and *-yo* as a "*derivational suffix forming abstract nouns* -ness, -hood, -ship."[139] This entry reflects her understanding of the concept as an "imperfective patientive nounstem of characteristic properties" with an abstracting *-yo(tl)* suffix.[140] We may render Karttunen's "image, likeness, representation" more literally as "that which is characterized by or pertains to a flayed surface or face."[141] Karttunen's canonical forms set the standard for Nahuatl orthography in this book, although I use the nonspecific human object prefix, *te-* (someone's), to remind readers of the concept's possessed condition.[142]

Whereas Karttunen's *Analytical Dictionary* standardizes *teixiptla*'s canonical form and precise meaning, Campbell's *Morphological Dictionary of Classical Nahuatl* (1985) amplifies our understanding of *teixiptla* by presenting its semantic range. In 1970, Campbell began collecting Nahuatl morpheme headings, "a combination of a form and a meaning . . . [that] are associated as a distinctive unit in the language," from the entries in Molina's dictionary.[143] We can access his work from three sources: the aforementioned *Morphological Dictionary*, an online database Campbell established, and increasingly through his contributions to the *Nahuatl Dictionary* hosted by the University of Oregon's Wired Humanities. In the *Morphological Dictionary*, the morphemes serve as headings for lists of their variants and meanings, and in order to determine the "true meaning of the morpheme," Campbell encourages readers "to read through the citations under the heading and abstract from them."[144] A morpheme heading's meanings should come through its variants, rather than through Campbell's translation of the heading. He explains that in compiling the morphemes from Molina's *Vocabulario*, his "aim has been to provide, without going too far afield into history, a reasonable set of morphemes for classical Nahuatl."[145]

Campbell glosses *teotl* as "god," and includes nearly 290 variants of the word. Terms included in this long list clearly demonstrate *teotl*'s wide semantic applicability, extensive use well into the colonial period, and adoption into the Nahuatl vocabulary of Catholics in New Spain. Campbell glosses *teixiptla* as "representative," and its variants compose two semantic fields, one substantive and the other verbal. The verbal semantic field encompasses to go in someone's place; to represent in a play; to make something in someone's image; to delegate or substitute someone in one's place; and to make a substitute. *Teixiptla*'s substantive semantic field includes representative; substitution; image of someone; substitute; delegate; representation; and painted image.[146] Campbell's work contributes to ongoing efforts by Nahuatl linguists to document the language's older and modern syntax and grammar, a project he contributes to through the Zacatecas Institute for Teaching and Research in Ethnology (IDIEZ). The work of these linguists establishes the canonical forms of *teotl* and *teixiptla* and provides us with a sense of the range of their meanings. This overview of the terms' meanings brings us to the question of how scholars have identified the embodiments of specific deities. In other words, how did the Aztecs know and how do we know who is who?

Putting a Face with a Name: Traditional Modes of Aztec Deity Identification

Generally speaking, Mesoamericanists identify the *teotl* present in a *teixiptla* using one of two approaches. Iconographers begin with the *teixiptla*'s physical appearance, thought to hold clues to the god's identity, and t(h)eologians start with the concept of *teotl*, presumed to be the embodiment's inner essence. Both of these interpretive modes are important to the study of Aztec deities and their representations, but used in isolation, each overlooks or obscures crucial distinctions between *teotl* and *teixiptla*.

For instance, t(h)eologians bring to the study of *teteo* a distinction between inner spirits and exterior matter(s). This distinction leads them to see *teteo* as substantially separable from their *teixiptlahuan* bodies. Said differently, they see the gods as essences poured into containers from which they maintained a physical and substantial distance; for t(h)eologians, *teteo* lie just beyond the firm grasp of the sensory world. "Images are vessels," López Austin explains, "portions of divine forces are poured into their visible receptacles"; Carrasco echoes this thought: "In a sense, gods fill up the human and natural images (rocks, trees, plants) that are thought to resemble them."[147]

Similarly, Clendinnen insists that *teixiptlahuan* manifested *in* multimedia everywhere.[148] The etymology of *teixiptla* and the process of their ritual manufacture, topics we shall explore later, suggest that such a division need not be drawn—indeed, that it may cause us to fundamentally misunderstand the nature and function of *teixiptlahuan* and *teteo* in Aztec religion.[149]

And yet, t(h)eologians' interpretations of a *teixiptla* as a vessel containing the divine essence—the *teotl*—raise basic and crucial questions regarding the relationship of the god to the visible physical forms the god embodied: namely, how can we determine which *teotl* embodies which *teixiptla*? Or, put differently, how did a *teotl* know who and what to embody? And how did a devotee recognize the *teixiptlahuan* of her *teteo*? These are questions iconographers have also asked and to which they have responded.

Say My Name: Iconicity and Identification

Eduard Seler's late nineteenth-century archaeological, ethnographic, iconographic, and linguistic studies in Mexico laid the foundation for Mesoamerican studies. He came to Mexico with a background in botany, and his training deeply informed his methods of studying Mesoamerican cultures:

> Rejecting all speculation and fantasy, he insisted that it was impossible to solve a problem—the meaning of a myth, for example—without understanding its component elements. Such understanding could only be gained by the most intensive analysis and comparison of the clues and information provided by Spanish and Indian sources, native picture writings, sculptures, and ceramics. This comparative, critical method was most exacting; it required a formidable mastery of the sources, documentary and archaeological, and above all of the Indian languages in which, Seler believed, the most authentic and reliable materials were preserved.[150]

The thought-rebus analogy Seler developed in "The Character of Aztec and Maya Manuscripts" (1888) bears out the influence of his background. Using this analogy, he argued that discrete iconographic symbols signified characteristics associated with—but not constitutive of—the person or place depicted. Seler cites names and toponyms in the *Codex Mendoza* as examples of rebuses.

Seler writes, "As a matter of fact, the pictures . . . are rebuses in the literal sense—word rebuses or syllable rebuses. The single words or syllables,

2.1. Toponym of Coatitlan illustrates Seler's rebus theory. The image of a *coatl* (serpent) over a set of *tlantli* (teeth) signifies Coatitlan (Place of the Serpent). *Codex Mendoza*, 17v. Line drawing by author.

of which the name of the place or person consists, are represented by pictures of objects of the same name or sound without regard, i.e. to intentional consideration of the idea that the corresponding word or syllable conveys."[151] Later he explains how Mesoamericans used the rebus system to create deity identities:

> Features of the face, painting, adornment, weapons, utensils which were given to the god or placed beside him—all are but means to characterize the god, to express in the clumsy mode of symbolic writing the attributes and peculiar nature of the god. This method is, as stated, also a rebus to some extent, but not a word-rebus; it is a thought-rebus.[152]

For Seler, the symbolic nature of "thought-rebuses" presented a problem of translation. While he recognized that some iconographic symbols conveyed phonetic information, Seler argued that spatially related glyphs from, say, the *Codex Mendoza* can "hardly be brought together into a linguistic sentence."[153] In other words, for Seler, the complex ideas glyphs express did not have a one-to-one linguistic correlation with alphabetic languages. He concluded that pictorial and sculptural representations of deities were not embodiments of those beings, but iconographic associations that symbolized the beings' characteristics or names. Thus, according to Seler, glyphs represented discrete ideas but could not articulate grammatically and syntactically complex thoughts.[154] Based on these observations, Seler encouraged scholars to use iconographic elements as primary indicators in deity identification.

Writing nearly a century later, Hanns J. Prem challenged the usefulness of Seler's thought-rebus analogy. He insisted that the notion of Aztec writing as "rebus-writing" offered no answer to the most basic question of writing systems: What are the system's potentials and restrictions? Because the idea of rebus-writing "originates from another culture, ours, where it was created as a kind of riddle, purposely constructed in a way to make it difficult to be solved . . . the term does not give any concrete information as to how the writing system really worked."[155] Prem urged scholars to consider the two types of glyphic writing he identifies among Central Mexican texts: pictographic and hieroglyphic (i.e., ideographic and phonetic) writing.[156] These two systems worked together to express everything from concrete ideas to toponyms to metaphorical notions. By contrast to Seler, Prem concluded that "it is not possible to press the Aztec hieroglyphic writing into formulae and rules."[157] Prem was not alone in criticizing and modifying Seler's ideas about Central Mexican writing.

In his landmark essay "Religion in Pre-Hispanic Central Mexico" (1971), Henry B. Nicholson modifies the iconographic trend initiated by Seler by introducing cult themes, deity complexes, and iconographic clusters as organizational principles. Nicholson organizes the Aztec deities according to "a few fundamental cult themes," including "Celestial Creativity-Divine Paternalism," "Rain-Moisture-Agricultural Fertility," and "War-Sacrifice-Sanguinary Nourishment of the Sun and Earth."[158] Although Nicholson describes the dual, quadruple, and quintuple principles of organization in Aztec religion as "fundamental characteristic[s] of Mesoamerican pantheonic systems," his cult themes quickly eclipse these organizational patterns.[159] Rather than orient his taxonomy in accordance with the Aztec classificatory principles, Nicholson adopts a method based on themes he identified in iconography and myth.

Nicholson cites a variety of alphabetic texts, pictorial manuscripts, and three-dimensional sculptures in his analysis and classification of Aztec deities. Under the heading of each cult theme he lists and describes individual deity complexes; for example, the Rain-Moisture-Agricultural Fertility cult theme includes the Tlaloc, Centeotl-Xochipilli, Ometochtli, Teteoinnan, and Xipe Totec complexes, each of which includes one or more individual *teotl*. In his descriptions of the complexes and their *teteo*, he draws on narrative descriptions of the *teteo* to provide a sense of each complex's orientation, and, like Seler, Nicholson emphasizes the importance of deities' insignia in their identification:

To each deity were assigned certain diagnostic insignia. The overall combination was usually unique, but the individual elements were often shared, particularly by other deities within the complex; these symbolic insignia were invested with considerable significance in their own right. The high development of Mesoamerican art permitted the effective representation of these deities displaying their diagnostic insignia, pictorially and plastically, which facilitated their identification by the instructed.[160]

Nicholson argues that devotees identified their deities by breaking down iconographic elements into recognizable components. In fact, he characterizes deities' appearance, their clothing and insignia, as "diagnostic." His instinct regarding the importance of deity insignia may point us in the right direction, but thinking of insignia as diagnostic, rather than as intrinsic to the deity, privileges our perspective over that of the Aztecs. After all, we are in the position of figuring out who is who, but devotees knew their gods by name, face, and substance—and perhaps by means that would not occur to outsiders.

Additionally, Nicholson bases his associations of different *teteo's teixiptlahuan* on their iconographic and mythological attributes without taking into account their ritual context or religious function. So we might ask if we should expect a *teotl* to wear the same headdress and carry the same insignia in a *tonalamatl* (divinatory book) that his or her human *teixiptla* did during a calendric festival. (Multiple factors, including the idea that the interlocking cycle of calendars might alter the presentation of a deity during his or her festival, an observation made by Catherine DiCesare, suggest we probably should not.[161]) Considering the context in which we assign deities identities based on their physical appearance is as important as reflecting on how we might employ additional resources or tools of analysis to understand the complexity of Aztec *teteo* and *teixiptlahuan*. For example, Nicholson identifies a relationship between the *teixiptlahuan* of Chantico, Xochiquetzal, and Coyolxauhqui through vaguely similar iconographic insignia and "mythologems" but does not account for their context or function:

> Chantico, a goddess who wears some of the insignia of Xochiquetzal and was probably merged to a certain extent with her, appears to have also possessed significant igneous associations. In myth, Chantico was transformed into a dog (the animal most closely connected with fire) for violation of a pre-offertory fast obligation. Chantico was also the special patron deity of the lapidaries of Mexico, originally of Xochimilcan affiliation, and, *to judge from her insignia* portrayed on a famous sculpture, may also have overlapped with Coyolxauhqui, the malevolent sister of Huitzilopochtli in the myth of his birth.[162]

If we consider the contexts and substances of these *teixiptlahuan* in addition to their form, their similarities seem less clear.

Both Chantico and Xochiquetzal appear in the *tonalpohualli* (day count) of the *Codex Telleriano-Remensis*, which Boone identifies as a *tonalamatl* (divinatory book). Boone explains that divinatory texts like the *Codex Telleriano-Remensis* contain the "accumulated knowledge of the calendar and of the mantic influences and festivals attached to different units of time," and that diviners consulted them "according to their pertinence to the divinatory situation."[163] We might imagine, then, that a diviner would encounter these images of the goddess during a situation in which she needed to be invoked. By comparison, the second image of Chantico, a three-dimensional diorite sculpture identified by Felipe Solís as Coyolxauhqui, "formed part of the Templo Mayor complex and was found in March 1830 in the old Convento de la Concepción near the street of Santa Teresa (now Guatemala Street)."[164] Regardless of the iconographic similarities Nicholson observes among these *teixiptlahuan*, their contexts suggest that they served quite different functions. Nicholson's deterministic approach—that deities' insignia determined their identities—eschews contextual interpretations of the *teixiptlahuan* and thereby ignores what may be crucial elements of their identities, including their day-sign associations and ritual functions.[165]

Nicholson bases his taxonomy on iconographic clusters because he sees them as reliable—able to resist change—and decipherable—capable of preserving information over long periods of time. A proponent of the direct

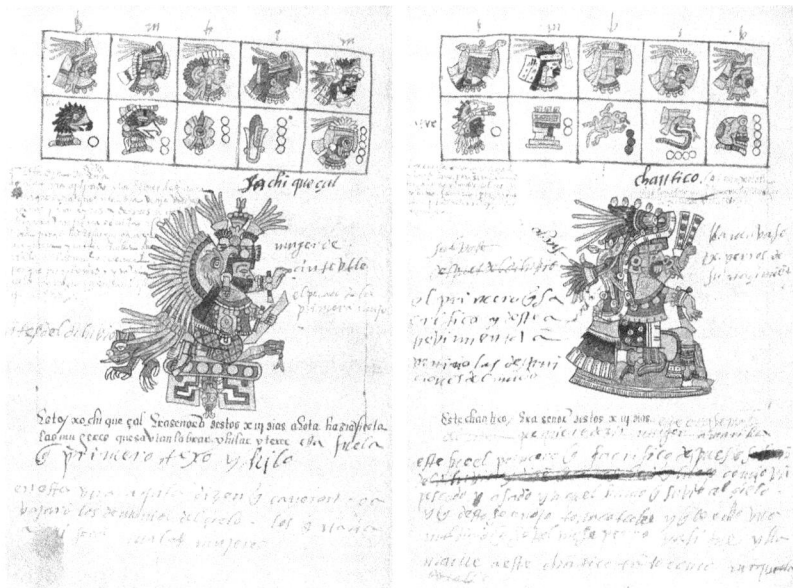

2.2. (left) Xochiquetzal. *Codex Telleriano-Remensis*, 22v. Courtesy of the Bibliothèque nationale de France.
2.3. (right) Chantico. *Codex Telleriano-Remensis*, 21v. Courtesy of the Bibliothèque nationale de France.

2.4. Diorite Chantico/Coyolxauhqui. Museo del Templo Mayor. Photograph by Elizabeth Aguilera.

historical approach, he values comparing images from chronologically later contexts with earlier ones or, as he writes in "Preclassic Mesoamerican Iconography," working "from the living to the dead."[166] Following Seler, Nicholson argues that the conservative religious context of pre-Contact Central Mexico preserved the meaning of iconographic elements over long periods of time. This continuity enables him to project meaning from post-Contact descriptions back to earlier historical periods: "Iconographic continuity can best be established by careful determination of similarity of images through time. And a single motif . . . would normally have less value than a consistently associated *cluster* of iconographic elements, the more complex the better."[167] This preference for groups of insignia also applies to the taxonomic scheme he articulates in "Religion in Pre-Hispanic Central Mexico," where iconographic continuity among deity representations (rather than through history) establishes complex and cult similarities.[168] And yet, Nicholson—ever reasonable and open-minded—describes his willingness to experiment with other methods, "I would also favor the utilization of possible other approaches, however, whenever cogent results seem likely to emerge. . . . In other words, a comprehensive, synthetic approach to the problems of the interpretation of early

Mesoamerican iconographic systems will probably eventually yield the most successful results."[169]

In *Aztec Art* (1983), Esther Pasztory attempts just such a systematic study of Mexica iconography. She begins by identifying deities as the most complex of four iconographic types: designs, symbols, emblems, and deities.[170] Designs, the simplest of her four types, ornament Mesoamerican art. They may convey some symbolic meaning, but they are essentially abstract and decorative. Symbols, she explains, conveyed more complex meanings than designs and included human hearts, skulls, skulls and crossbones, flowers, the planet Venus, corn, and maguey thorns. Pasztory defines emblems as "a complex image consisting of several symbolic units that generally occur together," and she identifies a discrete number of emblems: "the solar disk, the earth monster, the grass ball of sacrifice, the sky band, the jaguar-eagle pair, the feathered serpent, the fire serpent, the water-fire stream, and the smoking mirror." Pasztory explains that both emblems and deities are composed of symbols and denote onomastic associations, but she insists: "Emblems are concepts, not deities."[171]

Pasztory's typology culminates in deities, which she sees as complex arrangements of insignia that represent natural forces.[172] Essentially, she views deities as more refined and complex types of representations. "Sacredness," Pasztory explains, "does not reside in their bodies but in their costume and in associated insignia and symbols."[173] For example, in her taxonomic scheme, "The anthropomorphic sun deity is represented in different aspects by several gods—Tonatiuh, Huitzilopochtli, or Piltzintecuhtli[, but] the solar disk image stands for the more abstract concept of the sun as the equivalent of the Aztecs' cosmic era."[174] In her insistence on the importance of deity insignia, Pasztory undermines her typology. On the one hand, she insists that deities' bodily forms were simply armatures for the display of insignia; on the other hand, she characterizes Aztec deities as personified beings who manipulated natural forces. Like Nicholson, her emphasis on the primacy of individual iconographic elements leads her to deemphasize the importance of deities' bodies and embodiment. Yet her suggestion that deities control natural forces belies her feeling that *teteo* were more than complex symbols. Further, Pasztory's struggle to find a typology that explains how the deities related to other aspects of the cosmovision reveals the difficulties scholars have faced (and continue to face) as they attempt to understand Aztec religion.

The iconographic tradition Nicholson and Pasztory inherited from Seler and perpetuated in their own work disembodies deities by reducing complex figural forms to their simplest iconographic elements. As an analytic method, iconography isolates discrete symbolic elements within complex images, but without properly contextualizing *teixiptlahuan* and their insignia—both of which function(ed) in linguistic contexts that span spoken, performed, and pictographic forms of communication—iconography can assess only some aspects of a deity's identity.[175] Additionally, whenever iconographers gloss pictographic symbols without reference to Nahuatl, they ignore the intimate relationship between images, glyphs, and spoken language in older Nahuatl, because glyphs do, in fact, convey meaning on the level of spoken language.

As Boone explains, "Graphic systems of communication where marks communicate meaning directly and within the structure of their own system . . . convey ideas independently from language and on the same logical level as spoken language."[176] She describes Aztec glyphs as "conventionalized," and while she underscores the significance of the images' context, she also notes the dynamic quality of a pictorial script's reading order.[177] The flexibility of Aztec ideograms allowed a specialist's "reading" to change depending on the scenario's specific demands. Additionally, Boone insists, "In the semasiographic systems of the Mixtecs and Aztecs, the pictures *are* the texts. There is no distinction between word and image."[178] Her description of Aztec glyphic systems stresses the lack of disjuncture between image, concept, and word, a rupture that persists in iconographic analyses that dismiss the relationship between pictographic Nahuatl and spoken Nahuatl.

Indeed, Lacadena argues that the decipherment of older Nahuatl writing, by which he means the logograms of pictorial manuscripts, *is* possible. He further posits that three persistent presumptions regarding older Nahuatl writing have hindered its decipherment. The first two observations state that "(1) The written testimonies of the Mexica are the most representative of the Prehispanic writing system; [and] (2) documents that show a greater frequency of phoneticism do not represent the traditional indigenous system but rather a modified one, having been influenced as much by the alphabetic writing of the Spanish as by the novel necessities of transliterating foreign names."[179]

In regard to the study of Aztec *teteo* and their *teixiptlahuan*, the third presumption—that "Nahuatl writing is basically logographic, with an incipient or undeveloped phoneticism, restricted to the utilization of rebus for logograms and a limited repertory of signs used in phonetic mode, without integration into a true conventional syllabary"—has proved the most powerful.[180] Lacadena produces a partial syllabary based on a group of manuscripts produced in Tlatelolco and Texcoco, and his initial findings revealed that "the pending work depends on the identification of the repertory of signs, their reading values and functions, the identification and explication of the mechanisms that govern the scribal resources, and the orthographic conventions employed in Nahuatl writing."[181] Without a doubt, deciphering older Nahuatl (pictorial) writing will reveal important connections between *teteo*, their physical appearances, material substances, and the *teixiptlahuan* portrayed in two- and three-dimensional media.

Despite Lacadena's work, most scholars default to the iconographic method and rely on deities' insignia as identifiers. The complexity of deity representations calls for a more ample hermeneutic: one that allows for multiple significations and agglutination—both linguistic and material—while taking into account the presence of embodied figural forms and the particularities of context.

Conclusions

From the first moment of Contact, the concepts *teotl* and *teixiptla* preoccupied the Aztecs and Spaniards, and scholars still struggle to define and translate these elusive concepts. Moments of convergence and divergence in the terms' interpretive histories raise questions that I will pursue in the coming chapters. For example, the vast majority of scholars translate *teotl* as "god." While this strong concurrence reinforces this translation's strength, the question of what *teotl* as "god" meant to the Aztecs remains. Because of this lingering question and concerns that the translation "god" too easily evokes the Abrahamic God, some scholars prefer alternative expressions, such as Hvidtfeldt's "*mana*" and "sacred"; López Austin's "divine forces"; Read's "power"; and Maffie's "becoming."[182] These formulations reflect admirable intentions to understand Aztec religion through loosely defined comparisons, on the one hand, and to decouple it from Western religious concepts on the other. In regard to the former, it is important to remember that because *teotl* carries its own culturally specific connotations, it cannot function as an exotic synonym for comparison with other religious traditions. In order to distinguish *teotl* from the Western concept of God or that of any other god, we must first understand *teotl* on its own terms. Otherwise, it is impossible to assess alternative translations, like "the sacred" or "divine force," which may or may not convey the Aztec concept of *teotl* more effectively than "god."

The interpretive history of *teixiptla* raises similar questions about its canonical forms, translation, and relationship to *teotl*. In contrast to the relative consensus regarding *teotl*'s meaning, scholars recognize a wider semantic range for *teixiptla*. As Appendix A demonstrates, most verbal uses of *teixiptla* fall into one of three categories: to pay back or satisfy (as in a debt); to substitute for someone; and to make a representation or likeness of someone. These three senses of *teixiptla* clearly relate to one another, and by paying close attention to *teixiptla*'s etymology, we may determine how the variants relate and which of them reflect the concept's canonical forms.

Finally, several of the scholars discussed above raise questions about the relationship of a *teotl* to its *teixiptla*. Not all *teixiptlahuan* (localized embodiments) represent *teteo* (gods, deities). However, the *teixiptlahuan* of *teteo*—especially human *teixiptlahuan*—have drawn considerable attention from anthropologists and scholars of religion. The presence of deities in their representatives particularly concerns López Austin, Carrasco, and Clendinnen, who argue that a *teixiptla* acts as a container or vessel for a *teotl*'s divine force. The nature of a very particular type of representation, namely, that of religious effigies, is at issue in this question of a *teotl*'s presence or absence in its *teixiptla*. Unlike other types of representations (e.g., military delegates or painted portraits), devotees conceive of effigies as both deity representations and embodiments. Fortunately, the ritual creation and sacrificial destruction of *teixiptlahuan* in the calendric celebrations described by Sahagún and Durán provide rich contexts for understanding how *teteo* and their *teixiptlahuan* related to one another in Aztec religion.

In the following chapters, I respond to these questions through a comprehensive examination of *teotl*'s meaning and a detailed analysis of deities' localized embodiments and animation. In the next chapter, I explore the meaning of *teotl* employed in a variety of passages from the *Florentine Codex*, primarily those that describe two varieties of similar objects, such as *xihuitl* (turquoise) and *teoxihuitl* (*teo*-turquoise). Because these passages describe comparable objects, they facilitate a careful examination of the qualities that distinguish a *teotl*-modified object from its ordinary manifestation. Using this philological process, I highlight five qualities that inhere in a *teotl* or *teotl*-modified entity as the *Florentine Codex* describes them. Because these qualities are specific to *teotl*, they provide the basis for a more informed translation or more informed use of existing translations, including "god."

CHAPTER 3

Divining the Meaning of *Teotl*

>>> "auh in mexica quinnotz in inteouh quimilhui: oc nachcan tihui"

>>> And the god of the Mexica spoke to them; he said to them: "We go still farther."[1]

>>> "quinotza in teotl, in chalchihuitl icue, in atl"

>>> The midwife addressed the goddess, Chalchihuitlicue, the water.[2]

>>> "ca oquitotiaque, in tetepe ca teteo: ipampa quimpiquia in tepetl auh in imixiptlahuan, quintocayotiaya tepictoton"

>>> For they went on to say that the mountains were gods; wherefore they formed mountain [figures], and they called their representations Tepictoton.[3]

Aztec *teteo* (gods) acted in the world: they spoke to devotees, they inhabited and oversaw elements of the landscape, and they appeared in localized embodiments constructed by priests and practitioners. Hearing Aztecs call mountain-shaped dough figurines, human god-bodies, and bodies of water—let alone Cortés and company—"teteo" must have perplexed the conquistadors, friars, and chroniclers who encountered them and their stories. We know this in part from the awe they expressed regarding the Aztec gods and their embodiment. Bernal Díaz del Castillo wrote of the dazzling impression deity statues covered in precious stones made upon him, and Bernardino de Sahagún sensed a connection his informants denied between *teotl* (god) and *teoatl* (ocean): "inic mitoa teoatl, camo teotl, zan quitoznequi mahuiztic huei tlamahuizolli." (It is called *teoatl* [sea], not that it is a god; it only means wonderful, a great marvel.)[4] What was and was not a *teotl* was not always clear to sixteenth-century friars. Mesoamericans probably intentionally introduced some confusion and hid some information, but the nature of Aztec cosmology inhibited easy equivalences between native and European religions.

The meaning of *teotl*—what a speaker of older Nahuatl meant when she said "god"—lies at the heart of understanding Aztec religion. Gaining a sense of what a person meant when she invoked a *teotl* or identified someone/something as *teotl* requires investigating contexts that discuss deities, their *teixipt-*

lahuan (localized embodiments), and divine things, those objects modified and transformed by *teotl*. In this chapter, I identify the basic substantive uses of *teotl*, discuss variations on those forms, and explore properties associated with *teotl* based on its use in a variety of specific contexts documented in the *Florentine Codex*. These properties suggest that when *teotl* modifies another object or entity, it signals an ontological transformation in that which it modifies.

Because *teotl* is a morpheme, its meaning cannot be derived through further division, and, unfortunately, the Nahuatl-speaking scribes who compiled the *Florentine Codex* did not include an explicit definition of the concept.[5] In order to understand what *teotl* means, scholars may rely on the translations of *teotl* found in colonial chronicles and lexicons, including those discussed in the preceding chapter; they may compare and contrast different uses of the term; and they may search for contexts that illustrate how *teotl* functions in compounds. In the following, I incorporate two of these approaches: contextual examinations of the term's use and its meaning in three morphological configurations, including its canonical form, its use as a stem in a compound word, and its use as a modifier in a compound. As Arild Hvidtfeldt and Richard Andrews have noted, word order in Nahuatl compounds matters. When *teotl* functions as a prefix or modifier, it brings its complete set of connotations to the thing it modifies or transforms.[6] The first portion of this chapter examines the functions of *teotl* when it stands alone and when it appears as the stem in a compound. The remainder of the chapter works toward defining *teotl* by examining the meanings it conveys in compounds.

Neither Sahagún nor the scribes define *teotl* outright, but they do discuss words modified by *teotl*, and those passages provide rich contexts for *teotl*'s meaning. Sahagún's *Florentine Codex* represents one of the earliest and most comprehensive Nahuatl accounts of pre-Contact life as it was remembered in the decades following Contact. In fact, Sahagún intended other scholars to study the *Florentine Codex* as a record of Nahuatl and native culture: "It will be a great source of satisfaction, because with much less effort than it costs me here, those who may so desire will be able to know many of the ancient practices and all the language of this Mexican people in a brief time."[7] By identifying passages that elucidate elements of *teotl*'s meaning in the *Florentine Codex*, I compare how *teotl* functions in different constructions and contexts and examine the meaning *teotl* imports to the words it modifies. This approach yields a constellation of qualities that emerge from *teotl*'s use in the *Florentine Codex*. In the absence of an explicit definition from a Nahuatl source, these qualities serve as significant referents for our understanding of *teotl* and, more specifically, of *teotl* as "god."

My evidence gathering began with isolating passages that contain both comparative material and contextual clues about *teotl*'s meaning from among the more than 1,600 occurrences of *teotl* in the *Florentine Codex*. During this process, I compiled a list of approximately twenty-five pairs of words, like *calli* (house), with attested *teotl* modifications, like *teohcalli* (god house; temple).[8] These sets provide a comparative basis for determining *teotl*'s meaning. Examining how *teotl* changes a word/thing it modifies illuminates *teotl*'s semantic properties—the meanings it imparts to the words it transforms through prefixing.

This method proved especially fruitful because of the semantic nature of Nahuatl morphemes. *Teotl* retains the fullness of its meaning regardless of its occurrence as a prefix, stem, or noncompounded term. Comparing the *teotl* compound (*teohcalli*) with the compound's stem (*calli*) reveals how *teotl* alters the concepts it modifies. Admittedly, the transition from *calli* (house) to *teohcalli* (temple) may seem reasonably simple, but remember my concern about the ease with which scholars (and other non-Aztec, non-Nahuatl speakers) import foreign notions of god to *teotl*. That the Mexicas thought of temples as god-houses may sound sensible and even familiar, but it does not necessarily provide useful information about how they conceived of the "god" element in the concept. Other examples I encountered, including those of *teoxihuitl* (*teo*-turquoise), *teotetl* (*teo*-stone; jet), and *teocuitlatl* (*teo*-excrement; gold), proved quite instructive, though. Surprisingly, the differences between the three types of turquoises—*xihuitl*, *teoxihuitl*, and *tlapalteoxihuitl*—described in *Book 11: Earthly Things*, the *Florentine Codex*'s natural history, most strikingly illustrate several of *teotl*'s significant semantic elements (Figure 3.1).

In the following, I focus on three sets of words: *xihuitl*, *teoxihuitl*, and *tlapalteoxihuitl* (turquoise, *teo*-turquoise, and painted *teo*-turquoise); *tetl* and *teotetl* (stone and *teo*-stone/jet); and *cuitlatl* and *teocuitlatl* (excrement and *teo*-excrement/gold). These word sets prove particularly illuminating because they occur in passages that discuss their etymological origins, appearance, and artisanal use. Contrasting their meanings expands the semantic range of *teotl* and its nuances by highlighting, for example, the differences between ordinary turquoise and *teo*-turquoise. Comparing and contrasting these semantic sets isolates the compounds' distinctive elements and reveals a cluster of five *teotl* qualities:

(1) a *teotl* has *axcaitl* (possessions, property);
(2) a *teotl* has a *tonalli* (heat; day sign; fate, fortune, privilege, prerogative);
(3) a *teotl* has *neixcahuilli* (an exclusive thing, occupation, business, or pursuit);

3.1. *Xihuitl* (turquoise). *Florentine Codex*, 3:357r. Photograph courtesy of the Biblioteca Medicea Laurenziana.

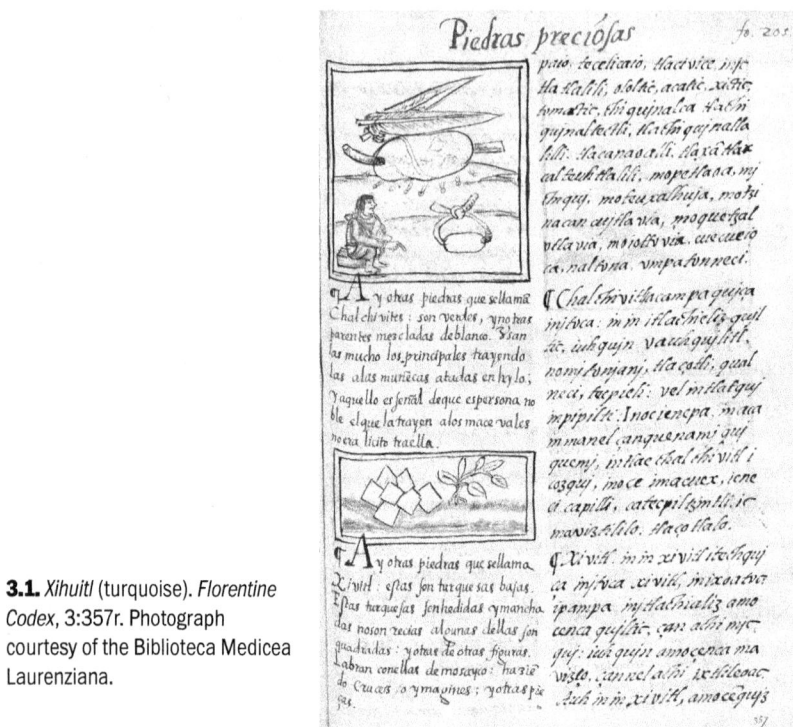

(4) a *teotl* is *mahuiztic* (something marvelous, awesome, worthy of esteem); and

(5) a *teotl* is *tlazohca* (valuable, beloved).

After examining *teotl* in its canonical and compound-stem forms, I explore its use in passages that describe these properties in relation to *teoxihuitl, teotetl,* and *teocuitlatl.* My interpretations of these passages provides a broader sense of what each of the qualities implies in Nahuatl. In essence, these five qualities define *teotl.*

Teotl in Its Canonical Form

In the *Florentine Codex, teotl* and its plural form, *teteo,* most often refer to a specific "god," various "gods," or "the gods," collectively. *Teotl* frequently occurs in formulaic phrases, and these may reflect the oral quality of spoken

Nahuatl and, by extension, the stock nature of ritualistic incantations. Alternatively (or additionally), formulaic uses of *teotl* may derive from the ways Sahagún and the scribes planned, composed, and edited the *Florentine Codex*. Chapter introductions from *Book 1: The Gods* provide examples of formulaic uses of *teotl*: "inic ei, capitulo, itechpa tlatoa in teotl, in itoca tezcatlipoca: in quimoteotiaya, ihuan in quitlamaniliaya, ye huecauh." (The third chapter, which tells of the god called Tezcatlipoca, whom they worshipped and to whom they offered sacrifices in distant times.)[9] In addition to the basic use of *teotl* as "god" or "deity" in this example, variants in the term's translations highlight the breadth of its significations. Significant semantic variants of *teotl* include its translation as "goddess," its specific function in the compound *cihuateotl* (woman god), and its presence in proper names. A close examination of *teotl* in these constructions reveals that while the basic semantic meaning of *teotl* is "god" or "deity," the concept also conveys specific nuances.[10]

According to its use in a variety of *Florentine Codex* passages, *teotl* most often means "god" or "deity" in the conventional sense.[11] A description of Quetzalcoatl from *Book 3: The Origin of the Gods* illustrates this sense of the term: "in yehuatl, in quetzalcoatl: iuhquinma teotl ipan quimatia, neteotiloya, teomachoya, in iquin ye huecauh, in ompa tollan." (This Quetzalcoatl they considered as a god; he was thought a god; he was prayed to in olden times there at Tula.)[12] Similarly, *teteo* often refers to various "gods" or collectively to "the gods." In *Book 7: The Sun, Moon, and Stars, and the Binding of the Years*, the gods discuss how to create the sun, "quitoque: quimolhuique tla xihualhuiyan, teteoye: aquin tlatzuiz? aquin tlamamaz? in tonaz, intlathuiz? . . . oc ceppa quitoque in teteo: aquin oc ce?" (They spoke; they said among themselves: "Come hither, O gods! Who will carry the burden? Who will take it upon himself to be the sun, to bring the dawn?" . . . And again the gods spoke, "[And] who else?")[13] These passages and others clearly establish *teotl*'s frequent use as "god" or "deity" in the *Florentine Codex*.

Another prominent use of *teotl* occurs in passages that identify *teteo* with their patron communities, and in many of these passages the scribes use the conventional phrase "[so-and-so] is the god of (*inteouh catca*) [some people]."[14] Most often the scribes associate deities with occupational or ethnic communities: "anahuatl iteouh: tzapoteca in huel inteouh catca." (He was the god of the seashore people, the proper god of the Zapotecs.)[15] Another example states, "ini yacateuctli: pochteca inteouh catca." (This one was Yiacatecutli, he was the merchants' god.)[16] Formulaic phrases like these demonstrate the scribes' use of *teotl* in a simple, noncompounded sense. In each of these contexts, the English gloss "deity" or "god" is an appropriate approximation of the entity being described. The prevalence of this basic use of *teotl* may predispose the *Florentine Codex*'s readers to assume that *teotl* is synonymous with the Western notion of god or deity. As we shall see, though, the transformations *teotl* brings about in the words it modifies clarify its pragmatic connotations and sharpen the culturally specific sense it brings to the translations "god" and "deity."

Teotl as a Stem in Compounds

In contrast to the profusion of words prefixed by *teotl*, only four common noun compounds include *teotl* as their stem: *cihuateotl* (woman *teotl*), *cihuateteo* (women *teteo*), *malteotl* (captive *teotl*), and *apizteotl* (hungry *teotl*). *Malteotl*, from *malli* (captive, prisoner), occurs near the end of the description of the festival Tlacaxipehualiztli in *Book 2: The Ceremonies* and refers to a masked thigh bone wrapped in paper.[17] *Apizteotl* comes from *apiztli* (hunger; hungry person) and is a characteristic attributed to thieves.[18] *Apizteotl* may be a synonym (or a nonce phrasing) of *teohcihui*, "to be hungry." Both *malteotl* and *apizteotl* occur only once in the *Florentine Codex*. Effectively, then, *cihuateotl* and *cihuateteo* are the only multiply attested *Florentine Codex* compounds with *teotl* stems.

Although *cihuateotl* and *cihuateteo* may at first appear to mean simply "goddess" and "goddesses," respectively, the scribes use them in specific contexts and surprising ways. In some contexts, the scribes refer to a female deity as *cihuateotl*, but in others they use the genderless *teotl*. For example, they refer to Chicomecoatl, Teteo Innan, Tzapotlan Tenan, and Chalchihuitlicue as *cihuateotl*, and yet their references to Chalchihuitlicue, Coatlicue/Coatlan Tonan, and Xochiquetzal as *teotl* raise questions about the terms' (in)distinction or the scribes' or redactors' care in using the terms.[19] Four of the six times the scribes refer to Chalchihuitlicue as a deity, they call her a *teotl*, and each time Anderson and Dibble translate *teotl* as "goddess":

> She was considered *teotl* (a god[dess]). They represented her as a woman. So it was claimed, it was said that she belonged to the rain-gods, as their elder sister.[20]

> Atoyatl [rivers from Tlalocan]—They are the property of, they issue from the *teotl* (goddess) named Chalchihuitlicue.[21]

> The midwife addressed the *teotl* (goddess) Chalchihuitlicue, the water.[22]

Behold, here is another way in which the midwife prayed as she prayed to the *teotl* (goddess) Chalchihuitlicue.[23]

Referring to Chalchihuitlicue as a *teotl* may signal overlooked or poorly understood aspects of her gender, perhaps that she is transgender, superficially gendered, or multigendered, as we might describe male priests who wore the flayed skins of females. Alternatively, this designation may point to a flexibility in *teotl*'s semantic denotation, indicate an evolution in Nahuatl terminology for female deities, or reflect a colonial adaptation of the term. Additionally, the translators' preference may reflect a Western (or Indo-European) insistence on gender agreement. To some extent, though, *cihuateotl* (woman *teotl*) and *teotl* seem to be interchangeable.

In contrast to the semantic similarity of *cihuateotl* and *teotl*, the term *cihuateteo* (women *teteo*) differs substantially from both *cihuateotl* and *teteo*. While *teteo* frequently refers to a plurality of gods, *cihuateteo* never simply means "goddesses."[24] In the *Florentine Codex*, *cihuateteo* designates a specific group of goddesses related to descent and sacrifices on Chicomecoatonalli (the day sign 7 Serpent) and during the feast of Ochpaniztli (sweeping). In addition to their veneration during Ochpaniztli, the *cihuateteo* descend on day signs ce mazatl (1 Deer), ce quiahuitl (1 Rain), ce ozomatli (1 Monkey), and ce ehecatl (1 Wind). On 1 Deer, "the Goddesses (*cihuateteo*) descended. There they made offerings to them, and there they clothed them in their paper vestments and paper adornments."[25] In the list of temples included in *Book 2*, priests venerated the *cihuateteo* at Aticpac, Xochicalco, and Atlauhco. At Aticpac, "oncan quintonaltiaia in Cihuateteo: ihcuac in quilhuia chicomecoatonalli." (There they were sacrificing to the *cihuateteo* when it says 7 Serpent.)[26] The *cihuateteo*'s veneration at Xochicalco during Ochpaniztli involved *netlatiloyan*, a cave or container for flayed skins: "oncan quintlatiaya in cihuateteo imehuayo, in ompa miquia xochicalco: cexiuhtica, ipan ochpaniztli." (Here they hid the skins of the *cihuateteo* who died there at Xochicalco every year at Ochpaniztli.)[27] Elsewhere, the text warns readers that *cihuateteo* linger at crossroads where they may injure passersby, especially children.[28] The differences between the *cihuateto* and related goddesses, including the *mocihuaquetzque*, have been debated by scholars, some of whom associate the physical characteristics of these deities with well-known statues, including the monoliths named coatlicue and Tlaltecuhtío.[29]

The *Florentine Codex* associates *cihuateteo* with *cihuapipiltin* (princesses); *ilhuica cihuapipiltin* (celestial princesses) or *ilhuicacihuatl* (celestial women); and *mocihuaquetzque* (women they departed).[30] The *mocihuaquetzque* are the spirits of women who died in childbirth, and "they believed in them like they believed in the *cihuateteo*."[31] Although the *Florentine Codex* compares these four goddess cohorts to one another, the scribes—for the most part—maintain a semantic distinction between them. According to their descriptions, none of these goddess cohorts is exactly equivalent, and I have little reason to consider them identical.[32] Instead, the scribes' denomination of different goddess cohorts signals a range of revered deity groups in pre-Contact religion. The semantic differences and similarities between *teotl*, *cihuateotl*, and *cihuateteo* present a complex and puzzling facet of Aztec deity classification, a reminder of the many gaps in our knowledge.

In addition to its use as a simple noun and as a stem in compounds, *teotl* occurs in seven onomastic compounds, or naming compounds, commonly thought to be the proper names of individual *teteo*, including Cinteotl (Maize God), Teotl Ehco (The God Arrives), Tlazolteotl (Trash God), Tlazolteteo (Trash Gods), Teteo Innan (Mother of the Gods), Teteo Inta (Father of the Gods) and Huehue Teotl (Very Old God).[33] In each of these compounds or phrases, *teotl* functions as the modified component of the name. For example, *cintli* (maize) and *teotl* combine to form Cinteotl (Maize God), a *teotl* whose *teixiptlahuan* manifest in corn ears and ritual actors.[34] The name Tlazolteotl (Trash God), from *tlahzolli* (trash) and *teotl*, alludes to mastery over "evil and perverseness—that is to say, lustful and debauched living. It was said that she ruled and was a mistress of lust and debauchery," and the scribes note that her veneration was widespread and especially popular among the Olmecs.[35] Additionally, the Tlazolteteo, the only collective onomastic in this list, refers to a group of four *teteo* associated with Tlazolteotl: "inic ce itoca tiacapan, inic ome, itoca teicu, inic eye, itoca tlaco: inic nahui itoca xocotzin. inique hin nahuintin cihuatl: quil teteo. inique in, ceceiaca intoca: tlazolteteo." (The first is named Tiacapan, the second Teicu, the third named Tlaco, the fourth named Xocotzin. These four women, it was said, were gods. Each one of these was called Tlazolteteo.)[36] According to descriptions like these, the Aztecs conceived of both Cinteotl, whose *teixiptla* took a variety of forms, and Tlazolteotl, who heard supplicants' prayers, as active *teteo* inscribed with individualized attributes.

The names Teteo Innan, Teteo Inta, and Huehue Teotl illustrate two other aspects of *teotl*'s naming functions. Scholars often treat these naming devices as proper nouns, because in many contexts they seem to refer to or indicate specific *teteo*. At other times, however, they function as an epithet or collective invocation. The eighth chapter of *Book 1* is dedicated to *Teteo innan*, and the phrase *Teteo innan* appears there as one of several names associated with

a specific *teotl*: "oncan motenehua, in cihuateotl, in itoca: teteo innan: no mo-
tocayotia, tlalli i yollo, huan toci. inna catca in teteo." (Here is named the goddess called Teteo Innan [Mother of the Gods], who is also named Tlalli Yiollo
[Heart of the Earth] and Toci [Our Grandmother]. She was the mother of the
gods.)[37] Similarly, the scribes explain that Xiuhtecuhtli (Green or Turquoise
Lord) was also known as Ixcozauhqui (Face Yellow), Cuezaltzin (Flame-
colored Thing or Scarlet Macaw, reverentially), Huehue Teotl, and Tota (Our
Father).[38] In *Book 6: Rhetoric and Moral Philosophy*, a midwife invokes Tic-
itl (Physician, Healer, Midwife) as both Teteo Innan and Tonan: "a ca nelle
axcan, anquimonochilia, anquimotzatzililia, anquiticinotza in teteo innan: in
tonan in yohualticitl, in quitquitica, in imac ca, in ipial in xochicalli, in tlal-
ticpac mitoa temazcalli." (Now truly, you call to her, you cry out to her, you
summon her, the mother of the gods, our mother, Yohualticitl, who bears in
her hands, in her care the flower house on earth, known as the sweathouse
for bathing.)[39] In these examples, Teteo Innan, Huehue Teotl, and Tota seem
to refer to identifiable and individual—though polynominal—*teteo*. Calling
these gods by multiple names emphasizes the deities' various—and sometimes overlapping—aspects, attributes, and responsibilities.

In other contexts, these names occur together and function as *difrasismos*
and as collective invocations, especially in the phrases "*teteo innan, teteo inta*"
(Mother of the gods, father of the gods) and "*in tonan, in tota*" (Our mother, our father). By contrast to the former examples, which refer to individual
teteo, these phrases invoke a parental pair joined through the *difrasismo*, a linguistic convention whereby two discrete words, when taken together, refer to
a third concept. For example, *in tonan, in tota* (Our mother, our father) pre-
cedes invocations of *tonatiuh tlaltecuhtli* (The sun, the earth-lord) and *mictlan
tecuhtli* (Mictlan lord): "oncan motenehua in tlatolli: inic quitlatlauhtiaya Tezcatlipoca, in quitocayotiaia titlacahua, moquequeloa, in iquac miquia tlatoani,
inic oc ce motlatocatlaliz . . . a ca oontlama, ca ocontocac in tonan, in tota in
mictlan tecuhtli." (Here are recorded the words which they asked of Tezcatlipoca, whom they called Titlacahuan, Moquequeloa, when the *tlahtoani* died, in
order that another be installed. . . . He knew, he had followed our mother, our
father Mictlan Tecuhtli.)[40] The *difrasismo* "*in tonan, in tota*" (Our mother, our
father) underscores the complementary duality present in Mictlan Tecuhtli,
who with his partner, Mictlan Cihuatl, was the divine mother-father (i.e., the
divine parent) governing the underworld. Notably, apart from this *difrasismo*,
there is no genderless word meaning "parent" in older Nahuatl.[41] These examples illustrate how "*teteo innan,*" "*teteo inta,*" and "*tonan, tota*" function in two
distinct ways: first, as the names of distinct *teteo* and, second, as *difrasismos*

that invoke divine parents. While they demonstrate the interchangeability of "*teteo innan, teteo inta*" with "*tonan, tota,*" the most metaphoric version of the collective invocation takes a third form and includes *huehue teotl.*

The three names, *teteo innan, teteo inta,* and *huehue teotl,* appear together in contexts with cosmic imagery and invocations of *teteo* whose names encompass the infinite. For example, in what the scribes identify as a prayer to Tezcatlipoca, a priest invokes *teteo innan, teteo inta,* and *huehue teotl* as one entity called *motechiuhcauh* (your authority)[42] and locates it/them in the center of the earth, a place known as *xiuhtetzacualco* (the turquoise enclosure): "in oncan motecahaltilitica, in motechiuhcauh, in teteo innan, in teteo inta, in huehueteotl in tlalxicco maquitoc . . ." (There your authority is being bathed, the mother of the gods, the father of the gods, the very old god, who dwelled in the navel of the earth . . .)[43] This example demonstrates the highly rhetorical quality of the phrase, in addition to its collective nature. Here the *difrasismo teteo innan, teteo inta* refers to one *huehue teotl,* who is one *motechiuhcauh,* one source of power and authority.

Another example of the phrase's encompassing nature occurs in a fascinating account in which a soothsayer prays to Tlazolteotl on behalf of a penitent.[44] In this passage, *teteo innan, teteo inta,* and *huehue teotl* appear in parallel structure with "in tlacatl, in totecujo, in tloqueh nahuaqueh: in totecujo, yoalli, in ehecatl" (Master, our lord of the near, the nigh, our lord the night, the wind), onomastic phrases that encompass the infinite:

> The penitent who would confess first explained to the soothsayer; he said unto him: "I wish to go to *in tlacatl, in totecujo, in tloqueh nahuaqueh: in totecujo, yoalli, in ehecatl* (Master, our lord of the near, the nigh, our lord the night, the wind). I wish to learn of his secrets." The soothsayer said: "Thou has done a favor." He instructed him when he should come; he chose the day. He consulted his sacred almanac, he noted the good day, the good time, the favorable time. . . . And when it was already the appointed time, he bought a new reed mat, and incense, and wood. . . . Then the soothsayer cast the incense into the flames. He [the soothsayer] addressed the fire; he said: "*Teteo innan, teteo inta, huehue teotl* (Mother of the gods, father of the gods, the old god), here hath come a man of low estate. He cometh here weeping, sad, anguished. . . . *Tlacatle, totecue, tloqueh nahuaqueh* (Master, our lord of the near, the nigh), receive, hear the torment of this lowly one."[45]

In this context, the collective invocation of *teteo innan, teteo inta,* and *huehue teotl* seems to signify an abstract entity—perhaps a presence in the fire—more akin to the metaphoric *tloqueh nahuaqueh* (Possessor of the adjacent, of the near) than to individual deities' names.[46] In some cases, *teteo innan*, *teteo inta* (or *tota*), and *huehue teotl* clearly refer to individual *teteo*. In others, such as the passages discussed above, the list operates at a metaphoric level on a par with highly rhetorical epithets like *tloqueh nahuaqueh*. This perplexing difference in usage may reflect a linguistic process, such as semantic "bleaching" whereby a specific term becomes more general, or it may highlight a distinction (or lack thereof) made by the Aztecs. In any case, the individual, collective, and metaphoric qualities of onomastic phrases like *teteo innan*, *teteo inta*, *huehue teotl*, *tonan*, and *tota* point to complex ways the Aztecs conceptualized, organized, identified, and invoked their *teteo*.

In its canonical form and as a stem in compounds, *teotl* signifies "god" or "deity," but particular compounds and contexts alter the concept's connotation. Whereas *cihuateotl* usually means "woman god," the scribes sometimes refer to a female deity as a *teotl*. Further, *cihuateteo*, which looks like the plural of *cihuateotl*, always pertains to a specific group of female deities: women who died in childbirth. Of the seven onomastic compounds that include *teotl* as a stem, four names refer to specific deities, Cinteotl, Teotl Ehco, Tlazolteotl, and the Tlazolteteo, while the other names, including Teteo Innan, Teteo Inta, and Huehue Teotl, denote individual *teteo* in some contexts but connote a cluster in others. The use of the composite phrase *teteo innan*, *teteo inta*, *huehue teotl* in proximity to and in parallel construction with *tlacatle, totecue, tloqueh nahuaqueh* (Master, lord of the near, the nigh) demonstrates its densely metaphoric and metaphysical resonances.

Our examination of *teotl* as a stem in compounds indicates that "god" or "deity" seems to be an appropriate gloss in most constructions. Words like *cihuateteo* reveal that *teotl* sometimes occurs in compounds with specific, rather than general, referents—in this case, a specific group of goddesses. Further, a close examination of *teotl*'s function as a modifier in compounds—rather than as the modified element—demonstrates that it signifies a transformation in the thing modified. In particular, several passages from *Book 11: Earthly Things* of the *Florentine Codex* demonstrate that *teotl* entails a specific set of qualities that reflect its specific cultural and linguistic context.

Teotl in *Earthly Things*: Documenting the Super(Natural) World

Earthly Things, the eleventh book of the *Florentine Codex*, contains an extensive taxonomy of the natural world as described and recorded by native speakers of Nahuatl in the mid to late sixteenth century. As with all colonial texts, *Earthly Things* reflects the increasingly hybrid perspective of Nahuatl speakers as they integrated traditional views of the world with those they adopted and adapted from the Spaniards.[47] Of all of the *Florentine Codex's* volumes, *Earthly Things* is most like a dictionary or encyclopedia in form and content, a reflection of the scribes' familiarity with European reference works.[48] To say that foreign models restricted the content of *Earthly Things* may be misleading. Even though Sahagún relied upon existing encyclopedias and dictionaries, a thought confirmed by his insistence that he was not prepared to compose a dictionary like Calepino's, his sense of what a reference book should be was quite broad in comparison to modern standards of specialization.

Sahagún believed that "the knowledge of natural things" was a critical element in his *Florentine Codex*.[49] Noting that *Earthly Things* is the lengthiest and most illustrated of the *Florentine Codex's* volumes, Walden Browne explains that "for Sahagún—as for all thinkers of the time—knowledge and beauty were not two clearly separate categories. . . . Sahagún was attempting to approach his knowledge of the Nahuas in a more totalizing fashion than the specialization of modern disciplines permits."[50] Although we might be tempted to think of *Earthly Things* as simply a natural history—that is to say, as a record of the world's natural objects and organisms—we should not discount its potential to contribute to our understanding of Aztec religion. Unlike in *The Gods* and *The Ceremonies* (Books 1 and 2), explicitly religious themes are not the focus of *Earthly Things*, and so this volume of the *Florentine Codex* may have escaped extensive redaction by the friar.

A taxonomy of the natural world, *Earthly Things* contains a series of classifications and subdivisions that order and explain elements of the physical environment. Each chapter focuses on a large-scale classification from which follow subdivisions that ultimately result in the identification and description of discrete animals, plants, stones, etc. For example, the classification *tlazohtetl* (precious stones) includes subdivisions devoted to green stones, "stones that appear like turquoise," and stones with other valuable properties.[51] Within the section devoted to "stones that appear like turquoise," the scribes include entries on *teoxihuitl* (god-turquoise) and *tlapalteoxihuitl* (painted god-turquoise).[52] As the names of these stones suggest, the taxonomic organization and encyclopedic layout of *Earthly Things* make it a fascinating reference work because it includes information on both the physical and metaphysical world(s).

Indeed, *Earthly Things* describes many of the relationships the Aztecs observed between the physical and metaphysical world, including those of the precious stones they valued. Because of the high value the Aztecs placed on *teoxihuitl* (*teo*-turquoise), *teotetl* (*teo*-stone), and *teocuitlatl* (*teo*-excrement), the scribes' alphabetic descriptions of the stones provide a starting point for understanding how they conceptualized *teteo*. Each of these texts begins by explaining how the stone received its name, an origin story that locates the stone in relation to *teotl*. By incorporating *teotl* into the stone's name, the Aztecs signaled a difference between an ordinary *tetl* (stone) and an extraordinary one. The varieties of turquoises described in *Earthly Things* provide contexts in which I explore the meaning *teotl* brings to a word it modifies, as well as the properties associated with *teotl*-modified objects and entities. Turquoise's importance in the Aztec world—and in the history of Mesoamerica—makes it an especially rich source.

Teotl and Turquoise: God Properties in the (Super)Natural World

As anthropologist Phil Weigand observes, "Turquoise became an extravagantly valuable possession and status marker, laden with so much symbolism that it is difficult for us to comprehend. Turquoise appears at almost every explanatory and symbolic juncture within the Mesoamerican ideological system."[53] The importance of *xihuitl* (turquoise, year, comet; herb) in Mesoamerican culture long preceded the Aztecs' rise to power.[54] Archaeological records of turquoise's value begin about 600 BCE in elite burials located in present-day Guerrero, but the demand for turquoise peaked approximately nine centuries later. Around 200–500 CE, extensive mining began in the Chalchihuites area of Zacatecas, where "there are about 800 individual mines from which millions of tons of spoil were taken."[55] Throughout the rise and eclipse of the Toltecs (900–1200 CE) the demand for turquoise continued to grow.

By the fourteenth century, the Aztecs associated turquoise with the Toltecs, whom they praised as master artisans, lapidaries, and goldsmiths. The Aztecs excavated highly valued goods from Toltec sites and attributed the discovery of turquoise to the Toltecs:[56]

> It is said that [the Toltecs] found it in this manner . . . when the sun came up, they took great care to look carefully in all directions . . . when the sun shone . . . a little smoke, a little mist, arose where the precious stone was, either in the ground or within a rock. . . . So is the account, so is their tradition, that they went to find a mine of the rock named turquoise. . . . They discovered, they knew of green stones, fine turquoise, common turquoise, the turquoise lands.[57]

When they excavated Toltec ruins, the Aztecs must have encountered turquoise goods and imagery, because, as Karl Taube notes, "there was a virtual cult of turquoise" at Tula.[58] In his overview of turquoise's use and importance in Tula, Taube explains that even before turquoise's popularity rose, the color blue had significance among the Toltecs, who would have known the "Maya blue" pigment and who represented blue birds, like the lovely cotinga, in their art.[59] Although turquoise's color made it valuable, its workability added to artisans' preference for it:

> Unlike precious carvings of jade . . . Postclassic artisans could easily sculpt wooden backings for turquoise mosaic surfaces . . . turquoise tesserae are typically much smaller and finer [than jade, bone, or shell], probably due to the fact that the stone occurs naturally in thin veins . . . once a turquoise mosaic object outlived its purpose, the stone tesserae could be readily dismantled from the wooden base to be used in another piece.[60]

In addition to its ease of use, turquoise offered artisans a variety of shades of blue—from pale blues to bright blue-greens—with which to work. Mesoamericans embraced the stone's variations in hue and identified different types of turquoise by name.

In her examination of the precious stone's place in the Aztec Empire, Frances Berdan identifies several types of turquoise known to the Aztecs: "*xihuitl*, common turquoise; *teoxihuitl*, fine turquoise; *matlalxihuitl*, blue turquoise; *uel popoca teuxihuitl*, very smoky fine turquoise; *xiuhtomolli*, turquoise that is half-round, half-flat; *xiuhtomoltetl*, a beautiful green and white stone; and *xixitl*, a soft low-grade turquoise that is flawed and spotted and may represent a misprint for *xihuitl*, which was considered less than perfect in any event."[61] In addition to these varieties, Berdan notes a few stones they associated with turquoise, including *xiuhmatlaliztli*, a turquoise-colored obsidian, and *tlapalteoxihuitl*, a red-colored fine "turquoise."[62] The number of names the Aztecs gave these stones reflects the range of "turquoises" associated with geological turquoise, a "blue-green hydrated copper aluminium phosphate $(CuAl_6(PO_4)_4(OH)_8.4H_2O)$."[63] In their analysis of turquoises in North America, Alyson Thibodeau et al. explain that geologists identify six chemically distinct "turquoise" stones that share a common characteristic: their variable composition.[64] "The prehispanic cultures of the American Southwest and Mexico," they write, "embraced these variations and used 'turquoise' of all colours and quality. In many of the famous Mixtec pieces, the artist used differences in colour of various mosaic pieces to achieve specific design features."[65] Despite the number of names by which they knew turquoises, the Aztecs used a standard and simple glyph, a circle containing two halved circles sometimes surrounded by four bosses, to signify the stone (Figure 3.2).

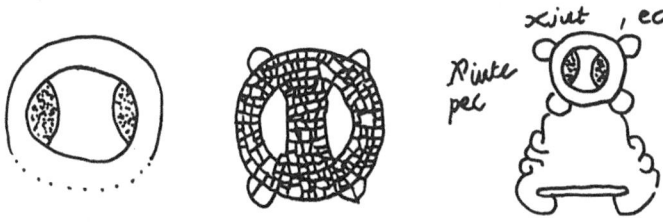

3.2 (a) turquoise sign appearing on Aztec brazier; (b) Aztec turquoise mosaic in form of turquoise sign from the Templo Mayor cache; (c) Aztec toponym for Xiuhtepec, *Matrícula de Tributos*, f. 3v. Line drawings by author after Taube 2012, fig. 12d–f.

The variations within and among types of turquoises has made determining the stones' geological origins difficult. In her study of turquoise's role in the Aztec Empire, Berdan observes that "despite the importance and intense use of turquoise in Aztec life, this precious material was not natively available in the Basin of Mexico and needed to be obtained through market exchange, foreign trade and imposed tribute."[66] Although some scholars argue that the Aztecs mined turquoise from sources used by the Toltecs and others, Berdan notes that the quality of the turquoise mined in the Zacatecas area was rather low. The high-grade turquoise the Aztecs demanded in tribute must have been traded from sources farther north or to the south.[67] Whether mined within Mesoamerica or imported from the north, turquoise continued to be regarded as an extraordinarily valuable item in Aztec culture, as it did throughout Mesoamerica. In addition to turquoise's association with the Toltecs, its relative rarity would have added to its value.[68]

Although geologists have difficulty identifying the sources of turquoises used by Mesoamericans, the Aztecs envisioned all turquoise as a product of the earth: precious stones born from deep within the ground. In his exploration of turquoise's cultural resonances, Patrick Johansson K. proposes that the Aztecs thought of the earth as the womb (*oztotl*) in which turquoise matured and caves as the stone's birth canals:[69]

And how is it with the turquoise? It comes out of a cave (*oztoio*). From within is removed the fine turquoise, the mature, the one that smokes; and that is called turquoise (*xihuitl*) or ruby (*tlapalteoxihuitl*).[70]

The Aztec cosmovision located turquoise in the depths of the earth, a place known as Tlalxicco (Place of the Earth's Navel), which Johansson K. suggests may once have been known as Tlalxiuhco (In the Place of Turquoise) or

Xiuhtetzaqualco (Turquoise Enclosure), where Xiuhtecuhtli (Turquoise Lord), commonly identified as the god of fire and considered to be the primordial parent of the gods, lived.[71] The Aztecs associated fire with both Xiuhtecuhtli and Huehue Teotl (Very Old God), but Taube points out that by contrast to Huehue Teotl's long history in Mesoamerica, "Xiuhtecuhtli is an entirely Late Postclassic phenomenon, and remains undocumented for the known corpus of deities at Tula or Chichen Itza."[72] Taube builds a convincing argument that Xiuhtecuhtli, the fire god who dwelt in the innermost enclosure of the earth, burned brightly as the turquoise that ornamented the ceremonial wares of Aztec *tlahtoque* (rulers): Xiuhtecuhtli "was explicitly evoked during Aztec rites of imperial coronation. However, in accession ceremonies, it was not only the god but the turquoise that he embodied in particular ornaments, such as the *xihuitzolli* crown and *yacaxihuitl* nosepiece," both of which the Aztecs adapted from Toltec devices.[73] Xiuhtecuhtli's emergence in the same era as Huitzilopochtli with his Xiuhcoatl staff signals an Aztec reappropriation of turquoise.

Indeed, the most striking uses of turquoise were in ceremonies and the ceremonial attire of elites. As part of the Aztec state-ceremonial program, "turquoise became the most esteemed form of royal regalia, including the *yacaxihuitl* nosepiece and the *xiuhuitzoli* diadem, in striking contrast to the jade items of more ancient, Classic period kings."[74] Woven into the *tlahtoani's xiuhtlalpilli tilmatli* (cape with knotted turquoise [stones]), arranged as a mosaic, or fashioned into elite nose rods, turquoise finery belonged to the *pipiltin* (nobles).[75] More specifically, Justyna Olko explains that the *xiuhtlalpilli tilmatli* "belonged to the complex of the turquoise royal insignia derived from the Early Postclassic . . . clearly associated with the fire god Xiuhtecuhtli, whose cult was also derived from earlier prestigious traditions."[76] Whereas the nobles owned *xihuitl*, *teoxihuitl* belonged to the *teteo* (see Figure 3.1).

Turquoises and the *Teteo*

Frances Karttunen glosses *xihuitl* as "grass; green stone, turquoise," and notes that the term may also modify heat with regard to its intensity.[77] In his examination of *xihuitl*'s significance in Aztec thought, Mutsumi Izeki argues that the most basic definition of *xihuitl* was herb or grass.[78] From this foundational sense of *xihuitl* evolved other meanings, including greenstone and turquoise, followed by year and its extended senses of fire, comet, red, preciousness, and soul or life.[79] Whether or not the progression from concrete to abstract meanings that Izeki proposes accurately represents the way in which *xihuitl* acquired its constellation of connotations, work by Taube, Johansson K., and others indicates that the Aztecs associated turquoise with blue-green hues, the year, firelight's intense reds and blues, and comets.[80] Figures like Xiuhtecuhtli and Xiuhcoatl, the fire god and turquoise fire serpent, embody and enliven the properties related to turquoise, and turquoise ceremonial attire invested rulers with a powerful intensity. Our primary interest in *xihuitl* lies in its relationship to *teoxihuitl*, which Arthur Anderson and Charles Dibble translate as "fine turquoise," as well as to other *teotl*-modified stones and metals, including *tlapalteoxihuitl*, *teotetl*, and *teocuitlatl*.

Comparing the *xihuitl* (turquoise) to that of *teoxihuitl* (*teo*-turquoise) reveals that the Aztecs attributed specific *teotl* characteristics to this second type, *teoxihuitl*.

XIHUITL

inin xihuitl itech quiza in itoca xihuitl, in ixoatoc: ipampa in itlachializ amo cenca quiltic, zan achi micqui: iuhquin amo cenca mahuizyo, zan nel achi ixtlileoac

auh inin xihuitl, amo cenquizqui, zan cacaiacaticac, iuhquin xalli, patlachtontli, patlachpipil, amo tlaquaoac, zan poxaoac. Inic monequi, inic tlaqualnextilo, zan momana, mozaloa, zan ic tlaixtzaqualo:

nixiuhzaloa, nixiuhtzaqua: nicxiuhtzaqua in huapalli, in teixiptla: nixiuhtemoa, nixiuhtataca, nixiuhquixtia.

TURQUOISE

Turquoise's name comes from grass, which sprouts out, for its appearance is not very herb-green, only a bit dull as if it is not very marvelous, only a little dark, actually.

Turquoise is not a perfect thing, but worn thin like sand, small and flat, small and wide, not hard, but soft. Thus it is used to beautify; it is merely set out, glued on and affixed to something.

I glue turquoise. I affix turquoise. I affix turquoise to the board, to the image. I search for turquoise. I excavate turquoise. I remove turquoise.[81]

According to this passage, turquoise took its name from *xihuitl* (grass) because of its color, a green that was neither exactly herb-green nor particularly marvelous. The description emphasizes turquoise's relative imperfections: its (dis)coloration, its thinness, its softness, and its lack of intrinsic beauty. Indeed, *xihuitl* was the type of turquoise the Aztecs used to ornament other objects. Even though informants likely produced the list of what they did with turquoise in response to a series of questions posed by Sahagún, this description demonstrates that *xihuitl* was not valued for its natural beauty. *Xihuitl* was, it seems, the turquoise used to make (and remake) objects adorned with tesserae. These characteristics of *xihuitl* become more clear by contrast to two finer types of turquoise, including *teoxihuitl*:

TEOXIHUITL

inin itoca itech quiza in teotl, ihuan in xihuitl, zan quihtoznequi iiaxca, itonal in teotl, ihuan, quihtoznequi cenca mahuizyo; ipampa acan cenca neci, canin zan queman in neci: inin teuxihuitl cenca mahuizyo, in itla in itech motta amo cenca mahuizyo: auh in achi huehca neci, huel tizatl, iuhquin xiuhtototl, nelli iuhquin popoca.

inin cequi patlachtic, cequi ololtic, itoca xiuhtomolli: inic xiuhtomolli, ca centlacotl in ololtic in tomoltic: auh in oc centlapal patlachtic, iuhquinma zan ic tlapanqui, cequi huel xipetztic, cequi chachaltic, cequi cocoioctic, cequi tezontic, patlachiuih, ololihui, ticeoa, popoca, teoxiuhpopoca, chachaquachiuih, quiquicahui, tetecahui.

TEO-TURQUOISE

The name of this one comes from *teotl* and turquoise because it means the possessions, the fate of the *teotl*, and it means something very marvelous, because it does not appear very much, because at times it does not appear anywhere. This *teo*-turquoise is very marvelous; when something is visible on it, it is not so marvelous, but from a little distance it appears rather chalky, like the blue cotinga, truly like smoke.

Some of these are wide, others are spherical. Their name is *xiuhtomolli* (turquoise blister)—"turquoise blister" because one half is spherical like a blister, and the other side is broad like something broken. Some are very slick, others roughened, others perforated, rough, wide. It becomes round; it becomes chalky; it smokes, it emits a vapor like turquoise. It is roughened; it becomes perforated; it becomes pale.[82]

In contrast to *xihuitl*, an imperfect and rather dull stone used for adorning other objects, the Aztecs highlight *teoxihuitl*'s relationship to *teotl*.

Teoxihuitl received its name because it both belongs to and is destined to be of a *teotl*: "It means the possessions, the fate of the *teotl*." Additionally, the scribes describe *teoxihuitl* as *mahuizyo*, a word that means "honored," "marvelous," and "something worthy of respect." Unlike ordinary *xihuitl*, the marvelous *teoxihuitl* was not used to ornament other objects; it was prized for its intrinsic beauty. Finally, the rarity with which the Aztecs encountered *teoxi-huitl* distinguishes it from the more common varieties: "It does not appear very much, because at times it does not appear at all." Like a *teotl*, *teoxihuitl* is scarce. The name "*teoxihuitl*," therefore, reflects the extraordinary attributes the Aztecs associated with the stone. The scribes highlight *teoxihuitl*'s remark-ableness again in their description of *tlapalteoxihuitl*, a red-colored stone that resembled turquoise.

TLAPALTEOXIHUITL

inin itoca, itech quizqui in tlapalli, ihuan in teoxihuitl: ipampa ca zan ye huel iehoatl in teoxihuitl, in quimotlatlalili, ic mopopoiauh chichiltic, ic cenca nelli mahuizyo, mahuiztic: zan cenca yequeneh tlazohnemi, mot-lapalpoiahua, meezcuicuiloa, mahuizyoa, tlazohneci tlazohpialo.

DYED TEO-TURQUOISE

Its name comes from *tlapalli* (ink, dye; metaphorically, blood) and *teo*-turquoise, because it is precisely already a lot [like] *teo*-turquoise. It is made red, it is darkened. In truth, it is very wonderful, marvelous. Last-ly, it is very rare, it is rose-colored, it is variously blood-colored. Es-teemed, it is rare. It is guarded as precious.[83]

Tlapalteoxihuitl's rosy and bloody red color distinguishes it from other va-rieties of turquoise. *Tlapalli* (dye, ink, something dyed; metaphorically, blood) modifies *xihuitl* and signals color as the feature that characterizes this stone.[84] *Tlapalteoxihuitl* may refer to turquoise colored with a red pigment, such as cinnabar or red hematite, or to a red stone, such as red agate. Although López Luján does not account for any red-colored turquoise at the Templo Mayor, he does describe several greenstone objects and *tecpame* (flint knives) deco-rated with red pigments.[85] He also mentions the presence of red agate in the sacred precinct.[86]

From the scribes' description of *tlapalteoxihuitl* as "precisely already a lot [like] *teo*-turquoise," we may assume that apart from its redness, the stone shared *teoxihuitl*'s physical and metaphysical characteristics. As with *teoxi-huitl*, the scribes emphasize the wonder and marvel (*mahuizyo, mahuiztic*) that *tlapalteoxihuitl* inspires, and they remark on the stone's rarity (*tlazoh-nemi*). By contrast to *xihuitl*, *teoxihuitl* and *tlapalteoxihuitl* highlight specific characteristics associated with *teotl* and signified by the *teo*- prefix, includ-ing *axcaitl* (possessions, property), *tonalli* (heat; day sign; fate, fortune, privi-lege, prerogative), *mahuiztic* (something marvelous), and *tlazohca* (valuable, beloved). These qualities resonate in the *Earthly Things* entries on two other important products of the natural world, *teotetl* (*teo*-stone; jet) and *teocuitlatl* (*teo*-excrement; gold).

Luminous *Teteo*: Perfectly Black *Teo*-stone and Glistening Gold

Teotetl and *teocuitlatl* reinforce characteristics of *teotl* highlighted in the *Florentine Codex*'s descriptions of the turquoises. Together, they deepen our understanding of *teotl*'s meaning through their associations with luminosity, especially in the form of sacrificial fires. The descriptions of each term's specific qualities—*teotetl*'s perfect blackness and *teocuitlatl*'s relationship to god-bodies—further enrich our sense of *teotl*.

To begin with, the scribes' emphasis on *teotetl*'s complete and perfect blackness, along with its scarcity (*tlazohnemi*) and preciousness (*tlazohca*), resonates with their descriptions of *teoxihuitl* and *tlapalteoxihuitl*.[87]

TEOTETL

itech quizqui in itoca teotl, ihuan tetl; ipampa acan centetl neci, iuhquin tetl inic tlitic, quitoznequi zan tlazohca zan tlazohnemi: iuhquinma ineixcahuil teotl, tliltic, tlilpatic, cemahcic tliltic, capotztic, chapopotic, huel cemahcic tliltic, huel ahcic in tlillan.

TEO-STONE

The name of this comes from *teotl* and stone, because nowhere does a single stone appear as black as this stone. That is to say, it is rare, precious, like the *teotl*'s exclusive thing. Black, very black, perfectly black; black like pitch. Indeed, perfectly black, it is really totally black.[88]

Mesoamericans associated the color black with blue and green, and the stone's absolute blackness—"Black, very black, perfectly black; black like pitch. Indeed, perfectly black, it is really totally black"—reflects the ritual significance of black body paint, pigments, unguents, and minerals.[89] Throughout Mesoamerica, priests, deity embodiments, and other ritual actors blackened their bodies in preparation for performing their ceremonial duties.[90] Olivier explains the role blackness—especially being covered in blackness—played in ritual contexts:

> By covering their bodies with soot or black paint, the penitents prepared for the divine confrontation but also performed an act of faith that was supposed to please the gods. The verb *tliltilia* [to push oneself up, to be-

come famous] probably translates the link that existed among blackening, penance, and the benefits or the prestige that could be derived from
these practices. . . . Coming before the meeting with the gods, blackening reduced the distance between people and their creators.[91]

For Olivier, the blackened skin of priests, deity impersonators, and ritual actors "could even represent a total identification with the deity." Drawing on
López Austin's association of blackness with *teotl*, Olivier defines *teotl* as "divine and black."[92] To the best of my knowledge, no etymological evidence
links the semantic denotation "black" with *teotl*; however, *teotetl*, glossed by
Anderson and Dibble as "jet," and the examples cited above and others by
López Austin, including *teotzinitzcan, teoquechol, teotzanatl,* and *teotetl,* demonstrate that *teotl* carried a pragmatic or contextual connotation associated
with blackness.[93] Ash, as the charred remains of fires, may be one facet of
blackness's connection to divinity; the intense red-to-blue firelight that consumed Nanahuatzin's body, for example, produced two residues: the ashes of
his earthly body and the sunshine of his celestial one.[94] In addition to the
teteo associated with blackness that Olivier discusses—Quetzalcoatl, Tezcatlipoca, and Ixtlilton—the *Florentine Codex* emphasizes a connection between
firelight, blackness, and Huehue Teotl (sometimes called Xiuhtecuhtli and
Milintoc).[95]

The celebration of Izcalli, the eighteenth and final ceremony of the *xihuitl*
(year), or solar calendar, honored "*tota, yehuatl in tletl*" (Our father, fire), and
involved the construction of two *teixiptlahuan* of fire *teteo*; the scribes identify
them as Xiuhtecuhtli (Year Lord) and Milintoc (Shining, Sparkling, Flaring).[96]
They describe Xiuhtecuhtli's mask as "made of green stone (*chalchihuitl*) diagonally striped with turquoise (*xihuitl*). It was awesome (*mahuizoticatca*); it
glistened, it glittered; it emanated brilliance exceedingly."[97] By comparison,
Milintoc's mask was "made of seashell. Its lips painted black, it appears black;
they, the black stones, were called *teotetl*, and the face was striped diagonally
with black mirror stones (*tezcapoctli*)."[98] Cumulatively, the *chalchihuitl* (green
stones), *xihuitl* (turquoise), *teotetl* (*teo*-stone; jet), and *tezcapoctli* (black mirror stones) adorning these images of Xiuhtecuhtli and Milintoc created lu-
minescent *teixiptlahuan* that sparkled, glistened, and glittered like firelight.[99]
The fiery light reflected in these stones reinforced the Mesoamerican association of luminosity with black, blue, and green and of these colors with *teteo*.

In addition to the passages describing how *teoxihuitl, tlapalteoxihuitl,* and
teotetl reflect *teotl* qualities, the scribes also explain the relationship of *teocuitlatl* (gold) to *teotl*:

COZTIC TEOCUITLATL

inin teocuitlatl in coztic, in iztac in itoca: itech quiza in itoca teotl, ihuan cuitlatl: ipampa in mahuiztic, in coztic, in cualli, in iectli, in tlazotli, in necuiltonolli, in netlamachtilli, intonal, imaxca, inneixcahuil in tlatoque, in totecuihuan:

itech quizqui, in queman cana neci tlahuizcalpan. iuhquinma apitztaltontli, quitocayotia tonatiuh icuitl, cenca coztic, cenca mahuiztic, iuhquin tlexochtli mani, iuhquinma coztic teocuitlatl, tlaatililli; ic neci itech tlaantli, y, in coztic teocuitlatl, amo yehuatl in ipalnemohuani, itechcopa mitoa, ye in tonatiuh: ca in ayamo iximacho in icel teotl, in nelli teotl in ca miequintin teteo neteotiloya. Auh in tonatiuh: zan huel itoca catca teotl, nepantla teotl, mitoaya hualquiza teotl, nizteotl: onmotzcaloa teotl, oncalaqui teotl: teotlac noma mitoa in axcan, quitoznequi onac, oncalac in teotl.

YELLOW TEO-EXCREMENT

The name of *teocuitlatl*, the yellow, the white, comes from *teotl* and excrement, because it is wonderful, yellow, good, pure, and precious. It is the wealth, the good fortune of the rulers, our lords; it is their prerogative, their property, their exclusive thing.

It comes from [this]: sometimes in some places it appears at dawn, as if a little bit of diarrhea. They call it the sun's excrement. It is very yellow, very wonderful, as if it is a live ember, as if it is molten yellow gold. So it appears that yellow gold is taken from this; it is not from He by whom living goes on. It is said that it comes from the sun, from before the only *teotl* was known. Before the true *teotl* was worshipped, there were many *teteo*. But the sun was the name of a *teotl*. It was called, "*Teotl* in the middle, *teotl* comes up, here is *teotl*, *teotl* leans on its side, *teotl* sets." Still now *teotlac*, "sunset," is said; it means the god entered, set.[100]

As with *teotetl*, *teocuitlatl*'s name reflects its appearance, including both its color and form. The scribes refer to *teocuitlatl* (*teo*-excrement) as yellow (*coztic*) and white (*iztac*, "silver"): "*teocuitlatl*, the yellow, the white . . . is wonderful, yellow, good, pure, and precious. . . . It is very yellow, very wonderful, as if it is a live ember, as if it is molten yellow gold."[101] The scribes explain that artisans designed objects with charcoal, and then with beeswax models "they cast *teocuitlatl*, the yellow and white."[102]

Returning to the scribes' discussion of precious metals, they expound on the popularity of gold and silver, "mitoa, in ye huecauh zan oc ye in coztic teocuitlatl neca, in mahuiltiaya . . . ayatle catca in iztac teocuitlatl, tel onnenca, zan oc canin necia: huel motlazotlaya. auh in axcan ye no cuele za moche in iztac teocuitlatl quinequi, in coztic ye huel motlazotla." (It is said that in times past only gold [was known to] exist. . . . Silver was not yet in use, though it existed; it appeared here and there. It was highly valued. But today, on the other hand, all is silver; they want gold; it is much treasured.)[103] Most of the gold and silver objects produced in the two centuries before Contact were copper-gold or copper-silver alloys. Bracelets, diadems, bells, and the like were

> gilded or silvered by hammering and annealing to form a gold or silver surface that represented the sacred colors. . . . Because of the surface color of the objects, the Spaniards probably thought them to be of pure gold or silver, but when melted down and assayed the resulting bullion carried low percentages of the precious metals, much to the chagrin of the looters, who labeled their take "*planta baja*" or "*oro de baja ley*."[104]

Although the scribes clearly state that "the goldbeaters, in times of old, hammered only gold," they do not elaborate on the increasing prevalence of silver in the post-Contact period. The shift from gold to silver may have accompanied the discovery of significant silver deposits by the Spaniards in the early 1530s.[105]

In addition to describing *teocuitlatl*'s colors, the scribes also remark on its form and possible sources. Physically, *teocuitlatl* resembles "iuhquinma apitzaltontli . . . iuhquin tlexochitli mani, iuhquinma coztic teocuitlatl, tlaatililli" (a little bit of diarrhea . . . as if a live ember, as if it is molten yellow gold), descriptions consistent with the shimmering flakes, grains, and nuggets of gold found in alluvial deposits.[106] The *Earthly Things* entry on *teocuitlatl* describes gold's appearance in waterways: "inic neci, inic motta in campa ca, ca onca inan: iquac in neci in inan in quihaui, in iaio (in quitoa) iiaxix cenca chihua, canin ixcoztic, canin xoxoxoctic: iuhquin xoxotla, cenca chihua inic neci." (It appears, it is seen in this manner: where it is, there is its mother. When its mother appears, when she rains her water (as they say), her urine stains deeply. Where it is yellow on the surface, where it is discolored as if glistening green, she stains deeply so that it appears.)[107] The same entry indicates that the Aztecs also knew of lode deposits of gold within the earth: "auh in mache inan ca tlalli, anozo tepetl itic in onoc, in ca coztic teocuitlatl: auh amo ma zan temi, in ma ololiuhtica; zan quimotlamiahualti in tlalli, in tepetl, tataconi, paconi pitzaloni." (But especially is its mother within the earth or the mountain, where gold lies, where it is. But it is not that it abounds; it is not heaped up; it just forms veins in the earth, in the mountain. It is that which can be excavated, can be washed, can be cast.)[108] The scribes' metaphoric descriptions of gold—as a nugget or little bit of diarrhea that shimmers like a still-hot ember—leave little room to doubt the metal's antiphrastic name.[109] Taken with Johansson K.'s suggestion that the Aztecs conceived of the earth as the womb that nurtured and birthed turquoise, *Earthly Things'* characterization of the earth as the mother that produced gold excrement—identified here with excrement and urine—suggests that women's (re)productive bodies were metaphors for the earth's relationship to precious stones and metals.[110]

Popularly translated as "divine excrement" or "holy shit," the compound word *teocuitlatl* contains both *teotl* and *cuitlatl* (excrement, residue, excrescence). In both older and modern Nahuatl, *teocuitlatl* carries broader connotations than "holy shit."[111] Cecelia Klein defines *cuitlatl* as "excrement, residue, excrescence" based on Molina and Siméon: "*mierda* [Molina]; *excremento, fiemo, inmundicia, residuo; llaga, tumor, absceso* [Siméon]."[112] In addition to Siméon's expansive glosses, López Austin cites other compounds containing *cuitlatl* as excrement, including *yacacuitlatl* (snot), from *yacatl* (nose) and *cuitlatl*; *nacazcuitlatl* (cerumen), from *nacaztli* (ear) and *cuitlatl*; and *ixcuitlatl* (sleep), from *ixtli* (eye) and *cuitlatl*.[113] The Aztecs conceived of other natural substances as excretions, including *metzcuitlatl* (mica), which they believed to be excreted by the *metztli* (moon), and *temetztli* (lead), which they also identified as the excrement of the moon because it appeared at night.[114] Similarly, according to modern Nahuatl speakers, *cuitlatl* refers to many types of bodily excretious, including cerumen; pus; and exudates of the eyes, boils, or blisters.[115] These definitions and uses of *cuitlatl* demonstrate that while it sometimes means excrement, its more general connotation is a form of excretion.

In addition to the issue of how *cuitlatl* should be translated, the question of *teotl's* referent in *teocuitlatl* is worth consideration. Eleanor Wake has explained the significance of gold, silver, and other precious materials, including crystal and iridescent feathers, as manifestations or reflections of "the sacred": "The Indian sacred was perceived as an abstract entity, manifest in the power and awesome living beauty of the natural world. To write the sacred [as the *tlacuiloque* (scribe-painters) had], therefore, was not just a case of reproducing its signs and symbols in, or through the particular manipulation of, a particular medium, but the nature of the medium itself."[116] Following the *Florentine Codex's* description of *teocuitlatl*, she identifies gold and silver, in particular, with *tonatiuh* (sun): "Gold and silver were defined as the yellow and white excrement of the sun: with them, 'I make things beautiful . . . I make things give off rays'. That is, the finished vessel or jewel was an embodiment of the divine celestial orb."[117] Wake specifically associates *coztic* and *iztac teocuitlatl* (yellow and white gold) with the sun's excrement, rather than with divine excrement, more generally.

Nanahuatzin (Pustules) provides a direct mythohistorical link between the sun and *teocuitlatl*. According to the *Florentine Codex*, Nanahuatzin's self-immolation brought about the creation of the sun, and his oozing skin directly bears on the second element of *teocuitlatl*. Nanahuatzin embodied excrescence. Before throwing himself in the fire, he offered his scabs, a dried excrescence, as incense: "he burned; his body crackled and sizzled."[118] Then when the new sun rose, "intensely did he shine . . . his brilliant rays penetrated everywhere."[119] The sun's brilliant rays—potentially blistering rays—emanated from Nanahuatzin's once-blistered, now-celestial body. Whether the Aztecs thought *teocuitlatl* came from the sun or the gods, they clearly associated gold with divine bodily waste.

Earthly Things's descriptions of *teoxihuitl* (*teo*-turquoise), *tlapalteoxihuitl* (painted *teo*-turquoise), *teotetl* (*teo*-stone; jet), and *teocuitlatl* (*teo*-excrement; gold) illustrate the metaphysical significance they held in Aztec culture. The passages detail the *tlazohtetl*'s (precious stones') colors—the dull green of *xihuitl*, the chalky blue of *teoxihuitl*, the perfect blackness of *teotetl*, and the radiance of *teocuitlatl*—and compare them to other prized ritual materials, including the blue cotinga's feathers and pitch. The colors associated with these *teotl*-modified stones also call to mind the range of colors present in fire's flame. The scribes marvel at these wonderful stones, their rarity and perfection. In essence, these passages describe precious materials whose metaphoric and mercantile value in Aztec culture—and in Mesoamerica more generally—motivated the widespread trade of luxury items, including intricately pieced mosaics.[120] In contrast to more ordinary materials, the Aztecs attributed extraordinary properties to *teoxihuitl*, *tlapalteoxihuitl*, *teotetl*, and *teocuitlatl*, and they signified the presence of those properties with the modifier *teotl*, "god" or "deity."

The Five Properties of *Teotl*

Teotl marks an ontological distinction between two or more varieties of some object or entity. Parallel descriptions of objects or entities in the *Florentine Codex*, such as *xihuitl* (turquoise) and its *teotl*-modified counterparts *teoxihuitl* and *tlapalteoxihuitl*, reveal five distinctive attributes of *teotl*: possessions, privilege, exclusive pursuits, marvelousness, and value. These five attributes appear in the descriptions of the *teotl*-modified entities (*teoxihuitl*, *tlapalteo-*

xihuitl, teotetl, and *teocuitlatl*) but not in the descriptions of their ordinary counterparts (*xihuitl, tetl,* and *cuitlatl*). Further, the descriptions of the *teotl*-modified entities explicitly associate these five qualities with *teotl*. In the following, I examine each of five characteristics in the contexts outlined above and underscore their significance through reference to examples from other portions of the *Florentine Codex.*

(1) A *teotl* has *axcaitl* (possessions, property).
Recall that the scribes explain that the name *teoxihuitl* "comes from *teotl* and *xihuitl* because it means *iiaxca* (the possessions) . . . of the *teotl*," and the phrase "*iiaxca*" (his/her/its property, possession), which does not appear in the description of regular *xihuitl*, functions as a defining property of *teotl*.[121] According to *axcaitl*'s use in other contexts, a *teotl*'s possessions are as feathers to birds and meat to a meat seller; in other words, like birds who need their feathers to fly and meat sellers for whom meat is a livelihood, particular possessions and property compose a defining characteristic of a *teotl*.[122] Indeed, these examples suggest that some property and possessions are essential to a given entity's identity or identification.

The story of Huitzilopochtli (Hummingbird Left-hand Side), the Mexica patron *teotl*, collecting the insignia of the Centzonhuitz Nahua (Four Hundred Southerners) defines the relationship between *axcaitl* and identity. In the myth of his birth at Coatepec (Serpent Hill), Huitzilopochtli decapitates Coyolxauhqui (Bells Painted), and then he chases his brothers, the Centzonhuitz Nahua: "And only very few fled his presence. . . . When he had slain them, when he had taken his pleasure, he took from them their goods, their adornment, the paper crowns. He took them as his own goods, he took them as *quimaxcati* (his own property); he assumed them as his due, as if taking the insignia to himself."[123] Huitzilopochtli takes the warriors' *tlahuiztli* (insignia, emblem)—that which had identified each individual in the Centzonhuitz Nahua—as his own property. In doing so, he acquires the signifying power of the four hundred he defeated.

Axcaitl designates personal property and possessions gained through one's own labor or service. *Book 9: The Merchants* distinguishes the personal property of the *pochteca* (merchants) from that which they carry on behalf of the *tlahtoani* (ruler) and those goods destined for the *cihuapipiltin* (princesses) and the *macehualtin* (commoners). For the *pochteca*, tradable wares were as essential to their professional identities as meat was to the meat seller. In this context *axcaitl* distinguishes the "*imaxca pochteca*" (merchants' personal property) from the commodities they carry on behalf of others.[124] The scribes equate property with livelihood—"that is, it is *naxca* (my property), my goods, my sustenance"[125]—and the results of hard work—"it is said of something which I guard for myself, which is really *naxca* (my property), really something mine which by my own toil, my own efforts I have produced, which I have not just picked up somewhere nor stolen."[126] As the fruits of labor, *axcaitl* designates a possession that belongs to the owner in both a personal and proprietorial manner.

In addition to referring to the things that compose personal property, *axcaitl* sometimes refers to humans or to the human body. In a description of a prostitute, the scribes clarify the woman's *axcaitl* relationship to her own body: "she sells her body, her flesh, her heritage, *in iaxca* (her possession), her vulva."[127] The prostitute's body was her own property, but one's body was not necessarily one's property. Some parents dedicated their children to the *calmecac* (religious academy), effectively giving their children to religious authorities, who "took up the baby; they cradled it in their arms *conmaxcatia* (to possess it), to make it forever *imaxca* (their possession), until it reached a marriageable age."[128] A *calmecac* priest offered children dedicated to the priesthood to Quetzalcoatl, and in the priest's invocation, he reminded Quetzalcoatl, "not [to] mistake her, for the poor thing is *maxcatzin* (your property). Receive her."[129] Parents transferred their children, their possessions, to religious leaders for upbringing and protection.[130]

Additionally, *axcaitl* denotes a domain or realm over which a *teotl* maintained control. Examples involving two *teteo* illustrate this sense of *axcaitl*. *Book 1: The Gods* describes the origin of the name Tlazolteotl (Trash God) as rooted in her domain, "that of evil and perverseness."[131] Tlazolteotl's domain—sexual desire and wanton decadence—distinguishes her from associated *teteo* and constitutes her identity.[132] In the *Earthly Things* description of an *atoyatl* (river), the scribes explain, "The people here in New Spain, the people of old, said: 'These [rivers] come—they flow—there from Tlalocan; they are *iiaxca* (the property of), they issue from the goddess named Chalchihuitlicue.'"[133] In this example, Chalchihuitlicue (Precious Green Stone Her Skirt) controls the rivers, which are her property and exist within her domain. According to the scribes, the Aztecs believed that Chalchihuitlicue controlled the waters; she "was esteemed, feared, held in awe; hence she caused terror. She drowned one, plunged one in water, submerged one; she caused the water to foam."[134] The domains of Tlazolteotl and Chalchihuitlicue have distinct qualities—the former being grounded in human relationships and the latter in the physical environment. In both instances, the *teotl's axcaitl* contributes to her identity and, in the case of Chalchihuitlicue, to her appearance and identification.

(2) A *teotl* has a *tonalli* (heat; day sign; fate, fortune, privilege, prerogative).

A second property of *teotl* relates to *tonalli* (heat; day sign; fate, fortune, privilege, prerogative) and is reflected in *teoxihuitl*'s onomastic origin: "The name of this one comes from *teotl* and *xihuitl* because it means the possessions, *itonal* (the fate) of the *teotl*."[135] The canonical form is *tonalli*, and its root comes from *tona* (to be warm, for the sun to shine).[136] A being's *tonalli* relates to his or her day sign or day name, which Aztecs acquired shortly after birth:

> Children took as their formal name the day on which they were born, and they took the influences of this day as their destiny. That day and its companions influenced the child's future occupation and even determined what kind of person the child was likely to become. A generally favorable birth day brought rejoicing. An unfavorable birth day could perhaps be mitigated by delaying the washing ceremony to a better day and by making special offerings and performing devotional acts.[137]

In the *Florentine Codex*, *tonalli* most often occurs in contexts where it means "day name" and consists of a day number (1–13) correlated with one of twenty day signs.

As noted, the Aztecs associated each day sign with specific fates and fortunes. For example, a person born on the day sign ce mazatl (1 Deer) inherited the deer's characteristics: "Verily, so was *itonal* (his lot); so was he born. Even as the deer is a great coward, just so was he, whose *itonal* (day sign) this is, a great coward; fearful."[138] Other day signs carried more positive connotations: "Of him who was born on the *itonal* (day sign) One Death it was said that he would prosper and be rich, whether a nobleman or only a poor vassal."[139] Additionally, the fates and fortunes of a given day sign were not immutable; rather, if those born on favorable days failed in their responsibilities, their fortune could change. For those born on ce miquiztli (1 Death), "Many were his gifts. Honor came his way and rested on him when he performed well his penances and humbled himself. But if he did not do well the penances, purely by his own act he forsook and harmed his *itonal* (day sign)."[140] Conversely, persons with unfavorable day names could improve their lot through religious rituals and observances. Those born on macuilli calli (5 House) or chicuacen cuetzpalin (6 Lizard) faced terrible fortunes: "He labored only in vain; his fate, deserts, and gifts were full of misery."[141] However, a person born on either of these days could "by his own penances, [cause] his day sign to result in good; he did it himself through penance."[142] A given day sign's fortunes and fates were not unyielding; bad fates could be improved, and good fortunes could

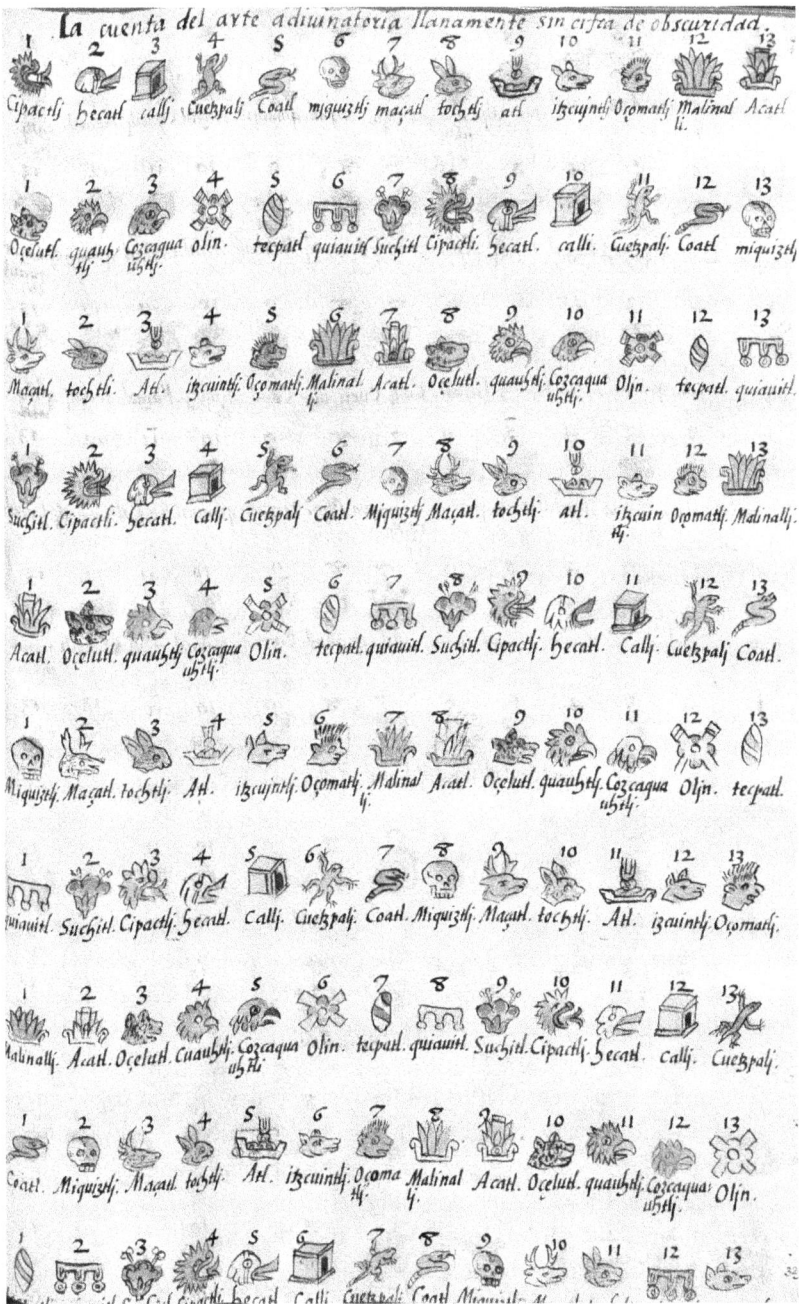

3.3. Day signs. *Florentine Codex*, 1:329r. Photograph courtesy of the Biblioteca Medicea Laurenziana.

be lost. However, once a person became associated with a day name, the connection was indelible even though some of the responsibility for maintaining a positive lot lay with the individual.

The day name is the foundation of a *tonalli*, and a day name signifies a series of characteristics, fortunes, fates, and responsibilities associated with an individual. Taken together, those associations compose a person's *tonalli*, which most specifically refers to a day sign, but more generally encompasses what we might call a prerogative, a responsibility or privilege exclusive to a certain person or group. The English words "fate," "fortune," and "lot" capture the temporality of *tonalli*, and "privilege" expresses the intensely private nature of one's *tonalli*.[143] However, as a right that is unique to a particular individual, "prerogative" best encapsulates the full sense of *tonalli*. My intention in glossing *tonalli* as "prerogative" is neither to redefine the term nor to detract from its most basic and specific meaning, "day sign," or the related concepts of fate and fortune. Rather, my aim is to encapsulate those meanings in a way that makes sense given the variety of contexts in which *tonalli* occurs in the *Florentine Codex*. "Day sign" would not adequately convey *tonalli*'s meaning all of the time, but "prerogative" captures a spectrum of meaning—from "day sign" to "fate" to "privilege"—implied by *tonalli*. According to the *Florentine Codex*, one's *tonalli* determined access to certain rights and privileges, including different types of shoes, qualities of clothing, and the right to travel on certain roads.[144] Everything included in an individual's *tonalli* is that person's prerogative to do with as she or he likes; essentially, *tonalli* is a person's malleable fate. As might be expected, the *tlahtoani*'s *tonalli* afforded him extraordinary rights and privileges.

The *Florentine Codex* mentions Moteuczoma Xocoyotzin's *tonalli* twice, and both instances occur in *Book 12: The Conquest*. In the first account, Moteuczoma sends a group of ambassadors with exceptional gifts to meet the Spaniards, and among them are elements of his *tonalli*:

> [His messengers] went as if to sell [goods] in order to go to spy upon them, to find out about them. They went to offer precious capes, precious goods: indeed, capes pertaining to Moctezuma alone, which no one else wore. They were his alone, *itonal* (his prerogative). . . . They offered them all the various things which they bore with them, the precious capes like those which are here named: the one with the sun design, the blue-knotted one, the one with the jar design, the one with eagle down.[145]

By sending gifts that belonged to him alone, Moteuczoma presented his *ton-alli* to Cortés.[146] Whether Cortés understood the gifts as elements of Moteuc-zoma's prerogative or not, he certainly valued them and sought other similarly valuable goods. Later in *Book 12*, the scribes recount the looting of Moteuc-zoma's *tonalli*:

> Thereupon they went to Moctezuma's own storehouse, where was kept Moctezuma's own property, a place called Totocalco. . . . Thereupon was brought forth [Moctezuma's] own property, that which was indeed his personally, *in huel itonal* (his very own lot), precious things all; the necklaces with pendants, the arm bands with tufts of quetzal feathers, the golden arm bands, the bracelets, the golden bands with shells, to fasten at the ankle, and the turquoise diadem, the attribute of the ruler, and the turquoise nose rods, and the rest of his goods without number. They took it all. They possessed themselves of all, they appropriated it all to themselves, they took all to themselves *comotonaltique* (as their lot).[147]

Without knowing the cosmological significance of the luxury goods they sought, Cortés and his companions stole and then appropriated possessions that were highly personal by right of Moteuczoma's *tonalli*.

In addition to the specific *tonalli* of an individual's day name, both the *Florentine Codex* and the *Codex Mendoza* describe the *tonalli* and *axcaitl* (possessions, property) given to male and female infants. The *Codex Mendoza*'s third section, a post-Contact account of pre-Contact daily life, begins with descriptions and depictions of infancy and Aztec birth rites (Figure 3.4):

> And at the beginning, when the infant was taken to be bathed, if it was a boy, they carried him with his symbol in his hand; and the symbol was the tool used by the infant's father, whether of the military or professions like metalworker, woodcarver, or whatever other profession. . . . And if the infant was a girl, the symbol they gave her for bathing was a distaff with its spindle and its basket, and a broom, which were the things she would use when she grew up. And they offered the male infant's umbilical cord, along with the little shield and arrows symbol used in bathing, in the place where they warred with their enemies, where they buried it underground. And likewise for the girl, they buried her umbilical cord under the *metate*, a stone for grinding tortillas.[148]

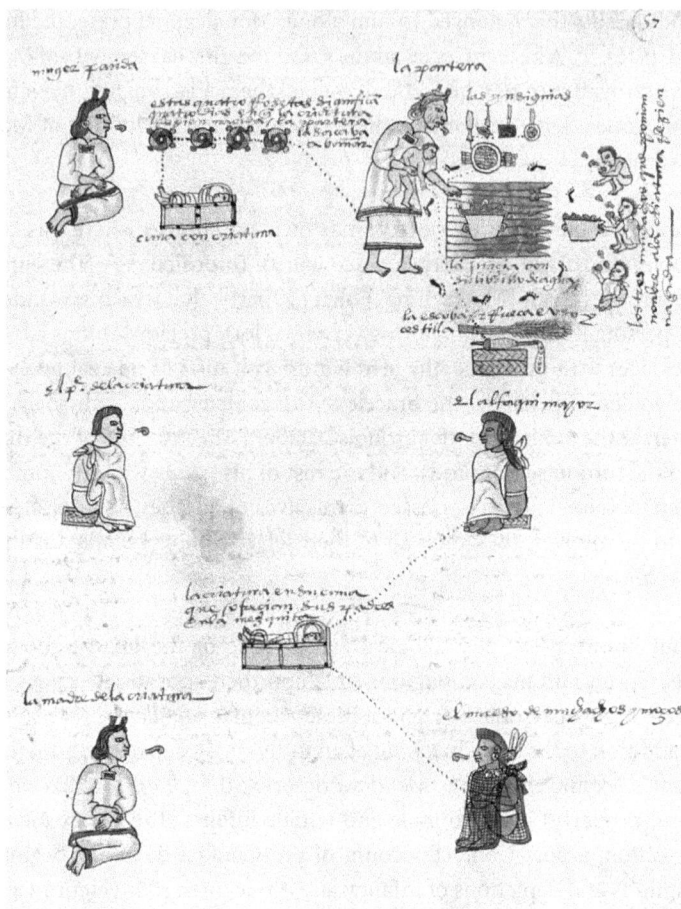

3.4. Birth rites. MS. Arch. Selden. A. 1, 57r. Courtesy of the Bodleian Libraries, the University of Oxford.

According to the *Florentine Codex*, midwives buried the umbilical cords of male infants on battlefields and dedicated them to those "*ixtlayoatl*" (wise in war).[149] Because women's "very task was the home life, life by the fire, by the grinding stone," midwives buried female infants' umbilical cords near the hearth.[150] Taken with the accounts of Moteuczoma's *tonalli*, these texts document that every Aztec individual—whether of elite or commoner status—had a specific *tonalli* that reflected her or his day sign, gender, and the familial-occupational group into which she or he was born. Similarly, *teteo* had prerogatives that derived from day-sign associations.

Book 4: *The Soothsayers*'s text associates four *teteo*, Quetzalcoatl, Tezcatlipoca, Huitzilopochtli, and Chalchihuitlicue, with day signs.[151] As in the description of *teoxihuitl*, the scribes attribute each of these *teteo* with "the possessions, the fate," a day sign, and a domain. *Book 4* associates Quetzalcoatl, a representative of the wind, with the two day signs *ce acatl* (1 Reed) and *ce ehecatl* (1 Wind): "It was held that One Reed was the day sign, the time, of Quetzalcoatl. For Quetzalcoatl represented the wind, and was therefore thought a god. And when the day One Reed set in, the lords and noblemen paid him great honors," and "This One Wind, they said, was evil. At this time they made offerings to the one called Quetzalcoatl, who was the representative of the wind, the whirlwind."[152] Of the four *teteo* associated with day signs, Quetzalcoatl and his association with 1 Reed may be the most debated.[153] Nonetheless, the scribes associate the *teotl* Quetzalcoatl with his domain, wind and whirlwinds, and his day signs, 1 Reed and 1 Wind.

In a similar manner, *Book 4* recounts the associations of Huitzilopochtli, Tezcatlipoca, and Chalchihuitlicue with ce tecpatl (1 Flint), ce miquiztli (1 Death), and ce atl (1 Water), respectively. For example, boat owners were particularly vigilant during 1 Water, because they believed that Chalchihuitlicue controlled the waters and their traffic: "She upset the boat, overturned it, lifted it up, tossed it up, plunged it in the water."[154] The scribes explain that "the sellers of water, the owners of boats—those who transported water with boats—and those who launched boats, made offerings to her. They formed her image; they set in place the framework [for her image] at her temple, in her *calpulco*."[155] Individuals who believed their livelihood depended on the *tonalli* of a given *teotl* secured the *teotl*'s favor through acts of devotion. Like Chalchihuitlicue, each *teotl* had a specific *tonalli* association, which both distinguished them one from another and endowed them with particular sets of rights and responsibilities. Like people, *teteo* received a *tonalli* association that correlated with a specific day sign and a prerogative.

(3) A *teotl* has *neixcahuilli* (an exclusive thing, occupation, business, or pursuit). The third property of *teotl* derives from the scribes' definitions of *teotetl*, "it is rare, precious, like a *teotl*'s *ineixcahuil* (its exclusive property)"[156] and *teocuitlatl*, "It is the wealth, the good fortune of the rulers, our lords; it is their prerogative, their property, *inneixcahuil* (their exclusive thing)."[157] According to the *Florentine Codex*, individuals acquired their *neixcahuilli* (an exclusive thing, occupation, business, or pursuit) through age, skill, status, and day-name associations.[158] An individual's *neixcahuilli* derived from and expressed his or her *tonalli*.

In several instances, an individual's given *neixcahuilli* became her or his responsibility as a result of age, occupation, or status. For example, with age, the restrictions against drinking pulque lessened to the point that "of the old men and the old women it was the *inneixcahuil* (exclusive business) that they drink pulque. Absolutely no one of the youths, the offering priests, the maidens drank pulque."[159] Similarly, at a certain point during the celebration of Huei Tecuilhuitl (Great Festival of the Lords), old women had the exclusive right to dance.[160] In other cases, people acquired an exclusive thing; for example, the Tlatelolcans gained a reputation as skilled boaters.[161] Additionally, some religious authorities oversaw exclusive occupational responsibilities. During Tlacaxipehualiztli (Feast of the Flaying of Men), Yohuallahuan (Night Drinker) had the exclusive privilege of sacrifice: "Because it was his office, *ineixcahuil* (his exclusive occupation) that he sacrifice to the gods, that he slay one; at his hands would perish, at his hands would be hacked open all the eagle men."[162] As might be expected, some exclusive things and occupations pertained only to *teteo* and *tlahtoque* (rulers).

The Aztecs attributed exclusive things, occupations, and, by extension, responsibilities to *teteo* and *tlahtoque*. As noted earlier, the scribes define *teocuitlatl* (*teo*-excrement; gold) as belonging exclusively to the *tlahtoque* and *teteuctin* (members of the high nobility). *Book 8: Kings and Lords* notes other rulers' exclusive things: "Flowers and tobacco, were the ruler's *ineixcahuil* (exclusive thing); a mirror in which the ruler looked at himself when he adorned himself."[163] During the celebration of Izcalli, "It was the *ineixcahuil* only of the *tlahtoque* (rulers) that they should dance the lordly dance."[164] The things exclusive to the *tlahtoque* and *teteuctin* (nobility)—gold, flowers, tobacco, and mirrors—signify at multiple levels and correlate with their *tonalli* and its signs.[165] The scribes attribute to elders, priests, and polities *neixcahuilli* that accord with their age, status, and occupation, but they make a less explicit distinction between the *tlahtoani's tonalli* and his *neixcahuilli*. In fact, the *tlahtoani's tonalli* and *neixcahuilli* are complementary and equivalent; all of his *neixcahuilli* stem from and manifest his *tonalli*.

The principle of *neixcahuilli* manifesting *tonalli* extends to *teteo*, as well. For example, the scribes list a series of eye maladies as Xipe Totec's *neixcahuilli*:

That which corresponded to his office, his particular creation, *ineixcahuil* (his exclusive thing) was that he struck people, he bewitched people, he visited people with blisters, festering pimples, eye pains, watering of the eyes, festering about the eyelashes, lice about the eyes, opacity, filling of the eyes with flesh, withering of the eyes, cataracts, glazing of the eyes.[166]

In contrast to Xipe Totec's publicly acknowledged exclusive things, a lengthy oration recorded in *Book 6: Rhetoric and Moral Philosophy* explains that the *neixcahuillin* of some *teteo* were secret: "Behold the mysteries of *in tloqueh, nahuaqueh* (Possessor of the near, of the nigh) which are not determined here, for they are *ineixcahuil* (his exclusive things)."[167] It seems reasonable to expect that, like Xipe Totec, some of whose *neixcahuilli* are recorded, and Chalchihuitlicue, whose *tonalli* included rivers and waterways, other *teteo* would also have had *tonalli* that manifested in particular *neixcahuilli*.

(4) A *teotl* is *mahuiztic* (something marvelous, awesome, worthy of esteem).
In addition to being the fate and property of the *teotl*, precious stones, including *teoxihuitl, tlapalteoxihuitl,* and *teocuitlatl,* are also *mahuiztic* (something marvelous, awesome, worthy of esteem).[168] The scribes contrast ordinary turquoise, which is "*amo cenca mahuizyo*" (not very marvelous) with *teoxihuitl* and *tlapalteoxihuitl*; when it is well formed, they explain, "*teoxihuitl* is *cenca mahuizyo* (very marvelous); when something is visible on it, it is *amo cenca mahuizyo* (not so marvelous)."[169] The *mahuiztic* quality of *teoxihuitl* and *tlapalteoxihuitl* distinguish them from common *xihuitl* and associate the precious stones with *teotl*. Similarly, the scribes explain that *teocuitlatl*'s name stems from its *mahuiztic* quality: "Its name comes from *teotl* and *cuitlatl*, because it is *mahuiztic* (marvelous)."[170] As with *teoxihuitl* and *tlapalteoxihuitl*, *mahuiztic* functions as a defining element of *teocuitlatl*'s association with *teotl*. The *mahuiztic* quality of these *tlazohtetl* (precious stones) derives from their *teotl* association, and *mahuiztic*—the marvel and the esteem they inspire—is rooted in a respect that derives from fear, an interesting quality with regard to *teteo*.

The root of *mahuiztic* (esteemed) is *mahui* (to be frightened).[171] Whereas *mahuiztic* things are respected because they are feared, *malhuilli* things are respected or cared for because they are delicate and important. Speakers of modern Nahuatl maintain this difference, too. For example, *malhuilli* describes the kind of respect with which women approach the process of making *chocolate*. If the ritual order of making *chocolate* is not followed properly—if it is not respected—something may go awry. The respect the women have for this process comes from their reverence for the powers at work in it. Additionally, objects that pose potential danger, including fire, electricity, or a hidden ravine, are *malhuilli*, as are delicate objects, like a borrowed book. A borrowed book is *malhuilli* (cared for) because if it were damaged, the borrower would feel responsible to the owner. A passage explaining the dedication of children to the *calmecac* (training academy) describes the chief *calmecac* priest as "*ca mahuizyo* (venerated), *tlamahutia* (feared), considered as a god."[172] Here the scribes use both *mahuiztic* (esteemed) and *tlamauhtia* (feared) to emphasize that the respect the priest commanded derived from peoples' fear of him.[173] In descriptions of *teoxihuitl*, *tlapalteoxihuitl*, and *teocuitlatl*, the element of fear that inspires marvel, esteem, and veneration originated in their connection to *teotl*.

In the *Florentine Codex*, the strong association of *mahuiztic* with *teotl* led Sahagún's informants to equivocate when asked if they understood the *teoatl* (ocean) to be a *teotl*.[174] According to the *Florentine Codex*, Sahagún informants ostensibly denied the ocean's divinity even as they implicitly affirmed it by describing the *teoatl* as *mahuiztic*: "It is called *teoatl* [sea], not that it is a god; it only means *mahuiztic* (marvelous), a great marvel. . . . It is great. It terrifies, it frightens one. It is that which is irresistible; a great marvel. . . ."[175] It would seem that by describing the ocean as marvelous and frightening, the scribes assert, rather than deny, its connection to *teotl*. Perhaps the fine point these Nahuatl speakers were making had to do with the ontological status of the ocean. It may have been that for them, *teoatl* was not (a) *teotl*. However, this distinction did not necessarily preclude the ocean having *teotl* qualities. In fact, its *teotl* modification suggests that it did.

(5) A *teotl* is *tlazohca* (valuable, beloved).

In addition to being *mahuiztic* (something marvelous, awesome, worthy of esteem), *teteo* are also *tlazohca* (valuable, beloved), a quality attested in the *tlazohtetl's* (precious stones') descriptions. Both *tlapalteoxihuitl* (painted *teo*-turquoise) and *teotetl* (*teo*-stone; jet) are "*tlazohca* (valuable, beloved)."[176] The scribes also characterize Moteuczoma's personal property and the gifts he gave triumphant warriors as *tlazohca*: "Moctezuma rewarded them all with *cenca tlazohtli* (very valuable) and *immahuizzo* (highly honorable) princely capes and breech clouts, and with expensive quetzal feather devices [ornamented] with gold, and with shields with, perhaps, quetzal feather garlands— *huel tlazohtli* (very valuable) shields."[177] Additionally, the *tlahtoani* (ruler) gave the *pipiltin* (nobles) similar gifts during the celebration of Ochpaniztli: "And those which they were given were *huel tlazohca* (very costly) insignia, with much gold, covered with gold, with many quetzal feathers, full of quetzal feathers."[178]

According to the descriptions of *teoxihuitl* and *teocuitlatl*—two items defined by their *teotl* qualities, the value of *tlazohca* goods correlates with their relative availability. The scribes note that *teoxihuitl* "does not appear much . . . at times it does not appear anywhere";[179] and of *teocuitlatl*, they say that it only "sometimes in some places appears at dawn."[180] In addition to these descriptions, archaeological evidence of extensive Mesoamerican turquoise trade structures supports the idea that their value derived, at least in part, from the effort that went into procuring the precious stones. The earliest (ca. 500 CE) Mesoamerican turquoise mines were located in the Chalchihuites region of Zacatecas, Mexico, but as Central Mexican populations expanded and cultural complexity increased, the demand for turquoise outpaced its local availability. By 1000 CE, powerful Central Mexican polities, such as Tula, may have been importing turquoise from as far north as Chaco Canyon.[181] Mesoamerican demand for turquoise continued to increase into the fourteenth century, and it expanded beyond the rulers and elites. An idealized description of Tula's affluence from *Book 3: The Origin of the Gods* may reflect the large-scale importation of turquoise and other *tlazohtetl* (precious stones):

> And also they were indeed rich. Of no value was food, all our sustenance. It is said that the gourds were exceedingly huge. . . . And there dwelt all [varieties] of birds of precious feather; the lovely cotinga, the resplendent trogon, the troupial, the roseate spoonbill. . . . And all the green stones, the gold were *amo tlazohtli* (not costly). . . . And these Tolteca were very rich; they were wealthy.[182]

This paradisiacal description of Tula's prosperity illustrates the tie between abundance and worth; goods that the Aztecs considered *tlazohca*—quetzal feathers, gold, and precious stones—were so abundant that they were practically valueless in Tula.

The abundance of *tlazohca* goods at Tula led to their devaluation, but the demand for *teocuitlatl coztic* (gold) after Contact outstripped its availability and probably contributed to the increased valuation of *teocuitlatl iztac* (silver). The scribes' description of goldsmiths' use of *teocuitlatl iztac* (silver) in the sixteenth century presents a striking comparison to the availability of *teocuitlatl coztic* (gold) in Tula: "It is said that in times past only gold [was known to] exist. . . . Silver was not yet in use, though it existed. . . . But today, on the other hand, all is silver; they want gold; *motlazohtla* (it is much treasured)."[183] In the early colonial period, the scarcity of gold increased the *tlazohca* of both gold and silver. Although the Aztecs clearly valued intrinsic aspects of *teocuitlatl* and *tlazohtetl* (precious stones), such as their color and brilliance, rarity also factored into their worth.[184]

As a valuation based on rarity, *tlazohca* (valuable, beloved) draws the physical world into closer proximity with the social and metaphysical worlds. *Teocuitlatl* and *tlazohtetl*, both *tlazohca* goods, were the property of those whose *tonalli* (day name) afforded them the prerogative to own exclusive goods. A sign of rarity and worth, *tlazohca* maintains the tension among these five *teotl* properties. A *tonalli* (day name and accompanying prerogative) associates a *teotl* with both *axcaitl* (possessions, property) and *neixcahuilli* (exclusive things) that are *tlazohca* (beloved) because they are rare. From the devotee's perspective, a *teotl* and his or her exclusive things are *mahuiztic* (esteemed) and *tlazohca* (precious). The Mexica *tlahtoani* Moteuczoma Xocoyotzin's delicate handling of the *teixiptla* during the festival of Toxcatl demonstrates the essential unity of these properties:

> At this time Moctezuma adorned [the impersonator]; he repeatedly adorned him; he gave him gifts; he arrayed him; he arrayed him with great pomp. He had all *tlazotlanqui* (costly things) placed on him, for verily he took him to be *itlazoteouh* (his beloved god). [The impersonator] fasted; hence it was said: "He fasteth in black," [for] he went with his face smoke-black. His head was pasted with feathers, with eagle down. They only covered his hair for him; it fell to his head. . . . And from his ears on both sides went hanging cured golden shell pendants. And they fitted [his ears with] ear plugs made of *teoxihuitl* (teoturquoise), *tlaxiuhcalolli* (turquoise mosaic). And a shell necklace was his necklace. Moreover, his breast ornament was of white seashells. . . . Then on both sides, on his upper arms, he placed *teocuitlamatemecatl* (golden bracelets), and on both sides, on his wrists, he went placing *xinmaquiztli* (turquoise bracelets) taking up almost all his forearms. . . . And then he went placing his bells on both sides, on his legs. All *teocuitlatl* (gold) were the bells, called *oyoalli*. These [he wore] because they went jingling, because they went ringing; so did they resound. And his obsidian sandals had ocelot skin ears. Thus was arrayed he who died after one year.[185]

Moteuczoma adorns the *teixiptla* with "*tlazohnemi* (costly goods)"—turquoise bracelets, golden bells, and shell ornaments, goods as *tlazohca* as his own exclusive possessions—because "he took him to be his beloved god."[186] Because of his *tonalli* and accompanying *neixcahuilli*, Moteuczoma was fated to adorn the *teixiptla*. By right of his *tonalli*, the *tlahtoani* was singularly obligated to transform the sacrificial victim into a *teixiptla* using his own *mahuizyo* (esteemed) and *tlazohca* (valuable) possessions. According to the scribes' descriptions of *teocuitlatl* and the *tlazohtetl*, the *teixiptla*'s brilliant jewels, tinkling bells, and precious green stones represent the quintessence of the natural and metaphysical worlds. The appearance of a *teotl's* embodiment, an event both rare (*tlazohca*) and ordinary (*ahmo tlazohca*) in the Aztec world, demanded *tlazohca* goods and *mahuiztic* treatment from Moteuczoma. Moteuczoma, whose day sign afforded him the most precious materials of the natural world, used his exclusive goods to ornament the god's *teixiptla*.

Conclusions

For more than four hundred years, scholars have glossed *teotl* as "god" or "deity," and thought of *teteo* either in terms of their own concepts of God, god, or gods or as their antitheses (idols, false gods, etc.). By 1571, the year Molina published his *Vocabulario*, the Tlatelolcan scholars, perhaps induced by Sahagún, had agreed that *teotl* meant *dios*, and with only a few exceptions, their consensus persists in contemporary analyses of Aztec religion. According to *teotl's* use in the *Florentine Codex*—both in overtly religious contexts and seemingly nonreligious ones—*teotl* does indeed mean "god," but the older Nahuatl concept of *teotl*-as-god conveys a culturally specific set of criteria and meanings. *Teotl* is neither the monotheistic God, the polytheistic gods, nor simply god. Instead, (1) a *teotl* has *axcaitl* (possessions, property); (2) a *teotl* has a *tonalli* (heat; day sign; fate, fortune, privilege, prerogative); (3) a *teotl* has a *neixcahuilli* (an exclusive thing, occupation, business, pursuit); (4) a *teotl* is *mahuiztic* (something marvelous, awesome, worthy of esteem); and (5) a *teotl* is *tlazohca* (valuable, beloved). Translations of *teotl* as "god" or "deity" should invoke these five properties (*axcaitl, tonalli, neixcahuilli, mahuiztic,* and *tlazohca*).

In addition to clarifying the concept of *teotl*, these attributes provide an alternative means for analyzing the intersection of religion and the natural world as they appear in Aztec material cultural. Presently, archaeologists recognize a symbolic relationship between the cosmos, monumental ceremonial structures, and the offering caches buried in those structures. The five attributes of *teotl* derived from the *Florentine Codex*'s descriptions enhance the interpretation of objects interred in ceremonial structures, such as the Templo Mayor, because they highlight the intimate connection between *teotl*-modified materials of the natural world and the ritual goods manufactured from those materials, including identifiable deity representations. The caches' location at the ritual nexus of the Aztec religion and state accentuates their symbolic importance, much like the private things Moteuczoma gave his be-

3.5. Templo Mayor offering cache with animate *tecpame*, ordinary *tecpame*, and a skull mask with eye inlays, Museo del Templo Mayor. Photograph by author.

loved god's *teixiptla*. The offerings interred at the Templo Mayor—and the structure itself—represent ritual obligations fulfilled by the *teteo, tlahtoani, pipiltin* (nobles), and *macehualtin* (commoners).

The Templo Mayor caches contain images of the Aztec universe that archaeologists, including Leonardo López Luján, consider analogous to the signs and symbols of pictorial manuscripts and spoken Nahuatl. Based on his comprehensive study of evidence uncovered at the Templo Mayor, López Luján argues that

> archaeological contexts have a great similarity to ritual syntax and to verbal language. If this is correct, we will find two kinds of archaeological syntax: an "internal" one, corresponding to the distribution of objects within a container or receptacle, and an "external" one, related to the arrangement of the offerings with respect to architectural structures. In this sense, we could speak of a "language" of the offerings that resembles the basic principles of writing—a language not only expressed in signs and symbols, but also with grammatical (or contextual) rules.[187]

Like the analogous languages of pictorial manuscripts and ritual gift exchanges, the symbolic language of caches buried at the Templo Mayor conveys information on multiple levels, including those of the objects and their interrelation, the caches and their architectural arrangement within the Templo, and the Templo as a phenomenological manifestation of Tenochtitlan's founding at the center of the Aztec cosmos.[188] Analyzing the relationship between *teotl*'s attributes and the caches' contents and material makeup lies beyond the scope of this book. However, the relationship of *teotl* to *teixiptla* (localized embodiment) is a vital aspect of the symbolic system underlying spoken Nahuatl, pictorial manuscripts, and ritual offerings.

CHAPTER 4

Gods in the Flesh
The Animation of Aztec *Teixiptlahuan*

>>> "the more masked the reality, the more striking the drama."[1]

Teteo (gods) and their *teixiptlahuan* (localized embodiments) frequently appear together in Nahuatl accounts of ritual activity, especially in those that describe devotees constructing and venerating a deity embodiment—whether human, dough, wood, or stone. Aztec rituals and devotional practices often involved multiple *teixiptlahuan* representing several *teteo*. This multiplicity has contributed to scholars' tendency to fuse the two concepts—*teotl* and *teixiptla* (localized embodiment)—into a single more manageable one. A description of Painal's appearance at the temple of Huitzilopochtli from the *Florentine Codex* exemplifies ritual contexts in which devotees interacted with multiple *teixiptlahuan*:

> Auh in otlathuic, niman ye ic hualquiza, in painaltzin, in zan no ye ixiptla Huitzilopochtli, quinapaloa: auh in ixiptla painal, zan cuauhitl tlacayetiuh: auh in quinapaloa, itoca topiltzin Quetzalcoatl: cenca mochichihuaya, iyapanecayouh: auh in ixiptla painal inic mochichihuaya, ihuitzitzilnahual, iianecuyouh, iteucuitlapan, ichalchiuhcozqui: auh in pilcatiuh, yehuatl in cuitlatezcatl, zan moche in teoxihuitl: auh in quiacana quitquitiuh icoatopil, xihuitl ic tlaquimilolli.

> And when day broke, then Painaltzin emerged, the very localized embodiment of Huitzilopochtli. He [Topiltzin Quetzalcoatl] carries him in his arms; the wooden embodiment of Painal was anthropomorphic. He who carries him in his arms is called Topiltzin Quetzalcoatl. He is greatly adorned with a feather device from shoulder to hip. And Painal's embodiment is adorned with his hummingbird disguise, his headdress, his gold banner hanging down, his greenstone necklace and back mirror. All were of *teo*-turquoise. And he led him, he carried his serpent staff covered in turquoise.[2]

In this passage, the Topiltzin Quetzalcoatl (the title of a priest in the temple of Huitzilopochtli) is the human *teixiptla* of Huitzilopochtli, and he carries the wooden *teixiptla* of Painal, Huitzilopochtli's representative.[3] Both the wooden *teixiptla* of Painal and the priest Topiltzin Quetzalcoatl wear ornate ceremonial garments made of feathers, gold, greenstone, mirror, and *teo*-turquoise, and the priest carries Huitzilopochtli's signature *xiuhcoatl* (turquoise serpent) staff. The multiple *teixiptlahuan* participating in this procession hint at the dizzying synchronicity and proliferation of Aztec gods during ceremonies; in the course of a few sentences, we encounter a wooden *teixiptla* of Painal, who is also Huitzilopochtli's *teixiptla*, and a priest carrying Huitzilopochtli's talismanic *xiuhcoatl* and his *tlaquimilolli*. By virtue of the *xiuhcoatl* staff, the priest embodies the god, while at the same time carrying the god in the sacred bundle. These three overlapping embodiments—the wooden Painal, Huitzilopochtli as Painal, and Huitzilopochtli as/in the priest, demonstrate the complex layers of representation that occur wherever the *teixiptlahuan* of *teteo* appear.

Rich passages describing multiple *teixiptlahuan* have attracted scholarly attention, as have those that detail the ritual sacrifice of *teteo*. The *Florentine Codex* documents the use of the term *teixiptla* outside religious contexts, but the literature tends to focus on localized embodiments in rituals, especially those involving human *teixiptlahuan*. However, it is important to note that *teixiptla* also occurs in contexts of familial succession and military representation.[4] Because of the number and relative detail of ritual descriptions like those in the *Florentine Codex* and Diego Durán's *Book of the Gods and Rites*, scholars who examine *teixiptlahuan* of *teteo* have been drawn to the question of a *teotl*'s presence or absence within a *teixiptla*, and many went on to define the embodiment's relationship to the deity it presents. As we saw in Chapter 2, t(h)eologians emphasize the importance of the *teotl*, the inner essence of the *teixiptlahuan*, "filling" the material embodiment (i.e., vessel) of the god, and iconographers identify *teteo* based on the appearance of their (anthropomorphic) *teixiptlahuan*. Doubtless these perspectives derive from the "habit of parsing the world into dull matter (it, things) and vibrant life (us, beings)" so prevalent in the modern West.[5] Studies of material culture, distributive agency, alternative ontologies, and "symmetrical" anthropology, especially as encountered in Bruno Latour's "factish," offer ways of engaging in the work of understanding what *teixiptlahuan* were and how they related to *teteo* without taking mind/body or ephemeral/material oppositions as given or even as necessarily relevant. This interdisciplinary work models Jane Bennett's notion that "we need both critique and positive formulations of alternatives, alternatives that will themselves become the objects of later critique and reform."[6]

In this chapter, my intention is to explain *teixiptla*'s etymology as it bears upon the ritual manufacture of deities' embodiments and then to propose some tentative alternatives to the ways in which scholars have traditionally understood *teixiptlahuan*. Drawing on the animation ceremonies of other religions, I suggest that the Aztecs ritually produced animate localized embodiments of their deities—*teixiptlahuan* who were living gods and goddesses—by focusing on specific elements of the *teixiptlahuan*'s construction and education. The embodiments' materiality and telltale signs of their constructedness did not disrupt their devotees' veneration. Rather, the process of a *teixiptla*'s ritual production facilitated its animacy: the god came to be (in) the localized embodiment by virtue of the *teixiptla*'s manufacture. The precise nature of that manufacture remains at least partly obscured because of the nature of the sources (or lack thereof) and the attempt to negotiate a cosmology that recognized ontologies and animacies outsiders have difficulty perceiving. Although my tentative positive alternatives may not describe exactly how a human body or an amaranth dough figurine came to be an Aztec god-body, they prompt us to consider how vital materialities functioned in Aztec religion.

On the Surface: Defining *Ixiptlatl*, *Ixiptlayotl*, and Their Functions

According to its semantic characteristics and lexical attestations, *teixiptla* occurs in two forms, the concrete *ixiptlatl* (representative, delegate) and the abstract *ixiptlayotl* (representation, image, likeness), and although the terms denote two forms of representation, one more concrete than the other, they share analogous modes of representation. Both forms of *teixiptla* appear in the *Florentine Codex* and early colonial lexicons, and they derive from three morphemic components: *ixtli* (eye; face; surface), **xip-* (refers to peeling, flaying, shaving, etc.), and the transitive suffix *-tla*, which means "to cause someone to be or to be treated as or to be characterized by (the entity denoted by the source noun stem)."[7] The resulting verbal form **ixxiptla* means "to cause someone or something to be/be treated as/be characterized by a flayed (sur)face."[8] Thus, a tentative morphological parsing of *teixiptla* reveals that it is a compound of *ixtli* (eye; face; surface) and **xip* (shaving; peeling; flaying); the term *teixiptla* signifies "a surface-flayed thing."

Like Nahuatl names for body parts, *teixiptla* is inherently possessed, and inherently possessed nouns always take a possessive prefix. *Nonaca* (my ear) is always "my ear," never just *naca*, or "ear." Similarly, a *teixiptla* (literally, "someone's surface-flayed thing") is never simply "a surface-flayed thing." What sounds like a complicated linguistic relationship makes sense materially, too. If *teixiptla* refers to the object or entity characterized by (i.e., wearing) the flayed skin, it would not make sense for us to think of it as other than possessed by or bound to that object or entity. Independent of that which (or she whom) it characterizes, the flayed skin would simply be a skin, not a *teixiptla*. Logically, then, a *teixiptla* cannot exist apart from the entity it embodies. Traditionally, scholars have translated *teixiptla* as "impersonator," "representative," and "representation," and indeed, the word occurs in a variety of contexts where it signifies a proxy, such as a military delegate. The phrase "*teixiptla, tepatillo*," translated by Anderson and Dibble as "one's deputy, one's vicar," describes the relationship between a ruler and his son who could act as the father's authoritative stand-in. However, in ritual contexts the term's condition of inherent possession and the fact of its performative embodiment direct us away from translations like "representation," which connotes a mental image or symbolic stand-in. A *teixiptla is* the being whom it embodies; it is neither an impression nor a representation of that being. *Teotl* transforms a person, idea, or object because of the cluster of qualities it conveys. *Teixiptla*'s etymology requires that it be in a relationship with someone else.

Given *teixiptla*'s meaning and semantic composition, most likely it originally designated the person who wore the flayed skin of a sacrificial victim, someone not only characterized by but also clothed in a flayed surface. We

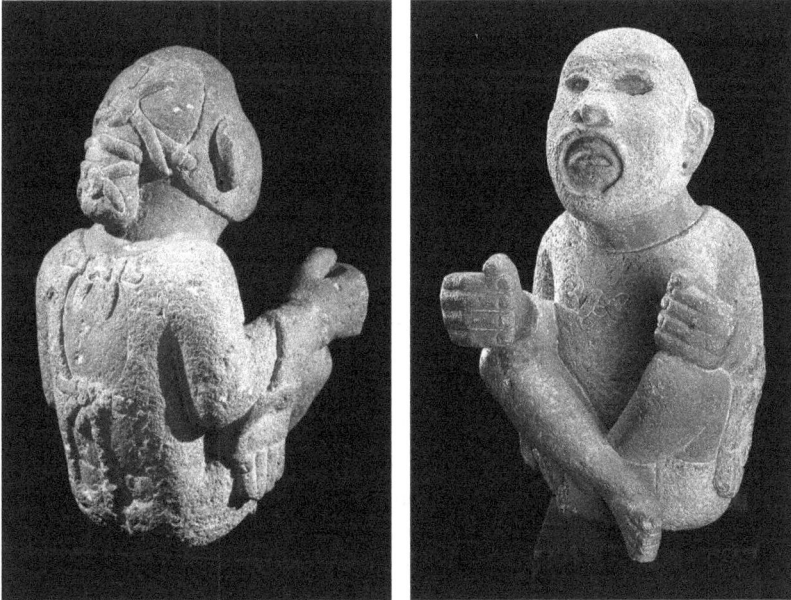

4.1a. (back) and **4.1b.** (front) Xipe Totec. Painted volcanic tuff, mid-fourteenth–mid-fifteenth century. © Museum der Kulturen, Basel, Switzerland.

encountered one such victim in the story of Huitzilopochtli's marriage to the Colhua princess. Huitzilopochtli simultaneously sowed discord between and bound together the Mexicas and the Colhuas by "marrying" the priest who wore the flayed skin of Achitometl's sacrificed daughter. Ceramic figures often identified as "Xipe Totec" (Flaying Lord) are literal *teixiptlahuan*; put simply, absent the clothing and insignia that adorned these effigies, scholars base objects' (mis)identification as Xipe Totec on the figures' most prominent characteristic: the flayed skins they wear (Figure 4.1).

Returning to *teixiptla*'s etymology, we find that the noun form *ixiptlatl* retains this ritual referent—a human's sacrifice and flaying—in its literal meaning, "someone that has been (sur)face flayed." *Ixiptlatl* denotes the concrete form of a representative, impersonator, substitute, or delegate, someone who stands in for another by wearing the other's surface or having the other's appearance, and *ixiptlayotl*, which also derives from **ixxiptla*, denotes an abstract sense of the concept. The suffix *-yotl* means "that which pertains to, that which is characterized by" or "that which is covered with" the entity denoted by the noun stem.[9] Thus *ixiptlayotl* means "that which pertains to/is characterized by/is covered with a flayed (sur)face."[10] Karttunen adopts *ixiptlayotl* as the term's canonical form and glosses it as "image, likeness, representation."[11] In this text, I retain the nonspecific object prefix *te-* (someone's) to remind us that a *teixiptla* belonged to the entity embodied.

The *Teixiptla's* Vital Skin

Literally a "surface-flayed thing or person," *teixiptla* semantically denotes a specific semiotic relationship between the "prototype" (that which is represented), its "index" (the representative or representation factually connected to the prototype), and its "icon" (connected by similarity in appearance). Here I follow anthropologist Alfred Gell, whose use of prototype and index derives from Peircean pragmatic semiotics wherein an "index" is "a 'natural sign', that is, an entity from which the observer can make a causal inference of some kind, or an inference about the intentions or capabilities of another person. The usual example of an 'index' is visible smoke, betokening 'fire'. Fire causes smoke, hence smoke is an 'index' of fire."[12] At the etymological level, the semantic elements of *teixiptla* appear to delimit its semiotic signification by naming both the concept's prototype—the flayed victim—and its iconic index—the individual who re-presents by wearing the flayed skin. The commonly held understanding of *teixiptla* as a representative or representation of a *teotl*, for instance, extrapolates from the paradigmatic ritual relationship of a skin-wearing *teixiptla*, the index that the flayed victim resembles, the prototype.

Regardless of *teixiptla*'s specific referent in a given context—a *tlahtoani* (ruler) or a *tlacochcalcatl* (commanding general), for instance—a *teixiptla* always functioned as a localized embodiment of that entity. A *teixiptla* at the behest of the *tlahtoani* would neither be mistaken for the *tlahtoani* himself nor for a powerless placeholder. The phrase *teixiptla, tepatillo* (one's deputy, one's vicar) further illustrates *teixiptla*'s representative function: "teixiptla, tepatillo inin tlatolli: itechpa mitoaya in tlatocatitlantli: anozo in ipiltzin tlatoani, in omic itatzin: ca oquimixiptlatitehuac in ipiltzin, ca ipatillo mochiuhtica." (One's deputy, one's vicar: This saying was said of the messenger of the ruler, or of the son of the ruler when his father died, for he had departed deputizing his son, who was acting as his vicar.)[13] Even if the son exercised the full extent of his father's authority, mistaking the person of the son for the person of the father would have been ludicrous. As messenger or heir, the *teixiptla* represented the ruler, but he was not the ruler. Similarly, a *teotl* (prototype) and its *teixiptla* (iconic index) are bound and distinguished by the representational relationship signified by *teixiptla*, a surface-flayed thing. However, in contrast to other types of representatives and representations, such as a military delegate or a painted portrait, the *teixiptla* of a *teotl* complicates the Peircean isolation of the index and icon from the prototype by paradoxically both representing and presenting the deity. In other words, a *teotl*'s *teixiptla* both looks like the *teotl* and embodies him or her, and the effect(iveness) of a *teixiptla* hangs on its physical imbrication of the *teotl*'s person.

A *teixiptla*'s ability to both represent and present a *teotl* emerges through its material manufacture and physical composition. In *The Inordinate Eye*, Lois Parkinson Zamora argues, "In Mesoamerican myth cultures, the body is coextensive with the world, an expressive space that contains—rather than filters or fixes—the world. Here, we may usefully speak of an embodied culture, a culture of embodiment."[14] In the case of *teixiptlahuan*, the embodiment marks its presence in the world through the overlay of exuviae. As a surface-flayed thing, a *teixiptla* is simultaneously image—the skin-wearer resembles the *teotl*—and exuviae—the skin or insignia that covers the index belongs to the *teotl*.[15] Although Gell discusses neither *teixiptla* nor *teteo*, the role of exuviae in his "distributed person" corresponds to a flayed skin's function in a *teixiptla*'s presentation of a *teotl*. Exuviae, he explains, "do not stand metonymically for the victim; they are physically detached fragments of the victim's 'distributed personhood'—that is, personhood distributed in the milieu, beyond the body-boundary."[16] Because exuviae are a detached part of the

prototype, they physically convey a portion of that prototype—the "distributed person"—in the index. So, in contrast to a painted portrait, which may
accurately represent an individual in oil, a medium unrelated to the person, a
teixiptla wearing a *teotl*'s skin presents that *teotl* in face, form, and substance.

A *teixiptla* is an iconic image of the prototype *because* it is a detached part
of the prototype. By virtue of its skin, a *teixiptla* is a *localized embodiment*.[17]
The *teixiptla* of a *teotl* complicates the Peircean divide between image, icon,
and prototype because the *teixiptla*, by virtue of its physical construction
from/of the *teotl*, presents not the original prototype (the image of the flayed
victim), but a new prototype (the god). The ritual manufacture of *teixiptlahuan* transposes the index: the skin, which once recalled the sacrificial victim,
comes to present the *teotl* because of its part(icipation) in the *teotl*'s distributed person.

The Skin(ny) on *Teteo*: *Teixiptlahuan* in Aztec Ceremonies

The in-the-flesh *teixiptlahuan* who embodied Xipe Totec during Tlacaxipehualiztli (Feast of the Flaying of Men) epitomized the relationship between
human *teixiptlahuan*, skins, and *teteo*. Tlacaxipehualiztli replicated the paradigm encapsulated in the etymology of *teixiptla* by clothing multiple humans
in the flayed skins of Xipe Totec. Durán describes Tlacaxipehualiztli as "a solemn, festive, bloody ceremony, which cost so many human lives that no other
rivaled it," and also as "the most popular of all the solemnities."[18] According
to Durán, "forty days before the feast the people dressed a man as a representation of the idol with his same adornments. . . . They honored him and glori-
fied him during the forty days, exhibiting him in public as if he had been the
god himself."[19]

Although Sahagún mentions simply "*oncan quixipehua*" (there they flayed
him), Durán describes the ritual process in more detail.[20]

> Acuados de desollar la carne dauan a cuio el yndio hauia sido y los cu-
> eros bestianlos a otros tantos yndios alli luego y poniale los mesmos
> nonbres de los dioses que los otros hauian representado bistiendoles
> encima de aquellos cueros las mesmas ropas y ynsignias de aquellos di-
> oses poniendo a cada vno su nonbre del dios que representaua tenien-
> dose ellos por tales.

When the heart had been removed and offered to the east, the skin-
ners (whose task it was) cast the dead body down and split it from the

4.2. Xipe Totec *teixiptla* from Tlacaxipehualiztli. *Florentine Codex*, 1:73v. Photograph courtesy of the Biblioteca Medicea Laurenziana.

nape of the neck to the heel, skinning it as a lamb. The skin came off complete. After the skinning had taken place, the flesh was given to the man who had owned the slave. Other men donned the skins immediately and then took the names of the gods who had been impersonated. Over the skins they wore the garments and insignia of the same divinities, each man bearing the name of the god and considering himself divine.[21]

Tlacaxipehualiztli clearly illustrates that as the original referent and conceptual foundation of *teixiptla*, the flayed skin covering, which came to include by extension face paint, headdress, clothing, and ornamentation, was both the prototype's image and its substance (Figure 4.2).[22]

Some *teixiptlahuan*, like those of Xipe Totec, literally wore the skins of flayed victims, but in the case of other *teteo*'s *teixiptlahuan*, physical attributes and costume elements replaced the flayed skin as indexical markers.[23] Fidelity to a *teotl*'s characteristic qualities in its material representation was key: "The artist has to produce a 'faithful' rendition of the features of the accepted image of the body of the god, triggering 'recognition' of the god among his worshippers."[24] Clearly, the role of exuviae—whether as flayed skins or prototypal insignia—enabled devotees' recognition of a *teotl* and, more importantly, the presence of a *teotl* in his *teixiptla*. In contrast to other types of *teixiptlahuan* (delegates, portraits, figurines, etc.), skin and insignia constituted a god's *teixiptla* at a fundamental level. These physical elements of the *teixiptla* facilitated its embodiment by a *teotl*.

The material and conceptual mimesis evoked by a *teixiptla*'s physical resemblance to and bodily participation in the *teotl* it presented made its religious animation possible. *Teteo* were solely imaginal; that is, what physically presented as a recognizable *teixiptla* was the material manifestation of a cluster of qualities that composed the *teotl*. I argued earlier that five defining characteristics distinguished *teteo* from other types of entities, and insofar as a specific set of associated qualities constituted a particular *teotl*, those qualities were "imaginal." Borrowing the words of Paul Ricoeur, they were imaginal "in the sense of being superefficacious while still remaining a part of common reality."[25] If we take Huitzilopochtli as an example, the *xiuhcoatl* (turquoise serpent) staff, the colors and patterning of his face paint, and his association with the Mexicas are elements in his cluster of qualities. As we saw in the description of Painal's appearance, those qualities were essential in the composition of his *teixiptlahuan*.

By calling *teteo* "solely imaginal," I mean to say that whereas *teixiptlahuan* were physical bodies (humans or plastic figures), *teteo* existed conceptually as qualitative clusters produced by the religious imagination. I identify *teteo* as products of the religious imagination not to remove them from the (profane) world to some other (sacred) realm, but to draw attention to the materiality of their embodiments. The moment a *teotl* manifests physically, she is a *teixiptla*. When a *teotl* manifests as a *teixiptla*, she brings all of the qualities that distinguish her as a *teotl* into a body manufactured for the purpose of presenting her in face, form, and substance. Describing *teteo* as imaginal highlights the requirement of their physicality. A *teixiptla* is necessarily possessed, and a *teotl* needs a *teixiptla*, a localized embodiment, in order to be present to devotees. The etymologies and ritual manufactures of deities' localized embodiments substantiate this fine point, and the emphasis on surface explicit in *teixiptla* calls our attention to the issue of recognizing a *teotl*.

Recall that as a surface-flayed thing or person, a *teixiptla* wore the skin (literally, figuratively, or both) of its *teotl* and, in so doing, physically re(as)sembled the deity. Although resemblance and recognition seem to determine the form of a *teotl's teixiptla*, the Mexica cosmovision facilitated endless graphic recombinations as it incorporated newly deified entities (like *cihuateteo*), absorbed the *teteo* of conquered polities, and met with unforeseen novelties (like the Spaniards). Devotees recognized a *teixiptla* because of its physical resemblance to (earlier bodily presentations of) the *teotl*, and they attributed appropriate (or expected) actions and responsibilities to it. Devotees' attribution of intention to a *teotl's teixiptla* endowed the *teixiptla* with agency, and a *teixiptla's* perceived participation in its *teotl*—a perception achieved through exuviae, appearance, and expectation—facilitated this process.[26]

What remains is the fact that *teixiptlahuan* were manufactured entities. In his discussion of the artist's relationship to the cult object, Gell explains, "Many objects which are in fact objects manufactured by (human) artists, are not believed to have originated in that way; they are thought to be of divine origin or to have mysteriously made themselves. The origins of art objects can be forgotten or concealed, blocking off the abduction leading from the existence of the material index to the agency of an artist."[27] Although the manufactured quality of *teixiptlahuan* had the potential to betray their human origins, it did not impede their veneration by devotees.[28] In fact, the abduction that occurred between the source materials and the final embodiment facilitated the *teixiptla's* possession by a *teotl*. In other words, that Aztec devotees perceived a human-made, handmade thing as a deity suggests that they conceived of ritual matter(s) not as inert and lifeless, but as the stuff of gods. Rather than animate lifeless materials, Aztec priests and devotees perceived the animacy already present in the vital materials—the human bodies or natural goods—from which they constructed *teixiptlahuan*.[29] In this sense, the "origins of art objects" of which Gell speaks were known to Aztec devotees, who were both aware of a material *teixiptla's* thingness and alert to its always-already animacy. Whether or not the Aztecs attributed a "mystical" origin to their *teixiptlahuan*—they seem to have done so with *tlaquimilolli*, as we shall see—the embodiments' materiality, and particularly their skin, whether flesh, precious stone, or cloth, absolutely mattered. The vital materiality of *teixiptlahuan* facilitated, rather than distracted from, the bodies' ability to embody gods.

Not only were the materials associated with properties of the gods, but they also conveyed a sense of vitality in the image they adorned. In both substance and appearance, they presented (aspects of) the god. Consider the god-stones that appeared on the masks identified with Xiuhtecuhtli (Turquoise

Lord) and Milintoc (Shining) described in the last chapter: both masks glistened with vital god-materials—*xihuitl* (turquoise) and *teotetl* (god-stone; jet)—made all the more vibrant in the flicker of firelight. Similarly, during the celebration of Xocotl Huetzin (Great Fruit Tree) the *tlenamacac* (fire priest) and other priests created a *teixiptla* of the *xocotl* (fruit) from amaranth dough: "auh in ixiptla xocotl, in quinacayotiaya: michihuauhtli quitlaliaya, zan ce-miztac in amatl in quimamaca, in itech quitlatlalia: amo ma tlacuilollo." (And they made the *xocotl*'s localized embodiment like flesh; they formed it from fish amaranth dough, and they gave it bright white papers. They placed the papers on it repeatedly. They did not have a painted design.)[30] Working without a design, the priests then dressed the *iixiptla xocotl* in paper clothes and placed it on top of the *xocotl* pole. At the end of Xocotl Huetzin, young men and boys climbed the *xocotl* pole and raced one another to reach the amaranth dough *teixiptla*: "in aquin yacatiuh, huel yehuatl caci in xocotl ixiptla, zan tzo-alli: mochi quicuilia in ichimal, in imiuh tlahuazomalli, huan iatlauh." (He who leads, he indeed seizes the *xocotl ixiptla*. It was only amaranth dough. He takes everything away from him: his shield, his pointless arrows, and his dart thrower.)[31] Although Sahagún may have included this description of these ritual objects' preparation for the benefit of his clerical colleagues, this example reveals that devotees' knowledge of a *teixiptla*'s manufacture did not compromise its value or veneration.[32] Even though the *teixiptla* was "only dough," the young participants raced to capture his insignia. Many ceremonies centered around the creation of one or more *teixiptlahuan*. Rather than prevent devotees from venerating *teixiptlahuan*, it seems that their process of manufacture and very materiality facilitated the localized embodiments' animation and endowed them with a vitality that made them venerable.

Deifying *Teixiptlahuan*: Animacy in Aztec Religion

As Gell observes, "to say that one attributes 'animacy' or 'anthropomorphism' to something does not explain what a thing must *be* or *do* to count as 'animate' or 'anthropomorphic,'" and even though the Aztecs perceived their world as highly animate, little evidence remains regarding exactly *how* they animated their *teixiptlahuan*.[33] Although no alphabetic text describes the precise moment in which a ritual event animated a deity's *teixiptla*, several clues as to what affected animation exist in ethnohistoric accounts. Together with comparative material from the animation ceremonies of other religions, those clues facilitate a tentative interpretation of what Aztec *teixiptlahuan* had to be and do in order to become animate. To begin with, the animacy of a *teixiptla* depended on its ability to see (and be seen) and on its ability to act (and look) like the *teotl* it represented.

The importance of a *teixiptla*'s ability to see stems from the word's etymology and semantic requirements. The etymological connection between *teixiptla* and *ixtli* (eye; face; surface) supports the role of sight in the lives of localized embodiments. The eyes, faces, and surfaces of *teixiptlahuan* are basic components of the word's meaning and the embodiments' materiality. Likewise, *teixiptla*'s morphology and meaning dictate that an embodiment is always someone's embodiment. In practice, this semantic requirement of belonging between a *teixiptla* and its prototype takes place as recognition occurs among the *teotl*, the *teixiptla*, and the devotees.

Teixiptlahuan existed to see and be seen. López Austin identifies *ixtli*, the eye, as, "the perceptive organ par excellence," and he cites *in ixtli, in yollotl* (the eye, the heart) as a metaphor for "that part of man where sensation, perception, understanding, and feeling unite in order to integrate a complete consciousness that is found in communication with the outside world."[34] Similar understandings of sight existed in the Maya world. Citing work by William F. Hanks and Evon Z. Vogt, Steven Houston explains, "It is probably relevant that, in most Mayan languages, to see something is also to discern and understand; thus, the act of perception is regarded as physiological, but equally cognitive, intellectual, and, in the case of shamans, at once visionary and spiritually omniscient."[35] The physiology of human *teixiptlahuan* facilitated their sensory experience of the world, but the manufacture of plastic *teixiptlahuan* ensured that they, too, could perceive their devotees. In particular, the placement of eye inlays on the faces of plastic *teixiptlahuan* materialized metaphoric and divinatory associations the Aztecs made between reflective surfaces and vision.

For the Aztecs, reflective surfaces, such as *itztli* (obsidian) and *tezcatl* (mirror stone), enkindled and reflected ocular metaphors and extraordinary modes of visual perception, including ocelots' night vision, astronomers' sight(ings), diviners' insight, and *teixiptlahuan*'s vision. For them, the eye served as "tezcatl . . . teiximati, tlaiximati, quitta, tetlauilia, tetlanextilia, teiacana, teuica, [and] tenemitia" (a mirror . . . [that] recognizes people, recognizes things, sees, illuminates one, enlightens one, leads one, guides one, [and] sustains one).[36] Both eyes and mirrors did more than reflect the onlooker's glance. Their reflective capacities facilitated a deeper knowing: one oriented toward a future direction while connected with the past through memory and the present in the moment of recognition. Some animals and humans distinguished themselves as extraordinary seers.

Book 11: Earthly Things begins with entries on the three species of *ocelotls* the Aztecs identified (Figure 4.3). All of them had especially keen vision after dark: "auh in yohualtica: huellachia, quimitta, in tlein quintemoa, in quinqua: cenca cualli, in itlachializ, chipactic: ca nelli, cenca huellachia, huel hueca tlachia: in manel tzontic, in manel ayauhtic: quitta." (And by night it watches; it seeks out what it hunts, what it eats. Its vision is clear, very good. Truly, it sees very well; it can see far. Even if it is very dark, even if it is misty, it sees.)[37] The *ocelotl*'s mirror-eyes, a naturally occurring shiny thing, enabled its night vision, because the animal's eyes featured a *tapetum lucidum*, a surface behind the retina that reflects light back toward the retina. Physiologically, a reflective surface—a mirror—within the ocelot's eye enabled it to see in darkness, much like visual apparatuses, including mirrors, facilitated a diviner's extraordinary vision. Ocelots' ability to see after dark paralleled that of astronomers, who observed the stars—painted in codices as half-opened eyes—in order to calculate calendrics (Figure 4.4).[38]

4.3. (right) *Ocelotl* (jaguar). *Florentine Codex*, 3:155v. Photograph courtesy of the Biblioteca Medicea Laurenziana.
4.4. (above) Astronomer observing night sky. *Codex Mendoza*, 63r. Line drawing by author.

Diviners' extraordinary vision facilitated communication between humans and the gods. In a penitent's statement of confession recorded in the *Florentine Codex*, a *tlapouhqui* (something open; diviner) functioned as the goddess Tlazolteotl's "*iix*" (her eye).[39] After preparing a fire and incense, the diviner invoked Tloque Nahuaque using the phrase *in tloqueh, in nahuaqueh, in totecuyo, in yoalli, in ehecatl* (the far, the near, our Lord the night, the wind) in his instructions to the penitent: "a ma no ceppa yeh nican timatoiauh, timotepexiuh: ma ixpantzinco ximopepetlaoa, ximomamaxauh, in tloque nahuaque, in totecuyo, in yoalli, in ehecatl. A cuix tictlacaittaz in totecuyo, a cuix mitztlacanotzaz: ca yoalli, ca ehecatl?" (No more shall thou err or sin. Before him of the near, the nigh, our lord the night, the wind, take off thy clothing, show thy nakedness. Wilt thou see our lord as a man and will he, as a man, address thee, for he is the night, the wind?)[40] The penitent then addresses the diviner:

> quilhuia, inic tehuihuiti, inic tepatiloti, inic teixiptla. Totecuyoe, tloque-he, nahuaquehe . . . mixpantzinco, ninopepetlaoa, ninomamaxauia: ca onax, ca onicchiuh: cuix ichtaca, ciux tlaihoaian, ca tezcac, ca tlahuil-pan in mixpantzinco, in onax. Niman compehualtia: in itlapilchihualiz, huel iuin quenin cah, huel iuin quenin quichiuh: in maca zan cuicatl, cenca zan iuin conehua, cencan ihuin conitoa, in iuh quichiuh, im maca zan otli, cencan quitocatiuh in itlachihual, in iuhui cencan quitocatiuh. Auh in otlamito in itlatol, in omochi quito itlachihual: quinanquilia, in tlapouhqui, in ixtli in nacaztli mochihua, in tehuihuiti, intepatilloti.

> He spoke as to a lieutenant, a deputy, a localized embodiment. "Our Lord of the near, the nigh . . . I take off my clothing and uncover, in thy presence, my nakedness—[that is] what I have perpetrated, what I have done. Can these things be hidden, can they be darkened, when that which I have perpetrated is reflected, is clear in thy sight?" Then he began [the tale of] his sins, in their proper order, in the same order as that in which he had committed them. Just as if it were a song, just as he intoned a song, in the very same way he told what he had done. As if on a road he went following his deeds; in the very same manner he went following them. And when he ended his words, when he had told all his deeds, then the soothsayer, the one who became the mediator, the lieutenant, the deputy, answered him.[41]

This account stands out from the many descriptions of public *teixiptlahuan*, because it both links a diviner with a *teotl*'s *teixiptla* and describes the embodiment of an invisible and enigmatic *teotl*—Tloque Nahuaque—

named by the epithet *in tloqueh, in nahuaqueh, in totecuyo, in yoalli, in ehe-catl* (the far, the near, our Lord the night, the wind). In *The Invisible War*, David Tavárez examines this naming practice in the context of Hernando Ruiz de Alarcón's *Treatise on Heathen Superstitions*, which contains numerous *nahualtocaitl* (Nahual names). Ritual specialists embodied *teteo* by invoking specific *nahualtocaitl* from among "an astounding number of epithets composed by two parallel elements for referring to oneself as a Nahua deity, calling forth propitiated entities, and designating a range of objects and entities during the course of the incantation."[42] Tavárez explains that "an important language ideology underlies this genre: every entity in the world, including deities, animals, natural features and objects, bears a unique personal or calendrical name associated with specific mythohistorical narratives, and uttering the appropriate name conferred on practitioners a form of authority."[43] In this instance, the diviner called upon and embodied a specific deity in order to facilitate the penitent's repentance. Embodying a god by invoking his *nahualtocaitl*, Tavárez notes, was a common and powerful practice in public and private religious practices:

> Nahua specialists believed that the effectiveness of their divination and propitiation activities derived from the illocutionary force of the speech act through which they designated themselves as deities. . . . Certainly, the rhetorical act of designating oneself as a particular deity through epithets was a significant departure from the deity personification practices of *teixiptlameh* in preconquest Mexica public ritual practices. The differences between both sets of practices highlight the contrast between the collective and elective spheres: Mexica state ceremonies targeted the well-being of the entire altepetl; colonial verbal deity personification was oriented toward pragmatic outcomes for an individual or family.[44]

By contrast to the public performances that took place during annual festivals like Tlacaxipehualiztli and Toxcatl, this diviner's transformation into a *teixiptla* occurred in private and for the express purpose of facilitating the penitent's confession. From the penitent's plea that the diviner hide his misdeeds, it is clear that the diviner's visual abilities extended far beyond plain sight. The diviner may have acquired extraordinary vision simply through his embodiment of the deity or with the aid of other ritual activities or paraphernalia, such as the *tlachiyaloni* (vision apparatus; see Figure 5.4). Much like humans who embodied deities, material *teixiptlahuan* acquired vision through the reflective quality of their (mirror) eyes.

Mesoamericans heightened the visual exchange between material *teixipt-lahuan* and devotees by placing highly valued reflective materials, including obsidian and iron pyrite, in the eye sockets of *teixiptlahuan*. The Aztecs recognized several varieties of *itztli* (obsidian) and *tezcatl* (mirror stone), both of which varied in color and use.[45] In *Book 11*, the scribes group the obsidians together with *teotetl* (jet) and *eztetl* (bloodstone) and characterize them as sharp blades and precious earspools that range in color from black and white to blue-green. According to Nicholas Saunders, obsidian derived its significance from a cross-cultural complex of brilliance: "Spiritual essence, manifested as brilliance, inhered in the celestial bodies, meteorological phenomena, fire, water, metals, minerals, shells, ceramics, feathers, bone, blood, and semen, amongst other things. Despite a multiplicity of individual significances, all revealed their inner sacredness by displaying light as surface glitter."[46] His argument that brilliance revealed sacredness reflects a tendency to divide outer appearance from inner essence that we have seen elsewhere, but the Aztecs clearly appreciated sparkling objects. As with obsidian, they associated *tezcatl* (mirror stone; magnetite) with other shiny or fiery stones native to Mesoamerica, including *tecpatl* (flint), *chopilotl* (hanging tears; crystal), and *huitzitziltetl* (hummingbird stone; opal), in addition to a variety of seashells. The Aztecs used these naturally occurring objects to increase the brilliance and value of ritual and luxury items:

> Material culture objectified these values at the same time as re-combining them into something new. . . . Making shiny objects was an act of transformative creation, converting—in a sense re-cycling— the fertilizing energy of light into brilliant solid forms via technological choices whose efficacy stemmed from a synergy of myth, ritual knowledge and individual technical skill. In this way, significance and meaning were given to the production, exchange and ritual display of brilliant objects.[47]

Polished obsidian and iron pyrite appear in the pupils of manufactured *teixiptlahuan* recovered by archaeologists; the mirror-eyes of a *teixiptla* and the light they caught took on a particularly powerful and enlivening cultural potency.

The reflective quality of a *teixiptla*'s mirror-eyes facilitated its animation, because the light-catching eyes enabled the embodied *teotl* to see his or her devotee and reflect the devotee's gaze. Gell argues that the eyes are a natural site for the location of animacy because "even if one does not take a mystical attitude towards images, one is none the less entitled to apply action verbs like 'look' (or 'smile', 'gesticulate', etc.) to them," and he cites as an example a non-believer, who he claims "is obliged to say, that an idol 'looks' in a particular direction; the remark would pass unnoticed because everybody accepts that the criterion for idols 'looking' is that their eyes should be open and pointed in a particular direction."[48] This observation is as applicable to the devotee, who would say the embodiment is animate, as it is to the skeptic, who would deny the idol's animacy. Gell's contention—that so long as the *teixiptla* has eyes, it "sees"—seems reasonable enough. But the extensive and intentional use of reflective materials in the construction of Aztec *teixiptlahuan* reveals a more complex cosmological relationship between the deity, the devotee, and the elements used in the *teixiptla*'s construction.

Colonial-era manuscripts, including the Tovar Calendar and Bernal Díaz del Castillo's *History*, contain descriptions of the elaborate and sparkling inlays that adorned prominent *teixiptlahuan*. In his description of the sacred precinct of Tlatelolco, Díaz del Castillo remembers the impression two grandiose *teixiptlahuan* made on him, one of Huitzilopochtli and another of Tezcatlipoca, both of which stood covered in precious stones:

> There were two altars. . . . On each altar were two figures, like giants with very tall bodies and very fat, and the first which stood on the right hand they said was the figure of Huichilobos their god of War; it had a very broad face and monstrous and terrible eyes, and the whole of his body was covered with precious stones, and gold and pearls, and with seed pearls stuck on with a paste . . . and in one hand he held a bow and in the other some arrows. . . . Then we saw on the other side on the left hand there stood the other great image the same height as Huichilobos, and it had a face like a bear and eyes that shone, made of their mirrors which they call Tezcat, and the body plastered with precious stones like Huichilobos, for they say that the two are brothers; and this Tezcatlipuca was the god of Hell and had charge of the souls of the Mexicans."[49]

The striking quality of these figures' eyes—and the remarkable use of mirrors among the dazzling display of other precious stones—underscores their importance. This description also calls our attention to the effect of layering a precious stone skin on the statue's subcutaneous structure: the stones' reflective surfaces caught the light and dazzled the onlooker. The fact that only after a lengthy description of these statues and others near them did Bernal Díaz del Castillo turn his attention to the temple's blood-soaked walls gives us a sense of the extent to which they captivated him.

The Tovar Calendar, a late-sixteenth-century manuscript compiled by Jesuit Juan de Tovar, also contains a description of a *teotl* venerated during Toxcatl whose *teixiptla* had a dough body and mirror-eyes. This passage indicates that the *teixiptla*'s face was like that of the "great idol" and that his eyes were valued so highly that they were protected in the temple when not in use:

> Hazian de diursas semillas de la tierra una masa y conella formavan vn rrostro qe era del gran ydolo en la forma esta encima de las armas, ponianle por ojos dos espejos q siempre estatua guardados en el templo alos quales llamauan los ojos de dios y assi quando los antiguos vieron alos españoles conantojos dezian q tenian los ojos desu dios vitzilopuchtli, ponian en este tiempo el rrostro y armas del ydolo ante elpueblo para significar queel sor todopoderoso cuyas eran aquellas insignias tenia el poder para dalles buen año, y assi se lo pedian congrandes rruegos y sacriff(icios) todo este mes.

> They made a dough from different cultivated seeds and with it they formed a face like the great idol in the form that was above the arms, and they placed two mirrors—called "the eyes of god"—as eyes and the statue was always guarded in the temple. And when the ancients saw the Spaniards with eyeglasses, they said that they had the eyes of their god Huitzilopochtli. At this time, they set the face and arms of the idol before the community to show that the all powerful one, whose insignia these were, had the power to give them a good year, and thus it was petitioned with great prayers and sacrifices all month.[50]

It seems likely that these mirrors belonged to the *teotl*—that they were part of his *axcaitl* (possessions, property)—and that they may have been kept inside his *tlaquimilolli* (sacred bundle), an idea we will consider later. As for how *teixiptlahuan* used their mirror-eyes to see, we might imagine, as have scholars working elsewhere in Mesoamerica, that the Aztecs incorporated an eye-opening ritual into the *teixiptla*'s manufacture.

An Eye-Opening Comparison

Limited evidence regarding eye-opening ceremonies exists in Mesoamerica, perhaps in part because of the secrecy that surrounded the construction of deity embodiments. Several sources document the manufacture of *teixiptlahuan* in and around the Central Valley, but similar practices may have been

4.5. Eye-opening ceremony.
Codex Fejérváry-Mayer, 23.
Line drawing by author.

less public in other areas. Diego de Landa describes the creation of a wooden image by Maya priests during the month of Mol as taking place behind closed doors: "The priests and sculptors shut themselves in the hut and began work on the gods, during which time they frequently cut their ears and anointed with the blood those devils and also burned incense before them. They continued in this manner until the idols were complete."[51] Yet, Houston, Stuart, and Taube point to inscriptions like those on Stela 3 at Machaquila, Guatemala, as indications that the Maya might have practiced an animation ceremony focused on the eyes. The stela "ends in an impersonal expression: *ila-aj / k'al-tuun / na-ho-tuun*, 'it is seen / wrapped [dedicated] stone / fifth stone'. In another publication, we argued that this refers to the first reading of the text, but it may also suggest that *the sight of the monument, probably by the ruler himself,* vitalizes and consecrates it to service as a royal representation."[52] Additionally, Ferdinand Anders and Maarten Jansen interpret a sequence of images in the *Codex Fejérváry-Mayer* as an eye-opening ceremony, and Boone identifies it as an element in the birth almanac:

[These scenes] very likely pertain to the painful action of birth, when the child comes into the world as a living, breathing human. The codices represent this by picturing a deity piercing the eye socket (occasionally another part) of an infant, who is represented by either a diminutive figure or only a head. This enigmatic imagery might seem unrelated or even antithetical to birth, but it surely should be read metaphorically. . . . The piercing in the Mexican almanacs may well refer to the Aztec understanding that humans were animated by having been breathed and bored by the creator couple.[53]

None of these instances provide us with much more than the suggestion that an eye-opening ceremony may have existed in Mesoamerica. However, comparative examples, such as those from the Hindu tradition, aid us in envisioning how the emplacement or opening of the *teixiptla*'s eyes may have contributed to the *teotl*'s animation.[54]

In the Hindu ceremony for the establishment (*pratiṣṭhā*) of a sculpted anthropomorphic image, the opening of the eyes (*unmīlana*) is the final stage of its creation. For the artisan, the creation of a *mūrti* (an embodiment, incarnation, manifestation) is an act of worship, and throughout the *mūrti*'s manufacture the sculptor follows scriptural guidelines regarding iconography and physical proportions. Then as the artisan releases the *mūrti*—a bronze sculpture, for instance—from its mold, "the priest immediately subjects this to further mantra recitations identifying the bronze with the deity who is to inhabit it. There is never a time when the image exists as an unconsecrated object; its very coming into being is within ritual."[55] Following the priest's recitations, the *mūrti*'s establishment culminates when the priest and artisan open its eyes and dress it:

> The priest uses a golden needle to draw on the outlines of Śiva's three eyes. The sculptor then opens the eyes with a diamond needle and opens the other apertures as well with a chisel. The priest rubs the eyes of the image with unguents and displays before it a series of highly auspicious objects: ghee, a pot of honey, heaps of grain, brahmans reciting praises, virgins in full decoration, and the assembled crowd of devotees. The priest immediately washes and purifies the image with clay, ashes, cowdung, and other substances, and then dresses it in clean clothes and adorns it with all suitable ornaments. Temple servants take the image on a palanquin and circumambulate the village. By this point the image has clearly reached an initial stage of livelihood, where it can see objects placed before it and is worthy of going in procession among its community of worshippers.[56]

The act of painting the image's eyes and opening them with a needle establishes the image's *prāṇa* (life breath). Diana Eck observes that the placement and opening of eyes continue to be regular practices in the consecration of Hindu images. She also emphasizes the potency of the deity's vision when his or her eyes first open: "The gaze which falls from the newly-opened eyes of the deity is said to be so powerful that it must first fall upon some pleasing offering, such as sweets, or upon a mirror where it may see its own reflection. More than once has the tale been told of that powerful gaze falling upon some unwitting bystander, who died instantly of its force."[57] The deity's vision fully consumes whatever it sees: something lovely and sweet, the deity's own reflection, or some unfortunate onlooker. Of the protective measures—providing something delightful for the deity to see or placing a mirror before the god—the second produces an infinite exchange of self-reflection as the god sees herself seeing herself. By "opening" the image's eyes, the artisan endows the Hindu *mūrti* with divine force; likewise, the addition of naturalistic eyes to Aztec *teixiptlahuan* invested them with lifelike animation.

Ritual animation, like the opening of a *mūrti*'s eyes or the emplacement of a *teixiptla*'s eyes, endowed the embodiment with life, but not biological life. Contrasting the animacy of embodiments with the liveliness of inanimate automata and the biological life of the animal world clarifies the meaning of ritual animacy. Automata mime life without actually partaking in it, and so they look alive without ever being alive.[58] Animals experience the fullness of biological animacy. Occupying a vital space somewhere between automata and animals (but seemingly closer to animals than automata), vibrant matter, "nonhuman or not-quite-human things" that have "distinctive capacities or efficacious powers," describes a class of stuff that acts in the world but has neither biological life nor divine inspiration.[59] Vital matter is "alive" by virtue of its material composition.

Teixiptlahuan and other animate deity embodiments participate in the life-world of their devotees by virtue of their material composition *and* because of their devotees, who endow them with animacy through social interactions: "Idols may be animate without, in other words, being endowed with animal life or activity. . . . It follows that 'ritual' animacy and the possession of 'life' in a biological sense are far from the same thing."[60] *Teixiptlahuan* lived in the social world of their devotees, and their animation occurred through rituals that recognized the vitality of their material assemblies and transformed them into the localized embodiments of *teteo*.[61]

Durán shares two stunning accounts of *teixiptlahuan* whose eyes endowed them with animacy. He recounts "a strange ceremony" that took place near Huitzilopochtli's temple and the *tzompantli* (skull racks) in Tenochtitlan's ceremonial center prior to the sacrifice of human victims. The ceremony began when a priest removed a *tzoalli* (amaranth) dough *teixiptla* from the temple, which facilitated visual exchanges between the *teotl* and his or her devotees:

> Desta massa traya este sacerdote hecho un ydolo con los ojos de unas cuentecelas berdes y los dientes de granos de maiz y baxaba con toda la priessa que podia por las gradas del templo abajo y subia por encima de una gran piedra . . . abracado con su ydolo subia á donde estavan los que havian de sacrificiar y desde uncanto asta otro yba mostrandoles aquel ydolo á cada uno en particular y diciendoles este es buestro dios.

> The priest brought down an idol made of this dough. Its eyes were small green beads, and its teeth were grains of corn. [The priest] descended the steps of the temple as swiftly as possible and climbed to the top of a great stone. . . . Still embracing the image, he ascended to the place where those who were to be sacrificed stood, and from one end to the other he went along showing the figure to each one saying, "Behold your god!"[62]

As the sacrificial victims stood staring into the beady-green eyes of the *tzoalli teixiptla*, the grinning god held their attention. Although no *teixiptlahuan* made from materials as temporary (and consumable) as *tzoalli*, maize, and small beads remain, a few three-dimensional *teixiptlahuan* identified as Huitzilopochtli attest to the importance of a *teotl*'s eyes. It takes little imagination to envision the inlays of white shell conjunctiva and black obsidian pupils that once adorned the eyes of a greenstone statuette in the collection of the Musée du Quai Branly, Paris (Figure 4.6). Perhaps they looked like those of the mask of Tezcatlipoca in the British Museum's collection, the standard bearer identified as Xiuhtecuhtli-Huitzilopochtli, or the skull masks in Templo Mayor caches (see Figure 3.5).

In addition to his description of Huitzilopochtli's *tzoalli teixiptla*, Durán also describes a series of *tzoalli teixiptlahuan* that represented *teteo* present in the mountains that encircled Tenochtitlan. His account of the *teixiptlahuan* created during the feast dedicated to the volcano Popocatepetl is one of the most expressive as to the role of eyes and mouth in the manufacture and animation of Aztec deity embodiments. The *tzoalli* dough mountains receive eyes, mouths, and names:

> Conviene á saber que llegado el dia solmne de la beneracion de este cerro toda la multitud de la gente que en la tierra había se ocupaba en

4.6. Anthropomorphic figure of a divinity (Huitzilopochtli). Aztec, jadeite. Courtesy of Musée du Quai Branly / Scala / Art Resource, NY.

moler semilla de bledos y maiz y de aquella masa hacer un cerro que representaba el volcan al cual ponían sus ojos y su boca y le ponían en un preminente lugar de la casa y al rededor de él ponían otros muchos serrillos de la misma masa de tzoalli con sus ojos y bocas los cuales todos tenían sus nombres que era el uno Tlaloc y el otro Chicomecoatl y á Itzactepetl y Amatlalcueye y juntamente á Chalchiuhtlyicue que era la diosa de los rios y fuentes que este volcan salían y a Cihuacoatl. Todos estos ceros ponían este día al rededor del volcan todos hechos de masa con sus caras los cuales así puestos en órden dos días arreo les ofrecían ofrendas y hacían algunas ceremonias donde el Segundo día les ponían unas mitras de papel y unos San Benitos de papel pintados donde despues de vestida aquella masa con la mesma solemnidad que mataban y sacrificaban índios que representaban los dioses de la mesma manera sacrificaban esta masa que habían representado los ceros donde despues de hecha la ceremonia se la comian con mucha reverencia.

When the solemn day of the feast of this hill [Popocatepetl] arrived a great multitude of people from the locality dedicated themselves to the grinding of amaranth seed and maize kernels, and with that dough they formed a hill representing the volcano. They gave him eyes, his mouth, and they placed him in an honored spot in the home. And around him were set many smaller hills of the same amaranth-seed dough, each with its eyes and mouth, each one possessing its own name: one, Tlaloc; another, Chicomecoatl, or Itzactepetl; Matlalcueye; together with Cihuacoatl and Chalchihuitlicue, the latter the goddess of rivers and springs which flowed from this volcano. On this day all these hills were placed around the [dough] volcano, each made of dough with its face. [They were] thus placed in order and left for two days [and] offerings and ceremonies were made to them. On the second day they were crowned with paper miters and sleeveless tunics of painted paper. After the dough had been dressed with the same solemnity customary in slaying and sacrificing the men who represented the gods, the dough representing the hills was sacrificed in the same way. The ceremony concluded, this dough was eaten as a sacred thing.[63]

Through the process of their ritual manufacture, ordinary grains became vital *teixiptlahuan* who had faces, names, and insignia. Durán repeatedly emphasizes the importance of the *teixiptlahuan*'s faces and facial features. Initially the *teixiptlahuan* represented mountains. With the addition of eyes and a mouth, they acquired *teteo*'s names, and finally their clothing—paper miters and sleeveless tunics—completed their transformation into sacrificial victims. Human hands brought these *teixiptlahuan* into the social world where they received individual names and appearances that facilitated their recognition and veneration. Durán carefully notes the "same solemnity" with which the priests attended both the *tzoalli* and human *teixiptlahuan*, suggesting that the Aztecs did not (and so today no one should) value one type of embodiment more than another. Heeding this advice, I turn to other artifacts that appear to have been animated through their ritual manufacture.

The Face of *Teotl*

Although the details of material *teixiptlahuan*'s animation may be irrecoverable, the acquisition of eyes and a mouth clearly played a significant role in the animation of earthly things. So far, I have drawn our attention to embodiments' eyes. If instead of comparing the Hindu eye-opening ceremony, we explored the Egyptian mouth-opening ceremony, we could focus our attention on the embodiments' toothy mouths. This comparison could prove equally profitable, especially if it were to link animacy, mouths, breath, and the inges-

4.7. Animate *tecpame*. Museo del Templo Mayor. Photograph by author.

tion of blood. *Tecpame*, flint knives uncovered in Templo Mayor excavations, underscore the importance of both eyes and mouths.

According to López Austin and López Luján, Templo Mayor archaeologists have recovered more than a thousand *tecpame*, flint knives "lanceolated with an acute point to penetrate the body before cutting out the heart," from the sacred precinct.[64] Significantly for us, they have recovered *tecpame* in two forms: some *tecpame* have faces with eyes and mouths, while others do not. Like the *tzoalli* mountains, *tecpame* may have been animated through the ritual process of their material manufacture.

The Mexicas buried two types of *tecpame* at the Templo Mayor: ordinary *tecpame*, like the ones used as sacrificial knives, and extraordinary *tecpame* adorned with wide-eyed, tooth-bearing faces (see Figures 3.5 and 4.7). Both types occur in caches with other penitential instruments, including bone bloodletters, manta ray spines, maguey spines, and obsidian blades.[65] Furthermore, Leonardo López Luján indicates that extraordinary *tecpame* have been recovered exclusively from Mexica caches:

> The Mexica offerings show certain innovations that give them a character of their own. Differing from the offerings of other regions and times, those deposited in Tenochtitlan and several other Mexica sites included

flint sacrificial knives, standardized statues of deities, stone containers, stone masks, divine insignia (scepters, earspools, noseplugs, and breast-plates), miniatures (of houses, braziers, canoes, tools, and musical in-struments), copper bells, and marine sand.[66]

In *The Offerings of the Templo Mayor of Tenochtitlan*, López Luján classifies personified *tecpame* as "deity images," along with skull masks, images of spe-cific deities, anthropomorphic masks and figures, deities made of copal, and deities portrayed on containers. In contrast, he groups sacrificial *tecpatl* along with other instruments of auto-sacrifice, animal sacrifice, and human sacri-fice.[67] This classification suggests that López Luján, too, suspects that the dec-orated *tecpame* were perceived differently from the unadorned flints. The co-occurrence of ordinary and extraordinary *tecpame* indicates that the knives served different purposes: "It is clear that the [adorned] knives were never used in actual sacrifices. It is more likely they were the personified symbols of the sacrificial instrument."[68] Furthermore, "other undecorated flint sacrifi-cial knives (*ixcuac*) were found near the remains of the beheaded. Their posi-tion and the lack of decoration suggest that these knives were used to kill the individuals buried in those offerings."[69] Significantly, the eyes, which repeat-edly feature a white shell conjunctiva inlayed with an obsidian pupil, are the most standardized element of the flints' animating features. The addition of the eyes, teeth, and eyebrows that compose the facial features of animate *tec-pame* transformed them from ordinary sacrificial knives into the *teixiptla-huan* of *teteo*.

The question of which *teotl* (or *teteo*) the *tecpame* embodied naturally fol-lows this description. *Tecpame* had a direct hand—or, perhaps better, mouth—in the sacrifice of human victims, including the *teixiptlahuan* of some *teteo*, and so they may embody any of a number of *teteo* involved in sacrifice. Giv-en their use in heart sacrifice, the *tecpame* must have shared a taste for blood with the other *teteo* associated with ritual sacrifice and death, including Mict-lan Tecuhtli, Mictecacihuatl, Tezcatlipoca, Itztli, Itzpapalotl, and Ixquimilli-Itztlacoliuhqui. However, it seems difficult, if not impossible, to identify the *tecpame* with any single *teotl*. Their appearances are too indistinct and too uniform to be defined so narrowly. Following the model of Tlaloc's relation-ship with the *tlaloque*, the "little Tlalocs" who looked like Tlaloc and assist-ed him in rainmaking, the *tecpame* could be the "distributed persons" of a death deity. Given their shape, sharpness, and use, they call to mind a *teotl*'s teeth. The prominence of teeth on adorned *tecpame* might support such an interpretation.

Extrapolating from the examples of dough mountain and flint *teixiptla-huan*, we may envision the ritual manufacture of other materials—carved wood, shaped stone, and molded clay, for instance—exiting the realm of ordinary things as they received eyes, faces, and names. Like human *teixiptlahuan*, these deity embodiments moved through the ritual landscape. Material *teixiptlahuan*, including those made of *tzoalli*, stone, wood, and ceramics, were periodically taken from their temples and paraded throughout the ceremonial precinct and Tenochtitlan: "It is crucial to emphasize that in the cosmomagical world of the Aztecs, these images often move and are alive with divine force, participate in ritual as much as humans do, and also (in various ways) see, hear, speak, taste, and touch the social world."[70] Earlier we saw that the priest carrying Huitzilopochtli's *tzoalli teixiptla* turned the deity's face toward each sacrificial victim. The priest and the *teotl* demanded face-to-face recognition: "Behold your god!" Drawing on the Hindu practice of *darśan*, the exchange of sight between a deity and a devotee, Gell argues that "union comes from eye contact. . . . The eyes of the god, which gaze at the devotee, mirror the action of the devotee, who gazes at the god."[71] The eyes invite the devotee to attribute interiority, agency, and intention to the *teixiptla*.[72] The play between attribution and expectation reaches a more acute realization in the *teteo* embodied by human *teixiptlahuan*.

Tezcatlipoca's Toxcatl *Teixiptla*

Teixiptla's connotations of eye, face, and surface lead us into a semantic field related to appearance. It was through a ritual process that resulted in appearing like the god—physically and behaviorally—that an effigy embodied Tezcatlipoca, Toci, or Xipe Totec. In other words, when a ritual actor donned the flayed skin of a sacrificial victim or the attire of a *teotl*, that person underwent a major ontological transformation from human to deity embodiment. Wearing the skin and participating in ritual activities brought about the god's localized embodiment in a living (formerly human?) body. Materially, mythohistorically, and linguistically, *teixiptla* literally tied flayed skins to god-bodies (see Figure 4.1).

Descriptions of these rituals and depictions of *teteo* in material culture and in the *tonalpohualli* (divinatory texts) corroborate the notion that specific sets of qualities clustered around particular *teteo*. These qualities both defined their personae and rendered them identifiable. In addition to the *teixiptla*'s ability to see and be seen, a *teixiptla* must also have acted and looked like the *teotl* it represented. Ritual accounts in the *Florentine Codex* describe human *teixiptlahuan*'s initiation through specific bodily and behavioral conditioning. In order for a *teixiptla* to be animate, that is, to participate in the social relationships devotees built around it, its body and behavior had to conform to the devotees' expectations—expectations that derived from their prior knowledge of and experiences with the *teotl*.

In the absence of flayed skins, human *teixiptlahuan*'s physical and behavioral conditioning functioned as ritual analogues to the assembly of material *teixiptlahuan*. Toxcatl, a month-long veneration of Tezcatlipoca (Smoking Mirror), is one of the many calendric rituals during which humans came to be the *teixiptlahuan* of *teteo*. Other festivals, like Tlacaxipehualiztli (Feast of the Flaying of Men), which focused on Xipe Totec (Flaying Lord), involved human sacrifice, skin flaying, and the wearing of skins by ritual actors. No skins were worn during Toxcatl, however, and my intention in discussing this festival is to call our attention to the marking of flesh as *the first step*, but not the only one, in transforming a human body into a god-body.

First, the prisoner of war who was to be the *teixiptla* of Tezcatlipoca during Toxcatl was selected:

> in aquin pepenaloia, in teixiptla, atle iyahyoca: iuhquin tlachictli, iuhquin tomatl, iuhquin telolotli, iuhquin quauitl tlaxixintli, amo quacocototztic, quacolochtic, huel tzomelahuac, tzompiaztic, amo ixquachachaquachtic, amo ixquatotomonqui . . . amo ixhuihuilaxtic, amo canhuihuilaxtic, amo ixpopotztic . . . amo tenmimicqui, amo tlanpantic, amo tlancuicuitztic, amo coatlani.

> He who was chosen as the localized embodiment was without defects. He was like something smoothed, like a tomato, like a pebble, as if sculptured in wood; he was not curly-haired, curly-headed; his hair was indeed straight, his hair was long. He was not rough of forehead; he had no pimples on his forehead . . . he was not mute, he was not of injured eyes; he was not of injured cheeks; he was not bulging of eye . . . he was not buck-toothed, he was not large-toothed, he was not fang-toothed.[73]

The description of how the person should look occupies an entire page, approximately one-tenth of the text dedicated to this month-long ceremony. In rhythmically repetitive Nahuatl, it describes the appropriate appearance of more than a dozen physical features requisite for Tezcatlipoca's *teixiptla*, including his face, forehead, hands, fingers, abdomen, and buttocks. The passage's length and level of detail give us a sense of how important the *teixiptla* candidate's appearance was in his selection. It also helps us understand what it meant for the candidate to be "without defects."[74] Note, too, that these presentational attributes *merely qualified* an individual to become Tezcatlipoca's *teixiptla*, a process that involved elaborate training and further transformation:

> For him who was thus, who had no flaw . . . there was taken the greatest care that he be taught to blow the flute, that he be able to play his whistle; and that at the same time he hold all his flowers and his smoking tube. . . . [V]ery great care was taken that he should be very circumspect in his discourse, that he talk graciously, that he greet people agreeably on the road if he met anyone. For he was indeed much honored when he appeared, when already he was a *teixiptla*.[75]

As we have seen, other accounts describe the materials that Aztec priests used to construct dough *teixiptlahuan* being submitted to similarly exacting standards. Seeing these standards as qualitative expectations facilitates our understanding of how a particular *teotl* came to be (in) his *teixiptla(huan)*. The description of the "perfect" candidate for Tezcatlipoca's *teixiptla* draws our attention to the significance of the body's physical form and representative ability (e.g., that the candidate not be mute), while the description and depiction of the candidate's training underscores the extent to which embodying the god involved more than physical appearance.

After finding the perfect candidate, the priests submitted him to extensive physical alteration and exacting ornamentation. The *teixiptla* spent a year receiving instruction concerning Tezcatlipoca's diction and musical abilities: "There was taken the greatest care that he be taught to blow the flute, that he be able to play his whistle; and that at the same time he hold all his flowers and his smoking tube. . . . Very great care was taken that he should be very circumspect in his discourse, that he talk graciously, that he greet people agreeably on the road if he met anyone."[76] The emphasis placed on the *teixiptla*'s appearance, both in his candidacy and throughout his training, reached its epitome when he met Moteuczoma.

At a critical point in the ritual, priests cut the *teixiptla*'s hair, and he presented himself to Moteuczoma, who "repeatedly adorned him; he gave him gifts; he arrayed him; he arrayed him with great pomp. He had all costly things placed on him, for verily he took him to be *itlazoteouh* (his beloved god)."[77] Recall that Moteuczoma's *itonal* (day sign) required that he dress the *teixiptla* with his own *tlazohca* (beloved) *axcaitl* (possessions, property) and *neixcahuilli* (exclusive things). Sahagún describes the *teixiptla*'s luxurious dress at length: he wore a flower crown, turquoise earplugs, a shell necklace, a sea-shell breastplate, an exquisite breechclout, and golden bell anklets.[78] As the year drew to a close and the subsequent Toxcatl approached, the *teixiptla* underwent another transformation: he began to dress and perform like an ascetic priest. The embodiment of Tezcatlipoca culminated in the *teixiptla*'s sacrifice, and then the festival of Toxcatl continued with the selection of a new *teixiptla*.[79]

Toxcatl foregrounds the significance of the human body in the selection of a perfect candidate for transformation into a *teotl*'s *teixiptla*. As Carrasco observes of the festival, "The image of Tezcatlipoca was alive, not only in the sense that a human being was the public image, but also in the changes he underwent at different stages of the year-long ceremony. The ideal person who started the ceremony was changed into the cultural paragon of Aztec society."[80] The priests selected, trained, and dressed a perfect candidate for the express purpose of manufacturing a *teixiptla* of Tezcatlipoca. The people of Tenochtitlan expected Tezcatlipoca's *teixiptla* to look and act like the one before him and the one before that (and so on), and they reacted to his appearance with solemn displays of veneration: "There was the assigning of lordship; he was importuned; he was sighed for; there was bowing before him; the commoners performed the earth-eating ceremony before him."[81]

Additionally, they expected Tezcatlipoca's human *teixiptla* to resemble his material *teixiptlahuan*. Tezcatlipoca's material localized embodiments included black stone and wooden statues adorned with golden earplugs, crystal labrets with blue-green feathers, and golden bracelets. In their left hands, the material *teixiptla* held "a fan of precious feathers, blue, green and yellow . . . [that emerge from] a round plate of gold, shining and brilliant, polished like a mirror. This [mirror] indicated that Tezcatlipoca could see all that took place in the world with that reflection."[82] The ritual manufacture of Tezcatlipoca's material *teixiptlahuan* and the ritual transformation of his human *teixiptla* facilitated his animation. Devotees recognized Tezcatlipoca's *teixiptlahuan* by their appearance, actions, and accoutrements, and Tezcatlipoca's ability to see—whether through obsidian or human eyes—and be seen seeing rendered his *teixiptla(huan)* believable.

Conclusions

As localized embodiments of *teteo*, *teixiptlahuan* met particular religious needs: they facilitated intimacy between deities and their devotees at the level of sensory experience and served as nexus points between levels of existence in the natural (material and physical) world and the metaphysical world. Like Hindus who give and take *darśan*, a potent visual exchange between the deity and devotee, the Aztecs experienced their *teixiptlahuan* as animate at least in part because of the *teixiptlahuan's* ability to see and be seen.[83] Given the use of mirror-eyes in the material *teixiptlahuan* made by the Aztecs, Gell's explanation of what transpires between the Hindu deity and devotee may more literally describe *teteo* and their devotees:

> What the devotee sees is the idol looking at him or her, performing an act of looking, mirroring his or her own. It is not mysticism on the devotee's part which results in the practical inference that the image "sees" the devotee, because we only ever know what other persons are seeing by knowing what they are looking at. . . . The devotee looks and sees. The image-as-mirror is doing what the devotee is doing, therefore, the image also looks and sees.[84]

Similar visual exchanges surely took place between Aztec devotees and the *teixiptlahuan* of their *teteo*. In a stunning account, Durán recounts the horrific appearance of a mirror-eyed *teixiptla* during the *tlahtoani* Tizoc's funeral:

> The King and Lord of the Underworld [was] dressed like a diabolical creature. In place of eyes he wore shining mirrors; his mouth was huge and fierce; his hair was curled; he had two hideous horns; and on each shoulder he wore a mask with mirror eyes. On each elbow there was one of these faces, on his abdomen another, and on his knees still other faces with eyes. With the shining of the mirrors that represented eyes on all these parts, it looked as if he could see in every direction. He was so hideous, so abominable, that no one dared look at him out of fear.[85]

The reflective quality of this *teixiptla's* many eyes clearly inspires fear—perhaps, even, a *mahuiztic* fear out of respect. Once open, the lifelike eyes of *teixiptlahuan* endowed them with an awesome vitality.

The visual exchanges devotees made with their deities reflect just one mode of sensory interaction they experienced. Devotees touched the *teteo* who processed through Tenochtitlan, and they gave their gods flowers. Grasping for a memento, they pulled off pieces of Xipe Totec's skin. Prostrating themselves before other *teteo*, they ate dirt in an act of supplication, all because "he was *mahuiztililoya* (greatly esteemed) when he appeared before the people; already he was a *teixiptla*."[86] As we have seen in other contexts, devotees carefully crafted *tzoalli teixiptlahuan* of mountains; transformed them into the *teixiptlahuan* of *teteo* by giving them eyes, mouths, and names; and then dressed them for sacrifice—much like Moteuczoma did for Tezcatlipoca's *teixiptla*. The care ritual participants took when crafting the *teixiptlahuan* of *teteo* reflects their desire, as devotees, for verisimilitude, but more importantly, their attentiveness to ceremony reflects their understanding of *teteo* as *mahuiztic* (esteemed) and *tlazohca* (beloved).

CHAPTER 5

Wrapped in Cloth, Clothed in Skins

Aztec *Tlaquimilolli* (Sacred Bundles) and Deity Embodiment

>>> They burned the temple of the Cuitlahuaca, which was a house of the devil Mixcoatl. And on this occasion Yaocuixtli of Mexicatzinco was the first to rush to the top of the Mixcoatl, seizing the ashes of Itzpapalotl—what was called the bundle, etc. [The ashes] were contained in two [lengths of] quetzal bamboo. Then Tenochtitlan's Citlalcoatzin and Iquehuatzin and Axicyotzin and Tenamaztzin spoke to Texoxomoctli: "O Texoxomoctzin," they said, "Mixcoatl the younger was burned, for you failed to pick up your shield and arrows. Now, there's this: Where did you put Mixcoatl? We must take him away. Give him to us."[1]

During the reign of Moteuczoma Ilhuicamina (ca. 1440–1469), the Aztecs waged war on the Cuitlahuacas under the pretext of returning a third group, the Atenchicalque, to their homeland. During the battle, Yaocuixtli of Mexicatzinco ran into the burning temple of the deity Mixcoatl to rescue the goddess Itzpapalotl's *tlaquimilolli* (something wrapped or bundled; sacred bundle). As the temple burned, Moteuczoma's representatives initiated an exchange with Texoxomoctzin in which they demanded that the ruler hand over the *teixiptla* (localized embodiment) of Mixcoatl. Texoxomoctzin directed his reply toward the story's audience as much as to the Aztecs standing before him. He explained that relinquishing the god would compromise his people's future. Unwilling to take such a risk, he tricked the Aztecs. Instead of giving them Mixcoatl, he handed over another *teixiptla*, that of Teuhcatl:

> It was not really the image of the so-called Camaxtle Mixcoatl. It was just the one named Teohcatl [*sic*]. It had the same costume as Mixcoatl, and this is what the Mexica took it for, thinking it was he. Thus the Mexica were deceived.[2]

Narrative digressions like this one punctuate the "Anales de Cuauhtitlan," which chronicles the reigns of Tenochtitlan's rulers, and Texoxomoctzin's clever ruse is clearly the point of this elaboration. The text draws us into the thrill of the battle and the capture of "Mixcoatl," and it would be easy for us to overlook an earlier event in the story: the rescue of Itzpapalotl's *tlaquimilolli* from Mixcoatl's temple. Yet the rescue's prominent place—first in the narrative—and the details surrounding it—the name of the bundle's owner, the identity of its rescuer, the materials of its construction, and their quantity— call our attention to the importance of *tlaquimilolli* in Aztec religion.

In his *Historia eclesiástica indiana* written in the late sixteenth century and published nearly two centuries later, Gerónimo de Mendieta cites an observation about *tlaquimilolli* made by his Franciscan colleague Andrés de Olmos. The *tlaquimilolli* was, Olmos explained, the "principal ídolo que tenían en mucha reverencia, y no tenían en tanta como a este a los bestiones o figuras de piedra o de palo que ellos hacían" (main idol, greatly revered [by them], so that they did not esteem as much as this one those large beasts or stone figures that they manufactured).[3] The centrality of *tlaquimilolli* in Aztec religion—and in indigenous American religions more generally—would be difficult to overstate. Curiously, though perhaps not surprisingly, their significance seems inversely proportionate to the amount we know about them. As sacred bundle expert Guilhem Olivier has noted, "Their study is difficult, partly because of the secret character of the rituals devoted to them [and partly because of] the discretion of indigenous informants."[4] Observations like this make even the briefest mention of a *tlaquimilolli*—like the one in the "Anales"—all the more significant. The rescue of Itzpapalotl's *tlaquimilolli* from Mixcoatl's temple raises questions we will pursue in the following pages: What were *tlaquimilolli*? What do we know about their origins? From what were they made? To whom did they belong? What purposes did they serve? And, ultimately, how did they relate to *teteo* (deities) and their *teixiptlahuan* (localized embodiments)?

According to the accounts we will examine, each *tlaquimilolli* enveloped the precious relics of an entity who had been instrumental in primordial progenitive events and actions, such as the first dawn.[5] It bound together the physical remains and *axcaitl* (property, possessions) of the *teteo* whose self-sacrifice animated the world. Additionally, the bundles were themselves active agents in the mythohistory of Mexica and Mixtec migrations from their places of origins through settlements and foundation. In fact, migration accounts—both pictorial and alphabetic—provide some of the richest sources for information about *tlaquimilolli*. In addition to the mythohistorical records of bundles' origins and their roles in migration and settlement, we find *tlaquimilolli* in the texts and images of several codices and post-Contact chronicles, including Bernardino de Sahagún's *Primeros memoriales* and *Florentine Codex*, Gerónimo de Mendieta's *Historia*, Fernando Chimalpahin's *Codex Chimalpopoca*/Alvarado Tezozómoc's *Crónica mexicana*, the anonymous *Historia de los mexicanos por sus pinturas*, and the *Codex Boturini*.[6]

While the word *tlaquimilolli* in its sense as "sacred bundle" occurs only

5.1. *Teomamaque* (god-carriers). *Codex Boturini*, 2. Line drawing by author.

once in Sahagún's *Florentine Codex*—"niman ic yaque, in teomamaque, in quimilli, in tlaquimilolli quitqui." (Thereupon the god-carriers departed; they carried him wrapped in a bundle, in a sacred bundle.)[7]—*tlaquimilolli* appear several times in the text's illustrations (Figure 5.1). What we can discern about *tlaquimilolli* derives from their representations in codices, their descriptions in mythohistories, chroniclers' accounts of their significance, *and* the difficulty extirpators encountered in attempts to uncover them. Records from the Inquisition in New Spain document the lengths to which officials went in search of *tlaquimilolli*—especially those they suspected to have been concealed within Tenochtitlan's Templo Mayor—often to no avail.[8]

Olivier's work documents the visual and textual evidence of *tlaquimilolli*, their origin narratives, and the roles they played in state society, including rites of accession and New Fire ceremonies.[9] His research provides a basis for our consideration of how *tlaquimilolli* related to *teotl* (deity) and *teixiptla*, conceptually, materially, and practically. Indeed, comparing and contrasting *tlaquimilolli* with both *teotl* and *teixiptla* provides us with a method for further distinguishing the three concepts, particularly as the specific qualities of *teotl* come to bear on the origins and manufacture of *tlaquimilolli*. That is to say, we will bring into focus how *tlaquimilolli* and *teixiptlahuan* presented or manifested *teteo* by considering the similarities, differences, and overlapping qualities of the two forms of deity embodiment as they relate to the Aztec concept of *teotl*.

A series of comparative and exploratory exercises aid us in refining our interpretations of *teteo* (gods), *teixiptlahuan* (localized embodiments), and *tlaquimilolli* (sacred bundles). In particular, examining the semantic range of *quimilli* (bundle) defines the relationship of sacred bundles to other types of bundles.[10] Mythohistorical and historical descriptions of *tlaquimilolli*'s origins and functions will give us a sense of how the Mexicas conceived of, produced, and interacted with these special bundles. Tradition tells us that the posthumous remains of deities—whether ashes, bones, or clothing—provided the materials from which devotees fashioned *tlaquimilolli*, and mythohistories recount their lives during migrations from caves of origin into the Central Valley. *Teteo* directed their migrating devotees by speaking to *teomamaque* (god-carriers) through *tlaquimilolli* and to priests in dreams. Devotees regarded a *tlaquimilolli* as their *teotl*'s material manifestation, and the precious bundle's presence in the community motivated migrants to build protective temples—like the one that housed Itzpapalotl's *tlaquimilolli*—immediately upon settling. Historically, *tlaquimilolli* occupied significant and signifying roles in state ceremonies, including the training of human *teixiptlahuan*, the accessions of rulers, and New Fire ceremonies. An overview of the functions of *tlaquimilolli* in Aztec religion and state ceremony leads to considering how the bundles' materiality contributed to their role in the religious community.

Covering and contents made up the essential elements of *tlaquimilolli*. Cloth, clothes, or animal hides formed the bundles' outermost layers, and these wrappings physically expressed the root of the concept *quimiloa* (to wrap someone or something in a blanket, to enshroud), nominalized as *quimilli* (bundle of clothes, blankets).[11] In addition to the bundles' coverings, their contents, which variously included biological remains, flints, mirrors, and precious stones, also figured in the regard in which devotees held the objects/entities. Given skin's prominence in the construction of *teixiptlahuan*, the role exuviae played in the formation of *tlaquimilolli*—from cloth exteriors to ash, bone, and *chalchihuitl* heart interiors—is striking. In a very real sense, the composite materials of *tlaquimilolli* both constituted the *teotl*'s body and made it recognizable. Regardless of the fact that *tlaquimilolli* were neither anthropomorphic nor zoomorphic, devotees identified the *teteo* they embodied by virtue of the bundles' (re)collection of a given god's constitutive qualities. That both *teixiptlahuan* and *tlaquimilolli* made *teteo* present in the lives of devotees raises questions about the distinctions between the two forms of deity manifestation and the specific purposes each served. I will return to these themes in closing.

Unwrapping the Meaning of *Tlaquimilolli*

The noun *tlaquimilolli* denotes a specific type of bundle, often glossed as a "sacred bundle," and has a rich and revealing etymology. Four components create this compound: *tla-*, a nonpersonal indefinite object prefix; the verbal root *quimiloa*, "to wrap someone or something in a blanket; to enshroud"; *-l*, a patientive suffix; and *-li*, the absolutive ending for a nonpossessed singular noun.[12] *Quimiloa*, the verb at the root of *tlaquimilolli*, formed around the noun *quimilli*, "bundle." *Quimilli* became the intransitive verb *quimilihui*, "to become a bundle," by acquiring the inceptive verber *-ihui* and then became transitive with the addition of the causative suffix *-oa*. The resulting verb *quimiloa* means "to make something into a bundle, to bundle something up." A *tlaquimilolli*, then, is "a bundle, something that has been bundled up."[13] By contrast to *quimilli*, defined by Frances Karttunen as "bundle of clothes, blankets," a *tlaquimilolli* signifies a more specific type of bundle, one that someone made.[14] As a patientive or deverbal noun, *tlaquimilolli* indicates "not the action of the verb, but the result of the action, that which has been acted upon."[15] Thus, *tlaquimilolli* refers to the completed bundle, the object that results from someone's bundling activity. As we shall see, the wrappings of *tlaquimilolli* bound together the personal property and material remains of *teteo*. A brief survey of the greater semantic context of *quimiloa* and *quimilli* provides us with a better sense of the terms' range and of *(tla)quimilolli*'s specificity.

Definitions and contextual uses of *quimilli* and *quimiloa* in post-Contact sources provide information about the words' various meanings and semantic ranges. According to the *Nahuatl Dictionary*, *quimilli* functions as "a counter (equivalent to 20)" and also denotes "a bundle."[16] In *L'imaginaire des nombres chez les anciens Mexicains*, Danièle Dehouve explains that *quimilli* belonged to a group of digital quantifiers that classified groups of twenty objects or entities according to their forms or shapes.[17] *Quimilli*, she writes, "designates 'twenty pieces of fabric.' This term was reserved for pieces of fabric enclosed in a *quimilli*, that is to say, in a bound package (from *quimiloa*, 'to wrap up'). In the expression *on-quimilli in cuachtli*, 'forty capes,' literally 'two times a pack of twenty capes,' it must be understood that capes were tied in bundles and not, as in the case of *ipilli* [a quantifier of flat objects], placed one over the other in layers."[18] *Quimilli*, then, is like words that count or quantify a specific amount of a particular object, including the English words "ream" (500 sheets of paper), "bushel" (64 US pints or 8 imperial gallons), and "peck" (an amount of dry goods equal to a quarter of a bushel).[19] Contextual uses of *quimilli* in the *Florentine Codex* demonstrate its use as a digital quantifier and provide a sense of its range of connotations.

Groups of cloths, most particularly of capes, are described as "bundles": "But the capes came in bundles. They were only in bales. Only by the bundle were they given and presented."[20] In the vigesimal counting system, *cem* (one) complete count includes twenty of a given thing. Thus, in the phrase "*cenquimilli in tecuachtli*" (one bundle of capes), *quimilli* signifies a complete count of twenty capes. In a marketplace exchange, a merchant trades "*cenquimilli*" one bundle (i.e., twenty capes) for tomatoes: "and he arranged to buy tomatoes; daily he bought tomatoes with perhaps twenty small capes."[21] In a discussion of merchants acquiring slaves for the celebration of Panquetzaliztli, the *Florentine Codex* explains that a buyer who selected a skilled dancer might pay "*cenquimilli onmactlactli*" (one bundle ten) or thirty large capes. In the marketplace, bundles of capes of varying quality carried different economic values in trade: "The value of a boat [of water] was one small cape given [for it]. The value of one small cape was one hundred cacao beans; this was the one [known as] *tototlaqualtequachtli*. And the value of the following small cape was eighty cacao beans. And finally the value of the last small cape was sixty-five cacao beans."[22] The monetary value of cape bundles depended upon their size and craftsmanship, but the *quimilli*, or bundle, was a standard unit of measure for capes in mercantile exchanges. With regard to capes, *quimilli* indicates a count (of twenty) rather than signifying a random number of cloths. By contrast to "ream," "peck," or "bushel" and even to other Nahuatl quantifiers, *quimilli* connotes the sense of completion, wholeness, and totality accorded twenty in the vigesimal system.

The semantic range of *quimilli* as "bundle" widens to signify wrappings that bind and expands *quimilli*'s sense of completion and complete sets. Some of the most common extensions of *quimilli* from bundles to bindings include paper wrappings used in ceremonies, bandages or wrappings used for medicinal purposes, wrappings that veil an individual's head or face, and wrappings that enshroud corpses. In both Ochpaniztli and Tititl, festivals dedicated to the goddesses Teteo Innan and Ilama Tecuhtli, respectively, paper bound together ritual structures. In Tititl, ritual officiants built and then burned a model of the goddess's "grain bin," which they joined together with paper: "They wrapped paper about it; they caulked it with paper."[23] During Ochpaniztli, *cihuatlamacazque* (offering priestesses) carried on their backs seven ears of dried maize covered in liquid rubber and bound with paper: "They carried the dried maize on their backs. . . . They wrapped them each in paper, and they carried them with precious capes."[24] In her study of Ochpaniztli, Catherine DiCesare argues that the dates associated with this ritual's depiction in the *Codex Borbonicus* and the "Leyenda de los soles" description of Quetzalcoatl's activities at the Mountain of Sustenance suggest that the priestesses' ritual use of maize recalled the *teotl's* primordial collection of food for humans.[25]

In the "Leyenda de los soles," Quetzalcoatl sets out in search of sustenance for human beings, and he transforms into a black ant in order to follow a red ant who knows where the maize is stored. Quetzalcoatl quickly confronts a problem: he can carry only a small amount of maize, not nearly enough to sustain humanity. And so, Cipactonal and Oxomoco summon thunder and the *tlaloque* (the Tlalocs; rain gods), "blue *tlaloque*, white *tlaloque*, yellow *tlaloque*, red *tlaloque*," to complete the task.[26] Thunder strikes the mountain and the *tlaloque* steal away with the staple foods of the Mesoamerican diet: "The white, black, and yellow corn, the red corn, the beans, the amaranth, the chia, the fish amaranth, all of the foods were stolen."[27] The seven ears of corn carried by Chicomecoatl's priestesses during Ochpaniztli likely resonated with this account and also would have signified maize's divinatory functions, including its use in curative practices.[28] Furthermore, the mention of precious capes in proximity to the bound ears of corn suggests that the priestesses may have carried the maize in a manner similar to that of a god carrier bearing a *tlaquimilolli*. In both Ochpaniztli and Tititl, paper bindings create a "bundle" of ritual objects that—taken together—compose a whole, either through complete representation, as with the maize, or through a completed structure, in the case of the grain bin.

Elsewhere in the *Florentine Codex*, bandages bind wounds and broken bones. *Book 11: Earthly Things* describes the Chiahuaitl or Chiauhcoatl, a large venomous snake, as "a terrifying one, a poisonous one; one that strikes one, spies on one, watches one on the road."[29] The bite of a Chiauhcoatl often led to the loss of a limb or to death, but there was a cure: "And the cure for the snakebite is to suck it at once. And many lines are slashed on the surface of the snakebite where it has proceeded to swell. And where he has been bitten is spread over, wrapped with a thin maguey fiber cloth. [Then] it is stretched over live coals and rubbed with fine tobacco."[30] In the case of wounds, such as the Chiauhcoatl's bite or broken bones, binding facilitated healing rather than a collection or count. Broken legs, for example, were treated with a compound of two roots, covered—literally "bound"—in cloth bandages, tied to splints, and left to heal for twenty days.[31] (Note the length of the cure: one complete count of twenty days.) The binding, bundling nature of *quimilli* restores a flesh wound or broken bone to wholeness. In these contexts—paper's use in ceremonies or bandages' use in cures—the *quimilli* (re)constructs a whole, be it a whole structure or a whole body.

Quimilli's binding action transformed materials by (re)joining parts into a whole, and *quimilli* also tied intangible qualities to the observable world through ritual. Historically, binding facilitated powerful transformations in rituals like the accession of a new *tlahtoani* (speaker; ruler). *Book 8: Kings and Lords* describes rites of accession on the occasion of a new ruler's selection, a process that involved the transformation of a *tlazopipil* (precious noble; prince) into a *tlahtoani*. The lords gathered to choose one of the *tlazopipiltin* (precious nobles) from among the sons of the noble lords, and guided by a list of characteristics desirable in a *tlahtoani*, they selected someone "experienced in war, who shrank not from the enemy, who knew not wine."[32] Once an appropriate candidate had been chosen, he and his four lords initiated ritual preparations for the transfer of power. The text emphasizes the five candidates' attire and ritual paraphernalia, all of which were decorated with a bone motif. The *teopixque* (god caretakers; priests) dressed the *tlahtoani*-elect first: "Then they veiled his face, they covered his head [with a] green fasting cape designed with bones."[33] Then they dressed the four lords: "Then they veiled and covered their faces, each one of them, with black fasting capes designed with bones."[34] The *tlahtoani* wore the *xicolli xoxouhqui* (green sleeveless jacket) and *nezahualcuachtli xoxoctic omicallo* (green fasting cape with bones), and his lords donned the same attire in black. Over the course of several days—including a four-day period of penitence during which the five candidates entered Huitzilopochtli's temple at midnight to make offerings of incense and blood—the candidates' ritual transformation took them from nobility to positions in which they became much more responsible to and for the *teteo*.

In the context of the *tlahtoani*'s accession, the veiling of the green and black fasting capes concealed the candidates as they underwent a process of transformation from one state (of being, social location, and responsibility) to another. Following Richard Townsend, Cecelia Klein suggests that in wearing the *xicolli*, the *tlahtoani*-elect and his staff ritually returned to the primordium.[35] Klein argues that the leaders' return to the beginning facilitated their transformation through "healing" contact with a time when Huitzilopochtli lived in skeletal form, a form represented in the *xicolli*'s skull-and-crossbones motif. According to Klein's analysis, the garments' designs wrapped the officials in Huitzilopochtli's osseous origins and healing capabilities. Patricia Anawalt's analysis of the *xicolli* as a memory cloth complements Klein's reading of the ceremonial garments. Anawalt argues that the *xicolli*, *quemitl,* and *quechquemitl*, all special-use garments associated with human sacrifice, "retain[ed] information regarding their pasts [, and] such clothing truly can be said to hold memory."[36] Based on *quimilli*'s meaning, we also know that the binding action of the garments worn by the officials facilitated change in their state and status. Indeed, the ritual of accession bound the *tlahtoani* to his new station and resulted in the presentation of five complete(ly) new rulers, an authoritative quincunx.

Quimilli occurs in more mundane ritual contexts as well, including those of mortuary preparations. Ximena Chávez Balderas explains that two variables affected funerary treatments: "the cause of death and the social position."[37] According to Sahagún, "When someone died—when [the sextons] adorned him, they wrapped him in his mantle and bound him [in wrappings]."[38] Other elements of the standard posthumous treatment of bodies in Aztec culture included enshrouding the corpse, adorning it with paper garments, cremating the corpse along with important personal articles, and gathering the ashes in a container.[39] These procedures prepared the person for Mictlan, the land of the dead to which "went all those who died on earth, who died only of sickness: the rulers, the commoners."[40] For the average person who died of natural causes, postmortem preparations involved "rituals in the presence of the corpse, cremation, collection of the ashes and their deposit, and burial of the human remains," but special circumstances called for special burial rites.[41] The appendix to *Book 3: The Origin of the Gods* describes mortuary treatments and their significance in detail.

At the time of death, family members prayed over the body before summoning a ritual specialist, an *amatlamatqui* (paper designer), who "kept on cutting, they kept on slicing it evenly, they kept on binding the paper. And when they had prepared the paper vestments, thereupon they arrayed the dead one; they sat him up; they poured water on his head."[42] The specialists ritually bathed the corpse and placed a bowl of water with the body before bundling in preparation for cremation: "They wrapped the dead one well, they wrapped him thoroughly, they bound him thoroughly, they bound him closely."[43] After wrapping the body, they dressed it in the paper garments cut for this occasion. Then along with the corpse, which they cremated, they burned the deceased's personal property because they believed the items would be helpful in navigating Mictlan. Upon arriving in Mictlan, Mictlan Tecuhtli (Lord of the Land of the Dead) returned to the person the items that had been burned with the individual's corpse. Men received back their weaponry, insignia, and captives' property and clothing, and women received their sewing paraphernalia and garments. The dead used these items for their protection from the extreme elements of Mictlan, like the obsidian blade winds they encountered: "It was said that they would make themselves an enclosure [with these things]; thus they would crouch protected from the obsidian-bladed winds; not much would they suffer."[44]

A passage from *Book 4: The Soothsayers* describing the fates of persons born on ce xochitl (1 Flower) underscores the importance of wrapping the corpse prior to its cremation. The Aztecs thought of this day sign as "a little miserable, and a little good," and the trouble with being born on ce xochitl had to do with how one handled success.[45] Those who paid too much attention to their success and wealth became proud and lost favor with Ipalnemohuani (He by Whom We Live). Of the proud, "He by whom we live, who had endowed him, took from and deprived him of his deserts."[46] When such an individual became so ill as to long for death, no one paid any attention to his suffering, because he had been so prideful. And so "when he died, he only aroused pity. Nothing was laid over him; he was only cast out naked; there was nothing at hand to be used as wrappings for the dead."[47] By contrast to individuals whose families bundled them prior to burial and who ensured their (relative) comfort in the afterlife by sending along their possessions to Mictlan Tecuhtli, those whose corpses were left uncovered would find only misery in the afterlife. In this discussion of mortuary treatments, we should not overlook the fact that the Aztecs collected crematory remains and placed them in urns. Most people interred family urns in a special location within their house complex, and archaeologists have identified some interments recovered from Templo Mayor caches as those of *tlahtoque*.

In special cases, the posthumous treatment of Aztec corpses followed other ritual procedures, some of which involved elaborate rebuilding and bundling. For example, when a body could not be recovered from the battlefield, they made a bundle to represent the fallen individual, because "in whichever case, a warrior—whether in flesh and bone or fashioned from pine—had to be placed into the crematory fire."[48] Durán describes the funerary bundles fashioned for Aztec warriors who died in Michoacán:

On the fifth day, images of the dead were made from slivers of resinous wood, each one with feet, arms, and head. Faces were made on these, the eyes and the mouth. They were dressed with breechcloths, sashes, and mantles. To their shoulders were attached wings of hawk feathers, as it was believed that in this way they would fly before the sun every day. The heads of these images were feathered and pendants for the ears, nose, and lips were placed upon them. The statues were taken to a room called Tlacochcalco. The widows then entered and each one placed in front of the statue of her husband a dish of a stew called *tlacatlacualli*, which means "food of human flesh." Together with these were offered some special tortillas called *papalotlaxcalli*, "butterfly bread," and a drink made of a little flour of toasted maize dissolved in water. . . . At dusk, when this ceremony was over, the widows rewarded the singers with ordinary mantles, breechcloths, and digging sticks. Then the elders ordered that all the statues be placed together and set on fire. Since they were made of resinous firewood and covered with paper, they burned with great fury. All the widows stood around the fire, weeping with great sorrow.[49]

When bodies could not be cremated, the Aztecs made and dressed images of the dead as proxies for cremation. Presumably, these "corpses," which Chávez Balderas refers to as *"bultos"* (bundles), were bundled in a manner similar to that described above. Most forms of death required cremation, and so it is curious that while the Aztecs bound human corpses *prior to* their cremation, they bound *teotl* bodies in sacred bundles *subsequent to* their cremation. The Aztecs bundled, cremated, and memorialized their deceased for ritually proscribed periods of time, but they reconstituted their *teteo* in *tlaquimilolli*, a process with significantly different results than the interment of remains in homes and temples.

Our brief survey of the semantic range of *quimilli* indicates that the term signified a complete count of twenty, especially with regard to *quimilli* of capes, and that its meaning extended to encompass other bundles or bindings that facilitated completion or wholeness through transformation. In its extended sense, *quimilli* encompassed paper bindings that completed ritual constructions and bandages whose bindings healed wounds and broken bones. Veils that covered the faces of the *tlahtoani*-elect and his lords facilitated their transformations into rulers and redefined their relationships with *teteo*. Finally, *quimilli* played an important role in securing a less arduous afterlife for those bound to Mictlan, and was thus crucial in the transition from life to death. By contrast to *quimilli*, *tlaquimilolli* signifies the bundle manufactured as part of the mortuary treatment of a cremated god-body, rather than a human body. Mythohistorical accounts of *tlaquimilolli*'s origins, composition, and functions bear out these connections to fire, beginnings, endings, and new beginnings.

Sacred Bundle Biographies

According to Aztec mythohistory, *tlaquimilolli* originated in progenitive, regenerative, and transformative events during the primordium that extended from before the birth of the sun until the foundation of Tenochtitlan. Surviving accounts of the creation of *tlaquimilolli* illustrate their production in the immediate aftermath of divine death and destruction: Mendieta describes the creation of several *tlaquimilolli* following the sacrifice of gods whose deaths caused the sun to move across the sky; the "Leyenda de los soles" and the "Anales de Cuauhtitlan" describe Itzpapalotl's death and the creation of her *tlaquimilolli*; Fernando de Alva Ixtlilxóchitl provides an account of Quetzalcoatl's *tlaquimilolli*; both Bartolomé de Las Casas and Juan Bautista de Pomar mention Tezcatlipoca's *tlaquimilolli*; and the *Historia de los mexicanos por sus pinturas*, the *Crónica Mexicayotl*, and Cristóbal del Castillo's *Historia* account for the origin of Huitzilopochtli's *tlaquimilolli*. Although our sources may occlude more than they reveal about sacred bundles, by drawing on them we are able to sketch a composite image of *tlaquimilolli*—however tentative it may be—that underscores the deep significance of death's regenerative and progenitive effects in Aztec religion. From the deaths of the gods—deaths often brought by their own hands—emerged *tlaquimilolli*, sacred bundles that enveloped the ashes and effects of those very deities. *Tlaquimilolli* (re)embodied *teteo*, and in so doing, they became a devotional focus and a source of counsel for the community. Prior to being born(e) by a *teomama* (god-carrier), the *teotl* first had to die, and through death, the god (re)emerged as a *tlaquimilolli*, unspeakably precious. The following mythohistorical accounts tell rich, enigmatic, and occasionally overlapping stories about the circumstances in which *tlaquimilolli* originated, and they greatly amplify our ability to understand the bundles' functions and significances.

Mendieta's account of the *tlaquimilolli* created after the gods' sacrifice at Teotihuacan appears in his *Historia eclesiástica indiana* (1596) and reads like the story of the originary *tlaquimilolli*. Having created the world and humans, the gods found themselves without a sun, and so they gathered at Teotihuacan, where they built an enormous fire and stationed themselves around each of its four sides. They announced that the one of them who most quickly threw himself into the fire would earn the honor of "*haberse criado el sol*" (having brought up the sun).[50] The most courageous and fearless of them rushed into the fire, descended into the underworld, and left the other gods wondering from which direction the sun would rise. After a while, the sun rose some distance into the sky and stopped. The gods sent a messenger to inquire about the sun's situation, and they learned that the sun refused to move until they—the gods—had been destroyed. Hearing this, some of the gods were afraid and others were angry. One of them, Citli, fired three arrows at the sun: the first flew beneath the sun, and the second and third also missed their mark. Enraged, the sun took hold of one of these arrows and hurled it back at Citli. The arrow pierced Citli's chest, and the *teotl* died. Witnessing this, the *teteo* agreed to sacrifice themselves in a desperate act that would force the sun across the sky. Xolotl administered this sacrifice. Using a large knife, Xolotl opened the *teteo*'s chests, killing them and then sacrificing himself. In the aftermath, "Each of them left behind the clothes they had worn (which was a blanket) for their devotees to have in memory of their devotion and friendship. And thus satiated, the sun made its way."[51]

After recounting the myth of the sun's origin and the gods' sacrifice for its life-sustaining movement, Mendieta describes how the *tlaquimilolli* were fashioned from the *mantas* of the *teteo*. Devotees found the *mantas* and placed within them "*ciertos palos*" (certain sticks) in which they made a notch to hold "*por corazon unas pedrezuelas verdes*" (some small green stones as hearts) along with snake and "*tigre*" skins placed in the bundle. Mendieta explains, "This bundle they called a *tlaquimilolli* and they gave each one the name of the demon who had supplied the blanket."[52] Following the chronology presented in this Aztec mythohistory, these were the first *tlaquimilolli*, and they held within them precious greenstones affixed to sticks covered in animal skins and bound within the sacred garments of the gods. Each *tlaquimilolli* received the name of the *teotl* who had worn the *manta*. These, like other *tlaquimilolli*, emerged in the immediate aftermath of the gods' sacrificial deaths, and insofar as they contained hearts, stick bodies, and skins tied in the *teotl*'s clothing, they re-presented the god and regenerated his/her life in the community.

In addition to the story of these first gods' sacrifice and the manufacture of their *tlaquimilolli*, other mythohistories account for the *tlaquimilolli* of specific *teteo*, including Itzpapalotl (Obsidian Butterfly), Quetzalcoatl, Tezcatlipoca, and Huitzilopochtli. Descriptions of the *tlaquimilolli* identified with these deities provide us with details about the specific characteristics of various *teteo*'s sacred bundles. Like the *tlaquimilolli* of the *teteo* in Mendieta's account, devotees or *teomamaque* (god-carriers) assembled other *tlaquimilolli* in the transitional wake of deities' auto-sacrificial deaths.

Although the "Anales de Cuauhtitlan" mentions Itzpapalotl's *tlaquimilolli*, the "Leyenda de los soles" provides the most detailed account of the goddess's death and the creation of her sacred bundle. According to the "Leyenda," the gods found themselves in a situation much like the one Mendieta describes.

Nanahuatzin (Pustules) sacrificed himself to create the sun, but after appearing in the sky, the sun refused to move for four days. When asked why he had not set, the sun replied, "Why? Because I'm asking for their blood, their color, their precious substance."[53] The gods arrived at a conclusion similar to that of other accounts: only their self-sacrifice could satisfy the sun. And so, the gods sacrificed themselves, and the sun began to move. The "Leyenda" then explains that in the year 1 Flint the four hundred Mixcoas were born, and in a subsequent birth event, five more Mixcoas appeared. The sun tasked the four hundred Mixcoas with the responsibility of using flying darts to satisfy the sun's thirst, but the young Mixcoas played with the darts instead of sating his thirst. When they hunted, they selfishly kept the game for themselves. They reveled in promiscuity and stayed drunk. Frustrated with the four hundred Mixcoas, the sun told the five youngest Mixcoa siblings to murder "the ones who fail to say, 'Mother, Father!'"[54] And they did.

Later, two of the five Mixcoas, Xiuhnel and Mimich, left to hunt a pair of two-headed deer that had descended from the sky. The deer transformed into women, and one of the women lured Xiuhnel into her bed with a bloody beverage. Once she had lain with him, she turned on Xiuhnel and chewed open his chest. After witnessing what had befallen his brother, Mimich said, "Alas, my elder brother is eaten."[55] The second woman invited Mimich to drink with her, but having grown wary of the women, he built a fire and jumped into it. She followed Mimich into the fire and chased after him until noon when a barrel cactus fell from the sky and st(r)uck her. Mimich showed the *xiuhteteuctin* (fire lords) where the body of this woman (now identified in the text as Itzpapalotl) lay, and "*tlatiya*" (they burn her).[56] Five colored flints "shined forth" from her pyre, and Mixcoatl, the soon-to-be husband of Chimalman, took the white one.[57] Of the five, this was the only flint they wrapped up, and "Mixcoatl made the white flint his spirit power, and when they had wrapped it up, he backpacked it. Then he goes off to make conquests in a place called Comallan, backpacking the flint. It's his spirit power, Itzpapalotl."[58] In the "Leyenda," Mixcoatl carried Itzpapalotl's *tlaquimilolli*, which contained her remains in the form of a white flint, on his back into battle. The text lists a series of successful conquests Mixcoatl made—among the Comalteca, and in Tecanman, Cocyama, Huehuetocan, and Pochtlan—before encountering his future spouse naked. Standing before Chimalman, Mixcoatl laid down his shield, took up his dart thrower, and shot at her repeatedly. He missed her eight times (with two shots sailing between her legs), but eventually won a night in her bed. Armed with his *tlaquimilolli* (Itzpapalotl), Mixcoatl experienced success on the battlefield and in the bedroom.

In the "Leyenda," Mixcoatl's conquests (and those of his progeny) have their beginning in primordial progenitive events, including the sun's creation, the *teteo*'s self-sacrifice, the Mixcoas' misbehavior, Itzpapalotl's death, and the creation of the *tlaquimilolli* (Itzpapalotl) that Mixcoatl carries. Despite her central role in this narrative, Itzpapalotl goes unnamed until the Mixcoas point Mixcoatl to her corpse. Itzpapalotl's descent in the shape of a two-headed deer, her hunt for Mimich, her death by cactus, and her cremation all stem from the creation of the sun, his refusal to move, and the disobedience of the Mixcoas. Viewed alongside Xiuhnel's blood thirsty lover, the other two-headed deer, Itzpapalotl seems practically a victim of circumstance.

In the "Anales," however, she actively advances upon the four hundred Mixcoas and devours them. In fact, only the White Mixcoatl escapes her by hiding inside a barrel cactus. Itzpapalotl finds this Mixcoatl, who emerges from the cactus and resurrects his Mixcoa siblings. Together with his siblings, he turns on and kills the goddess: "They shot her. And when she was dead, they burned her. Then they rubbed themselves with her ashes, blackening their eye sockets. And when their bundle was finished being made, they all decorated themselves in a place called Mazatepec."[59] The "Leyenda" and the "Anales" converge and diverge in the details of their accounts. In both, Itzpapalotl pursues Mixcoatl, identified as/with white(ness), and their chase hinges on the appearance of a barrel cactus. In one, the cactus traps and kills the goddess, and in the other, it aids and abets Mixcoatl's (and the Mixcoas') murder of Itzpapalotl. In both, Mixcoatl/the Mixcoas cremate Itzpapalotl and incorporate her biological remains (in the form of either a flint or ashes) into the *tlaquimilolli* they create. Although their details differ, both texts describe Itzpapalotl's *tlaquimilolli* as containing her crematory remains.[60]

The story of Itzpapalotl's *tlaquimilolli* underscores sacred bundles' transformative and regenerative properties upon their emergence from the afterbirth of divine self-sacrifice. Although Itzpapalotl's death at the hand of Mixcoatl (and the Mixcoas) results in her transformation into a bundle that contains her remains, the *tlaquimilolli* is more than mere(ly what) remains. The rescue of her bundle from a burning temple in Cuitlahuacan (quoted above) reveals its material and symbolic significance. Itzpapalotl's account is in keeping with the mythohistorically established paradigm of *teteo*'s sacrificial deaths at Teotihuacan: the gods perform (auto-)sacrifice; *tlaquimilolli* are produced in the mortuary treatment of their remains; and the newly manufactured *tlaquimilolli* embody the physically transformed *teteo* for their devotional community. *Tlaquimilolli* manifested the recently deceased, recently rehabilitated *teteo*. Although the "Anales" and "Leyenda" may not catalogue all of the contents of Itzpapalotl's *tlaquimilolli*, I maintain that by their nature, *quimilli* contained complete sets of things or bodies transformed through the curative powers of binding. With regard to *tlaquimilolli*—these extraordinary bundles set apart from other *quimilli* through the transformative event of death—the complete sets corporeally (re)constituted the *teotl* and contained material assemblages specific to him/her. A bundle's unique contents or coverings were most often produced during the *teotl's* mortuary preparations; this was the case with Itzpapalotl's white fire flint and ashes, and as we will see, it will be the case with the biological remains included in the *tlaquimiloltin* of Quetzalcoatl, Huitzilopochtli, and Tezcatlipoca.

Alva Ixtlilxóchitl recounts the end of Topiltzin Quetzalcoatl's life and the origin of his *tlaquimilolli* in a digression from his discussion of "the order and ceremony for making one a lord":

> And this Topiltzin was made a lord, and after a certain time, he wanted to go to the place where the sun comes out and it would come within a certain time, and he pointed out on his own in which year it would come . . . *ce acatl* (1 Reed). . . . Many people left with him, and in each of the villages at which they arrived, he left one of them, and they took the person for an idol, and because of that they adored him/her. He went to die in a town called Matlapalan . . . and at the time that this Topiltzin died, he demanded that all of the treasure that he had be incinerated with him. It took four days to burn, after it had burned they took the ashes from his body and placed them in a bag made from a tiger skin, and because of this, to this day the lords are cremated.[61]

Much like the *tlaquimilolli* of other *teteo*, Quetzalcoatl's sacred bundle consisted of his ashes (likely mixed with the charred remains of his personal property) wrapped inside the animal hide. The details surrounding Quetzalcoatl's death provide us with interesting comparative material for the accounts of the divine self-sacrifices of the *teteo* at Teotihuacan and of Itzpapalotl.

In each of these three cases, the deaths of the gods preceded the manufacture of their *tlaquimilolli*, but in the first two instances, the sun's demand of divine auto-sacrifice led to the deities' deaths either directly, as at Teotihuacan, or indirectly, as with Itzpapalotl. By contrast, Alva Ixtlilxóchitl's version of Quetzalcoatl's death takes us away from the scene of first dawn. Unlike others, this account makes no mention of Quetzalcoatl witnessing the sun's birth.[62] Rather, it presents Quetzalcoatl anticipating his own death in the time and place of the sun's rising, a reflection of the life/death complementarity in Aztec religion or an artifact of Alva Ixtlilxóchitl's self-conscious attempts to harmonize pre-Contact and post-Contact traditions.[63] Chávez Balderas opens *Rituales funerarios en el Templo Mayor de Tenochtitlan* by characterizing life and death as unopposed pairs, a view she shares with López Austin: "Life and death are not opposites on a straight line, but two points diametrically situated on a circle that is in motion."[64] Like the cyclical dualism of life and death, the sun's path begins with the dawn and leaves darkness in its wake. The Aztecs embedded the parallel cycles of life/death and sunlight/darkness in their stories of beginnings and endings, and they bound these stories in the materials of their *tlaquimilolli*.

Tlaquimilolli bundled the complete set of things that composed the deity's transfigured body, including greenstone hearts, stick bodies, animal skins, and woven garments. Despite the fact that *tlaquimilolli* did not take an anthropomorphic or zoomorphic shape, colonial accounts suggest that devotees attributed to them the capabilities of communication, sensation, and perception. In particular, accounts describing the origins, contents, and functions of the *tlaquimilolli* of Huitzilopochtli and Tezcatlipoca present what Olivier has called a "double tradition."[65] Both deities' *tlaquimilolli* are described as containing bones and objects emblematic of the deities, but none of the sources account for the presence of *both* the bone *and* the objects in a single bundle. The divergence of these accounts complicates interpretive work, but it provides an opportunity to examine each of these narratives in relation to these two prominent *teteo*. This more detailed interpretive work leads to a clearer picture of how *tlaquimilolli* embodied *teteo*, as well as how they functioned in devotional contexts.

Huitzilopochtli's *tlaquimilolli* frequently appears in and directs the path taken by the Mexicas in their migration story. By contrast to the accounts of other *tlaquimilolli*'s origins in death, Huitzilopochtli's *tlaquimilolli* enters the Mexica migration narrative sometime after his birth and ensuing conquest over the Centzonhuitz Nahua (Four Hundred Southerners) at Coatepec. To my knowledge, no account of Huitzilopochtli's death or cremation exists, but the mythohistorical importance of his *tlaquimilolli* implies either his death or a similarly momentous transitional experience. According to two different sources, the notable material features of Huitzilopochtli's *tlaquimilolli* were his loincloth and bones. Several *teteo* contributed mantas, capes, or cloths to their bundles, but Olivier notes that based on the accounts available, only those describing the *tlaquimilolli* of Huitzilopochtli and Tezcatlipoca specify the inclusion of bones.[66] Given that the *Historia de los mexicanos* describes Huitzilopochtli's primal body as one of fleshless bone—"nació sin carne" (he was born without flesh)—it is interesting that this same source emphasizes the significance of the bundle's covering—the *teotl*'s loincloth—without mentioning the presence of skeletal material.[67] However, the inclusion of bones in these deities' *tlaquimilolli* is enough to call our attention to the osteological remains present in the bundles and signified in other representations of the gods.

In Huitzilopochtli's case, the inclusion of a bone seems apt, given his personal history as a skeletal figure and the frequency with which anthropomorphic embodiments of the *teotl* were fashioned from *michihuatli* ("fish" amaranth). Practitioners used *michihuatli*, a type of *tzoalli* (amaranth-seed dough), in the manufacture of *teixiptlahuan* exclusively. In fact, *tzoalli*'s use in rituals led to the Nahuatl word being "translated as 'bones of the gods.'"[68] During Panquetzaliztli, priests crafted Huitzilopochtli's *teixiptla* by molding *michihuatli* on a wooden frame.[69] It is quite possible, too, that the inclusion of a bone in Huitzilopochtli's *tlaquimilolli* was analogous to the ashes of other *teteo* insofar as it signified his prior and present physicality.

Indeed, the striking features of Huitzilopochtli's *tlaquimilolli* were its sensational abilities to sense, perceive, and communicate. The *Historia de los mexicanos*, Chimalpahin's *Mexican History or Chronicle*, /Alvarado Tezozómoc's *Crónica mexicana*, Durán's *History*, the *Codex Boturini*, and the *Codex Azcatitlan* recount Huitzilopochtli's guiding presence among the Mexicas from the moment they left their place of origin. As Boone has observed, the *Codex Boturini* shows a *teomama* named Tezcacoatl (Mirror Serpent) holding Huitzilopochtli's *tlaquimilolli*. Other *teomamaque* accompanying them carry three more bundles, which Boone believes to have contained cult objects belonging to the god (see Figure 5.1).[70] Chimalpahin emphasizes Huitzilopochtli's activity among the Mexicas: "And in their keeping was he to whom they supplicated, whom they considered a god, he whom they named the portent Huitzilopochtli. He spoke; he conversed with the Azteca; he lived among them and was their friend."[71] This description of Huitzilopochtli's lively companionship might lead some to a Euhemerist reading of the text, that is, one that would see the *teotl* Huitzilopochtli as having originally been a great man or "culture hero," but such an interpretation would distract from our interest in *teteo*'s embodiments, materiality, and animacy.[72]

Multiple sources document the importance of building a temple to house the patron deity's *tlaquimilolli* immediately upon settling—even in temporary locales. The *Historia de los mexicanos* tells us that as they left Aztlan, the Mexicas "carried with them the figure and manner of constructing their temples, so as to be able to erect them to *Vchilobi* [Huitzilopochtli] wherever they arrived."[73] Similarly, Durán explains:

The Aztecs left the Seven Caves and embarked upon their journey in or-der to seek the land promised them by their gods. . . . In a painting that I was shown in Santiago Tlatelolco, I saw depicted many towns . . . now abandoned because the people there have died off. Only vestiges remain of the buildings and temples erected to their god; the first thing the peo-ple did in each place was to construct a temple.[74]

Chimalpahin corroborates these accounts: "And wherever they tarried long they built a temple; there they erected the house of their god Huitzilopoch-tli."[75] Indeed, codices and *mapas*, including the *Boturini, Historia Tolteca-Chichimeca*, and *Mapa de Cuauhtinchan No. 2*, also document the presence of the *teteo* among migrating peoples, the Mexicas and Mixtecs included, leaving their places of origin. Like the *Boturini*, the documents frequently depict four *teomamaque* leading the migrants, but their names vary.[76] According to Chi-malpahin, "As the Azteca set out from Culhuacan there were four who on their backs carried the portent Huitzilopochtli lying in a coffer. Of the god-carriers one man was named Iztac Mixcoatzin; and the second was named Apanecatl; the third was named Tezcacoacatl. The fourth, a woman, was named Chimal-man. These were the aforesaid god-carriers."[77] Huitzilopochtli figures promi-nently among the gods bundled on the backs of the *teomamaque*, whom he often used as intermediaries in his contact with the people.

Huitzilopochtli interacted with the Mexicas in person and through reli-gious specialists who bore the responsibility of conveying his messages to the migrating community. He commonly communicated with the community by appearing in his priests' dreams. Durán recounts that near the beginning of the migration the Mexicas arrived at Pátzcuaro and wished to settle there. The priests asked Huitzilopochtli if some of the group might remain in Pátzcu-aro even if it was not the place they had been promised. Huitzilopochtli "an-swered the priests in dreams, telling them he was happy to do what they asked of him."[78] Similarly, when the Mexicas stopped at Temazcaltitlan, "some Mex-icans who carried *Vchilogos* went astray, murmured against him, and *Vchi-logos* told them in their dreams that things must be as they had been, but that they were near to the place where they were to take their final rest and home."[79] Dreams were not the *teotl's* only means of contact with the Mexi-cas, though. According to one of Chimalpahin's sources, mestizo elder Alonso Franco, Huitzilopochtli spoke to the Mexicas directly from his *tlaquimilo-lli*. Franco told Chimalpahin, "They brought what was in their keeping, their bundle. To it they prayed; to it the Azteca listened when it spoke, and they an-swered it; but they did not see in what way it talked to them."[80]

Later Chimalpahin identifies Huitzilopochtli exclusively as a *tlamacazqui*, glossed by Molina as *"ministros y servidores de los templos de los ídolos"* (priests and servants of the temples of the idols), and traditionally thought of as a priest or, in Karttunen's words, a penitent.[81] Chimalpahin frequently refers to Huitzilopochtli as a *tlamacazqui*: "And then the offering priest Huitzilopocht-li spoke; he spoke to his senior auxiliaries known as the god-carriers . . . and he said to them . . ."[82] As a *tlamacazqui*, Huitzilopochtli not only spoke to the Mexicas, but he also participated in ritual activities. When the Mexicas settled at Coatepec, for instance, they built a temple to Huitzilopochtli in which they placed an eagle vessel and the images of many other deities, a process in which Huitzilopochtli took an active hand: "Right there Huitzilopochtli assembled, arranged, and counted all the devils. For he was the leader, the chief, of the devils."[83] In sum, these accounts describe Huitzilopochtli as an offering priest and as a "portent" kept in a coffer, which sounds suspiciously like a *tlaqui-milolli*. Read with the *Codex Boturini* and *Codex Azcatitlan* in hand, it would seem that Huitzilopochtli's *teomamaque* carried his *tlaquimilolli* through-out the Mexica migration. The mythohistories of Mexica migration describe Huitzilopochtli manifesting in different modes, which prompts us to explore both when and why he appeared differently.

Boone suggests that Huitzilopochtli's different pictorial depictions—as a *tlaquimilolli* or in anthropomorphic modes—may indicate the varying de-grees to which or the differing ways in which he was involved in events of the migration. "His bundle," she explains, "is pictured in the codices in ways that affirm Huitzilopochtli's guidance and supervision of the migration, and when circumstances seem to call for more direct support, he is pictured in full figure, often with the shield and spears of the warrior."[84] It is, of course, im-portant to keep in mind that the codices and the accounts contained in eth-nohistories represent mythohistories that were originally inscribed pictori-ally and recounted orally: "The images in the manuscript gave meaning, by recording the sense or the gist of the story, and they directed them as read-ers or interpreters to the elaborate oral exposition of the story they already knew."[85] In other words, depending on his action in the mythohistory's script, Huitzilopochtli appears as a figure and as a *tlaquimilolli* in both the *Boturini* and *Azcatitlan*. This is not to deny the historicity of Huitzilopochtli's *tlaqui-milolli* or *teixiptlahuan*. Rather, the anomalies among Huitzilopochtli's em-bodiments—for example, the existence of his *tlaquimilolli* despite no account of his death—raise questions about the relationship of mythohistorical rep-resentations to ritual practices. This particular discrepancy prompts us to in-quire why devotees manufactured other deities' *tlaquimilolli* in the aftermath of their deaths, while Huitzilopochtli's existed independently of his death (or, at least, descriptions of it).

With regard to the reconstitution of the *teotl* in his *tlaquimilolli*, the recently deceased *teotl* contributed the bundle's contents, its wrapping, or both.[86] With this observation, I return to the challenge of the "double tradition," wherein sources attest to differing materials in the *tlaquimilolli* of Huitzilopochtli and Tezcatlipoca. Las Casas and Pomar indicate that Tezcatlipoca (Smoking Mirror) left his devotees "*el hueso de su muslo*" (the bone of his thigh) and a mirror.[87] Las Casas embeds the thigh bone detail in a footnote explaining that Popocatepetl (Smoking Mountain) takes its name from Tezcatlipoca, whose descent into the volcano incited it. The Popocatepetl narratives differed, Las Casas explains, as to whether Tezcatlipoca merely penetrated the volcano or died there. Regardless, the *teotl* sent his thigh bone to Texcoco, and the Texcocans, his patrons, proudly devoted themselves to the god and to the veneration of his relic, which they placed in his temple. This last detail—the bone's location—may indicate that they included it in his *tlaquimilolli*, but Las Casas stops short of saying so.[88] Las Casas explains the origin of one of Tezcatlipoca's relics, an item that may have been wrapped inside his *tlaquimilolli*, and Pomar elaborates on the bundle's various contents: "There was a polished mirror, the size and measure of half of a large orange, set in a crude black stone. With it were many loose fine stones, including greenstones, emeralds, turquoises, and many other kinds. And the cloth that was closest to the mirror and stones, it was painted with a human skeleton."[89] According to Pomar, the bundle contained a variety of loose greenstones along with a small mirror set in crudely hewn black stone. Cloths decorated in a skeletal motif surrounded the mirror and greenstones, but he mentions no bones. In sum, these descriptions account for the presence of a mirror or a bone or both in Tezcatlipoca's *tlaquimilolli*.

These colonial accounts of the *tlaquimilolli*'s contents reveal the multiple narrative threads present in Mexica theogonies. By keeping the narrative threads separate, I can examine each independently for the frays left by linguistic, thematic, or iconographic wear that suggest where the various accounts once intersected or knotted. Resisting the temptation to harmonize accounts like those of Las Casas and Pomar—that is, to assume that the *tlaquimilolli* contained both a mirror and a thigh bone (though it certainly may have)—is important for at least two reasons. First, I prevent myself from making easy elisions that would lead to conclusions rather than tentative interpretations, and second, I create space to develop a hermeneutic appropriate to the polysemic signifiers of Aztec religion. If I take seriously the nature of mythohistories as Andeanist Gary Urton characterizes them—as having a "potentially equal and simultaneous, and thus fully ambiguous, mythical and historical status"[90]—tentatively interpreting tangled narratives and contradictions allows me to consider their many possibilities. This hermeneutic helps me avoid distorting or manipulating the sources by permitting multiplicity rather than enforcing unity. With respect to Tezcatlipoca's *tlaquimilolli*, tentative interpretations that attend to the polysemic signifiers of Nahuatl and Aztec visual and material cultures facilitate a richer understanding of the god's relationships to his various embodiments.

That Tezcatlipoca's *tlaquimilolli* contained a mirror should come as no surprise, given the god's onomastic, corporeal, and mythohistorical connections to smoking mirrors, in particular, and to obsidian, generally.[91] Tezcatlipoca both *is* (Lord of) the Smoking Mirror and *is identified by* the visual or material smoking mirror, which complicates attempts to distinguish the eponym from its embodied apotheosis (Figure 5.2). Perhaps, though, this (in)distinction points to other qualities of the *teotl*. Olivier suggests as much in the opening lines of *Mockeries and Metamorphoses*: "One must say that the Lord of the Smoking Mirror, as he appears under a variety of guises and names, seems

5.2. Tezcatlipoca with smoking mirror prosthetic. *Codex Borgia*, 21. Line drawing by author.

to strive against any attempt at identifying or reducing him. Sorcerer god, master of transformations, he seems to amuse himself in ceaseless metamorphoses to the detriment of the Cartesian investigator."[92] If, however, I were forced to select one identifying and identifiable (though not invariant) feature of this shadowy sorcerer *teotl*, the smoking mirror seems most obvious and relevant.[93] A curious object, the smoking mirror reflects a distorted image of the onlooker; acts as a vision apparatus comparable to the *tlachiyaloni* (instrument for seeing); and emits (or at least affects) smoke, a signifier of fire, volcanic activity, and rain clouds.

According to Sahagún, the Aztecs identified two types of mirror stone—one white and one black—and they varied in their surface quality and reflective properties. He explains, "Of these mirror stones, one is white, one black. The white one—this is a good one to look into. . . . They named it the mirror of the noblemen, the mirror of the ruler. The black one—this one is not good. It is not good to look into. . . . They say it is an ugly mirror, a mirror which contends with one's face."[94] Tezcatlipoca's smoking mirror was of the black variety, and may have been fashioned from pyrite or obsidian.[95] Tezcatlipoca held deep connections to obsidian, a volcanic rock. We have already seen Tezcatlipoca enter and excite the volcano Popocatepetl. According to Olivier, the *teotl* Itztli (Obsidian) was "one of Tezcatlipoca's avatars."[96] Nicholas Saunders draws an even more intimate connection by identifying "obsidian's apotheosis as Tezcatlipoca."[97] Materially and pictorially, the mirror clearly (re)presented Tezcatlipoca. In fact, archaeologist Michael Smith goes so far as to say that "most or all obsidian mirrors suggest the presence of the cult of Tezcatlipoca."[98] It seems fair to say, then, that the Lord of the Smoking Mirror stood in/as both *tezcatl* and *itztli*, and that the mirror bundled inside the *teotl's tlaquimilolli* stood in/as Tezcatlipoca. The mirror simultaneously signified his corporeality, his mythohistory, and his name.

Tezcatlipoca's mythohistorical embodiment of the reflective stones *tezcatl* and *itztli* locate him at, with, or as significant places, peoples, events, and animals. For instance, the *ocelotl* (jaguar), a frightening predator popular among transmogrifying *teteo* and *nanahualtin* (sorcerers), figures prominently in Tezcatlipoca's imagery (see Figure 4.3). *Ocelotls*' ability to see after dark paralleled that of diviners, whose ability to see in ways, times, and places unavailable to ordinary humans contributed to their singularity. Saunders situates the Aztecs' fascination with the shiny surfaces of mirrors in the nexus between *ocelotls* and diviners: "The widespread notion [that a mysterious light enabled diviners' night vision] appears linked to the 'divinatory seeing' and hunting of game animals by human and animal predators that, in Central

5.3. Tezcatlipoca's Toxcatl *teixiptla* holding a *tlachiyaloni*. *Florentine Codex*, 1:84v. Photograph courtesy of the Biblioteca Medicea Laurenziana.

and South America, associates shamans with the brightly colored and mirror-eyed jaguar (*Panthera onca*)."[99] The Aztecs understood *ocelotl*s in relation to themselves. Like *ocelotl*s, humans were efficient predators; like *ocelotl*s, diviners used mirror-eyes to see into the dark; and like *ocelotl*s and diviners, Tezcatlipoca had extraordinary vision.

From a devotee's perspective, the mirror's presence in Tezcatlipoca's *tlaquimilolli* reflected the *teotl*'s extraordinary ocular abilities, abilities that he extended to his religious associates through two of the *teotl*'s enchanted technologies/technologies of enchantment: the smoking mirror and *tlachiyaloni*.[100] The smoking mirror and *tlachiyaloni* exemplify Tezcatlipoca's vision(ary) capabilities by enabling devotees to see and communicate with the *teotl*. The *tlachiyaloni* appears in several codices, and both the *Florentine Codex* and Pomar's "Relación" describe its use in association with Tezcatlipoca (Figure

5.4. Figure holding *tlachiyaloni*. *Huamantla Codex*. Line drawing by author.

5.3).[101] According to Durán, the *tlachiyaloni* was, "like a mirror, a highly pol-ished and glistening round plate of gold, and it was understood that in this mirror he could see all that happened in the world."[102] Sahagún records a similar description and use of the *tlachiyaloni*. Tezcatlipoca and other deities, including Ixcozauhqui, Tlacochcalco, Yaotl, and Omacatl, carried the ocular instrument and looked through the hole in its center, which Sahagún char-acterizes as "like a small window (Figure 5.4)."[103] Drawings of Tezcatlipoca and Omacatl in the *Florentine Codex* show them holding a *tlachiyaloni*, and the text indicates that the apparatus was essential to Omacatl's *inechichihual* (array).[104]

Together, the smoking mirror and *tlachiyaloni* facilitated visual exchanges between Tezcatlipoca or his *teixiptla* and his devotees. For his part, Tezcatli-poca used the *tlachiyaloni* to extend the range of his vision, and perhaps to see into the *tonalli*, the fate or fortune, of his devotees.[105] Sahagún does not mention the *tlachiyaloni* in his overview of Toxcatl, but in three of the accom-panying images, Tezcatlipoca's *teixiptla* holds the vision apparatus in his left hand.[106] These images raise the question of how the device might have altered, enhanced, or extended the vision of the *teotl*'s *teixiptla*. Given the extensive training this *teixiptla* underwent in becoming Tezcatlipoca, including learning to speak like the *teotl* and play his flute, it seems likely that he would have learned how to magnify his vision using the *tlachiyaloni*, as well.

The *tlachiyaloni* extended the *teotl*'s vision (or that of the *teixiptla*) deeper into the human lifeworld (and possibly even into the minds of people), and conversely, the mirror enhanced devotees' ability to see their god. Mythohistorical accounts explain that priests, *teomamaque*, and dedicated devotees saw Tezcatlipoca through the mirror in his *tlaquimilolli*. Pomar reports, "They say that in this mirror, they saw Tezcatlipoca many times in the form that has been described and painted."[107] Taken together, Tezcatlipoca's reflective array facilitated a visual exchange, not unlike that of Hindu *darśan*, between the *teotl* and his people, including both priests and lay adherents. Not only did Tezcatlipoca's devotees see the deity in the mirror, but they also heard his voice through it. Pomar's account continues:

> and that, when the ancestors of those from Huitznahuac came . . . he spoke with them in a human voice through this mirror, so that they would continue and neither stop nor settle in the places that in coming along they wanted to stop and stay until they arrived at the land of the Chichimec Aculhuaque. When they arrived, he did not say anything else, and because of this, they settled there. And they found that afterward it no longer spoke to them, except sometimes they saw it in dreams and it told them some things that they did afterward: and they were the priests of his temple that were his caretakers and servants, that this was a very rare occurrence.[108]

We know from the descriptions of other *tlaquimilolli*'s origins that the bundles were almost always manufactured after the death of a deity, and Pomar's account gives the impression that the bundle did much more than simply "represent" the *teotl*. According to this story, the mirror included in Tezcatlipoca's *tlaquimilolli* brought him—face and voice—to the eyes and ears of his caretakers. The *tlaquimilolli* was the functional—if not ontological—equivalent of Tezcatlipoca's body. Tezcatlipoca's *tlaquimilolli* sensed, perceived, and communicated on behalf of the deity, much as his *teixiptla* did.

Tezcatlipoca's bodily presence in the *tlaquimilolli* calls to mind Las Casas's point about the significance of the thigh bone the *teotl* sent to the Texcocoans. Tezcatlipoca and Popocatepetl share an onomastic element: *popoca* (to smoke, give off vapor). Their shared signifier—smoky steam—began with Tezcatlipoca's descent into the fiery mountain, where he lost his leg and gained an obsidian mirror prosthetic. Olivier identifies the leg bone that Tez-catlipoca sent to the Texcocoans as "the most important element of his bundle."[109] Given the connotation of completeness associated with *tlaquimilolli*, I am hesitant to follow Olivier's valuation of one element in the bundle over another. However, the significance of the thigh bone in ritual sacrifice deserves our attention, and devotees' understanding of the femur in relation to *teotl* extends beyond the importance of including the physical remains of *teteo*, be they ash or bone, inside *tlaquimilolli*.

Itzpapalotl's *tlaquimilolli* demonstrates the importance of including in the bundle some physical rem(a)inder of the *teotl*'s corporeality. The femur stands out as having received special ritual attention during Tlacaxipehualiztli (Feast of the Flaying of Men), and femurs recovered by archaeologists substantiate colonial accounts of their posthumous modification. During Tlacaxipehualiztli, Aztec priests honored Xipe Totec (Flaying Lord) by sacrificing a captive and flaying his corpse. Ritual participants wore the flayed skins as an act of atonement, and the penitents shared the offerings they received with the captor. After the skin wearers had removed the skins and deposited them in a cave, the captor cleaned himself—he had fasted for twenty days for his captive—and erected an *itlacaxipehualizquauh* (flaying men tree) in his courtyard as a sign of his status. From the pole, he hung the captive's femur, *xicolli*, and heron feathers: "And he completely wrapped the thigh bone in paper; he provided it with a mask; and this was called the *malteotl* (captive-god)."[110] The word *malteotl* occurs in the *Florentine Codex* only once, but its significance relative to Tlacaxipehualiztli and to the (leg) bones included in *teteo*'s *tlaquimilolli* bring to mind the prominence of osteological material and skeletal symbolism in Aztec religion.

Despite the absolute proliferation of images and accounts detailing human sacrifice and the related practices of flaying and dismemberment, on one hand, and the pronounced place of skeletal motifs in Aztec iconography, on the other, we seem to know surprisingly little about what the Aztecs thought about human bone(s).[111] That is, the display of skulls on Templo Mayor structures and the presence of human and animal bones in sacred precinct caches make the skeleton's importance undeniable. By contrast to their descriptions of other body parts, our sources are largely silent as to Mexica philosophical or physiological articulations of bones. In *The Human Body and Ideology*, López Austin briefly addresses the importance of bone with reference to the femur of sacrificial victims, observing that its name—*malteotl*—"gives some idea of its sacred nature."[112] Others, including Jill Furst, argue that bones, semen, and seeds are mythohistorically homologous, meaning they symbolize the potential of life, the former by returning to the earth and the latter by bringing forth new life from it.[113]

Grégory Pereira's analysis of femurs and other osteological remains recovered from gravesites in Michoacán suggests that locals modified skeletal material for use in ritual. Specifically, Pereira observes that the notched femurs he examines may be like the *omichicahuaztli* (bone strength; bone rasp) described by Durán and Alvarado Tezozómoc. According to the chroniclers, the *omichicahuaztli* was a percussive instrument used exclusively in the funerals of men who had died on the battlefield. Pereira cites studies of incised bones from the Valley of Mexico, including those of Leopoldo Batres, Hermann Beyer, and Hasso Von Winning, but he admits that the poor records of bones' provenances often complicate drawing close connections between osteological material and the Aztecs.[114] The presence of bones in images depicting funerary bundles and their recovery from burials in Mesoamerica emphasizes the prominent role osteological materials played in funerary rituals.

The inclusion of osteological remains in *tlaquimilolli* attests to the theological significance of the material, the corporeal, and the human/zoological in Aztec religion. The instrument Tezcatlipoca used to present his visage and communicate his desires during the Texcocoan migration bundled the physical remains of his body: his femur and his (smoking) mirror. Given *quimilli's* semantics, it seems likely that the Texcocoans conceived of the *tlaquimilolli* as Tezcatlipoca, the Smoking Mirror completely refashioned. This bundled god-body, like its depictions in codices, carried the insignia appropriate to the *teotl*. The *tlaquimilolli* presented Tezcatlipoca with the mirror, his *axcaitl* (possessions, property), and *neixcahuilli* (exclusive thing), as well as with signifiers of his status as *mahuiztic* (marvelous) and *tlazohca* (valuable, beloved). In so doing, the *tlaquimilolli* exemplified the constructed or manufactured nature of *teixiptlahuan*.

Tlaquimilolli Wrap-Up

Quimiloa (to wrap somebody or something in a blanket) constituted a basic ritual action in Aztec culture and throughout the Americas.[115] Among the living, the process of wrapping healed broken bones and cured snake bites; it bound the joints of ritual structures; and it prepared humans for their trials in the afterlife. In addition to effecting cures, bundles brought with them a sense of the whole. *Quimilli* (bundle of cloths) referred specifically to a count of twenty capes, a number that connoted completeness in the Mesoamerican vigesimal system. In thinking through *tlaquimilolli*, those bundles specifically associated with *teteo*, the use of bundles in funerary practices provides an especially important frame of reference. The Aztecs wrapped human corpses prior to cremation, and they included personal belongings, such as women's weaving implements and men's weaponry, in the bundles. They believed that the individual's possessions would help them weather the ordeals of Mictlan, and not bundling a corpse amounted to abandoning a person to the harsh elements of the afterlife. Wrapping the corpse was so essential that the Aztecs rebuilt the bodies of warriors whose remains could not be recovered by making "corpses" from pine sticks, which they adorned with faces and dressed in ceremonial attire—replete with hawk feathers—prior to their cremation and burial. For the Aztecs, wrapping somebody or something in a blanket (re)constituted the person or the thing. In the case of deity bundles, wrapping facilitated the reconstitution of the healed, whole, and complete god-body. Simply put, *tlaquimilolli* were both made gods and gods-made material.

Although disentangling *tlaquimilolli*'s mythic origins from their historical uses may be tempting, their fabulous mythic lives made possible their powerful historical functions. At their simplest, *tlaquimilolli*, like *teixiptlahuan* and other living creatures, were mere skin and bones. The cloth, clothing, and hides that covered a *tlaquimilolli* bound together a *teotl*'s corporeal remains and *axcaitl* (possessions, property). Already these bundles straddle the ambiguous territories of mythohistory: to say that *teteo* had bodies and property suggests that they existed physically, that they were more than metaphors. And yet, clearly they did and were. The Aztecs (and other peoples throughout Mesoamerica and the Americas) created and re-created their gods' localized embodiments from a multitude of materials, including human ones. They produced *teteo* who became active agents in the world. The *teteo*, whether as *teixiptlahuan* or *tlaquimilolli*, were vital products of human labor and the religious imagination. *Teixiptlahuan* became the localized embodiments of *teteo* by virtue of presenting gods in (sur)face—literally in the skin—and the amorphous aniconic mass of *tlaquimilolli* were localized embodiments of the gods, too.

There is no reason to elide *teixiptlahuan* and *tlaquimilolli* or even classify *tlaquimilolli* as a type of *teixiptlahuan*. Strictly speaking, the two types of embodiments take different shapes and they performed different functions. *Teixiptlahuan* manifested *teteo* in elaborate anthropomorphic and zoomorphic forms whose verisimilitude must have transfixed onlookers, while *tlaquimilolli* looked like ordinary bundles of cloths. *Teixiptlahuan* presented recognizable manifestations of *teteo* in state and local ceremonies, and devotees saw, touched, and sometimes tasted the flesh of these localized embodiments.

By contrast, *tlaquimilolli* lived protected lives under the watchful guard of *teo-mamaque* or inside the innermost sanctuaries of their temples. Earlier, I argued that the animacy of *teixiptlahuan*—their ability to participate as agents in social relations—derived in part from the reflective capacity of their eyes, which held the devotee's attentive gaze. *Tlaquimilolli*, by contrast, had no eyes, nor did they reflect the onlooker's devotion. Rather than highlight the significance of sight and vision in relation to Mexica *teteo*, *tlaquimilolli*—this "principal" form of deity embodiment—reveal the importance of the gods' materiality and tangibility.

Teomamaque carried *tlaquimilolli*—the gods' bodies—on their backs as they followed (the directives of) these same *teteo* across the arid and mountainous terrain of Mesoamerica. The lives—past, present, and future—of the *teteo*, *teomamaque*, and priests were bound together: the *tlaquimilolli*'s physical presence weighed on the god-carriers even as their divine guidance urged them forward, and because of the gods' persistent physical presence, devotees felt an obligation to protect their *tlaquimilolli* by building a temple for it, even when they settled for the short-term. Among the Mexicas, Huitzilopochtli's *tlaquimilolli* functioned as an active agent in the social and religious events that led to their arrival in Tenochtitlan and prominence in the Central Valley. He communicated with his devotees, he motivated the community, and he ensured the foundation of his *altepetl* (water mountain; community). Aztec cities built up around the *tlaquimilolli* protected in the heart of their ceremonial centers, which replicated places of origin and embodied cosmological order.

At base, a *tlaquimilolli* simply presented what was left of the god: her skin, her ashes/bones, her heart, and her *axcaitl* (possessions). Of course, none of these materials was more (or less) than symbolic. *Teixiptlahuan* were wrapped in skins, and by virtue of being wrapped in cloth, *tlaquimilolli* were clothed in skins. The cloth-wrapped pine-stick bones and greenstone heart *made up* the *tlaquimilolli*. They made up the *tlaquimilolli* physically and imaginatively. They embodied the god, perhaps not in face, but certainly in form and signifying substance. Not unlike human corpses bundled with the skills of their trade before cremation, a *teotl*'s *tlaquimilolli* contained the *axcaitl* that derived from their *tonalli* (prerogative) and enabled their ongoing pursuit of *neixcahuilli* (exclusive pursuit). To the extent that *teteo* were products of the religious imagination, *tlaquimilolli* manifested one more mode of deity embodiment. They replicated neither the form nor substance of *teixiptlahuan*. Instead they presented *teteo*—once again—in body/embodied, and in this bodily form the *teotl* did not look like anybody.

Fates and Futures
Conclusions and New Directions

>>> No one, in practice, has ever displayed a naïve belief in any being whatsoever. If there is such a thing as belief at all, it is the most complex, sophisticated, critical, subtle, reflective activity there is.[1]

>>> Nopa Chicomexochitl yanopa niñoh.

>>> This Chicomexochitl is a baby boy.[2]

The Fate of the *Totiotzin*

In the summer of 2007, the year after I first witnessed Chicomexochitl, the community and several of my colleagues performed the ceremony again. The *tepahtihquetl* (ritual specialist) brought a new apprentice, and they changed the order of the ritual activities. He began the ritual at the *pozo* (well) where it usually concludes and arranged the *altepetl* (mountain) altars differently than before. After the ceremony ended, the participants returned to their respective homes and most of the visitors left the community. Everyone who remained agreed that the new ritual sequence seemed askew.

As my colleague Kelly McDonough was preparing to leave, she realized the home altar had caught fire. Several people quickly extinguished the fire, but some of the paper effigies had been singed. The mother and father of the sponsoring family held the Chicomexochitl and cried. The mother bounced the baby in her arms in an effort to comfort him; she and her husband soothed the Chicomexochitl figures as they would their own children.

These devoted parents' concern and grief illustrate the intimate familial relationship they share with the Chicomexochitl: what may appear to outsiders to be barely distinguishable paper dolls cut by human hands are, for them, localized embodiments of Tohueyinanan, Tohueyitatah, and their four children. The figures eat, their clothes become dirty and need to be changed periodically, and they see what goes on in the house (and, perhaps, everywhere). When accidental injury befalls them, their devotees sense and respond to their pain. Drawing a direct connection between Chicomexochitl and Aztec rituals centered on deity embodiment, whether state ceremonies like Tlacaxipehualiztli or private divinatory practices, seems at once obvious and obviously impossible. The destructive and creative disruptions of Contact prohibit me from making any claims to uncomplicated continuity between pre- and post-Contact cultures. There is, quite frankly, a lot I can't say.[3]

What I can say is that the devotional practices of the Aztecs and modern Nahuatl speakers reveal the ability of *teotl*, a marvelous and beloved entity with its own possessions, fate, and pursuits, to act and be acted upon and to create and re-create in the evolving form of *teixiptlahuan*, the localized embodiments of deities. Bruno Latour contends that "even though the fetish is nothing but what a human makes of it, it nevertheless adds a little something: it invents the origin of the action, it dissimulates the human work of manipulation, and it transforms the creator into a creature."[4] If I go along with him for a few minutes, the magic of the religious imagination at work in the ritual manufacture of Nahua god-bodies, the *teteo* and the *totiotzin*, becomes visible.

The *teixiptla*, which Latour would call a fetish and Alfred Gell an idol, is physically and conceptually made by and through its social relationship with the devotional community that brings it to life. Despite the fact that the mother of the sponsoring family had watched the *tepahtihquetl* cut the baby Chicomexochitl from a sheet of colored paper before she herself dressed the paper deity in the clothes she had made for him, her reaction to his accident demonstrates the depth of her feeling for the infant/deity.[5] Immediately she went to him, picked him up, held him in her arms, and soothed him as she would have her own (human) child. Their interaction was familiar and familial, in a word: intimate.

To those who witnessed the sequence of events, the mother responded with genuine concern for the infant she held in her arms. She did not react to the fire "as if" the effigy were alive; she treated it as her injured baby. "The essence of idolatry," Gell asserts, "is that it permits *real physical interactions* to take place between persons and divinities. To treat such interactions as 'symbolic' is to miss the point."[6] Treating this woman's relationship with the Chicomexochitl child as symbolic would certainly miss the point. And really, I think it would risk missing quite a bit more.

If the point is to see the *teixiptla* as an animate entity—a seemingly inanimate object brought to life by the devotional community—then treating the object-now-entity as symbolic would ignore the *teixiptla*'s real nature. But if I focus solely on the *teixiptla* and its ontological transformation, I miss another crucial point. In making the god-body, the devotional community made itself; the community members also underwent a process of becoming—one through which they became devotees of/to an entity they could see, touch, taste, and give to and take from. To borrow Latour's words, they the creators have become creatures, and these are words that should be heard less in reference to a Creator-creature relationship than to a world in which such dualisms (though operative in Mexican Catholicism and its many vernacular instantiations) dissipate in the face of a wholly animate cosmology.

The paper effigies created during Chicomexochitl offer one contemporary illustration of the powerful experience of fabricating and venerating a deity's localized embodiment (see Figure I.4). They also illustrate the relevance of two points driving this text: one, the importance of the meanings (and not just the translations) of *teotl* and *teixiptla*, and two, the incredibly imaginative variety and various natures of deity embodiments in Nahua religions.

Early in the book, I suggested that the challenges scholars face in explaining how and why *teteo* manifested in *teixiptlahuan* have as much to do with inherited (Western, somewhat iconoclastic, sometimes agnostic, and often religiously antagonistic) attitudes toward suspending belief in a differentiated (super)natural as they do with penetrating these complex and foreign, though indigenous, religious systems. In other words, to conceive of a world in which nature manifests the "supernatural" without relegating it (the manifestation) to the symbolic realm or designating it (the supernatural) as the transcendent brought immanent is to collapse the divisions that justify the firmament. These divisions—ones I might classify as generally Cartesian—support distinctions between familiar dualisms: mind/body, ephemeral/material, and life/death.

Nahua languages and cultures also recognize dualisms, but they treat opposition as an opportunity for creative thought and action through juxtaposition. The effect of a *difrasismo*, "pairing two metaphors which together give a symbolic means of expressing a single thought," illustrates this tendency most clearly: *atl* (water) and *tepetl* (mountain) become *altepetl*, a community's sustenance mountain and identifying mark on the local landscape; together *in xochitl* (flower) and *in cuicatl* (song) mean poetry; and *in mitl* (the arrow) and *in chimalli* (shield) mean war.[7] There is a similar effect—the bringing together of two different things to make a third—in the manufacture of deities' localized embodiments. But the ability to make that observation—to see the new third term—depends on having a clear sense of the initial terms: in this case, *teotl* and *teixiptla*.

The Fate of *Teotl*

In Chapter 3, I identified five properties that characterize "*teotl*" in the *Florentine Codex*: a *teotl* has *axcaitl* (possessions), a *tonalli* (prerogative), and a *neixcahuilli* (an exclusive pursuit) and is *mahuiztic* (marvelous) and *tlazohca* (beloved).[8] One conclusion I draw from these semantic associations is that the Aztecs connected individual gods and goddesses with qualitative clusters that shaped the deities' identities and today, if not historically, facilitate their identification. Isolating *axcaitl, tonalli,* and *neixcahuilli* as elements that constituted *teotl* means that we should expect individual deities to have their own possessions, property, day signs, fates, and exclusive businesses or pursuits.

This mode of interpreting the world—expecting its human, animal, and divine beings to have their own unique sets of properties—reflects the logic of folk taxonomies typically associated with the anthropological study of natural history: "People universally create a hierarchical ordering of living things based on how living things appear, that is, on similarities and dissimilarities in how they look, smell, sound, and act. . . . People might or might not produce other additional orderings based on such factors as how they use or interact with those living beings."[9] It is easy enough to understand how folk taxonomies order the natural world based on people's observations of and interactions with it. For example, the Aztecs described the *ocelotl* as follows:

quauhtla chane, texcalco chane, atlan chane: tecpilli, tlazopilli: quil inpillo, intlatocauh in iolque . . . Hueiac tlachueiac, melactic, temimiltic, pachtic, amo huecapan: tomaoac, tlaque, nacatetic, nacatepul, cuitlapilhuiuiac . . . ixpechtic, ixtletlexochtic; tlancuicuitztic, tlancuinene . . . cuicuiltic . . .

It is a dweller of the forests, of crags, of water; noble, princely, it is said. It is the lord, the ruler of the animals. . . . It is long: long bodied, straight, round like a pillar, squat, not tall; thick, corpulent; hard-fleshed, very hard-fleshed; long-tailed . . . of wide face with eyes like live coals; toothy, with small pointed front teeth. . . . It is varicolored. . . .[10]

The description of the *ocelotl* is the first entry in *Book 11: Earthly Things*. As the "ruler of the animals" and a noble creature, the *ocelotl* occupies the first place in the animal kingdom. The creature's physical description—the shape of its body, its ember-like eyes, and its sharp front teeth—follows these important considerations. The Aztecs located the *ocelotl* first in the animal kingdom and, according to *Book 11*, first in their natural history. Put simply: like the rest of the world's peoples, the Aztecs ordered the life around them.[11]

Reflecting on the ways in which Nahuas have discussed and depicted their *teteo* and *totiotzin*, one might be tempted to say that they extend their folk taxonomies to include deities. In other words, I could argue that their folk tax-onomy encompassed the supernatural as well as the natural. This might be a misguided assertion, though. It seems, rather, that the spectrum of animacy and the linguistic and ontological transformations god-bodies underwent in Aztec rituals and undergo during Nahua ceremonies point to an inclusive tax-onomic system, that is, one that does not distinguish (or is content to ignore) the line so often drawn between the supernatural and the natural.

Aztec religion centered around a cosmovision that recognized a wide spec-trum of animate entities, ranging from features of the natural world to ritually animated deity effigies. It wove the this-worldly and the otherworldly into the tangible and observable environment. Rather than delineating the immanent from the transcendent or the natural from the supernatural, the Aztecs, like other Amerindians, conceived of the world and its inhabitants as predomi-nantly animate (or able to be animated).[12] They identified some elements of the world, such as mountains, as innately animate, while in other cases, their ritual activity facilitated the transformation of inanimate "objects" into ani-mate entities. In this view of the world, Chalchihuitlicue *was* the water: "in ci-huateotl, in itoca chalchiuhtli icue, yehuatl in atl" (the goddess, the one called Chalchihuitlicue, she is the water).[13]

It may be, then, that understanding a god as bearing *teotl*'s five character-istics helps us interpret deity (re)presentations in the codices. For instance, the *Codex Borbonicus*, which begins with a *tonalamatl* (divinatory book) and concludes with depictions of rituals, including the New Fire ceremony and Ochpaniztli, contains a variety of images of deities. Catherine DiCesare has suggested that the final section of this codex may illustrate a sequence of fes-tivals that occurred during a specific year rather than a generic script of how the observances were typically performed.[14] Understanding a given deity's *ax-caitl*, *tonalli*, and *neixcahuilli* in more depth may help scholars recognize oth-er situations in which codices depict specific celebrations rather than general scenarios of a given ritual. Furthermore, these characteristics could aid in bet-ter understanding the deity presentations and associations in the *tonalamame* (divinatory books).[15]

Elizabeth Boone has described the *tonalamame* as books that "concern themselves with the way things now are in a present that continues into the future; they yield potentials, for they are windows into the future that allow one to see dangers and successes ahead."[16] We might expect, then, that the de-ities depicted in the largest frames of the *Codex Borbonicus*'s *tonalamatl* have with them the temporal and ritual associates and instruments that facilitated a diviner's interpretation of the present and future. Understanding the relationship between a deity's day sign, her possessions, and her exclusive pursuits will lead toward more specific analyses of these images and entities in relation to Aztec ritual and religion.

The Future of the Gods

This work with Aztec religion may, in turn, prompt new and different questions about contemporary Nahua beliefs and practices. When I visited the community in 2010, Victoriano de la Cruz and I asked the people we interviewed to describe the *totiotzin*'s physical appearance. The *tepahtihquetl* (ritual specialist) and the women we spoke with told us that the *totiotzin* (gods) look like adults and that the Chicomexochitl, who are also gods, look like children. The Chicomexochitl, they explained, have parents, too.

The mother of the host family—the same woman who three years earlier had held the burned child—told us that the ritual's hosts dreamed about when we (the outsiders) would arrive and when Chicomexochitl would take place. When Victoriano and I asked her about the deities' appearance, she explained that in dreams, "quemantzin tiquintemiquiz cocuetzitzin cocuetzitzin quemantzin huehhueyih tiquintemiquiz quen ni inihhuantin, chipactiqueh . . . pero nopa totiotzin titemiquiz, nopa titiotzin axcanah eliz cristiano nopa totiotzin." (Sometimes you're going to dream that they're very small, very small, sometimes large. You'll dream that they're white like them [pointing to my colleagues and I]. . . . But it's God that you're going to dream of, this is a god. It's not a person, it's truly a god.)[17] These gods inhabit the natural world. As the women explained, they are the mountains and the water.[18]

They are also the heat with whom the community negotiates during Chicomexochitl, a ritual meant to bring the rains. The *tepahtihquetl* insisted on this point:

Ese huallah niña, huallah niño. Como namantzin yauhque chamaquitos queuhne nenticateh, nochi chocah nochi monenecticateh, quipaxaloa totatah quipaxalotoh tonana, patzmiquih, techmaquilia ce tlitl ayoc ticxicoah tinequizquiah ce vasitos agua para tiatlizceh, a ver eso si.

Tinequizquia matlacehui como namantzin tlaehecaticah quentzin ticiauhtoqueh, techlahlamiquih pero cuando . . . ce calor moquetzaz tlen quinequi quichihuaz de la seca quichihua, tres años la seca quichiuhtoc para na niquittac la seca, a ver.

Quimahcahuilih ce lumbre a tres años, axcanah ticahuantarohqueh, miac mocauhqueh terrenos nican, parcelas. Nochi yahqueh miquitoh ceccoyoc pan pueblo ayoccanah quiahuantarohqueh la seca, eso tlanqui tlacualiztli, tlanqui cintli, ayocelqui, nochi niquiztoc.

A baby girl comes; a baby boy comes. Like just now, they were little kids, like those everyone is coddling. They visit our father; they visit our mother. They are hot; the heat hits us. We can't endure the heat. We want a few glasses of water to drink, see. This is how it is.

We would like for the heat to ease up a little, like now there's a little wind. We're tired, but we remember when . . . a hot spell is going to stop what you want to do, the dryness does it. There have been three years of dryness—I've seen the dryness, you see.

There was a heat wave three years ago, many of us didn't endure, many fields and plots died here. Everyone left, they left to die in another town. They couldn't endure the dryness. It killed the food, it killed the maize. I've seen everything.[19]

What remains, then, is to see if and, if so, how the characteristic qualities of *teteo* might help us understand the *totiotzin* and Chicomexochitl. Do they, like the Aztec deities, also have their own possessions and pursuits? From this ethnographic fragment, it seems that the Chicomexochitl have a close relationship to the sun (and presumably to temporal markers) because of their "*calor*" (heat). Is that actually the case?

The important point here is not to determine a definitive answer to these or other similar questions. Rather, it is that the similarities and differences scholars might identify by comparing Aztec and Nahua religions may offer insights that the kinds of comparisons that have been made—with Greek and Roman pantheons, with Polynesian *mana*, or with Hindu *darśan*—do not facilitate. The animate cosmovision of modern Nahuas is not that of the Aztecs, but they share linguistic, spatial, temporal, human, and divine elements: They live in and off of a similar landscape, and they face heat and winds that threaten their livelihood. In response, they manufacture gods that take on life before their very eyes. They clothe and feed their gods. They pray, and then they watch and wait for the rain.

The Fate of *Teixiptla*

Historically, Nahuas have recognized the powerful animacy of the world around them, and (m)any of its elements that are not already (highly) animate may be made so by ritually wrapping them in skin, cloth, or clothing.

Yoltoc, "someone alive, among the living," describes animate entities and has its root in the verb *yoli*: "to live; to come to life, to hatch."[20] These terms convey the process of becoming reflected in the ritual manufacture of *totiotzin* and *teteo*, like Xipe Totec's *teixiptla*, his god-body. Not just any man wearing any skin or any assortment of insignia could become Xipe Totec. Rather, each *teixiptla* of each deity came into being through a process: a specific human or material assimilation adopted the appearance and, in some cases, the behavior of a particular deity. In the Aztec context, a seemingly lifeless thing could take on life by adopting the appearance—the flesh—of a god (see Figure 4.1).

The extent to which a *teixiptla* looked like the deity he embodied depended on the materials that composed the physical effigy as well as the circumstances that demanded the deity's apotheosis. Diviners who embodied deities in order to receive penitents' confessions, like the *tlapouhqui* (something open; diviner) who became Tlazolteotl's "*iix*" (her eye), functioned as the gods without necessarily taking on their physical appearances. By contrast, the physical fidelity of material *teixiptlahuan* like the *tepictoton* (mountain figures) and *totiotzin* constructed in local and state ceremonies mattered more. As we have seen, both the *Florentine Codex* and the *tepahtihquetl* describe the importance of material *teixiptlahuan*'s shape and dress. Colonial sources stress the significance of a *teixiptla*'s facial features, and modern devotees invest significant amounts of time in sewing and dressing each Chicomexochitl in his or her own clothing and accessories (see Figures 1.4 and 4.7).

In addition to the importance of their appearance, the specific educations of human *teixiptlahuan* draw our attention to their socialization in state ceremonies and devotional communities. *Teixiptlahuan* commanded ritual stages specifically arranged to frighten and impress dependent polities, but they also shared intimate, if brief, relationships with devotees, who would kiss the earth (or eat it) as the gods paraded through the city. Devotees gave *teixiptlahuan* gifts, and they touched the gods—sometimes picking off a dry bit of flayed skin as a keepsake. But the importance of god-bodies' social roles was not limited to human *teixiptlahuan*. *Tlaquimilolli* (sacred bundles) also interacted with their devotees. Indeed, the lives of *tlaquimilolli*, the principal form of deity embodiment, make for fascinating god-body biographies. Accounts from the early colonial period indicate that Aztecs fashioned sacred bundles from deities' posthumous remains: the deity's *manta* (blanket) or an animal skin enshrouded her relics, including ashes, bones, and personal possessions. Wrapped in cloth, the remains and effects of the deity reincorporated her bundle-body so that she became, once again, an active agent living in the religious community. The stories and rituals surrounding this form of *teixiptlahuan* cross the boundaries conventionally drawn between myth and history, material and ephemeral, past and present, and life and death. The aniconic appearance and simple composition of *tlaquimilolli* challenge conventional notions of deity embodiment and expand our sense of how the Aztec religious imagination engaged in and enchanted the material world.

The common factor underlying the divine activity of all kinds of *teixiptlahuan* in Nahua religions was the recognition of the potential animacy or the potential for increased animacy in the materials that made up the god-bodies. Bennett describes this sort of animacy as "a liveliness intrinsic to the materiality of the thing formerly known as an object."[21] Whether made of packed amaranth-seed dough, wrapped deity relics, or dressed human bodies, *teixiptlahuan* embodied deities because their ritual manufacture invoked and transfigured the abundant animacy present in the natural world. In other words, the rituals—when rightly done—facilitate a process of becoming, an ontological transformation, in the materials that make up the god-body. This transformation results in the recognition of the *teotl*, and the act of recognition goes beyond simple name and appearance because it involves an exchange.

The Future of Earthly Things

The *teixiptla*'s ritual manufacture and education prepared the god-body to engage in the exchanges that occurred between the priest/devotee and the deity. Material *teixiptlahuan* received the facial features, clothing, and insignia necessary for them to see and be seen by devotees and to consume offerings. Similarly, human *teixiptlahuan* engaged in ceremonial activities that brought about their new identities. These processes resulted in the creation of new bodies, bodies that engaged in the world from uniquely constituted and highly animate perspectives.

Eduardo Viveiros de Castro's work among Amazonian Amerindians points to the centrality of "perspectivism," meaning "the ideas in Amazonian cosmologies concerning the way in which humans, animals and spirits see both themselves and one another."[22] The cosmologies Viveiros de Castro studies understand all beings as having different bodies that participate in the same soul, so that the viewer's unique body (whether that of a human, a bee, or a lizard) affords her a unique perspective. The viewer's perspective is at the heart of Viveiros de Castro's theory of Amerindian being and knowing:

A perspective is not a representation because representations are a property of the mind or spirit, whereas the point of view is located in the body. . . . The differences between viewpoints (and a viewpoint is nothing if not a difference) lie not in the soul. Since the soul is formally identical in all species, it can only perceive the same things everywhere. *The difference is given in the specificity of bodies.*[23]

By comparison, the localized embodiments of gods occupy specific perspectival locations in Nahua religions, namely a highly animate subjectivity acquired through a ritual process of becoming that is initiated when one person gets inside another person's skin. Once inside the skin (and/or attire), the *teixiptla* sees the world as Toci, Tonantzin, Xipe Totec, Tezcatlipoca, Tohueyinanan, Tohueyitatah, or a *totiotzin*. The perspective is not only divine, it is also deictic with respect to the set of qualities that characterize the specific *teotl*.

In contrast to Amazonian cosmology, Nahuas seem unconcerned with the sameness of souls and deeply invested in the differences of bodies. Nahua cosmologies recognize specific perspectives in the highly animate world, and they ritually invoke those perspectives in their respective god-bodies through the construction of *teixiptlahuan*. Neither transcendent nor immanent, the divinity of *teteo* and *totiotzin* embodiments derives from their materiality, their locality, and their perspective, including those qualities that compose each *teteo*'s identity. Together, the perspectives of the devotee and the god-body facilitate a social relationship and an exchange. The devotee makes and names the god-body:

in cihuateotl, in itoca chalchiuhtli icue, yehuatl in atl.

The goddess, the one called Chalchihuitlicue, she is the water.[24]

And:

nopa Chicomexochitl yanopa niñoh.

This Chicomexochitl is a baby boy.[25]

And in turn, the god (re)makes and (re)names the devotee as devotee and, every so often, the *teixiptla* as *teotl/totiotzin*.

Ixiptla Variants in Early Lexicons

Verbal Forms: By Resolution and Object

Verb	Form*	English Translation (Bassett)	Spanish Translation	Source
ixiptlayoua	*ni*	to pay back or satisfy something	recompensarse o satisfazarse algo	Molina
ixiptlayohua	*ni*	to pay back, to satisfy a debt	quedar pagada o satisfecha la deuda	Clavijero
ixiptlatia	*ni / nin*	to hand over one's post to somebody	entregar su cargo a alguien	Siméon
ixiptlayotia	*nin*	to delegate; to substitute in its place	delegar o sostituir a otro en su lugar	Molina
ixiptlayotia	*nicn*	to make something in one's image or likeness	hazer algo a su imagen y semejanza	Molina
ixiptlatia	*nite*	to paint a portrait of someone or to represent	retratar, representar	Clavijero
ixiptlati	*nite*	to attend in the place of another or to represent a person in a comedy	asistir en lugar de otro, o representar persona en farsa	Molina
ixiptlati	*nite*	to substitute for someone, to represent a role by a person	sustituir a alguien, representar un papel, a un personaje	Siméon

Verbal Forms: By Definition

English Translation	Verb	Spanish Translation	Form	Source
to pay back or satisfy something	*ixiptlayoua*	recompensarse o satisfazarse algo	*ni*	Molina
to pay back, to satisfy a debt	*ixiptlayohua*	quedar pagada o satisfecha la deuda	*ni*	Clavijero
to attend in the place of another or to represent a person in a comedy	*ixiptlati*	asistir en lugar de otro, o representar persona en farsa	*nite*	Molina
to substitute for someone, to represent a role by a person	*ixiptlati*	sustituir a alguien, representar un papel, a un personaje	*nite*	Siméon
to delegate; to substitute in its place	*ixiptlayotia*	delegar o sostituir a otro en su lugar	*nin*	Molina
to hand over one's post to somebody	*ixiptlatia*	entregar su cargo a alguien	*n / nin*	Siméon
to make something in one's image or likeness	*ixiptlayotia*	hazer algo a su imagen y semejanza	*nicn*	Molina
to paint a portrait of someone or to represent	*ixiptlatia*	retratar, representar	*nite*	Clavijero

Substantive Forms

Noun	English Translation	Spanish Translation	Source
teixiptla	image of someone, substitute or delegate	imagen de alguno, sustituto, o delegado	Molina
teixiptlatini	representative of a person in a comedy	representador de persona en farsa	Molina
tlaixiptlayotl	a thing restored in another kind, or a thing that is given in the place of another	cosa restituida en otra especie, o cosa que se da en lugar de otra	Molina
tlaixiptlayotl	painted image	imagen pintada	Molina
ixiptlayotl	image, portrait	imagen, retrato	Clavijero
ixiptlatl	representative, delegate	representante, delegado	Siméon

*Verbal form abbreviations: *ni* (transitive); *nite* (transitive, takes a living object); *nin* (transitive, reflexive); *nicn* (transitive, takes an object, reflexive).

A List of Terms Modified by *Teo-* in the *Florentine Codex* (English translations from Anderson and Dibble)

	Canonical Form	Translation	Modified Form	Translation	Citation by Book and Page Number
1.	*atl*	water	*teoatl*	sea, ocean	1:64, 10:88
2.	*calli*	house	*teocalli*	temple	2:178, 11:269
3.	*cuitlatl*	excrement	*teocuitlatl*	gold	11:231
4.	*octli*	maguey wine, pulque	*teoctli*	sacred pulque	9:63
5.	*cuahuitl*	oak	*teocuahuitl*		10:81, 11:108
6.	*ithualco*	courtyard	*teoithualco*	temple courtyard	2:109, 134
7.	*pixeque*	guardians of tradition	*teopixqui*		1:33, 3:69
8.	*miquiz*	he will die	*teomiquiz*	he will die sacrificed as a war captive	4:35, 6:171
9.	*tetl*	stone	*teotetl*	jet	2:161, 11:228
10.	*xihuitl*	turquoise	*teoxihuitl*	fine turquoise	11:224
11.	*teoxihuitl*	fine turquoise	*tlapalteoxihuitl*	red or ruby turquoise	11:224
12.	*quemitl*	clothing	*teoquemitl*	sacred cape	2:72, 12:81
13.	*tlachtli*	ball court	*teotlachco*	sacred ball court	2:145
14.	*xochitl*	flower	*teoxochitl*	sacred flower	2:157
15.	*tlalli*	dirt, earth	*teotlalli*	desert waste	6:23, 9:13
16.	*tzanatl*	grackle (bird)	*teotzanatl*	boat-tailed grackle	2:160, 11:50
17.	*xalli*	sand	*teoxalli*	abrasive sand	9:81, 11:237
18.	*nantli*	mother	*teonantli*	godly mother	6:155
19.	*cocoliztli*	illness, sickness	*teococoliztli*	divine sickness (leprosy?)	3:11, 10:157
20.	*aztatl*	heron, snowy egret	*teoaztatl*	snowy egret (intensely white)	11:28
21.	*texcalli*	oven	*teotexcalli*	hearth	7:4–5
22.	?	?	*teteopohualli*	sacrificial paper	9:65

Turquoise, Jet, and Gold

The Nahuatl passage is followed by translations by *Bassett and **Anderson and Dibble.

XIHUITL

inin xihuitl itech quiza in itoca xihuitl, in ixoatoc: ipampa in itlachializ amo cenca quiltic, zan achi micqui: iuhquin amo cenca mahuizyo, zan nel achi ixtlileoac

auh inin xihuitl, amo cenquizqui, zan cacaiacaticac, iuhquin xalli, patlachtontli, patlachpipil, amo tlaquaoac, zan poxoaoac. Inic monequi, inic tlaqualnextilo, zan momana, mozaloa, zan ic tlaixtzaqualo:

nixiuhzaloa, nixiuhtzaqua: nicxiuhtzaqua in huapalli, in teixiptla: nixiuhtemoa, nixiuhtataca, nixiuhquixtia.

*TURQUOISE

Turquoise's name comes from grass, which sprouts out, for its appearance is not very herb-green, only a bit dull as if it is not very marvelous, only a little dark, actually.

Turquoise is not a perfect thing, but worn thin like sand, small and flat, small and wide, not hard, but soft. Thus it is used to beautify; it is merely set out, glued on and affixed to something.

I glue turquoise. I affix turquoise. I affix turquoise to the board, to the image. I search for turquoise. I excavate turquoise. I remove turquoise.

**TURQUOISE

The name of this turquoise comes from the herb which lies sprouting; because its appearance is [not highly colored,] not very herb-green, just a little dull; as if it were not highly estimable. It is really a little dark-surfaced. And this is not in one piece. It is just broken up in little pieces like sand, small and flat, small and wide, not hard, just soft. It is required for use in adorning; it is just set on, glued on, for which there is gluing of the surface. I glue turquoise. I affix turquoise. I affix turquoise to the beam, to the image. I search for turquoise. I excavate turquoise. I remove turquoise. (Sahagún, *Book 11*, 11:223)

TEOXIHUITL

inin itoca itech quiza in teōtl, ihuan in xihuitl, zan quihtoznequi iiaxca, itonal in teōtl, ihuan, quihtoznequi cenca mahuizyo; ipampa acan cenca neci, canin zan queman in neci: inin teuxihuitl cenca mahuizyo, in itla in itech motta amo cenca mahuizyo: auh in achi huehca neci, huel tizatl, iuhquin xiuhtototl, nelli iuhquin popoca.

inin cequi patlachtic, cequi ololtic, itoca xiuhtomolli: inic xiuhtomolli, ca centlacotl in ololtic in tomoltic: auh in oc centlapal patlachtic, iuhquinma zan ic tlapanqui, cequi huel xipetztic, cequi chachaltic, cequi cocoioctic, cequi tezontic, patlachiuih, ololihui, ticeoa, popoca, teoxiuhpopoca, chachaquachiuih, quiquicahui, tetecahui.

*TEO-TURQUOISE

The name of this one comes from *teotl* and turquoise because it means the possessions, the fate of the *teotl*, and it means something very marvelous, because it does not appear very much, because at times it does not appear anywhere. This *teo*-turquoise is very marvelous; when something is visible on it, it is not so marvelous, but from a little distance it appears rather chalky, like the blue cotinga, truly like smoke.

Some of these are wide, others are spherical. Their name is *xiuhtomolli* (turquoise blister)—"turquoise blister" because one half is spherical like a blister, and the other side is broad like something broken. Some are very slick, others roughened, others perforated, rough, wide. It becomes round; it becomes chalky; it smokes, it emits a vapor like turquoise. It is roughened; it becomes perforated; it becomes pale.

**FINE TURQUOISE

The name of this comes from *teotl* [god] and *xihuitl* [turquoise], which merely means that it is the property, the lot, of the god; and it means that it is much esteemed, because it does not appear anywhere very often. It seldom appears anywhere. This fine turquoise is much esteemed. When in it, when on it [something] is seen, it is not much esteemed. And when it appears some distance away, it is quite pale, like the lovely cotinga, verily as if smoking. Some of these are flat. Some are round; their name is *xiuhtomolli*. They are called *xiuhtomolli* because one side is round, swollen, but the other side is flat, just as if broken in half. Some are quite smooth, some roughened, some pitted, some like volcanic rock. It becomes flat, it becomes round, it becomes pale. It smokes. The fine turquoise smokes. It becomes rough, it becomes perforated, it becomes pale. (Sahagún, *Book 11*, 11:224)

TLAPALTEOXIHUITL

inin itoca, itech quizqui in tlapalli, huan in teoxihuitl: ipampa ca zan ye huel iehoatl in teoxihuitl, in quimotlatlalili, ic mopopoiauh chichiltic, ic cenca nelli mahuizyo, mahuiztic: zan cenca yequeneh tlazohnemi, motlapalpoiahua, meezcuicuiloa, mahuizyoa, tlazohneci tlazohpialo.

*DYED *TEO*-TURQUOISE

Its name comes from *tlapalli* (ink, dye; metaphorically, blood) and *teo*-turquoise, because it is precisely already a lot [like] *teo*-turquoise. It is made red, it is darkened. In truth, it is very wonderful, marvelous. Lastly, it is very rare, it is rose-colored, it is variously blood-colored. Esteemed, it is rare. It is guarded as precious.

RUBY

**The name of this comes from *tlapalli* [red] and *teoxihuitl* [fine turquoise], because it is the same as the fine turquoise. However, it is so constituted as to be colored chili-red. Thus it is truly very wonderful, marvelous; in short, it is very rare. It is rose-colored, blood-speckled, esteemed, rare; it is guarded as precious. (Sahagún, *Book 11*, 11:224)

TEOTETL

itech quizqui in itoca teotl, ihuan tetl; ipampa acan centetl neci, iuhquin tetl inic tlitic, quitoznequi zan tlazohca zan tlazohnemi: iuhquinma ineixcahuil teutl, tliltic, tlilpatic, cemahcic tliltic, capotztic, chapopotic, huel cemahcic tliltic, huel ahcic in tlillan.

*TEO-STONE

The name of this comes from *teotl* and stone, because nowhere does a single stone appear as black as this stone. That is to say, it is rare, precious, like the *teotl*'s exclusive thing. Black, very black, perfectly black; black like pitch. Indeed, perfectly black, it is really totally black.

**JET

Its name comes from *teotl* [god] and *tetl* [stone], because nowhere does a stone appear as black as this stone. That is to say, it is precious, rare, like the special attribute of a god. It is black, very black, completely black; black, the color of bitumen; completely black, perfect in its blackness. (Sahagún, *Book 11*, 11:228)

COZTIC TEOCUITLATL

inin teocuitlatl in coztic, in iztac in itoca: itech quiza in itoca teotl, ihuan cuitlatl: ipampa in mahuiztic, in coztic, in cualli, in iectli, in tlazotli, in necuiltonolli, in netlamachtilli, intonal, imaxca, inneixcahuil in tlatoque, in totecuihuan:

  itech quizqui, in queman cana neci tlahuizcalpan. iuhquinma apitztaltontli, quitocayotia tonatiuh icuitl, cenca coztic, cenca mahuiztic, iuhquin tlexochtli mani, iuhquinma coztic teocuitlatl, tlaatililli; ic neci itech tlaantli, y, in coztic teocuitlatl, amo yehuatl in ipalnemohuani, itechcopa mitoa, ye in tonatiuh: ca in ayamo iximacho in icel teotl, in nelli teotl in ca miequintin tēteoh neteotiloya. Auh in tonatiuh: zan huel itoca catca teotl, nepantla teotl, mitoaya hualquiza teotl, nizteotl: onmotzcaloa teotl, oncalaqui teotl: teotlac noma mitoa in axcan, quitoznequi onac, oncalac in teotl.

*YELLOW *TEO*-EXCREMENT

The name of *teocuitlatl*, the yellow, the white, comes from *teotl* and excrement, because it is wonderful, yellow, good, pure, and precious. It is the wealth, the good fortune of the rulers, our lords; it is their prerogative, their property, their exclusive thing.

  It comes from [this]: sometimes in some places it appears at dawn, as if a little bit of diarrhea. They call it the sun's excrement. It is very yellow, very wonderful, as if it is a live ember, as if it is molten yellow gold. So it appears that yellow gold is taken from this; it is not from he by whom living goes on. It is said that it comes from the sun, from before the only *teotl* was known. Before the true *teotl* was worshipped, there were many *teteo*. But the sun was the name of a *teotl*. It was called, "*Teotl* in the middle, *teotl* comes up, here is *teotl*, *teotl* leans on its side, *teotl* sets." Still now *teotlac* [sunset] is said; it means the god entered, set.

**GOLD

The name of this gold, the yellow, the white [silver]—its name comes from *teotl* [god] and *cuitlatl* [excrement], because it is wonderful, yellow, good, fine, precious. It is the wealth, the riches, the lot, the possession, the property of the rulers, our lords. It derives from [the fact that] sometimes, in some places, there appears in the dawn something like a little bit of diarrhea. They named it "the excrement of the sun"; it was very yellow, very wonderful, resting like an ember, like molten gold. So it appears that [the name] gold is taken from this. It is not from God. It is said that this is the sun, for the only God, the true God, was not yet known; for many gods were worshipped. And "sun" was really the name of a god. It was said, "The god comes up; the god is in the middle; here is the god; the god leans on his side; the god enters." *Teotlac* is still said today; it means "the god [the sun] has entered, has set." (Sahagún, *Book 11*, 11:233–234)

NOTES

All citations in the notes to the *Florentine Codex: General History of the Things of New Spain* by Bernardino de Sahagún have been shortened to Sahagún, *Book No.*, vol. no.:pg. no., as the book number is what distinguishes one volume from another, with the exception of Vol. 1, *Introductions and Indices*, which does not have a book number. Additionally, the translators' names in the text and citations are given as Anderson and Dibble throughout; however, the correct order of the translators' names as they appeared on the copyright page is given in the bibliography entry for each volume.

INTRODUCTION

1. Scholars differ in their preference regarding the use of the terms "Aztec," "Mexica," or "Nahua" to identify the peoples who lived in and around Tenochtitlan prior to Contact. Some, including James Lockhart, prefer the term "Nahua" over "Aztec," which he says "has several decisive disadvantages: it implies a kind of quasi-national unity that did not exist, it directs attention to an ephemeral imperial agglomeration, it is attached specifically to the preconquest period, and by the standards of the time, its use for anyone other than the Mexicas (the inhabitants of the imperial capital, Tenochtitlan) would have been improper even if it had been the Mexica's primary designation, which it was not." *Nahuas after the Conquest*, 1. By contrast, others, such as John F. Schwaller, opt to use "Aztec," because it is more easily understood by readers less familiar with the polities of the pre-Contact Central Valley. "Expansion of Nahuatl," 688n682. When used to capture the populations of the Central Valley, "Aztecs" or "the Aztec Empire" usually refers to the Triple Alliance of Tenochtitlan, Tlacopan, and Texcoco. "Mexica" designates those people living in Tenochtitlan, and "Nahua" refers to a broader population: those who spoke (older or classical) Nahuatl, the lingua franca of the Aztec Empire. Today approximately 1.5 million people speak modern Nahuatl, a variant of the Nahuatl spoken by the Mexicas and their neighbors. In this work, "Mexica" refers to the culture group led by Huitzilopochtli from the place of origin into the Central Valley, where they founded Tenochtitlan; "Aztecs" incorporates the peoples who formed the Triple Alliance; and "Nahuas" includes present and past native speakers of Nahuatl.

2. Anderson and Schroeder, *Codex Chimalpahin*, 95; translation by Anderson and Schroeder. Unless otherwise indicated, as here, all translations are my own. In this retelling, I draw upon the *Codex Chimalpahin* (1621) and Diego Durán's *History of the Indies of New Spain* (ca. 1581).

3. Ibid., 94–95; translation by Anderson and Schroeder.

4. Durán, *History of the Indies*, 36.

5. Anderson and Schroeder, *Codex Chimalpahin*, 96–97; translation by Anderson and Schroeder.

6. Durán, *History of the Indies*, 37.

7. Ibid. Durán explains, "It is she whom the Aztecs worshiped from that time on as mother of the gods. . . . She is called Toci, which means "mother" or "grandmother.""

8. Anderson and Schroeder, *Codex Chimalpahin*, 96–97; translation by Anderson and Schroeder.

9. Ibid.; translation by Anderson and Schroeder.

10. Ibid., 97–98; translation by Anderson and Schroeder.

11. Durán, *History of the Indies*, 38.

12. Navarrete Linares, *Orígines de los pueblos indígenas*, 11–35.

13. Navarrete Linares, "Las fuentes indígenas," 231–238.

14. Trouillot, *Silencing the Past*, 2.

15. Urton, *History of a Myth*, 141n144.

16. See Navarrete Linares, *Orígines de los pueblos indígenas*, 18–22; and Lockhart, *Nahuas after the Conquest*, 416.

17. Pagden, "Introduction," l. On the same page, Pagden also notes that "no other royal official, either in America or Europe, had two complete scribal copies made of his correspondence."

18. Ibid., li.

19. Doniger, *Other Peoples' Myths*, 28.

20. Austin, *How to Do Things with Words*, 6.

21. Silko, *Ceremony*, 135–138.

22. Doniger, *Other Peoples' Myths*, 28.

23. "Cosmovision" refers to the Mesoamerican mode of being-in-the-world that "integrates the structure of space and the rhythms of time into a unified whole." Carrasco, *Religions of Mesoamerica*, 166.

24. Doniger, *Other Peoples' Myths*, 2.

25. Patton, *Religion of the Gods*, 8.

26. Andrews, *Introduction to Classical Nahuatl*, 18.

27. Ibid.

28. Ibid., 20.

29. See Gómez Martínez, *Tlaneltokilli*, 66.

30. Catalina Cruz de la Cruz, Sabina Cruz de la Cruz, and Delfina de la Cruz de la Cruz, personal communication, June 1–July 31, 2006.

31. This classificatory scheme ties modern Nahuatl to the speakers' observation of life in (or attribution of life to) other members of and materials in the world, and it prompted me to consider whether clues to the animacy of *teixiptlahuan* might be found within older Nahuatl. Unfortunately, older Nahuatl has only one "to be" verb, *ca* (to be), that functioned with regard to place and existence but without regard to animacy.

32. C. Cruz de la Cruz, S. Cruz de la Cruz, and D. de la Cruz de la Cruz, personal communication; and "Nahuatl Dictionary."

33. In his exposition of semiotic ideology, Webb Keane explains the relationship be-

tween social relations, language, and a speaker's linguistic awareness: "Language ideologies do not just express social difference, they play a crucial role in producing—in objectifying and making inhabitable—the categories by which social difference is understood and evaluated. Moreover, since the power effects of language (and of semiotic form more generally) are not fully determinate—the 'same' forms can, for example, have quite different implications in different contexts—ideological mediation is a necessary component of any political consequences that might follow from form. At the same time, *ideology* here does not mean false consciousness or systematic deception. By using the word *ideology*, most linguistic anthropologists are stressing the productive effects of reflexive awareness." Keane, *Christian Moderns*, 17.

34. These conversations took place from 2006 through 2012, and during that time, Kelly McDonough and I compiled a Nahuatl word list akin to a Swadesh list that records how native speakers classify a wide variety of modern Nahuatl nouns.

35. In modern Nahuatl, *teteo* are called *totiotzin* (our *teteo*, reverentially).

36. Ofelia Cruz Morales and Abelardo de la Cruz de la Cruz, personal communication, September 12, 2007.

37. C. Cruz de la Cruz, S. Cruz de la Cruz, and D. de la Cruz de la Cruz, personal communication; John Sullivan and Delfina de la Cruz de la Cruz, personal communication, October 9, 2008; and "Nahuatl Dictionary."

38. "Nahuatl Dictionary."

39. Kelly McDonough, personal communication, 2011.

40. Author interview with ritual participant A, August 4, 2010.

41. One participant indicated that *relámpagos* (lightning bolts) receive this offering so that it will rain. Author interview with ritual participant B, August 4, 2010.

42. These interviews were conducted informally with the agreement that I would not use the informants' names. They are not comprehensive; instead they represent initial inquiries into how animacy occurs during Chicomexochitl. I appreciate Victoriano de la Cruz's willingness to sit in on the interviews, transcribe them, and translate the modern Nahuatl into Spanish.

43. Author interview with ritual participant A.

44. Author interviews with ritual participant B, ritual participant A, and ritual participant C, August 4, 2010.

45. Medina Hernández, "La cosmovisión nahua actual," 195.

46. Author interview with ritual participant C.

47. Ibid.

48. Latour, "On the Cult of the Factish Gods," 3–4.

49. Ibid., 22–23.

50. Keane, *Christian Moderns*, 18.

51. In *Corn Is Our Blood* (229–322), Alan Sandstrom examines religion in Amatlan, the pseudonym he provides for the Nahuatl-speaking village in which he conducted decades of ethnographic and linguistic research.

52. Author interview with ritual participant D (the *tepahtihquetl*), August 4, 2010.

This *tepahtihquetl* is Otomí, and in addition to speaking his own language, he speaks Spanish and some Nahuatl.

53. Ibid.

54. In *Tlaneltokilli*, Gómez Martínez describes the Nahua pantheon and provides line drawings of several *tlatecmeh*, including one identified as Chicomexochitl.

CHAPTER 1

1. López de Gómara, *La conquista de México*, 161.

2. Muñoz Camargo, *Historia de Tlaxcala*, 181–182.

3. In Lockhart, *We People Here*, 1:62; translation by Lockhart.

4. Schroeder et al., *Chimalpahin's Conquest*, 178.

5. Sometime between 1593 and 1620, Chimalpahin, who authored "the most comprehensive extant corpus of the history of Indian Mexico written by a known indigenous author in his own language," copied and emended *Historia de las Indias y conquista de México*, first published by López de Gómara in 1552. Schroeder describes López de Gómara as Cortés's biographer and notes that he may have served as his priest. Ibid., 3–4.

6. One such encounter includes, as Gananath Obeyesekere argues, the accounts of how Hawai'ians perceived Captain Cook. Although they go about it differently, both Diana Taylor and Tzvetan Todorov also identify Cortés's invasion of the Aztecs as the paradigm for later European explorers. Taylor explains that "scenarios, by encapsulating both the setup and the action/behaviors, are formulaic structures that predispose certain outcomes and yet allow for reversal, parody, and change. The frame is basically fixed and, as such, repeatable and transferable. Scenarios may consciously reference each other by the way they frame the situation and quote words and gestures. They may often appear stereotypical, with situations and characters frozen within them. *The scenario of conquest has been replayed again and again—from Cortés's entrance into Tenochtitlán, to the meeting between Pizarro and Atahualpa, to Oñate's claiming possession of New Mexico.*" Todorov argues that Cortés became "the type" for later conquistadors: "It required a remarkably gifted man to crystallize into a unique type of behavior elements hitherto so disparate: once the example is set, it spreads with impressive speed. The difference between Cortés and those who preceded him may lie in the fact that he is the first to have a political and even a historical consciousness of his actions." Obeyesekere, *Apotheosis of Captain Cook*, 19, 124; Taylor, *The Archive and the Repertoire*, 31, emphasis added; and Todorov, *Conquest of America*, 99.

7. Pratt, *Imperial Eyes*, 7, emphasis added.

8. Townsend ("Burying the White Gods" and "No One Said It Was Quetzalcoatl"), Susan Gillespie ("Blaming Moteuczoma"), and Louise Burkhart ("Meeting the Enemy") argue that the myth of Cortés as Quetzalcoatl was a post-Contact invention; Carrasco (*Quetzalcoatl* and "Spaniards as Gods") and Henry B. Nicholson (*The "Return of Quetzalcoatl"*) argue that the Aztecs identified Cortés with the deity, at least initially.

9. Townsend, "Burying the White Gods," 668. See Gillespie, *The Aztec Kings*, 197–198.

10. Lockhart, *We People Here*, 4.

11. León-Portilla, "Have We Really Translated," 35.

12. Sahagún, *Book 12*, 12:26.

13. Lockhart, *We People Here*, 65. By contrast, the Nahuatl text lists this same element as "a serpent mask, made of turquoise; a quetzal-feather head band." However, the Nahuatl text identifies specific bird species from which the feathers come, the *quetzal* (quetzal) and *aztatl* (heron). Ibid., 64.

14. Kevin Terraciano notes that the Spanish descriptions of the gifts are uncharacteristically lengthier than those in Nahuatl, and he suggests that the Nahuatl text may be shorter because the "details were already familiar to a Nahua." Elsewhere he observes that Sahagún may have drawn upon other manuscripts of his, perhaps *Book 1* or the *Primeros memoriales* for the lengthier descriptions, but that the Spanish descriptions in *Book 12* contain more details than either of those sources. Terraciano, "Three Texts in One," 60 and 70n4.

15. Boone, *Stories in Red and Black*, 232.

16. Ibid.

17. Durán, *History of the Indies*, 515.

18. Alvarado Tezozómoc, *Crónica mexicana*, 32–35; and Durán, *History of the Indies*, 74–77.

19. Durán, *History of the Indies*, 76.

20. Ibid., 77.

21. Ibid., 451.

22. Boone, *Stories in Red and Black*, 34.

23. Durán, *Book of the Gods and Rites*, 297.

24. Ibid.

25. Durán, *History of the Indies*, 124.

26. Ibid., 291.

27. Sahagún, *Book 12*, 12:19; and Schroeder et al., *Chimalpahin's Conquest*, 183–184. Although no necklace appears among Moteuczoma's gifts for Cortés depicted in the *Codex Mexicanus*, a necklace does appear among the gifts given by Cortés to Moteuczoma.

28. Boone, *Stories in Red and Black*, 232–233.

29. Anawalt, "Analysis of the Aztec Quechquemitl," 41.

30. Sahagún, Sullivan, and Nicholson, *Primeros memoriales*, 96 and folio 261v.

31. Bierhorst, *History and Mythology of the Aztecs*, 31–32.

32. Ibid., 32.

33. Ibid., 32–33; translation by Bierhorst.

34. Ibid., 36; translation by Bierhorst.

35. Russo, "Plumes of Sacrifice," 232.

36. Ibid., 231–232.

37. Ibid., 231. See also Durán, *Historia de las Indias*, 116.

38. Russo, "Plumes of Sacrifice," 232.

39. Russo, "Cortés's Objects," 232–233 and 48n17.

40. Russo, "Plumes of Sacrifice," 234.

41. Ibid.

42. Baird, "Sahagún and the Representation of History," 117–120.

43. The Nahuatl text of *Book 12* was first written in 1555, and Sahagún sent the twelve finished books to Spain in 1579. Six years later, he redacted *Book 12*—and *Book 12* alone—following what was likely clerical criticism regarding its presentation of the Conquest. See Terraciano, "Three Texts in One," 53 and 64.

44. On mythohistory, see Urton, *History of a Myth*, 141n4; on myth, see Doniger, *Other Peoples' Myths*, 28; and on history, see Trouillot, *Silencing the Past*, 2–4.

45. Cortés, *Hernán Cortés: Letters from Mexico*, 85.

46. Nicholson, *The "Return of Quetzalcoatl,"* 13.

47. See Gillespie, "Blaming Moteuczoma," 25–28. Moteuczoma devised a test in order to discover the foreigner's identity: "If he eats and drinks he surely is Quetzalcoatl, for this will show that he is familiar with the foods of this land, that he ate them once and has come back to savor them again. . . . If by any chance he does not like the food you give him and is desirous of devouring human beings and wishes to eat you, allow yourselves to be eaten." Durán, *History of the Indies*, 497.

48. Durán, *History of the Indies*, 498. Sahagún continued to redact the text of *Book 12* until 1585, and this later edition reflects his perspective more often than does the version of *Book 12* found in the twelfth volume of the *Florentine Codex*.

49. Sahagún, *Conquest of New Spain: 1585 Revision*, 41.

50. Lockhart, *We People Here*, 62.

51. Burkhart, "Meeting the Enemy," 15.

52. Townsend, "Burying the White Gods," 667. Thanks to one of UT Press's anonymous readers for pointing out that Townsend bases this criticism on conjecture.

53. Magaloni Kerpel, "Painting a New Era," 130.

54. Terraciano, "Three Texts in One," 67.

55. See ibid., 53–54; and Boone, "Ruptures and Unions," 197–225.

56. García Márquez, "Nobel Lecture," http://nobelprize.org/nobel_prizes/literature/laureates/1982/marquez-lecture-e.html.

57. Obeyesekere, *Apotheosis of Captain Cook*, 124. For another perspective on Cook's reception, see Sahlins, *How "Natives" Think*.

58. Boone, *Cycles of Time and Meaning*, 32.

59. Ricoeur, *Hermeneutics and the Human Sciences*, 187.

CHAPTER 2

1. See Ruiz de Alarcón, *Treatise on the Heathen Superstitions*, 803–836; Hamann, "Chronological Pollution"; and Sandstrom, *Corn Is Our Blood*.

2. Townsend, "Burying the White Gods," 661; and "No One Said It Was Quetzalcoatl," 2.

3. Townsend, "Burying the White Gods," 670–671.

4. Terraciano, "Three Texts in One," 68–69.

5. The classifications "older Nahuatl" and "modern Nahuatl" distinguish between the Nahuatl of the pre-Contact and colonial periods and the dialects spoken in Mexico today.

6. Townsend, *State and Cosmos*, 28.

7. See Boone, *Cycles of Time and Meaning*, 43; Pohl and Lyons, *The Aztec Pantheon*, 34–35; Stone, *The Jaguar Within*, 6; and Townsend, *State and Cosmos*, 28.

8. My discussion of these genealogies presents a significant, though not exhaustive, account and analysis of Mesoamericanists' interpretations of *teotl* and *teixiptla*. A more expansive survey would consider the work of Eduard Seler, Ángel María Garibay Kintana, Alfonso Caso, Miguel León-Portilla, and others.

9. Archives of Nahuat-l conversations are available online via the Foundation for the Advancement of Mesoamerican Studies website (www.famsi.com) by following the links "Resources" and "Discussion Lists." The Nahuat-l archives are searchable by keyword.

10. Rao, "Florentine Codex," 488.

11. Sahagún, *Introductions and Indices*, 53.

12. Ibid., 47.

13. Clayton, "Trilingual Spanish-Latin-Nahuatl Manuscript." It seems that Sahagún's collaboration with Colegio de Santa Cruz colleagues, including Molina, who did prepare a Spanish-Nahuatl dictionary, was as close as he came to achieving his dream. For more on the linguistic models familiar to Sahagún, see Léon-Portilla, *Bernardino de Sahagun*, 38–44.

14. Mendieta, *Historia eclesiástica indiana*, 663.

15. Sahagún, *Introductions and Indices*, 50.

16. Ibid.

17. León-Portilla, "Bernardino de Sahagún," 2–3.

18. Browne, *Sahagún and the Transition to Modernity*, 93–94.

19. Sahagún, *Book 10*, 10:95.

20. Karttunen, *Analytical Dictionary*, xv.

21. León-Portilla, "Estudio preliminar," xxxi.

22. Molina, *Vocabulario*, aviso segundo.

23. León-Portilla, "Estudio preliminar," xxxvi–xxxvii.

24. Each lexicographer uses a (mostly) standardized orthography within his or her own work, but spelling and use of diacritics vary among them. In the following discussions, I replicate the orthography of each text. On canonical forms, see Karttunen, *Analytical Dictionary*, xi and xv.

25. Molina, *Vocabulario*, 101r.

26. For a comprehensive discussion of word formation in Nahuatl, see Andrews, *Introduction to Classical Nahuatl*, 13–14, 42, and 143.

27. Molina, *Vocabulario*, 45v. In addition to providing the first-person present tense verb form, Molina sometimes lists preterite forms. The abbreviations that accompany

verbs in Nahuatl dictionaries indicate the verb's possible formations. The first-person singular prefix *ni-* signals transitive verbs; *nin-* verbs are transitive and reflexive; *nicn-* verbs are transitive, take an object, and are reflexive; and *nite-* verbs are transitive and take a living object. Refer to "Verbal Forms" in Appendix A for a list of *ixiptla*'s verbal forms as provided by Molina, Siméon, and Clavijero, and for more information on these annotations, see Lockhart, *Nahuatl as Written*, 154 and 207–208.

28. Browne suggests that Sahagún would have been interested in the question of *teixiptla*'s referent, given the medieval understanding of linguistic origins and universal significance with which he was familiar. Browne, *Sahagún and the Transition to Modernity*, 123–124.

29. Portraits and other representations of people, including casta paintings, gained popularity in eighteenth-century Mexico. See, for example, Katzew, *Casta Painting*; and Bailey, *Art of Colonial Latin America*, 65–68 and 326–330.

30. Siméon, *Diccionario de la lengua náhuatl o mexicana*, xxxi.

31. Ibid., 490.

32. "Unido a otras palabras, *teotl* significa sagrado, maravilloso, raro, sorprendente, penoso." Ibid., 490.

33. See Appendix A to compare the forms listed by Molina, Clavijero, and Siméon.

34. Hvidtfeldt, *Teotl and *Ixiptlatli*, 19.

35. Wagoner, "Mana," 5631.

36. Although engaging in a more informed comparison of *teotl* to *mana* departs from my focus, Roger M. Keesing's linguistic analysis of *mana* suggests that comparing these terms may merit reconsideration. Tracing a path back to the grammatical confusion that puzzled early-twentieth-century anthropologists, Keesing explains that *mana* "is in Oceanic languages canonically a stative verb, not a noun: things and human enterprises and efforts are *mana*. *Mana* is used as a transitive verb as well: ancestors and gods *mana*-ize people and their efforts. Where *mana* is used as a noun, it is (usually) not as a substantive but as an abstract verbal noun denoting the state or quality of *mana*-ness (of a thing or act) or being-*mana* (of a person). Things that are *mana* are efficacious, potent, successful, true, fulfilled, realized: they 'work.' *Mana*-ness is a state of efficacy, success, truth, potency, blessing, luck, realization—an abstract state or quality, not an invisible spiritual substance or medium." Significant differences between *mana* and *teotl* emerge from even a cursory reading of Keesing's study, but a careful comparison of *mana* with both *teotl* and *teixiptla* may prove valuable. Keesing, "Rethinking *Mana*," 138.

37. In his preface, Tregear presents his book as a synthesis written with "the settler, the anthropologist, and the tourist" in mind. Indeed, influential anthropologists, including Mauss, relied upon *The Maori Race*. Mauss himself cites Tregear's definition: "The Polynesian word *mana* itself symbolizes not only the magical force in every creature, but also his honour, and one of the best translations of the word is 'authority', 'wealth.'" Mauss, *The Gift*, 38; and Tregear, *The Maori Race*, iv.

38. Hvidtfeldt, *Teotl and *Ixiptlatli*, 20.

39. Tregear, *The Maori Race*, 317.

40. The Maori believe that their rulers descended from the gods, and so the leaders' *mana* comprises part of their "god-inheritance." Ibid., 317 and 321–323.

41. Ibid., 317.

42. Durkheim, *Elementary Forms*, 196; emphasis added.

43. Ibid., 194.

44. Keesing, "Rethinking *Mana*," 137–138.

45. Hvidtfeldt, *Teotl and *Ixiptlatli*, 20 and 23.

46. Ibid., 78.

47. Ibid., 99–100.

48. Ibid., 84.

49. Ibid., 20–22 and 84.

50. Ibid., 82.

51. See Furst, "Skeletonization in Mixtec Art"; Bierhorst, *History and Mythology of the Aztecs*, 145; and Haly, "Bare Bones," 289.

52. Townsend, *State and Cosmos*, 28.

53. Hvidtfeldt, *Teotl and *Ixiptlatli*, 81.

54. Ibid., 17.

55. Ibid., 98n1.

56. Ibid., 98.

57. Sahagún, *Book 2*, 3:159. Hvidtfeldt cites a portion of this passage, but he does not refer back to it in his argument for image as mask. Hvidtfeldt, *Teotl and *Ixiptlatli*, 97–98.

58. Ibid., 99.

59. J. Z. Smith, *Drudgery Divine*, 51.

60. Kirchhoff, review of *Teotl and *Ixiptlatli*, 439.

61. "La palabra náhuatl *téutl*, que significa 'dios', parece tener el valor de 'negrura' en algunos compuestos." López Austin, *Los mitos del tlacuache*, 188; and *Myths of the Opossum*, 145.

62. López Austin, *Myths of the Opossum*, 368n7.

63. Ibid., 139.

64. Sahagún, *Book 12*, 12:20.

65. Ibid., 12:50n3.

66. For more on blackness and sacredness, see Bassett and Peterson, "Coloring the Sacred," 49–56; López Austin, *Myths of the Opossum*, 145 and 368; and Olivier, *Mockeries and Metamorphoses*, 184–191.

67. López Austin, *Myths of the Opossum*, 139.

68. In addition to this discussion of *teotl*, López Austin includes an extensive exploration of *calpulteteo*, patron deities of the *calpulli* (neighborhood-like kin-based societies in the Basin of Mexico). The term *calpulteotl* appears in neither the *Florentine Codex* nor Molina. See López Austin, *Human Body and Ideology*, 68–72.

69. López Austin traces connections between the brothers' parentage and their parents' cosmic significance to determine that, ultimately, the *hombres-dioses* were born of the Milky Way and the (mother) earth. According to various traditions, their par-

ents were, "Iztacmixcoatl, Mixcoatl, Mixcoatl Camaxtle, Camaxtle, Totepeuh y Cit-
lalatonac . . . Coatlicue, Chimalma, Ilancueitl." López Austin, *Hombre-Dios*, 145–146.

70. Ibid., 107.

71. Ibid., 120.

72. Molina, *Vocabulario*, 43v; and López Austin, *Hombre-Dios*, 120nn519–521.

73. López Austin, *Hombre-Dios*, 120. López Austin acknowledges that Anderson
and Dibble translate the verb as "possessed" elsewhere.

74. Ibid., 121.

75. Anderson and Schroeder, *Codex Chimalpahin*, 29, 69–71, 75, 95, 105, 183, 191,
197, and 211.

76. López Austin, *Hombre-Dios*, 127.

77. Ibid., 119.

78. Ibid., 115; López Austin, *Human Body and Ideology*, 1:377-378.

79. Ibid., 119–120. The asterisk following *xip** indicates that this stem, which carries the sense of flaying, peeling, and shaving, is not found in free form in older Nahuatl sources.

80. Ibid., 127.

81. Martínez González, *El nahualismo*, 290–291.

82. Ibid., 291; emphasis added.

83. In later works, López Austin limits the temporal and cultural scope of the sources he uses, but he also defends his syncretic approach: "In previous works, and especially in *The Myths of the Opossum*, I have worked with the entire dimension of
Mesoamerican religious tradition. In *The Myths of the Opossum* I covered all of the
Mesoamerican territory and even dared to cross 'official borders' and include information extending from Preclassic archaeological remains to modern oral traditions. This
allowed me to discover congruencies and meanings that, with a lesser scope, I would
not otherwise have perceived." López Austin, *Tamoanchan, Tlalocan*, 7.

84. López Austin, *Human Body and Ideology*, 1:377–378.

85. Ibid., 377, and see 181–184 and 203. López Austin's reference to an essence draws
on his understanding of *teyolia* (someone's means of living, someone's spirit or life
principle), one of three animistic entities he identifies in Mexica and modern Nahua
culture. The form *teyolia* consists of the indefinite personal object prefix *te-* (someone), the modifying element *-yol-*, and the applicative ending *-ia*. Karttunen associates *-yol-* with "emotion, volition, strength, valor and heart." Karttunen, *Analytical
Dictionary*, 340.

86. He devotes the first chapter of *Tamoanchan, Tlalocan* to the "relationship of
essences," which in the case of deities pertain to the "original matter of the Gods."
Here, matter refers to the substance of deities. López Austin, *Tamoanchan, Tlalocan*,
22–26.

87. Ibid., 23.

88. Ibid.

89. López Austin, *Myths of the Opossum*, 137.

90. Gruzinski, *Man-Gods in the Mexican Highlands*, 22.

91. Carrasco, *Religions of Mesoamerica*, 169.

92. Ibid., 88 and 90; Carrasco, *City of Sacrifice*, 84 and 131.

93. Carrasco, *City of Sacrifice*, 83.

94. Ibid., 132.

95. Ibid., 130.

96. Ibid., 131–132; see also Carrasco, *Religions of Mesoamerica*, 88–90.

97. Carrasco, *City of Sacrifice*, 136; Sahagún, *Book 2*, 3:71.

98. Clendinnen, *Aztecs*, 249.

99. Ibid., 252.

100. Ibid., 251.

101. Ranere et al., "Cultural and Chronological Context," 5014–5018.

102. Sahagún, *Book 2*, 3:63 and 124–125.

103. Ibid., 3:62, 105, and 187; Sahagún, *Book 9*, 9:79–80.

104. Clendinnen, *Aztecs*, 251.

105. Ibid., 252.

106. Ibid., 253.

107. The neologism "teoyoism" is an Anglicization of the Nahuatl word *teoyotl*. *Teoyotl* stems from *teotl* and a suffix that forms abstract nouns (*-yo*); literally, *teoyotl* would mean *teotl*-ness or *teotl*-hood. Karttunen glosses *teoyotl* as "divinity, spirituality" (*Analytical Dictionary*, 228). Klor de Alva, *Spiritual Warfare*, 66.

108. Ibid., 65.

109. Ibid., 66–67.

110. Ibid., 67. Somewhat surprisingly, Louise Burkhart concludes her discussion of *teotl*'s meaning with Klor de Alva's neologism. After summarizing the sixteenth-century Christian dualistic conception of good versus evil, she notes, "Nahua cosmic dualism was not cast in terms of good and evil. Despite the many dual aspects of Nahua thought, its theology was monist. A single divine principle—*teotl*—was responsible for the nature of the cosmos, negative aspects as well as beneficial ones. It was a polytheist monism: that is, the divine principle manifested itself in multiple forms, some ambivalent, some expressing opposite principles in their different manifestations. More accurate would be Klor de Alva's term *teoyoism* (from *teoyotl*, the abstract form of *teotl*), since *teotl* could manifest itself in ritual objects, images, and human deity-impersonators—forms not necessarily consistent with the Western conception of deity." Burkhart, *The Slippery Earth*, 36–37.

111. Klor de Alva, *Spiritual Warfare*, 68 and 77–83.

112. Ibid., 68.

113. Cline, "Missing and Variant Prologues," 245.

114. Ibid., 239, 245, and 250.

115. Klor de Alva, *Spiritual Warfare*, 67–68. I have included Klor de Alva's glosses for these Nahuatl words.

116. Ibid., 68. Klor de Alva's definition of hierophanies is erroneous. According to

Mircea Eliade, a hierophany is "the *act of manifestation* of the sacred," a term that "expresses no more than is implicit in its etymological content, *i.e.*, that *something sacred shows itself to us*." Eliade, *The Sacred and the Profane*, 11; emphasis in original.

117. Read, *Time and Sacrifice*, 271n41.

118. Read, "Sacred Commoners," 45. Her list of Nahuatl terms basically duplicates that of Klor de Alva quoted above. She reiterates the importance of *teo-* as potency in Read, "Sun and Earth Rulers," 365; and *Time and Sacrifice*, 145–146.

119. Read, *Time and Sacrifice*, 271n41.

120. Ibid., 145.

121. Kidwell, "Systems of Knowledge," 396.

122. Read, *Time and Sacrifice*, 147.

123. Maffie, "Centrality of Nepantla," 15.

124. Ibid., 11 and 16.

125. Ibid., 16.

126. Ramiro Medrano, e-mail, December 4, 2006. This exchange may be found in the Nahuat-l archives at: http://www.famsi.org/pipermail/nahuatl/2006-December/index.html.

127. Craig Berry, e-mail, December 4, 2006. In an e-mail from 1999, Karttunen suggests translating *teo-* as "super" or "supernatural" and provides *teomazatl*, "horse," as an example: "So if a deer is a big hooved animal, and one sees a horse for the first time, one might quite naturally refer to the beast as teomazatl 'super deer' (or 'hooved beast bigger than any deer heretofore known to us'). It doesn't necessarily mean 'deer of the gods' as it has often been translated."

128. Michael Swanton, e-mail, December 6, 2006.

129. Kay Read, e-mail, December 6, 2006.

130. Ibid.

131. Ibid.

132. Andrews, *Introduction to Classical Nahuatl*, 446.

133. Ibid., 470.

134. In three cases, Andrews uses "god": *teocalli*, "god house, i.e., temple, church"; *teopan*, "god site, i.e., temple"; and *teopixqui*, "god guarder, i.e., priest." Ibid., 470–471.

135. Ibid., 471. In his list of Nahuatl morphemes, Campbell includes *teohpohua*, "to suffer," as a separate entry from *teotl*. This morphological division indicates that he sees the two words as having different origins. Similarly, Karttunen recognizes that the short "o" in the *teoh-* stems of these words is an indication that they are not, strictly speaking, *teotl* compounds.

136. See R. Joe Campbell, "Nahuatl Morphemes," http://www2.potsdam.edu/schwaljf/Nahuatl/nahmor2.txt; and Karttunen, *Analytical Dictionary*, 27.

137. Karttunen, *Analytical Dictionary*, 228. Elsewhere Karttunen has suggested translating *teo-* as "super" or "supernatural." Frances Karttunen, e-mail to Nahuat-l, April 20, 1999. See also the Nahuatl-l discussion at the end of this chapter.

138. Karttunen, *Analytical Dictionary*, 114.

139. Ibid., 121, 325, and 339; italics in original.

140. A verb stem may take one of two aspects, "the *perfective* (which catches the event at the moment of either its beginning or end), [and] the *imperfective* (which catches the event during its career without regard to beginning or end)." A patient noun "names the patient of the action (i.e., the entity affected or the state produced) . . . [and] may be translated as 'an entity that can be ——ed,' 'an entity that has been ——ed,' or 'an entity that has become ——.' In these two latter senses it frequently has the meaning of a product or result." Karttunen's *ixiptla* entry begins as *ixiptlatl* (the imperfective patientive noun stem meaning 'a surface-flayed thing'), and incorporating -yo-, an abstracting suffix, alters its meaning to 'that which is characterized by a surface-flayed thing' (i.e., an image, representation, or likeness). Andrews, *Introduction to Classical Nahuatl*, 13–14; and *Workbook*, 13–14.

141. John Sullivan, personal communication, April 13, 2008.

142. As with human body parts in Nahuatl, *teixiptla* is inherently possessed, that is to say, it does not occur (linguistically) except in relation to someone.

143. Andrews, *Introduction to Classical Nahuatl*, 471.

144. Campbell, *Morphological Dictionary*, vi.

145. Ibid., iv. The variants of both *teotl* and *teixiptla* include colonial neologisms, but without seeing the variants in context, it is difficult—if not impossible—to distinguish between colonial inventions and pre-Contact terms.

146. Ibid., 142. The reader should keep in mind that these semantic fields represent the forms contained in Molina's *Vocabulario*, all of which Molina extracted from their original spoken contexts: "With respect to the origin or provenance of the Nahua voices gathered by Molina, it may be said generally that they came principally from the central region of Mexico. About this Molina notes in the 'Second Notice' (from the first 'Prologue') that 'at first they will be given (the words) that they use here in Tetzcoco and Mexico, where the language is better spoken and more peculiar.'" León-Portilla, "Estudio preliminar," 53.

147. López Austin, *Myths of the Opossum*, 132; and Carrasco, *City of Sacrifice*, 132.

148. Clendinnen, *Aztecs*, 252.

149. As we saw earlier, though, t(h)eologians do insist on the vitality of *teixiptla-huan*. In their view, Aztec deity embodiments were animate entities, not lifeless images. Carrasco, in particular, underscores this point's centrality in Aztec religion. In his *City of Sacrifice* discussion of the festival Toxcatl, he explains, "The image of Tezcatlipoca was alive, not only in the sense that a human being was the public image, but also in the changes he underwent at different stages of the year-long ceremony," adding that, "studies of iconography and image do not afford us much help in understanding this series of transformations" (134). Carrasco criticizes the iconographic approach and prompts us to consider the importance of the ontological transformations *teixiptlahuan* experienced through ritual.

150. Keen, *Aztec Image*, 448.

151. Seler, "Character of Aztec and Maya Manuscripts," 113.

152. Ibid.

153. Ibid., 113 and 115.

154. The brilliant work of diligent epigraphers and iconographers both in the Maya and Central Mexican contexts has refuted Seler's underestimation of glyphs' communicative ability and sophistication. In particular, Elizabeth H. Boone's work with Central Mexican pictorial manuscripts demonstrates the complexity of Mexica and nearby cultures' semasiographic capabilities; see Boone, "Introduction," 3–26. Additionally, epigraphers' decipherment of an amazing variety of texts has opened previously unimagined avenues for understanding and interpreting Maya cosmology and culture; see the "Resources" available through Peter Mathews et al., "Mesoweb," http://www.mesoweb.com/resources/resources.html; and Bricker, "Advances in Maya Epigraphy."

155. Prem, "Aztec Hieroglyphic Writing System," 159.

156. Ibid., 160.

157. Ibid., 164.

158. Nicholson, "Religion in Pre-Hispanic Central Mexico," 408 and Table 3. These "cult themes" also organize "Table 3: Major Deities of the Late Pre-Hispanic Central Mexican Nahua-Speaking Communities."

159. Ibid., 409.

160. Ibid., 408.

161. DiCesare, "History and Time"; and *Sweeping the Way*, 123–154.

162. Nicholson, "Religion in Pre-Hispanic Central Mexico," 413–414; emphasis added.

163. Boone, *Cycles of Time and Meaning*, 18, 83, and 239.

164. Solís, "Head of Coyolxauhqui," 464.

165. Deity images may have developed in more organic ways, perhaps undergoing transformations through the periodic accumulation and abandonment of particular elements through history. A Coyolxauhqui stone accompanies at least two (and potentially more) of the seven stages of the Templo Mayor's reconstruction, and these layered images may be one example of a deity accumulating or abandoning insignia over time. In a personal communication, Rudy Busto suggested that the symbols the stone accumulates may be metaphoric markers for historic events that occurred between building stages. Emily Umberger argues that the most recent stone (ca. 1473) commemorates Axayacatl's defeat of the Tlatelolcan ruler Moquihuix by depicting him as Coyolxauhqui; see Umberger, "Coyolxauhqui's Body." For a discussion of the stones relative to the Templo Mayor site, see López Luján, *Offerings of the Templo Mayor*, 72–78. Byron Hamann's study of the relationship between temporality, destruction, and renewal may offer additional insights into artifacts like the Coyolxauhqui stone. (In a response that follows Hamann's article, Emily Umberger mentions the Coyolxauhqui stones as images that were buried successively at the Templo Mayor.) See Hamann, "Chronological Pollution," 812 and 829.

166. Nicholson, "Preclassic Mesoamerican Iconography," 159.

167. Ibid., 163.

168. By looking for clusters of iconographic elements, Nicholson aims to trace "developmental-sequential chains" of identified or identifiable deities through time. Ibid.

169. Ibid., 172.

170. Pasztory, *Aztec Art*, 79–81.

171. Ibid., 81.

172. Ibid., 84.

173. Ibid; and see Nicholson, "Religion in Pre-Hispanic Central Mexico," 408.

174. Pasztory, *Aztec Art*, 81.

175. An isolationist iconography risks positing impossible comparisons as plausible by removing images from the contexts in which they appear. For instance, in his discussion of the "Teteo-Innan Complex," Nicholson disregards differences among the codices (*Borbonicus*, *Magliabecchiano*, and *Telleriano-Remensis*) from which he extracts images of "similarly" depicted (and, therefore, associated) female *teteo*. Without the images' contexts, it is impossible to know if shared symbols indicate shared referents. See Nicholson, "Religion in Pre-Hispanic Central Mexico," 422; and van der Loo, "Codices, Customs, Continuity," 7–10.

176. Boone, "Introduction," 15.

177. Ibid., 18–19.

178. Ibid., 20.

179. Lacadena, "Regional Scribal Traditions," 2.

180. Ibid., 2–3.

181. Ibid., 19.

182. Hvidtfeldt, *Teotl and *Ixiptlatli*, 19; López Austin, *Tamoanchan, Tlalocan*, 7; Read, "Sacred Commoners," 45; and Maffie, "Centrality of Nepantla," 16.

CHAPTER 3

1. Sahagún, *Book 10*, 10:195; translation by Anderson and Dibble.

2. Sahagún, *Book 6*, 6:175; translation by Anderson and Dibble.

3. Sahagún, *Book 1*, 2:74; translation by Anderson and Dibble.

4. Sahagún, *Book 11*, 11:247; translation by Anderson and Dibble.

5. Campbell, *Morphological Dictionary*, 312.

6. Hvidtfeldt, *Teotl and *Ixiptlatli*, 77; Andrews, *Introduction to Classical Nahuatl*, 236.

7. Sahagún, *Introductions and Indices*, 1:47. In the same passage, he describes the *Florentine Codex* as "like a dragnet [that brings] to light all the words of this language with their exact and metaphoric meanings, and all their ways of speaking and most of their ancient practices, the good and evil."

8. See Appendix B for other examples.

9. Sahagún, *Book 1*, 2:5; translation by Anderson and Dibble. For other similar examples, see the introductions of *Book 1* Chapters 2, 4, 5, 14–20, and 22.

10. Colonial uses of *teotl* affected its post-Contact meaning. As we might expect, Christianity inflected the concept's meaning in colonial neologisms. In my analysis,

I have tried to avoid including obviously Christian applications of *teotl* in its seman-tic range. Many of the Christian-influenced uses of *teotl* in the *Florentine Codex* are fairly obvious because they appear in introductions or appendices, sections of the text clearly set apart from the books' contents. For instance, the appendix to *Book 1* tran-scribes several chapters from the apocryphal Wisdom of Solomon, and so I omit the forty-two examples of *teotl* that occur in these passages. Apart from the appendix, *teotl* occasionally occurs in contexts that seem to have been influenced by a Christian per-spective, including the neologisms *teotlatolli* (word of God) and *tlateotoquiliztli* (idola-try). I have also omitted these terms. Louise Burkhart's *Slippery Earth* (1989) addresses Christian rhetoric in the colonial period.

11. The term occurs in its canonical form 219 times in the *Florentine Codex*; of those, 122 are singular forms, and the remaining 97 are plural. In the majority of these cases, *teotl* may be translated as "god" and *teteo* as "gods."

12. Sahagún, *Book 3*, 4:13; translation by Anderson and Dibble.

13. Sahagún, *Book 7*, 7:4; translation by Anderson and Dibble.

14. *Book 10: The People* contains a variation on this formula; in this case, the name of the people derives from the name of their deity: "The name of the god of these [peo-ple] was Taras; hence they are now named Tarascos. This Taras is called Michoacatl in the Nahuatl language. He is the god of the Chichimeca." Sahagún, *Book 10*, 10:189; translation by Anderson and Dibble.

15. Sahagún, *Book 1*, 2:39; translation by Anderson and Dibble. Lockhart relates the association of patron gods with ethnic groups to the *altepetl*: "A special ethnic god (like the Mexica's Huitzilopochtli, often at once a deified ancestor and a variant of one of the general Mesoamerican deities) was one of the main unifying forces of the altepetl, and his temple was the primary symbol of its sovereignty and power. A lesser god with a lesser temple fulfilled the same function for each calpolli; and it appears that the per-vasive if little understood gods or spirits of the household may have done the same at that level. In theory, the god gave his people their land and clothed their rulers with title and authority." Lockhart, *Nahuas after the Conquest*, 203–204.

16. Sahagún, *Book 2*, 3:129; translation by Anderson and Dibble. The *Florentine Co-dex* also names the patron deities of the palace folk, merchants, water folk, reed mat makers, and goldworkers, as well as the Mexicas, Otomís, Huexotzincas, Toloques, Chichimecas, and Huitznahuacs.

17. Ibid., 3:60; translation by Anderson and Dibble.

18. Sahagún, *Book 10*, 10:39; translation by Anderson and Dibble.

19. For Chicomecoatl as a *cihuateotl*, see *Book 1*, 2:13; for Teteo Innan, *Book 1*, 2:15; for Tzapotlan Tenan, *Book 1*, 2:17; and for Chalchihuitlicue, *Book 1*, 2:21 and *Book 6*, 6:175. For Coatlicue or Coatlan Tonan as a *teotl*, see *Book 2*, 3:56, and for Xochiquetzal, see *Book 4*, 5:7 and *Book 6*, 6:34. Other examples of *teotl* as "goddess" occur at *Book 2*, 3:226 and 238.

20. Sahagún, *Book 1*, 2:21; translation by Anderson and Dibble. Note that the trans-lators inserted the bracketed "a god[dess]."

21. Sahagún, *Book 11*, 11:247; translation by Anderson and Dibble.

22. Sahagún, *Book 6*, 6:175; translation by Anderson and Dibble.

23. Ibid., 6:176; translation by Anderson and Dibble.

24. See *cihuateteo* at *Book 1*, 2:19; *Book 2*, 3:189 (2 occurrences); *Book 4*, 5:10, 41, 79, 93 (2), and 107 (2); and *Book 6*, 6:161. Four colonial uses of *cihuateteo* as "the goddesses" occur in the *Florentine Codex*; see *Book 1*, 2:7, 11, 64, and 72.

25. Sahagún, *Book 4*, 5:10; translation by Anderson and Dibble.

26. Sahagún, *Book 2*, 3:189; translation by Anderson and Dibble.

27. Ibid.; translation by Anderson and Dibble. See *netlatiloyan* at ibid., 3:186.

28. See Sahagún, *Books 4 and 5*, 5:1, 79, and 93.

29. See Boone, "The 'Coatlicues,'" 189–206; Klein, "The Devil and the Skirt," 1–26.

30. For *cihuapipiltin*, see Sahagún, *Book 1*, 2:19 and 72; for *ilhuica cihuapipiltin* or *ilhuicacihuatl*, see *Book 6*, 6:164; and for *mocihuaquetzque*, see *Book 6*, 6:161–165.

31. Although scholars commonly describe the *cihuateteo* as the spirits of parturient women, "auh intla ic miqui iiti, mitoa, motocaihuatia: mocihuaquetzqui" (if she died in the midst of it [childbirth], she is called, she is named mocihuaquetzqui"). Sahagún, *Book 6*, 6:161. See Nicholson, "Religion in Pre-Hispanic Central Mexico," 422 and Table 3; and Boone, "The 'Coatlicues' at the Templo Mayor," 199.

32. See Klein, "The Shield Women," 47; Seler, *Gesammelte Abhandlungen*, 840–841; Boone, "The 'Coatlicues,'" 199–200; and Barnes, "Partitioning the Parturient," 20–21.

33. Teotl Ehco (The God Arrives) names the twelfth month in the festival cycle. See Sahagún, *Book 2*, 3:127–130; and *Book 12*, 12:81–82. Following English conventions, deity names are capitalized and appear in roman type throughout the text: Teotl Ehco (The God Arrives). When names occur as epithets, they appear in lowercase italics in the Nahuatl, and only the initial word in the phrase is capitalized in the gloss: *in tloqueh, nahuaqueh* (Possessor of the near, of the nigh).

34. See Sahagún, *Book 2*, 3:184, 186, 191, and 238.

35. Sahagún, *Book 1*, 2:23; translation by Anderson and Dibble. Also known as Ixcuina and Tlaelquani, the Tlazolteteo were called Tiacapan (First Born), Teicu (Younger Sister), Tlaco (Middle Sister) and Xocotzin (Beloved Youngest Sister). The only other mention of the Tlazolteteo occurs in *Book 6*, which notes that the Huastecans venerated them in particular. Sahagún, *Book 6*, 6:34.

36. Sahagún, *Book 1*, 2:23; translation by Anderson and Dibble. See also ibid., 2:70.

37. Ibid., 2:15; translation by Anderson and Dibble. See also ibid., 2:70; Sahagún, *Book 2*, 3:226; *Book 6*, 6:153.

38. Sahagún, *Book 1*, 2:72.

39. Sahagún, *Book 6*, 6:153; translation by Anderson and Dibble.

40. Ibid., 6:21 and 74; translation by Anderson and Dibble.

41. Thanks to Julia Madajczak, who pointed this out to me.

42. Karttunen defines *chiuhqui* as "someone in authority, someone in power," which does not necessarily connote parentage as does Anderson and Dibble's translation "progenitor." Karttunen, *Analytical Dictionary*, 53.

43. Sahagún, *Book 8*, 8:19; translation by Anderson and Dibble; see also *Book 6*, 6:88.

44. The phrase *teteo innan, teteo inta, huehue teotl* also occurs in *Book 6*, 6:41.

45. Sahagún, *Book 1*, 2:24–25; translation by Anderson and Dibble.

46. Guilhem Olivier identifies both *yohualli ehecatl* (Night wind) and *tloqueh na-huaqueh*, whom he glosses "Unknown God," as invisible deities, and he addresses their possible connections to Tezcatlipoca in Olivier, *Mockeries and Metamorphoses*, 20–23, 26–27, 175, 217–218, and 274–275. With regard to the meaning of *tloqueh nahuaqueh*, Karttunen explains *tloqueh* as, "the possessor derivation from -TLOC [that] is conventionally paired with a possessor derivation from -nahuac, the whole phrase tloqueh nahuaqueh referring to the universal and all-pervading deity." She defines *-tloc* as "adjacent to, close to" and *nahuaqueh* as "the one that is close to all things, god." At *nahuaqueh*, she adds, "This is conventionally paired with tloqueh<-tloc, which also has the sense of vicinity, the whole phrase being an epithet for divine presence." Highly metaphoric onomastic phrases like *tloqueh nahuaqueh* occur often in *Book 6* and deserve further study, in relation to both the concept of *teotl* and the rarified Nahuatl of rhetoric and philosophy. Karttunen, *Analytical Dictionary*, 308–309.

47. Elizabeth Boone indicates that writers and illustrators in New Spain drew on the resources of both Western and European writing in ways that impacted native and foreign texts. See Boone, "Ruptures and Unions," 197–225.

48. Pablo Escalante Gonzalbo addresses the similarities between the images contained in the *Hortus sanitatis* and *Earthly Things* in Escalante Gonzalbo, "The Painters of Sahagún's Manuscripts," 167–192. As I noted in Chapter 2, Sahagún and the scribes seem to have modeled the *Florentine Codex*'s layout on late fifteenth-century natural histories, and I intend to investigate connections related to the texts' form and contents in a later work.

49. Sahagún, *Book 11* prologue in *Introductions and Indices*.

50. Browne, *Sahagún and the Transition to Modernity*, 73.

51. Sahagún, *Book 11*, 11:222, 224, and 226.

52. Ibid., 11:224.

53. Weigand, "Observations on Ancient Mining," 22.

54. For more on the importance of turquoise and other green stones in Central Mexico, see Aguilera, "Of Royal Mantles and Blue Turquoise," 3–19; McEwan et al., *Turquoise Mosaics from Mexico*; Johansson K., "Teoxihuitl"; Weigand, Harbottle, and Sayre, "Turquoise Sources and Source Analysis," 15–34; and Weigand, "Observations on Ancient Mining," 21–35.

55. Weigand, "Observations on Ancient Mining," 23. Weigand catalogs the variety of stones mined in the Chalchihuites region: "a variety of blue/green stones, especially malachite and azurite (some of which looks remarkably like chemical turquoise); cinnabar; limonite; hematite; a weathered chert/flint (a highly carveable, white stone); iron pyrite; and possibly native copper." Extensive turquoise trade networks extended from the Anasazi and Hohokam cultures south through Mesoamerica. For more on turquoise trade, see Vokes and Gregory, "Exchange Networks for Exotic Goods."

56. Diehl, "Previous Investigations at Tula," 13 and 27; and Healan, "Tula, Tollan, and the Toltecs," 3 and 5.

57. Sahagún, *Book 10*, 10:168; translation by Anderson and Dibble.

58. Taube, "Symbolism of Turquoise," 124.

59. Ibid., 124–125.

60. Ibid., 124. Patricia Meehan and Valerie Magar describe the restoration of a turquoise mosaic disk found at Tula in Meehan and Magar, "Conservation of a Turquoise Mosaic Disk," 45, fig. 8.

61. Berdan, "Turquoise in the Aztec Imperial World," 92.

62. Ibid.

63. Thibodeau et al., "An Alternative Approach," 65.

64. Ibid., 68.

65. Ibid.

66. Berdan, "Turquoise in the Aztec Imperial World," 96.

67. Harbottle and Weigand, "Turquoise in Pre-Columbian America," 83–84; and Berdan, "Turquoise in the Aztec Imperial World," 97. See also Thibodeau et al., "An Alternative Approach to the Prehispanic Turquoise Trade," 66–72.

68. On Aztec sources of turquoise and the stone's role in tribute systems, see Berdan, "Turquoise in the Aztec Imperial World," 96–101.

69. Johansson K., "Teoxihuitl," 135.

70. Sahagún, *Book 11*, 11:222; translation by Anderson and Dibble.

71. Johansson K., "Teoxihuitl," 135–136 and 140; and Olivier and López Luján, "Images of Moctezuma," 86.

72. Taube, "Symbolism of Turquoise," 130.

73. Ibid.; and see Olko, *Turquoise Diadems and Staffs of Office*, 113–136.

74. Taube, "Symbolism of Turquoise," 128.

75. For more on the use of turquoise in nobles' dress and adornment, see Aguilera, "Of Royal Mantles and Blue Turquoise," 3–19.

76. She goes on to explain that it was also associated with Tezcatlipoca, who wears it in the *Codex Borgia* and the *Florentine Codex*, but not with Quetzalcoatl. Olko, *Turquoise Diadems and Staffs of Office*, 231.

77. Karttunen provides separate entries for *xihuitl* (year), which forms a different abstraction than *xihuitl* (grass; green stone), and for *xihuitl* (comet), which Carochi indicates had a long initial "i" vowel. See Karttunen, *Analytical Dictionary*, 324.

78. Ibid.; and Izeki, *Conceptualization of 'Xihuitl,'* 31–32.

79. Izeki: *Conceptualization of 'Xihuitl,'* 31–36.

80. Johansson K., "Teoxihuitl," 137–142; Gutiérrez Solana, "Xiuhcóatl tallada en piedra," 5–18; and Taube, "Symbolism of Turquoise," 128–132.

81. Sahagún, *Book 11*, 11:223. See Appendix C for translations by Anderson and Dibble.

82. Ibid., 11:224.

83. Ibid.

84. In an email to the Nahuat-l listserv, Karttunen observes, "Tlapalli also can mean 'ink' as well as paint, but probably not black ink. Its core meaning seems to be derived from palli, a type of clay used in dying cloth." Frances Karttunen, e-mail, May 31, 2001.

85. López Luján, *The Offerings*, 274, 280, 281, 283, and 289.

86. Ibid., 77.

87. See MacLaury, *Color and Cognition*, 329–332.

88. Sahagún, *Book 11*, 11:228.

89. In *Book 10: The People*, the scribes explain that *chapopohtli* (a type of tar, asphalt; pitch, bitumen), "[is] *tliltic, tlilpatic, capotztic* (black, very black, black); [it is] that which flakes, crumbles, breaks up." Sahagún, *Book 10*, 10:88.

90. For an overview of blackness's significance in the Aztec and Maya religions, see Peterson, "Perceiving Blackness, Envisioning Power," 186.

91. Olivier associates *tliltilia* (to push oneself up, to become famous), which appears in Siméon alone, with *"tliltiani [sic]*, 'to stand up, to become black.'" Molina defines *tliltia* as *"pararse* (to stop; to stand up), *hacerse negro* (to make oneself black)," and Siméon as *"ponerse moreno* (to make oneself dark), *atezarse* (to bronze oneself)." Molina, *Vocabulario*, 148r; Olivier, *Mockeries and Metamorphoses*, 188; Siméon, *Diccionario*, 208.

92. Olivier, *Mockeries and Metamorphoses*, 191.

93. Recall, also, that López Austin associates blackness with *teotl*. The description of the *teotzanatl*, one of the birds he mentions, emphasizes the bird's absolute blackness: "the *huel tliltic* (very black one), very curved of bill, glistening, is the cockerel" (Sahagún, *Book 11*, 11:50). Similarly, the *teotzinitzcan*, another bird whose blackness López Austin notes, was both black and green: "and for this reason is it called teotzinitzcan: on its breast and its underwing it is varicolored, *centlacotl tliltic, centlacotl xoxoctic* (half black, half green)" (Sahagún, *Book 11*, 11:20). See Chapter 2, above, and López Austin, *Tamoanchan, Tlalocan*, 145 and 368n7.

94. See Bassett and Peterson, "Coloring the Sacred," 50; and Olivier, *Mockeries and Metamorphoses*, 188.

95. See Olivier, *Mockeries and Metamorphoses*, 184–191.

96. Milintoc comes from *milini* (to shine, sparkle, flare) and the -*ti*- ligature combined with -*onoc* (to be lying, to stretch out), which reduces to -*toc* and conveys a progressive sense. For a discussion of *xihuitl* as solar year, grass, and fire, see Izeki, *Conceptualization of 'Xihuitl,'* 92–97.

97. Sahagún, *Book 2*, 3:159. Although Anderson and Dibble translate *"ixtlan tlatlaan"* as "horizontally striped" here, they translate the same phrase as "diagonally striped" three times in the description of a Huitzilopochtli amaranth dough *ixiptla* created during the post-Contact observance of the festival Toxcatl; see Sahagún, *Book 12*, 12:52; translation by Anderson and Dibble.

98. Sahagún, *Book 2*, 3:161. Anderson and Dibble translate *motentlilhui* as "the lower part of the face was blackened," but according to López Austin, *tentli* refers specifically to "lips (the parts covered with skin and mucous)." López Austin, *Human Body and Ideology*, 1:106–107.

99. Elsewhere, Xiuhtecuhtli and Huehue Teotl are associated with one another and with black; see Bassett and Peterson, "Coloring the Sacred"; and Sahagún, *Book 2*, 3:209.

100. Sahagún, *Book 11*, 11:233–234.

101. Other *Florentine Codex* uses of *coztic* and *iztac* with *teocuitlatl* suggest that the Aztecs used the colors to differentiate gold (*coztic*) from silver (*iztac*). Anderson and Dibble interpret *iztac* as "silver," but Karttunen glosses *iztac* as "something white" and refers readers to *itzatl* (salt). Ibid., 233; and Karttunen, *Analytical Dictionary*, 123–124. For a description of artisans' work with precious metals, including gold and silver, see Sahagún, *Book 9*, 9:69–71.

102. The Nahuatl reads, "inic quipitza teocuitlatl, in coztic, ihuan iztac." Sahagún, *Book 9*, 9:75–76; translation by Anderson and Dibble. The gold-casting method described in the *Florentine Codex* involves beeswax, and although two genera of stingless bees are indigenous to Mesoamerica (*Melipona* and *Trigona*), the *xicomeh* (bees) described in *Earthly Things* sting: "It is round, small and round, yellow-legged, winged. It is a flyer, a buzzer, a sucker, a maker of hives, an earth excavator, a honey producer, a stinger (*teminani*)." Sahagún, *Book 11*, 11:93–94. European bees were introduced into New Spain as early as 1520–1530. While beeswax would have been available to pre-Contact artisans, the *Florentine Codex*'s description may conflate pre- and post-Contact gold casting, as it does *xicomeh* (bees).

103. Sahagún, *Book 9*, 9:75–76; translation by Anderson and Dibble.

104. West, "Aboriginal Metallurgy and Metalworking," 10.

105. Otis Young reports that by the 1550s, "the great silver lodes of Zacatecas, Guanajuato and Pachuca were prospected, all lying within a week's travel of Mexico City. These surface silver ores were cheap to excavate with impressed and unskilled labor, easily reduced with a minimum of fuel and experience, and required little refining preparatory to being minted. The initial phase produced a recorded 22 million pesos of silver, not to mention what may have escaped the notice of the royal tax-gatherers." Young, "Black Legends and Silver Mountains," 110.

106. Sahagún, *Book 11*, 11:233.

107. Ibid.; translation by Anderson and Dibble. *Inan* (its mother) also produces precious stones. See the description of the "mother of precious stone" in ibid., 11:221–222.

108. Ibid.; translation by Anderson and Dibble.

109. Nothing in the discussions of *tlazohtetl* (precious stones) or *teocuitlatl* in *Earthly Things* indicates that this *nantli* (mother) is associated with Teteo Innan or with material representations of earth-associated entities like Tlaltecuhtli. Rather, numerous passages in the *Florentine Codex*, and especially in *Book 6: Rhetoric and Moral Philosophy*, liken children to elite goods and precious stones: "She said to him: 'Precious necklace, precious feather, precious green stone, precious bracelet, precious turquoise, thou wert created in the place of duality, the place [above] the nine heavens." Sahagún, *Book 6*, 6:233; translation by Anderson and Dibble.

110. This metaphoric relationship may be reflected and reinforced by language that describes children as precious stones. In an exhortation to maintain honor, a father

addresses his daughter as, "tichalchihuitl, titeoxihuitl." (You are a precious greenstone, you are a *teo*-turquoise.) Ibid., 6:94; translation by Anderson and Dibble.

111. Some scholars who translate *teocuitlatl* as "divine excrement" include: Carrasco, *City of Sacrifice*; Klein, "Teocuitlatl, 'Divine Excrement'"; Miller, *The Art of Mesoamerica*; Miller and Taube, *An Illustrated Dictionary*.

112. Molina and Siméon define *cuitlatl* as "shit," and "excrement, dung, filth, residue; sore, tumor, abscess," respectively. Karttunen, *Analytical Dictionary*, 73–74.

113. López Austin, *Vieja historia de la mierda*, 65.

114. See Sahagún, *Book 11*, 11:234–235; and López Austin, *Vieja historia de la mierda*, 70–71.

115. John Sullivan, personal communication, October 9, 2008.

116. Wake, "Contact: Indo-Christian Art," 344.

117. Ibid.

118. Sahagún, *Book 7*, 7:6; translation by Anderson and Dibble.

119. Ibid., 7:7; translation by Anderson and Dibble.

120. On turquoise trade routes, see Harbottle and Weigand, "Turquoise in Pre-Columbian America," 78–85; Weigand and Harbottle, "The Role of Turquoises," 159–177. On turquoise mosaics, especially in masks, see McEwan et al., *Turquoise Mosaics from Mexico*, 42–84.

121. The canonical form of this word is *axcaitl*, and Karttunen defines it as "possessions, property"; *iiaxca* and *iaxca* are two spellings of *axcaitl*'s possessed form. Karttunen, *Analytical Dictionary*, 14.

122. "The property, *iaxca* (the possession), which belongs to all the different birds and to turkeys is feathers." In Nahuatl, "in ixquich nepapan tototl: ihuan in totolin, in itech ca, in itlatqui, in iaxca: ihhuitl." Sahagún, *Book 10*, 10:54; translation by Anderson and Dibble. On meat sellers and their meat, see ibid., 10:80.

123. "auh ca quezquitoton in ixpampa ehuaque . . . auh in ye iuhqui in oquinmicti, in oyiellelquiz quincuili in intlaqui, in innechichioal in anecuiotl, quimotlatlaquiti, quimaxcati, quimotonalti, iuhquin quimotlahuizti." Sahagún, *Book 3*, 4:4–5; translation by Anderson and Dibble. Huitzilopochtli's collection serves as an interesting model for the Mexica practice of collecting the patron *teixiptlahuan* of defeated polities.

124. Sahagún, *Book 9*, 9:17–18; translation by Anderson and Dibble.

125. "quitoznequi. ca naxca, ca notlatqui, ca nonetlayecoltiliz." Sahagún, *Book 6*, 6:241; translation by Anderson and Dibble.

126. "itechpa mitoa: in tlein nicnopialia, in huel naxca, in huel noyocauh, in nociahuiliztica, notlatequipanoliztica onicnonextili, in amo zan cana oniccuic, anozo oniquichtec." Ibid.; translation by Anderson and Dibble.

127. "quinamaca in itlalnacayo, in inacayo, in iiyohcauh, in iaxca, in ineneu . . ." Sahagún, *Book 10*, 10:94; translation by Anderson and Dibble.

128. "conana, connapaloa in piltontli: inic conmaxcatia, cemicac imaxca, ixquichca in tlapaliuhcatitiuh . . ." Sahagún, *Book 6*, 6:209; translation by Anderson and Dibble.

129. "ca tel amo ticmotlanehuilia, ca maxcatzin, motolinia." Ibid., 6:210; translation by Anderson and Dibble.

130. During a male infant's ritual bath, the midwife describes the child as property: "Our mother, our father, Tonatiuh, Tlaltecuhtli . . unto thee I declare him, unto thee I commend him, unto thee I raise him as an offering . . . he is thy possession, thy property; he is dedicated to thee." In Nahuatl, "tonan, tota tonatiuh, tlaltecuhtli . . . mohuic noconitoa, mohuic noconpoa, mohuic niconiiaya . . . ca maxcatzin, ca motlatquitizn, ca motechtzinco pouhqui." Ibid., 6:203; translation by Anderson and Dibble.

131. Sahagún, *Book 1*, 2:23; translation by Anderson and Dibble.

132. The chapter mentions two other names associated with Tlazolteotl: Ixcuina, who was four women, and Tlaelcuani (Liver-Eater). Note that although *tlahzolli* (trash) and *tlazohtli* (someone or something beloved, rare, or expensive) sound similar, they have distinct etymology. Ibid.; Karttunen, *Analytical Dictionary*, 271 and 306.

133. "ca iiaxca, ca itech quiza in teotl, in itoca, chalchihuitli icue." Sahagún, *Book 10*, 10:247; translation by Anderson and Dibble.

134. Sahagún, *Book 1*, 2:21; translation by Anderson and Dibble.

135. "inin itoca itech quiza in teotl, ihuan in xihuitl, zan quihtoznequi iiaxca, itonal in teotl." Sahagún, *Book 10*, 10:224.

136. The initial *i-* of *itonalli* (sweat) has not been identified, but *itonalli* is both distinct from and related to *tonalli* (warmth of the sun, day sign, fate). According to R. Joe Campbell, "The 'tona' part looks straightforward enough (with a /ton/ stem and a /a/ verbalizer). The /ton/ stem appears also with a /i/ verbalizer in 'atotonilli'. But the initial 'i-' of 'itonal' is not yet identified—Fran Karttunen believes that it is a long vowel, which would make it unrelated to the 'ih' of 'ihmati'—I'm still scratching my head over it." R. Joe Campbell, e-mail, November 23, 2008. In order to maintain consistency, I restrict my discussion of this term to its uses in the *Florentine Codex*. Because of its popularity, though, López Austin's work on Mexica concepts of the human body merits mention. He understands *tonalli* as one of three animistic entities that facilitate "the processes that give life and movement to the organism and permit the fulfillment of psychic functions," and he lists several definitions of *tonalli*: "a. irradiation; b. solar heat; c. summer; d. day; e. day sign; f. the destiny of a person according to the day of his birth; g. 'the soul and spirit' (Molina: *totonal*); h. something meant for, or the property of, a certain person (Molina: *tetonal*)." These definitions, he explains, "[come] from the concept of the tie existing between mythical time, in which what is contingent is present, and the moment in which, by calendrical order, one of the forces of that time penetrates and becomes active in the time of man." López Austin, *Human Body and Ideology*, 1:181 and 204–205.

137. Boone, *Cycles of Time and Meaning*, 29.

138. "ca nel iuhqui itonal, iuhqui ipan motlacatili: in iuhqui mazatl, cenca momauhtiani: zan no iuhqui in aquin itonal catca, huel mauhca tlacatl, mahuitzoco: ic zan ica mellacuaoa, in ihuaniolque, in itahuan, aque commatia." Sahagún, *Book 4*, 5:10; translation by Anderson and Dibble.

139. "auh in aquin ipan tlacatia itonal ce miquiztli: mitoaya mocuiltonoz, motlamachtiz, intla pilli, anozo zan macehualtzintli . . ." Ibid., 5:34; translation by Anderson and Dibble.

140. "muchi inemactia, itech acia, itech pachihuia, in mahuizotl: icuac in tlahuella-macehua, mocnomati: auh intlacamo huellamacehua, ca zan inehuiyan conmocahuil-ia, quimitlacalhuia in itonal." Ibid.; translation by Anderson and Dibble.

141. Ibid., 5:49; translation by Anderson and Dibble.

142. Ibid., 5:50; translation by Anderson and Dibble.

143. Anderson and Dibble translate *itonal* as "heat," "day sign," "lot," and "fortune, fate, privilege, and prerogative."

144. Sahagún, *Book 10*, 10:91; *Book 11*, 11:169 and 268.

145. "zan iuhquinma quintlanamaquiltito, inic quinnahualittato, inic quinnemilito: quinmacato tlazotilmatli, tlazotlanqui, zan huel itech itilma in Moctezuma, in huac ac oc ce quiquemi, zan huel ineixcahuil, huel itonal." Sahagún, *Book 12*, 12:5–6; translation by Anderson and Dibble.

146. The gift exchange between Moteuczoma and Cortés that I discuss in Chapter 1 takes place after this early exchange. Following their first encounter with the Spaniards, Moteuczoma's emissaries return with their report, and Moteuczoma sends a second group of lookouts to wait for the Spaniards to land again. According to the *Florentine Codex*, about a year passes before lookouts report that the Spaniards had landed again. Following this report, Moteuczoma sends messengers with a set of gifts the scribes call *teotlatquitl* (*teo*-property). Cortés reciprocated by giving Moteuczoma's emissaries "green and yellow necklaces which resembled amber." The emissaries also convey the Spaniards' message about their gift: "They said: 'If in truth ye have come from Mexico, behold what ye shall give the ruler Moctezuma by which he will know us.'" Ibid., 12:1–13; translation by Anderson and Dibble.

147. "niman ye ic huallaquixtilo in huel ixcoyan iiaxca, in huel ineixcahuil, in huel itonal, mochi tlazotlanqui, in chayahuac cozcatl, in machoncotl, in teocuitlamatem-ecatl, ihuan in matzopetztli, teocuitlaicxitecuecuextli, ihuan in xiuhuitzolli tlatocat-latquitl, ihuan in yacaxihuitl, ihuan in ixquich in oc cequi in itlatqui in amo zan tl-apoalli muchi quicuique, moch intech compachoqui moch comotechtique, moch comotonaltique." Ibid., 12:49; translation by Anderson and Dibble.

148. Berdan and Anawalt, *The Essential Codex Mendoza*, 118.

149. Sahagún, *Book 6*, 6:171; translation by Anderson and Dibble.

150. Ibid.; translation by Anderson and Dibble.

151. *The Gods* names each of these figures as a *teotl*. See Sahagún, *Book 1*, 2:1, 5, 9, and 21.

152. Sahagún, *Book 4*, 5:29 and 101; translation by Anderson and Dibble.

153. Indeed, the scribes note the designation of 1 Reed as Quetzalcoatl's day sign: "So they said that then they dedicated and assigned the day sign to Quetzalcoatl." None of the other three passages contains a similar annotation about the designation or assignation of a day sign to a *teotl*. The scribes' commentary may substantiate arguments that Quetzalcoatl's association with 1 Reed developed during and after Contact. However, it is also worth noting that humans were assigned a day name; children born on

unfavorable day signs could receive a day name other than that of their birth day. Sahagún, *Book 6*, 6:29. On the debate about Quetzalcoatl and 1 Reed, see Hassig, *Time, History and Belief*; Lockhart, *We People Here*; Townsend, "Burying the White Gods."

154. Sahagún, *Book 1*, 2:21; translation by Anderson and Dibble.

155. Sahagún, *Book 4*, 5:99; translation by Anderson and Dibble.

156. "zan tlazoca zan tlazohnemi; iuhquinma ineixcahuil." Sahagún, *Book 11*, 11:228.

157. "in necuiltonolli, in netlamachtilli, intonal, imaxca, inneixcahuil in tlatoque, in totecuihuan." Ibid., 11:233.

158. *Ineixcahuil* is the possessive form of the nominalized verb *moixcahuia* (to be single-minded, preoccupied with one's own affairs; to have or do just one thing to the exclusion of others). When nominalized, the nonspecific reflexive object prefix *ne-* replaces *mo-*, and the resulting forms include the singular *neixcahuilli* (an exclusive thing, occupation, business, or pursuit) and the plural *neixcahuillin*. *Neixcahuilli* often appears with the possessive prefix *i-* (his, her, its) or *in-* (their). Anderson and Dibble translate *neixcahuilli* variously as "exclusive thing(s)," "exclusive privilege," "personal privilege," and "attribute." Thanks to Michael McCafferty, R. Joe Campbell, and Lindsay Sidders for their helpful responses to my query about *neixcahuilli*'s etymology on the Nahuat-l listserv (December 8, 2008).

159. "auh in huehuetque, han in ilamatque, zan inneixcahuil atca in tlahuanaya: zan niman ayac tlahuanaya in telpuchtli, in tlamacazqui, in ichpuchtli." Sahagún, *Book 2*, 3:106; translation by Anderson and Dibble.

160. Ibid., 3:105; translation by Anderson and Dibble.

161. Sahagún, *Book 12*, 12:125; translation by Anderson and Dibble.

162. "yehica ca itequiuh, ineixcahuil atca, in tlamictiz, in tetlatlatiz, imac polihuaz, imac xamanizqui in ixquich cuauhtecatl." Sahagún, *Book 2*, 3:52; translation by Anderson and Dibble.

163. "xochitl, iyetl, ineixcahuil tlatoani, tezcatl inic motta tlatoani, inic mochichihua." Sahagún, *Book 8*, 8:28; translation by Anderson and Dibble.

164. Sahagún, *Book 2*, 3:164; translation by Anderson and Dibble.

165. Recall the scribes' account of Moteuczoma's *itonal*, including the capes he gave Cortés in their first exchange and the luxury goods Cortés later looted from Totoalco. See Sahagún, *Book 12*, 12:5 and 48; translation by Anderson and Dibble.

166. "in itequiuh pohua, in ixcoian itlachihual, in ineixcahuil: ic temolaya, ic texoxaya, yehuatl quitemacaya, in totomoniliztli, papalaniliztli, cacahuatiliztli, ixcuculiztli, ixchichitinaliztli, ixtenpipixquiliztli, ixtamacoliciuiztli, ixayauhpachiuiliztli, ixnacapachihuiliztli, ixhuahuaciuiztli, ixtotoliciuiztli, ixtezcaiciuitli." Sahagún, *Book 1*, 2:39; translation by Anderson and Dibble.

167. "auh iz nelle axcan: ca itoptzin, ca ipetlacaltzin in tloque, nahuaque: aiz in nican in motenehua, ca ineixcahuiltzin." Sahagún, *Book 6*, 6:138; translation by Anderson and Dibble.

168. Karttunen defines *mahuiztic* as "something marvelous, awesome, worthy of es-

teem" and *mahuizyotl* (or *mahuizzotl*) as "honor." For the sake of brevity and clarity, I gloss *mahuiztic* as "esteemed," which denotes both respect and admiration. Karttunen, *Analytical Dictionary*, 133.

169. Sahagún, *Book 11*, 11:223–224.

170. Ibid., 11:233.

171. Catalina Cruz de la Cruz, Sabina Cruz de la Cruz, and Delfina de la Cruz de la Cruz, personal communication, June 1–July 31, 2006.

172. "in mitoa Quetzalcoatl: iampa amo campa tepan calaqui, ca mahuizyo, ca tlamauhtia iuhquinma teomacho: zaniyo tecpan, tlatocan in huel calaqui." Sahagún, *Book 6*, 6:210; translation by Anderson and Dibble. In other contexts, the *cuacuacuiltin* are the priests responsible for collecting the corpses of sacrificial victims. See Sahagún, *Book 1*, 2:44, 48, 81, 83, 85, 112, 115, 117, 122, 214, and 245; *Book 3*, 4:61; *Book 6*, 6:210.

173. Both *mahuiztic* and *tlamauhtia* contain the stem *mahui*. On *mauhtia* and *mahui*, see Karttunen, *Analytical Dictionary*, 132.

174. In the compound *teoatl*, *teotl* modifies *atl* (water).

175. "inic mitoa teoatl, camo teotl, zan quitoznequi mahuiztic huei tlamahuizolli . . . huei temauhti, teicahui, aixnamiquiliztli, tlamahuizolli." Sahagún, *Book 11*, 11:247; translation by Anderson and Dibble.

176. Ibid., 11:224 and 228; translation by Anderson and Dibble.

177. "auh in quintlauhtia moteuczoma moch yehuatl in tlatocatilmahtli. in tlatocamaxtlatl. i cenca tlazohtli immahuizzo. ihuan tlazotlanqui quetzallahuiztli teocuitlayo. ihuan chimalli. ahzo quetzalcozcayo i huel tlazohtli chimalli." Sahagún, *Book 8*, 8:83; translation by Anderson and Dibble. On Moteuczoma's personal property, see my discussion above and Sahagún, *Book 12*, 12:12.

178. "auh in quimomacaya, cenca tlazotlanqui in tlauiztli, cenca teocuitlayo, moca teocuitla cenca quetzallo, moca quetzalli." Sahagún, *Book 2*, 3:124; translation by Anderson and Dibble.

179. Sahagún, *Book 11*, 11:224.

180. Ibid., 11:233.

181. Several of the blue-green minerals that occur in Mexico, including malachite and azurite, look like chemical turquoise; however, geologists differentiate between "chemical turquoise" (copper-aluminum hydrous phosphate) and "cultural turquoise." Central Mexican importation of chemical turquoise from Chaco Canyon and other northern mines raises the question of how subtly they differentiated between cultural and chemical turquoise, and whether *teoxihuitl* referred to chemical turquoise or a cultural variety. Weigand and Harbottle, "The Role of Turquoises," 171–173; and Weigand, "Observations on Ancient Mining," 171–173. More recently, several of the contributors to *Turquoise in Mexico and North America* argue that it is extremely difficult, if not presently impossible, to determine the provenance of turquoise excavated in Aztec sites. See King et al., *Turquoise in Mexico and North America*, 29–40 and 65–74.

182. "auh huan huel mocuiltonoaya, ahtlazotli catca, in cualoni, in ixquich in tonacaiotl, quilmach in ayotetl, cenca huehueitepopol catca . . . auh ixquich nenca in

tlazototol, y xiuhtototl, in quetzaltototl, y zacua, in tlauhquechol. . . . auh huan in ix-quich in chalchihuitl, in teocuitlatl, amo tlazotli catca. . . . ah in yehuantin in Tolteca, cenca mocuiltonohuaya." Sahagún, *Book 3*, 4:14; translation by Anderson and Dibble.

183. "mitoa, in ye huecauh zan oc ye in coztic cuitlatl nenca . . . ayatle catca in iz-tac teocuitlatl, tel onnenca . . . auh in ascan ye no cuele ca moche in iztac teocuitlatl quinequi, in coztic ye huel motlazotla." Sahagún, *Book 9*, 9:75–76; translation by An-derson and Dibble. The claim that only gold was known is inaccurate; on the use of al-loys, see Hosler, "Sound, Color and Meaning," 100–115.

184. On the importance of brilliance, see Hosler, "Sound, Color and Meaning," 100–115; Saunders, "'Catching the Light,'" 15–47; and "Biographies of Brilliance," 243–257.

185. Anderson and Dibble translate *xinmaquiztli* as "turquoise bracelets," but the *xin-* element of this compound may come from *xinachtli* (seed) and be combined with *maquiztetl* (bracelet, ornament). Sahagún, *Book 2*, 3:69–70; translation by Anderson and Dibble.

186. "ipampa canel ic itlazoteouh ipan quimati." Ibid., 3:69; translation by Ander-son and Dibble.

187. López Luján, *The Offerings*, 113.

188. On the symbolism of the Templo Mayor, as a whole, see Broda, Carrasco, and Matos Moctezuma, *The Great Temple of Tenochtitlan*.

CHAPTER 4

1. Taussig, *Defacement*, 254.

2. Sahagún, *Book 2*, 3:175–176. Traditionally, the headdress *aneucyotl* has been spelled "*anecuyotl.*" I have maintained the Nahuatl spelling, because I think this trans-literation reflects the same misleading spelling as when older sources spell *teuctli* (lord, member of the high nobility) "*tecuhtli*" or "*tecutli.*" See Karttunen, *Analytical Diction-ary*, 237. Thank you to R. Joe Campbell for helping clarify the translation of *tlaquimilol-li* as "covered in turquoise" rather than "contained in a bundle."

3. Some scholars spell Painal according to colonial orthography (Paynal); the name derives from the verb *paina*, which Molina defines as "*correr ligamente,*" to run hastily. Molina, *Vocabulario*, 79r.

4. On familial succession, see Sahagún, *Book 4*, 5:114; *Book 6*, 6:246; and *Book 10*, 10:6, 19. On military delegates, see Sahagún, *Book 1*, 2:3, 25, 55; *Book 2*, 3:114; *Book 6*, 6:54, 246; *Book 10*, 10:32.

5. Bennett, *Vibrant Matter*, 35.

6. Ibid., xv.

7. Andrews, *Introduction to Classical Nahuatl*, 357.

8. John Sullivan, personal communication, April 13, 2008. This transitive verb *teixi-ptla* is unattested, but it is retained in the noun form *ixiptlatl*, which is formed by add-ing the absolutive *-tl* to the verb *ixiptla*. All of the sources document a reduction from *ixxiptla* to *ixiptla*.

9. Andrews, *Introduction to Classical Nahuatl*, 243–244 and 258.

10. John Sullivan, personal communication, April 13, 2008.

11. Karttunen, *Analytical Dictionary*, 15.

12. Gell, *Art and Agency*, 13-14.

13. Sahagún, *Book 6*, 6:246; translation by Anderson and Dibble.

14. She concludes her brief discussion of "Indigenous American cultures," by noting that they "recognize a shared cultural substratum ... that allows us to generalize an indigenous *image-as-presence*." Although she does not discuss *teixiptlahuan*, her recognition of the image as an embodied presence approximates my argument. Zamora, *The Inordinate Eye*, 10-13.

15. Of course, the skin also belonged to the sacrificial victim. On resemblance and iconicity, see Peirce, *Writings of Charles S. Peirce*, 53-56.

16. Gell, *Art and Agency*, 99 and 104. See my discussion of Tlacaxipehualiztli (Feast of the Flaying of Men) below and Carrasco, *City of Sacrifice*, 140-163.

17. See a similar use of "localized" in Davis, *Lives of Indian Images*.

18. Durán, *Book of the Gods and Rites*, 173-174.

19. Durán's description of Tlacaxipehualiztli seems more linear than that of Sahagún, but both account for the presence of sacrificed captives whose posthumous treatment included heart extraction and flaying. According to Durán, slaves served as the *teixiptlahuan* of Xipe Totec, Huitzilopochtli, et al., and captives later wore the flayed skins of the (slave) *teixiptlahuan*. Sahagún does not mention slaves participating in Tlacaxipehualiztli. Although it may be impossible to determine which account most accurately represents the ritual, both attest to humans embodying Xipe Totec. Ibid., 174-176. See Sahagún, *Book 2*, 3:3-4 and 47-60.

20. Durán, *Book of the Gods and Rites*, 176; and Sahagún, *Book 2*, 3:54; translation by Anderson and Dibble.

21. Durán, "Ritos y fiestas," 149.

22. Gell explains, "But with indexes [representation] is not the same as with proper signs. Abduction from an index does characteristically involve positing a substantive part-whole (or part-part) relation. Smoke is a kind of 'part' of fire, for instance. A person's smile (the Cheshire cat excepted) is a part of the friendly person it betokens. From this point of view, it is not senseless to suppose that Constable's picture of Salisbury cathedral is a part of Salisbury cathedral. It is, what we would call, a 'spin-off' of Salisbury cathedral." Gell, *Art and Agency*, 104.

23. Because flayed skins are both sign and signifying substance, the (un)recognition of ritual participants wearing them must have been horrifically traumatic and deeply unsettling. Recall Achitometl's shock upon realizing the Mexica priest wore his daughter's skin: "He attended the ceremony and witnessed with horror the priest who wore the flayed skin of his daughter." López Austin, *Hombre-Dios*, 151.

24. Gell, *Art and Agency*, 99. Citing the record of Don Carlos Ometochtzin's trial in *Inquisición Libro 2 Expediente 10* held in the Archivo General de la Nación, Mexico City, Byron Hamann reports that mid-sixteenth-century Texcocoans recognized "20

of the revealed gods by name (e.g., Tlaloc, Quetzalcoatl, Xipe), but 30 were unrecognizable." Hamann, "Chronological Pollution," 809.

25. Paul Ricoeur borrows Henri Corbin's expression "*imaginal* (Fr.)" in his discussion of phenomenological manifestations. Following Eliade, Ricoeur notes, "That a stone or a tree may manifest the sacred means that this profane reality becomes something other than itself while still remaining itself. It is transformed into something supernatural—or, to avoid using a theological term, we may say that it is transformed into something superreal (*surréel*), in the sense of being superefficacious while still remaining a part of common reality." Ricoeur, *Hermeneutics*, 49–50.

26. Gell defines an agent "as one who has the capacity to initiate causal events in his/her vicinity, which cannot be ascribed to the current state of the physical cosmos, but only to a special category of mental states; that is, intentions," and he eliminates the paradox of things acting as agents by virtue "of the fact that objectification in artefact-form is how social agency manifests and realizes itself, via the proliferation of fragments of 'primary' intentional agents in their 'secondary' artefactual forms." Further, the concept of agency Gell employs is "exclusively relational" and context dependent, so that objects typically thought of as inanimate (in Western paradigms) may be considered animate agents because of their perception and reception by humans in their vicinity. Gell, *Art and Agency*, 19, 21, and 22.

27. Ibid., 23.

28. Gell cites the Kula shells used in Melanesian rituals as objects that ceremonially acquire an origin (in addition to their manufactural origin) and observes, "Often an art object indexes, primarily, not the moment and agent of its manufacture, but some subsequent, purely transactional, 'origin.'" Ibid., 24. Since Gell's primary interest is in idol artifacts as social agents, he addresses their original manufacture and subsequent ritual re-creation, but in the introduction to *Lives of Indian Images*, Richard Davis reminds us that objects continue to be reimagined. Following Igor Kopytoff's "cultural biographical" approach, Davis argues, "Hindu priests and worshipers are not the only ones to enliven images. Bringing with them differing religious assumptions, political agendas, and economic motivations, others may animate the very same objects as icons of sovereignty, as polytheistic 'idols,' as 'devils,' as potentially lucrative commodities, as objects of sculptural art, or as symbols for a whole range of new meanings never foreseen by the images' makers or original worshipers." Davis, *Lives of Indian Images*, 7. Both the Aztecs and (post-Contact) Europeans destroyed and (re-)created or reimagined pre-Contact idols and icons. On Aztec processes of destruction and re-creation, see Hamann, "Seeing and the Mixtec Screenfolds." Fernando Cervantes addresses the post-Contact demonization of Mexica images in *The Devil in the New World*.

29. See Bennett, *Vibrant Matter*, vii–xix.

30. Sahagún, *Book 2*, 3:112.

31. Ibid., 116.

32. Ritual prescriptions also appear in pictorial manuscripts, including the *Codex Fejérváry-Mayer*; see Boone, *Cycles of Time and Meaning*, 162 and fig. 97 on 66.

33. Gell, *Art and Agency*, 121; emphasis added.

34. López Austin, *Human Body and Ideology*, 1:196–197.

35. Houston, Stuart, and Taube, *The Memory of Bones*, 173.

36. Sahagún, *Book 10*, 10:103.

37. Sahagún, *Book 11*, 11:2.

38. On stargazing and calendrics, see Aveni, *Skywatchers*, 15–28. Saunders has argued that the mirror-vision of diviners, whom he calls shamans, parallels that of jaguars, were-jaguars, and other beings in the "mirror-image spirit worlds." Although Saunders's inspiration for these jaguar-shaman connections comes via Gerardo Reichel-Dolmatoff's adoption of Eliade's "shaman," research along the lines of that conducted by Barbara Tedlock, Timothy Knab, or Rebecca Stone may support his position, as could further investigation of the jaguar and eagle warrior schools. Saunders, "Chatoyer," 10–11.

39. Sahagún, *Book 1*, 2:24.

40. Ibid., 2:25; translation by Anderson and Dibble. Olivier identifies Tloque Nahuaque as the "Unknown God," and notes that apart from a temple dedicated by Nezahualcoyotl to the Unknown God in Texcoco—where Tezcatlipoca was the tutelary deity—Tloque Nahuaque took no form and had no temples. Olivier speculates that the association of Tezcatlipoca, in the form of Yohualli Ehecatl, the "Night Wind," with Tloque Nahuaque may have related to both deities' invisibility. Later, though, Olivier warns against interpreting the Texcocoan version of Tloque Nahuaque too literally, because Alva Ixtlilxóchitl, the source of this material, "obviously [intended] to present a pre-Columbian religious model announcing the coming of the Christian message." See Olivier, *Mockeries and Metamorphoses*, 48 and 275.

41. Ibid., 2:25–27; translation by Anderson and Dibble.

42. Tavárez, *The Invisible War*, 77.

43. Ibid., 79.

44. Ibid., 80.

45. Brumfiel, "Meaning by Design," 252.

46. Saunders, "Stealers of Light," 226.

47. Saunders identifies these qualities as present throughout the Americas in "Biographies of Brilliance," 246.

48. He bases this observation on his analysis of the Hindu practice of *darśan* (*darshan*), a blessing conveyed through sight between the deity and the devotee. Gell, *Art and Agency*, 116 and 118. Notably, "the dead are shown throughout Mesoamerican art with closed eyes." Houston, Stuart, and Taube, *The Memory of Bones*, 170.

49. Díaz del Castillo, *Discovery and Conquest of Mexico*, 219–220.

50. The manuscript's editors acknowledge the passage's identification of Huitzilopochtli's *teixiptla* during the observance of Toxcatl, a month typically dedicated to Tezcatlipoca. The illustration that accompanies this month's description in the calendar

suggests that Tezcatlipoca was also venerated. They note that both Durán, from whom Tovar borrowed heavily in other of his texts, and Torquemada associate Huitzilopochtli with Toxcatl. Kubler and Gibson, *The Tovar Calendar*, 24–25.

51. Landa, *Account of the Affairs of Yucatán*, 121.

52. Houston, Stuart, and Taube, *The Memory of Bones*, 170; emphasis added.

53. Anders and Jansen, *La pintura de la muerte*, 251; and Boone, *Cycles of Time and Meaning*, 140.

54. Other models for comparison include the Egyptian funerary practice of "Opening the Mouth" (of a mummy) so that the deceased is able to sense and perceive: "The eyes must be given the capacity to see, the mouth to speak and to eat and drink. This animation of the statue could be done only by the performance of the ritual known as the 'Opening of the Mouth', or sometimes more fully the 'Opening of the Mouth and Eyes'. This ritual was performed at the completion of the statues, while in the workshop. . . . In the same way the 'Opening of the Mouth' was performed on other types of image which served to support the *ka* of the owner, such as anthropoid coffins, and even on two-dimensional images carved in relief. Most importantly it was carried out on the mummified body itself at the completion of the embalming, in order to revivify it." See Taylor, *Death and the Afterlife*, 164–165. The painting of Greek Orthodox icons and the animation of Buddhist statues and Shinto images provide other salient comparisons that would require further, rigorous study.

55. Davis, *Lives of Indian Images*, 35.

56. Ibid., 35–36.

57. Eck, *Darshan*, 7.

58. RadioLab explored animacy in an episode devoted to a 450-year-old automaton, available here: http://www.radiolab.org/blogs/radiolab-blog/2011/jun/14/clockwork-miracle/.

59. Bennett, *Vibrant Matter*, ix. Bennett provides several examples of vital materials and their ability to act, including "the way omega-3 fatty acids can alter human moods or the way our trash is not 'away' in landfills but generating lively streams of chemicals and volatile winds of methane as we speak" (vii).

60. Gell, *Art and Agency*, 122.

61. On the vitality of "objects" in the study of religions, see Hughes, "Mysterium Materiae," 16–24.

62. Durán, *Book of the Gods and Rites*, 80; and "Ritos y fiestas," 85–86.

63. Durán, *Book of the Gods and Rites*, 255–256; and "Ritos y fiestas," 204.

64. López Austin and López Luján, "Aztec Human Sacrifice," 140.

65. López Luján, *The Offerings*, 124–125.

66. Ibid., 100. See also Nagao, *Mexica Buried Offerings*, 62–82.

67. López Luján, *The Offerings*, 122–125.

68. Ibid., 199.

69. Ibid., 200. See also Nicholson and Quiñones Keber, *Art of Aztec Mexico*, 40.

70. Carrasco, *City of Sacrifice*, 130.

71. Gell, *Art and Agency*, 118.

72. As Gell observes, "The idol may not be biologically a 'living thing' but, if it has 'intentional psychology' attributed to it, then it has something like a spirit, a soul, an ego, lodged within it." By intentional psychology, Gell means that intention or agency that the devotee attributes to the image. Ibid., 18–19 and 129.

73. Sahagún, *Book 2*, 3:67; translation by Anderson and Dibble.

74. Ibid., 3:66; translation by Anderson and Dibble.

75. Ibid., 3:68; translation by Anderson and Dibble.

76. Ibid.; translation by Anderson and Dibble.

77. Ibid., 3:69; translation by Anderson and Dibble.

78. Ibid.; translation by Anderson and Dibble.

79. Ibid., 3:71; translation by Anderson and Dibble.

80. Carrasco, *City of Sacrifice*, 134.

81. "netecuyotilo, tlatlauhtilo, ica elcicihuoa, ixpan nepechteco, ixpan ontlalcua in macehualtzintli." Sahagún, *Book 2*, 3:68; translation by Anderson and Dibble.

82. Durán, *Book of the Gods and Rites*, 98. The mirrorlike object Durán describes was a *tlachiyaloni*, a vision apparatus.

83. As Diana Eck explains, "In popular terminology, Hindus say that the deity or the *sadhu* 'gives darśan' (*darśan dena* is the Hindi expression), and the people 'take darśan' (*darśan lena*)." Eck, *Darshan*, 6.

84. Gell, *Art and Agency*, 118.

85. Durán, *History of the Indies*, 308.

86. Sahagún, *Book 2*, 3:68; translation by Anderson and Dibble.

CHAPTER 5

1. "quitlatito yn inteocal cuitlahuaca in ical mixcoatl Diablo yquac mexicatzinco yaocuixtli yn achto tlecotihuetzyn icpac mixcoatl yn quicuito ytzpapalotl ynexyo yn mitoaya tlaquimilolli et. Ome yn quetzallotlatl yc temiya: auh niman ye quilhuiya y teçoçomoctli yn çitlalcohuatzin Tenochtitlan yhuan yn yquehuacatzin yhuan axicyotzin yhuan tenamaztzin quilhuique teçoçomoctze: ca otlatlac yn mixcoatl yn xocoyotl can el aocmo toconcuic yn mitl yn chimalli auh ynin can otictecac yn mixcoatl tichuicazque xitechmaca." Bierhorst, *History and Mythology*, 106; and *Codex Chimalpopoca*, 63. The "Anales de Cuauhtitlan" and the "Leyenda de los soles" are two of the three texts collected in the *Codex Chimalpopoca*. Bierhorst's edition of the *Codex Chimalpopoca* contains only these two parts; the third, by seventeenth-century cleric Pedro Ponce de León, is "Breve relación de los dioses y ritos de la gentilidad."

2. "amo nelli yehuatl yxiptla yn mitoaya camaxtle mixcohuatl ca çan yehuatl yn itoca teohcatl can no yuhqui yn inechichihual yn mixcohuatl çan no yuh ypan quttaque yn Meixca yn momatque aço nelli yehuatl ca çan yc ynca necayahualloc yn Mexica yn mochiuh yn ye." Bierhorst, *History and Mythology*, 106; and *Codex Chimalpopoca*, 63.

3. Mendieta, "Historia eclesiástica," 79–80. Thanks to María Isabel Ramos and León García Garagarza for their consultation on this translation.

4. Olivier, "Sacred Bundles," 199.

5. Molina, *Vocabulario*, 134r.

6. On the authorship of Chimalpahin's *Codex Chimalpopoca* and Alvarado Tezozómoc's *Crónica mexicana*, see Schroeder, "The Truth about the *Crónica Mexicayotl*."

7. Sahagún, *Book 10*, 10:191. The Spanish text also mentions the *bulto* (bundle): "se
partieron con su dios, que llevaban en buelto, en un enboltorio de mantas" (fol. 141r).

8. Sepúlveda y Herrera, *Procesos por idolatría*, 115–140.

9. On *tlaquimilolli* and the New Fire ceremony, see Olivier, "Sacred Bundles."

10. John M. D. Pohl examines Mixtec sacred bundles and provides a brief overview
of bundles in other Amerindian cultures in *The Politics of Symbolism in the Mixtec Codices*, 19–41.

11. Karttunen, *Analytical Dictionary*, 211.

12. Alternatively, *tlaquimilolli* may be analyzed as *tlaquimilo-l(o)-li*, where the *-lo-*
is a passive ending that loses the final vowel when, according to Andrews, *-li* is added
during derivation. Compared to Andrews, Lockhart is less certain regarding whether
-l- is *-lo-* or an independent patientive affix. Thanks to one of the University of Texas
Press's anonymous reviewers for calling this to my attention.

13. Thanks to John Sullivan for refining my understanding of the *tlaquimilolli*'s
etymology.

14. Karttunen, *Analytical Dictionary*, 211.

15. Lockhart, *Nahuatl as Written*, 29.

16. "Nahuatl Dictionary," whp.oregon.edu/dictionaries/nahuatl/index.lasso.

17. Other quantifiers include *tecpantli* for beings, *ipilli* for flat objects, and *tlamic* for
ears of corn. See Dehouve, *L'imaginaire des nombres*, 42–43.

18. Ibid., 43.

19. Thanks to Ellen Logan for helping me think of English words that signify specific quantities of things.

20. "auh in tilmatli zan quiquimiliuhtiuh, zan quiquimilietiuh, zan quimiltica in
quimomaca, in, in quimotlauhtia." Sahagún, *Book 4*, 5:88.

21. "ihuan tomatl quicouhtihuia, in cecemilhuitl ic tomacohua, ahzo cenquimilli in
tecuachtli." Sahagún, *Book 9*, 9:48.

22. "in cemacalli ipatiuh catca, centetl in tequachtli momacaia: in centetl tequachtli, ipatiuh catca, macuilpohualli in cacahuatl, yehuatl in tequachtli nappohuali ipatiuh
catca in cacahuatl auh in zan yequene tlazacuia tequachtli, Epohualli onmacuilli in cacahuatl, ipatiuh catca." Ibid., 48. In a footnote, Anderson and Dibble observe that the
Spanish text distinguishes between the three types of capes as *tototlaqualtequachtli*,
"first grade, fine, small capes, at 100 cacao beans"; *tequachtli*, "second grade, fine, small
capes at 80"; and *quachtli*, "third grade, large capes, at 60—not the 65 mentioned in
the Nahuatl text."

23. "ic quitlaliaya camaquimiloaya, camapepechoa." Sahagún, *Book 2*, 3:124 and 157.

24. "quimomamaltiaya in cintli . . . amatica in quinquiquimiloaya huan tlazotilmat-
ica in quinmama in cihuatlamacazque." Ibid., 3:124.

25. DiCesare, *Sweeping the Way*, 151–152.

26. Bierhorst, *History and Mythology*, 147.

27. "in tonacayotl in iztac in yahuitl in coztic in xiuhtoctli in etl in huauhtli in chian in michihuauhtli ixquich namoyaloc in tonacayotl." Ibid.; and *Codex Chimalpopoca*, 90; see also DiCesare, *Sweeping the Way*, 151.

28. DiCesare, *Sweeping the Way*, 95 and 151–152.

29. "temauhti, tequani, techopiniani, motepachihuiani, tehuchiani." Sahagún, *Book 11*, 11:77.

30. "auh in ipayo tecooaqualiztli: niman iciuh ca mochichina, huan moxoxotla in pani pozaoatiuh, tecoaqualli: huan motemilia, meciotica moquimilhuia in icooaqualocauh, tlexochpan moteca: huan picietica momatiloa." Ibid.

31. Sahagún, *Book 10*, 10:161. The *Florentine Codex* identifies the Toltecs as the inventors of *ticiotl*, the art of medicine.

32. "in tiacahuan in ihuac mantini, in amo quitlazotla in intzonteco, in imelchiquiuh, in amo quiximati in octli." Sahagún, *Book 8*, 8:61.

33. "niman ic conixtlapachoa, ic quicuaquimiloa nezahualcuachtli xoxoctic." Ibid., 8:62.

34. "niman ic quimontlapachoa, quimonixquimiloa, cecemme, ica nezahualcuachtli, tliltic omicallo." Ibid., 8:63.

35. Klein, "The Devil and the Skirt," 22.

36. Anawalt, "Memory Clothing," 165.

37. "la causa de muerte y la posición social." Chávez Balderas, *Rituales funerarios*, 72.

38. "yehica, in ihcuac aquin miquia, in oconchichiuhque, in oconquiquimiloque, in oconiilpique." Sahagún, *Book 7*, 7:21.

39. Chávez Balderas, *Rituales funerarios*, 72–78. For a description of contemporary Maya internment practices that involve a second burial likened to bundling, see Astor-Aguilera, *Maya World of Communicating Objects*, 158–161.

40. Sahagún, *Book 3*, 4:41.

41. "ritos en presencia del cadaver, cremación, recolección de las cenizas y depósito, y sepultura de los restos mortales." Chávez Balderas, *Rituales funerarios*, 78.

42. "in amatl quixoxotlaya, quitetequia quihilpiaya. auh in oquicencauhque in amatlatquitl, niman ye ic quichichioa in micqui, quicocototztlalia, icpac conteca atl." Sahagún, *Book 3*, 4:42; translation by Anderson and Dibble.

43. "niman ye ic quiquiquimiloa, quiteteuhquimiloa, quiteteuhilpia, quicacatzilpia in micqui." Ibid., 4:43.

44. "quilmach quimotenati, ic mehecatzacuiliz in itzeheciaya, amo cenca motoliniz." Ibid.

45. "achi tetolini, huan achi cualli." Sahagún, *Book 4*, 5:24.

46. "in tel ye oquimanili, in ipalnemohuani, in oquimotzitzquili, conmocahualtilia in imacehual." Ibid.

47. "inic onmiqui, zan tetlaoculti, aoc tle itech huetztotiuh, za petlauhtiuh, aoc necini in tlein iquimiliuhca." Ibid.

48. "En cualquier caso, un guerrero—de carne y hueso o de ocote—debía ser entregado al fuego." Chávez Balderas, *Rituales funerarios*, 79.

49. Durán, *History of the Indies*, 284–285.

50. Mendieta, *Historia eclesiástica indiana*, 79.

51. "Dejaron cada uno de ellos la ropa que traia (que era una manta) á los devotos que tenia, en memoria de su devocion y amistad. Y así aplacado el sol hizo su curso." Ibid.

52. "Este envoltorio decian tlaquimilolli, y cada uno le ponia el nombre de aquel demonio que le habia dado la manta." Ibid., 80.

53. "tleica ca noconitlani in imeço in intlapallo in in tlacoca." Bierhorst, *Codex Chimalpopoca*, 90–91; *History and Mythology*, 148. Bierhorst published the *Codex Chimalpopoca* as a two-volume set: one contains the Nahuatl text with a glossary, and the other his English translation and a concordance. In my discussion of Itzpapalotl's *tlaquimilolli*'s origin, I quote the Nahuatl transcribed by Bierhorst and then his English translation. My commentary on the meanings and significances of some of the Nahuatl terms appears below.

54. "amo quitoa in tonan in tota." Bierhorst, *Codex Chimalpopoca*, 92; *History and Mythology*, 150.

55. "in mimich iyo ca ye qua llo in nachcauh." Bierhorst, *Codex Chimalpopoca*, 93; *History and Mythology*, 151.

56. Bierhorst, *Codex Chimalpopoca*, 93; *History and Mythology*, 152.

57. "cuecueponi." Bierhorst, *Codex Chimalpopoca*, 93; *History and Mythology*, 152.

58. "auh in iztac tecpatl niman ye quimoteotia in mixcohuatl niman quiquimiloque niman ye quimama niman ye yauh in tepehuaz itocayocan comallan quimamatiuh in tecpatl in iteouh in itzpapalotl." Bierhorst, *Codex Chimalpopoca*, 93; *History and Mythology*, 152.

59. "auh yn omic niman quitlatique auh yn inexyo yc mixconòque yhuan yc mixtetlilcomoloque: auh yn mocauh yntlaquimilol mochiuh oncan moçenchichiuhque yn itocayocan maçatepec." Bierhorst, *Codex Chimalpopoca*, 3; *History and Mythology*, 23.

60. The *Historia de los mexicanos por sus pinturas* also describes Mixcoatl's activities in the aftermath of the sun's creation. Although the *Historia* does not mention Itzpapalotl, in this version a single two-headed deer descends, and Camasale (Camaxtle) ordered the people of Cuitlahuaca to catch the deer and consider it a god. Later, the text explains, "Los chichimecas traían guerra con el Camasale. y le tomaron el cierro que traía, por cuyo favor él vencía, y la causa porque lo perdió fué porque andando en el campo topó con unal parienta de Tezcatlipuca que descendía de las cinco mujeres que hizo cuando crió los cuatrocientos hombres, y ellos murieron y ellas quedaron vivas, y esta descendía dellas, y parió dél un hijo que dijeron Ceacalt [*sic*]." The deer in this account sounds suspiciously like a *tlaquimilolli*: the Cuitlahuacans venerate it as a

god, and the Chichimeca take it from Camaxtle like other polities take the *tlaquimilolli* of conquered peoples. If we are willing to elide the details in this account with those in the "Leyenda" and "Anales," together they suggest that Itzpapalotl's *tlaquimilolli* may have included, or been wrapped in, a deer hide. García Icazbalceta, *Historia de los mexicanos por sus pinturas*, 3:217.

61. "Y este Topiltzin hecho señor, a cabo de cierto tiempo, que él quería ir a donde salía el sol y que vendría dentro de cierto tiempo, y señaló por su cuenta en qué año vendría . . . ce ácatl . . . con él se fue mucha gente, y en cada pueblo a donde llegaba, dejaba alguna de ella, y teníanle por ídolo, y por tal lo adoraban. Fue a morir en un pueblo que se llama Matlapalan . . . y al tiempo que este Topiltzin murió, mandó que con él quemasen todo el tesoro que tenía. Tuviéronlo cuatro días por quemar, al cabo de los cuales lo quemaron y cogieron la ceniza que se hizo de su cuerpo, y echáronla en una bolsa hecha de cuero de tigre, y por esta causa todos los señores que aquel tiempo morían los quemaban." Alva Ixtlilxóchitl, *Obras históricas*, 1:387.

62. The *Florentine Codex* includes Quetzalcoatl among the gods who witnessed the sunrise. Further, Quetzalcoatl was one of four *teteo* who were looking east at the time of the first dawn. Elsewhere, Jeanette Peterson and I have suggested that the redness of the dawn and the redness of the location to which Quetzalcoatl fled (in the *Florentine Codex*) and where he may have died (per Alva Ixtlilxóchitl) may "bind [him] to creative and destructive forces through the vibrant and vital reds of blood, fire and sunlight." See Sahagún, *Book 7*, 7:7; and Bassett and Peterson, "Coloring the Sacred in the New World."

63. Thanks to one of the anonymous readers of the version of this material published by *History of Religions* for reminding me of Alva Ixtlilxóchitl's perspective, which involved efforts both to reconcile the two worlds in which he lived and to present them to non-native audiences.

64. "Vida y muerte no son extremos de una línea recta, sino dos puntos situados de manera diametral en un círculo que está en movimiento." Chávez Balderas, *Rituales funerarios*, 24.

65. More specifically, Olivier identifies a "double tradition" in the mythohistories of the *tlaquimilolli* belonging to Tezcatlipoca and Huitzilopochtli. Olivier, *Mockeries and Metamorphoses*, 74; and "Sacred Bundles," 202.

66. Olivier, "Sacred Bundles," 202.

67. García Icazbalceta, *Historia de los mexicanos*, 210.

68. Boone, "Incarnations of the Aztec Supernatural," 35–36.

69. Ibid., 40. Boone identifies depictions of the *teotl's tzoalli teixiptlahuan* in the codices by their lack of legs and feet. See her Figure 20 in "Incarnations." In contrast to images of *teixiptlahuan* fashioned in other media, those of *tzoalli* figures typically appear wearing cloaks that cover or conceal their lower bodies. Taking the Magliabecchiano images as a representative corpus, Boone observes, "Since all the other deity images in the Magliabechiano Group pictorials are fully painted with legs and feet, the lack of the lower body here unquestionably distinguishes it as the *tzoalli* form; it is as if

the legs and feet of the seated *tzoalli* image were being obscured by the richly designed cloak, as is nearly the case in the Durán illustration."

70. Ibid., 22.

71. "auh yntlapial catca quitlatlauhtiaya quiteomatia yn aquin quitocayotiaya tetzahuitl Huitzilopochtli. ca tlahtohuaya. quinnotzaya. yhuan oyntlan ne oquinmocniuhtiaya. in yehuatin azteca." Anderson and Schroeder, *Codex Chimalpahin*, 66–67. English translations of the *Mexican History and Chronicle* (*Codex Chimalpahin*) are by Anderson and Schroeder. Alvarado Tezozómoc has it this way, "Tetzahuitl Huitzilopochtli," as he calls the *teotl*, "catlahtohuaya. quinnotzaya. ihuan oyntlanne oquin mocniuhtiaya. in yehuantin Azteca." (Huitzilopochtli, the portent, was speaking to them, they were summoning him, and he was living among them; afterward he became the friend of these Aztecs.) Alvarado Tezozómoc, *Crónica mexicana*, 12. *Tetzahuitl* (something extraordinary, frightening, supernatural; an augury, a bad omen) is related to *tetzahuia* (to be beset by forboding; to frighten others, for something to augur ill for someone). Karttunen, *Analytical Dictionary*, 236–237.

72. For a Euhemerist reading, see González de Lesur, "El dios Huitzilopochtli."

73. "traían asimismo la figura y manera de cómo hacían sus templos, par le hacer á Uchilobi doquiera que llegasen." García Icazbalceta, *Historia de los mexicanos*, 218.

74. Durán, *History of the Indies*, 21–22.

75. "auh y cana cenca huecahuaya. Moteocaltiaya. oncan quiquetzque yn ical yn iteouh yn Huitzilopochtli." Anderson and Schroeder, *Codex Chimalpahin*, 76–77.

76. See Boone, *Incarnations of the Aztec Supernatural*, 21n20.

77. "auh yn ompa yc huallehuaque Azteca yn culhuacan nahuintin yn quihualmamaque yn tetzahuitl Huitzilopochtli. Topco hualonotia. Yn teomamaque ce tlacatl. Ytoca yztac mixcohuatzin Auh ynic ome ytoca apanecatl. Yniquey ytoca tezcacohuacatl ynic nahui cihuatl ytoca chimalma yehuantin y motenehua teomamaque." Anderson and Schroeder, *Codex Chimalpahin*, 70–71. Alvarado Tezozómoc explains that "nahuíntin inquihualmamaque in tetzahuitl Huitzilopochtli to[p]cohualonotia in teomamaque ce tlacatl itoca Iztacmixcohuatzin, auh inic ome itoca Apanecatl, inic ey itoca Tetzcacohuacatl, inic nahui cihuatl itoca Chimalma yehuantinin imotenehua teomamaque" (four carried Huitzilopochtli's portent in a coffer; the god-carriers were one man called Iztacmixcohuatzin, a second called Apanecatl, a third named Tetzcacohuacatl, and a fourth, a woman, named Chimalma; these were called "god-carriers"). Alvarado Tezozómoc, *Crónica mexicana*, 19. Note, too, that the first god-carrier, Iztac Mixcoatzin (White Mixcoatl), and the fourth god-carrier, Chimalman, figure in the story of the creation of Itzpapalotl's bundle.

78. Durán, *History of the Indies*: 23.

79. "Algunos mexicanos que dónde los llevaba Uchilogos perdidos, y murmuraron dél, y el Uchilogos les dijo entre sueños que ansí convenía haber pasado, y que ya estaban cerca de do habían de tener su reposo y casa." García Icazbalceta, *Historia de los mexicanos*, 227.

80. "quihualhuicaya yn telyn intlapial yn intlaquimilol catca yn quimoteotiaya qui-

caquia yn tlahtohua, auh quinanquiliaya yn azteca auh yn amo tuittaya yn quename quinotzaýa." Anderson and Schroeder, *Codex Chimalpahin*, 68–69. According to Alvarado Tezozómoc, the *teotl* communicated with them in the form of his *tlaquimilolli*: "hualhuicaya in tleinin tlapial inintlaquimilolcatca ìn quimoteotiaya quicaquia in tlatohua, auh quinanquiliaya in Azteca in amoquittaya inquename quin notzaya." Alvarado Tezozómoc, *Crónica mexicana*, 17.

81. Molina, *Vocabulario*, 125r; and Karttunen, *Analytical Dictionary*, 278.

82. "auh niman oquihto yn tlamacazqui. yn Huitzilopochtli. auh quimilhuia yn itahua yn motenehua yn teomamaque . . . auh oquimilihui . . ." Anderson and Schroeder, *Codex Chimalpahin*, 78–79.

83. "in yehuatl. yn Huitzilopochtli. ca yehica ynteyacancauh ymachcauh yn diablosme." Ibid., 80–81. It is worth noting that the *Historia de los mexicanos* describes Huitzilopochtli "appearing" to Tiunche, whom he "told that his home was to be in this spot . . . which afterwards was called Tenustitan [Tenochtitlan]." García Icazbalceta, *Historia de los mexicanos*, 227.

84. Boone, "Incarnations of the Supernatural," 29.

85. Boone, "Aztec Pictorial Histories," 72.

86. Olivier, "Sacred Bundles," 201.

87. Las Casas, *Apologética historia sumaria* 1:643; and Pomar, "Relación de Tezcoco," 59.

88. Las Casas writes, "Y de este nombre [Texcatepócatl] tomó nombre Popocatépetl, el volcán que está en la sierra Nevada; este, después de muerto, lo tuvieron los de Tezcuco y su tierra por dios. Algunos dicen que no murió sino que se metió en el dicho volcán y que de allí les envió el hueso de su muslo, el cual pusieron en su templo y lo reverenciaron y sacrificaban por dios y dello se jactan los de Tezcuco." (And from this name [Tezcatlipoca] the volcano that is in the Sierra Nevada took the name Popocatepetl; this one, after he died, was taken by those from Texcoco and the vicinity for their god. Some said that he did not die, but that he got into this volcano and that from there he sent them his thigh bone, which they put in their temple and they revere and sacrifice to it as a god and the Texcocoans tend to brag about it.) In *Mockeries and Metamorphoses*, Olivier misquotes Las Casas as "el hueso de su muslo, el cual pusieron en su temple [sic] por su principal dios y dello se jactan much los de Tezcoco," which he translates as "the bone of his thigh, they placed it in their temple like their principal god and the Tezcocans are prone to boast much about that." The 1967 edition of the *Apologética*, which both Olivier and I cite, indicates that the Texcocoans venerated the bone like a god without identifying it as their "*principal dios.*" Olivier, *Mockeries and Metamorphoses*, 77; *Tezcatlipoca*, 643n1.

89. "Estaba un espejo de alinde, del tamaño y compás de una media naranja grande, engastada en una piedra negra tosca. Estaban con ella, muchas piedras ricas sueltas, como eran chalchihuites, esmeraldas, turquesas, y de otros muchos géneros. Y la manta que estaba más cercana del espejo y piedras, era pintada de osmenta humana." Pomar, "Relación de Tezcoco," 59.

90. Urton, *History of a Myth*, 142n4.

91. Olivier's comprehensive exploration of Tezcatlipoca dedicates an entire chapter to the deity's fascinating prosthetic, the smoking mirror, and his missing leg and foot. See Olivier, *Mockeries and Metamorphoses*, 231–268.

92. Ibid., 11.

93. See also Smith, "Archaeology of Tezcatlipoca," 5.

94. "inin tezcatl cequi iztac, cequi tliltic, in iztac yehuatl in cualli in tlachia . . . quitocaiotia tecpiltezcatl, tlatocatezcatl, in tliltic, yehuatl in amo cualli, in amo tlachia . . . quitoa tlaeltezcatl, teixahuani tezcatl." Sahagún, *Book 11*, 11:228; translation by Anderson and Dibble.

95. Obsidian mirrors appear in the archaeological records of the Epiclassic, Early Postclassic, and Late Postclassic periods, but archaeologists have also recovered numerous pyrite mirrors from Classic- and Postclassic-era Mesoamerica despite the objects' popularity among post-Contact looters. Olivier refrains from promoting the tempting notion—first proposed by Alden Mason—that pyrite might produce the clear image of the white mirror, and obsidian, the distorted image of the black one, and Smith asserts that "there is abundant evidence in the codices that mirrors in Aztec and central Mexico—both those associated with Tezcatlipoca and other mirrors—were black and circular in form." Olivier, *Mockeries and Metamorphoses*, 241–242; Mason, "Mirrors of Ancient America," 203; and Smith, "Archaeology of Tezcatlipoca," 6.

96. Olivier, *Mockeries and Metamorphoses*, 242.

97. Saunders, "A Dark Light," 222.

98. Smith, "Archaeology of Tezcatlipoca," 5.

99. Saunders, "Stealers of Light," 226.

100. Gell, "Technology of Enchantment."

101. Thanks to David Wright for pointing me toward the *Huamantla Codex* (available online via the World Digital Library at www.wdl.org/en/item/3244) and other sources related to the *tlachiyaloni*.

102. "una chapa de oro muy relumbrante y bruñida, como un espejo, que era dar a entender que en aquel espejo veía todo lo que se hacía en el mundo." Olivier, *Mockeries and Metamorphoses*, 249; and Durán, *Book of the Gods and Rites*, 99.

103. Olivier, *Mockeries and Metamorphoses*, 249; and Sahagún, *Historia general*, 52.

104. Sahagún, *Book 1*, 2:34.

105. On the relationship between the mirror, transgression, and fate, see Olivier, *Mockeries and Metamorphoses*, 253–256. In his discussion of these topics, Olivier draws on a geographically dispersed collection of ethnohistoric and ethnographic accounts relating mirrors to confessional and prophetic divinatory practices.

106. The other images show the *teixiptla*: (1) before he has been dressed in the *teotl*'s array; (2) using both hands to play the flute; and (3) after being sacrificed—all situations in which holding the *tlachiyaloni* would have been difficult, if not impossible.

107. "Dicen que, en este espejo, vieron muchas veces al Tezcatlipoca en la forma que se ha dicho y pintado." Pomar, "Relación de Tezcoco," 59.

108. "y que, cuando vinieron los antepasados de los del barrio de Huitznahuac . . . venía hablando con ellos este espejo en voz humana, para que pasasen adelante y no parasen ni asentasen en las partes que, viniendo, pretendieron parar y poblar hasta que llegaron a esta tierra de los chichimecas aculhuaque. Donde llegados, no les habló más; y, por eso, hicieron en ella su asiento. . . . Y no se halla que después les hablase más salvo que algunas veces, lo veían en sueños y les mandaba algunas cosas que después hacían: que eran los sacerdotes de su templo, que estaban en su guarda y servicio, y que esto era muy raras veces." Ibid.

109. Olivier, *Mockeries and Metamorphoses*, 77.

110. "auh in queztepolli, amatica quiquiquimiloaya, quixaiacatiaia: auh inin moto-caiotiaia, malteotl." Sahagún, *Book 2*, 3:60.

111. By comparison, Mayanists have studied bones and bodies from etymological, glyphic, (bio)archaeological, and ethnographic perspectives. See Houston, Stuart, and Taube, *Memory of Bones*, 31, 72, and 221.

112. López Austin, *Human Body and Ideology*, 1: 166.

113. See Furst, "Skeletonization in Mixtec Art"; Klein, "The Devil and the Skirt," 22; and Chávez Balderas, *Rituales funerarios*, 30–31.

114. Pereira, "Utilization of Grooved Human Bones," 295–297.

115. Stuart, "Kings of Stone," 156–157 and 65n16.

CONCLUSION

1. Latour, "On the Cult of the Factish Gods," 42.

2. Author interview with ritual participant D, August 4, 2010.

3. On writing narrative fragments, see Flueckiger, "Writing with Fragments and Silences."

4. Latour, "On the Cult of the Factish Gods," 9.

5. On the bundling of infant and infant-sized deities in Mesoamerican and contemporary Mexican religion, see Hughes, "Cradling as a Ritual Posture."

6. Gell, *Art and Agency*, 135.

7. Garibay Kintana, *Historia de la literatura náhuatl*, 1:19.

8. Because these properties emerge from the *Florentine Codex*, they may not represent a comprehensive definition of *teotl*. In combination with early lexicons, the *Florentine Codex* offers an unparalleled (though not unproblematic) source for older Nahuatl studies, and in my research, no roughly contemporary texts contradicted these qualities or substantially altered them. The *teotl* properties I extrapolate may be modified with reference to later texts, such as Ruiz de Alarcón. I have consulted his work and others in the chapters that surround my investigation of *teotl*'s semantic denotation, but I was careful to avoid the complications that might arise in the years between the Nahuatl of Sahagún's time and that of Ruiz de Alarcón's—to take just one example—by restricting my linguistic analysis to the *Florentine Codex*.

9. Yoon, *Naming Nature*, 11.

10. Sahagún, *Book 11*, 11:1; translation by Anderson and Dibble.

11. Of course, the extent to which Sahagún's questionnaire elicited the content or form of this response is difficult to determine. Given its similarity to other descriptions we have encountered, such as the body of Tezcatlipoca's *teixiptla* during Toxcatl, the questions may have prompted similar responses, the redactor may have made the texts similar, or they may reflect typical responses from older Nahuatl speakers. See Yoon, *Naming Nature*, 12–13.

12. See Dean, *A Culture of Stone*, 8–13 and 35–40; Houston, Stuart, and Taube, *Memory of Bones*, 72–76; Hughes, "Mysterium Materiae," 16–24; Zedeño, "Bundled Worlds," 362–378.

13. Sahagún, *Book 1*, 2:21.

14. DiCesare, "History and Time"; and *Sweeping the Way*, 123–154.

15. Apart from Francisco del Paso y Troncoso's commentary, Christopher Couch's analysis, and Elizabeth Boone's examination of the trecenas in the *Codex Borbonicus*, the scholarship analyzing the elements of this extraordinary codex is rather limited. See Paso y Troncoso, *Descripción, historia y exposición*; Couch, *The Festival Cycle*; and Boone, *Cycles of Time and Meaning*, 88–95.

16. Boone, *Cycles of Time and Meaning*, 2.

17. Author interview with ritual participant B, August 4, 2010.

18. Ibid.; and author interview with ritual participant A, August 4, 2010.

19. Author interview with ritual participant D, August 4, 2010.

20. Karttunen, *Analytical Dictionary*, 340 and 343.

21. Bennett, *Vibrant Matter*, xvi.

22. Viveiros de Castro, "Cosmological Deixis," 469. He argues that unlike in the West, where we operate on the assumption that there is one way of being with many ways of knowing, "Amerindian thought proposes the opposite: a representational or phenomenological unity that is purely pronominal or deictic, indifferently applied to a radically objective diversity. One culture, multiple natures—one epistemology, multiple ontologies." Viveiros de Castro, "Exchanging Perspectives," 474.

23. Ibid., 474; emphasis added.

24. Sahagún, *Book 1*, 2:21.

25. Author interview with ritual participant D (the *tepahtihquetl*), August 4, 2010.

BIBLIOGRAPHY

Aguilera, Carmen. "Of Royal Mantles and Blue Turquoise: The Meaning of the Mexica Emperor's Mantle." *Latin American Antiquity* 8, no. 1 (1997): 3–19.

Alva Ixtlilxóchitl, Fernando de. *Obras históricas.* Edited by Edmundo O'Gorman. 2 vols. Mexico City: Instituto de Investigaciones Históricas, Universidad Nacional Autónoma de México, 1975.

Alvarado Tezozómoc, Fernando. *Crónica mexicana, escrito hacia el año de 1598.* Mexico City: Editorial Leyenda, 1944.

Anawalt, Patricia. "Analysis of the Aztec Quechquemitl: An Exercise in Inference." In *The Art and Iconography of Late Post-Classic Central Mexico,* edited by Elizabeth Hill Boone, 37–72. Washington, D.C.: Dumbarton Oaks, 1982.

———. "Memory Clothing: Costumes Associated with Aztec Human Sacrifice." In *Ritual Human Sacrifice in Mesoamerica,* edited by Elizabeth Hill Boone, 165–193. Washington, D.C.: Dumbarton Oaks, 1984.

Anders, Ferdinand, and Maarten Jansen. *La pintura de la muerte y de los destinos: Libro explicativo del llamado Códice Laud.* Mexico City: Fondo de Cultura Económica, 1994.

Anderson, Arthur J. O., and Susan Schroeder. *Codex Chimalpahin.* Edited by Wayne Ruwet and Susan Schroeder. 2 vols. Norman: University of Oklahoma Press, 1997.

Andrews, J. Richard. *Introduction to Classical Nahuatl.* Austin: University of Texas Press, 1975.

———. *Workbook for Introduction to Classical Nahuatl.* Rev. ed. Norman: University of Oklahoma Press, 2003.

Astor-Aguilera, Miguel Angel. *The Maya World of Communicating Objects: Quadripartite Crosses, Trees, and Stones.* Albuquerque: University of New Mexico Press, 2010.

Austin, J. L. *How to Do Things with Words.* Cambridge: Harvard University Press, 1975.

Aveni, Anthony F. *Skywatchers.* Austin: University of Texas Press, 2001.

Bailey, Gauvin Alexander. *Art of Colonial Latin America.* New York: Phaidon Press, 2005.

Baird, Ellen T. "Sahagún and the Representation of History." In *Sahagún at 500: Essays on the Quincentenary of the Birth of Fr. Bernardino de Sahagún,* edited by John F. Schwaller, 117–136. Berkeley: Academy of American Franciscan History, 2003.

Barnes, William L. "Partitioning the Parturient: An Exploration of the Aztec Fetishized Female Body." *Athanor* 15 (1997): 20–27.

Bassett, Molly H., and Jeanette Favrot Peterson. "Coloring the Sacred in the New World." In *The Materiality of Color: The Production, Circulation, and Application of Dyes and Pigments, 1400–1800,* edited by Andrea Feeser, Maureen Daly Goggin, and Beth Fowkes Tobin, 45–64. London: Ashgate, 2012.

Bennett, Jane. *Vibrant Matter: A Political Ecology of Things*. Durham, NC: Duke University Press, 2010.

Berdan, Frances. "Turquoise in the Aztec Imperial World." In *Turquoise in Mexico and North America: Science, Conservation, Culture and Collections*, edited by J. C. H. King, Max Carocci, Caroline Cartwright, Colin McEwan, and Rebecca Stacey, 91–102. London: Archetype Publications, 2012.

Berdan, Frances F., and Patricia Anawalt, eds. *The Essential Codex Mendoza*. Consists of vols. 2 and 4 of the authors' four-volume work, *The Codex Mendoza* (1992). Berkeley: University of California Press, 1997.

Bierhorst, John, ed. *Codex Chimalpopoca: The Text in Nahuatl with a Glossary and Grammatical Notes*. Tucson, AZ: University of Arizona Press, 1992.

——. *History and Mythology of the Aztecs: The Codex Chimalpopoca*. Tucson: University of Arizona Press, 1998.

Boone, Elizabeth Hill. "Aztec Pictorial Histories: Records without Words." In *Writing without Words: Alternative Literacies in Mesoamerica and the Andes*, edited by Elizabeth Hill Boone and Walter D. Mignolo, 50–76. Durham: Duke University Press, 1994.

——. "The 'Coatlicues' at the Templo Mayor." *Ancient Mesoamerica* 10 (1999): 189–206.

——. *Cycles of Time and Meaning in the Mexican Books of Fate*. Joe R. And Teresa Lozano Long Series in Latin American and Latino Art and Culture. Austin: University of Texas Press, 2007.

——. *Incarnations of the Aztec Supernatural: The Image of Huitzilopochtli in Mexico and Europe*. Vol. 79, Transactions of the American Philosophical Society. Philadelphia: The American Philosophical Society, 1989.

——. "Introduction: Writing and Recording Knowledge." In *Writing without Words: Alternative Literacies in Mesoamerica and the Andes*, edited by Elizabeth Hill Boone and Walter D. Mignolo, 3–26. Durham: Duke University Press, 1994.

——. "Ruptures and Unions: Graphic Complexity and Hybridity in Sixteenth-Century Mexico." In *Their Way of Writing: Scripts, Signs, and Pictographies in Pre-Columbian America*, edited by Elizabeth H. Boone and Gary Urton, 197–225. Washington, D.C.: Dumbarton Oaks Research Library and Collection, 2011.

——. *Stories in Red and Black: Pictorial Histories of the Aztec and Mixtec*. Austin: University of Texas Press, 2000.

Bricker, Victoria A. "Advances in Maya Epigraphy." *Annual Review of Anthropology* 24 (1995): 215–235.

Broda, Johanna, Davíd Carrasco, and Eduardo Matos Moctezuma. *The Great Temple of Tenochtitlan: Center and Periphery in the Aztec World*. Berkeley: University of California Press, 1987.

Browne, Walden. *Sahagún and the Transition to Modernity*. Norman: University of Oklahoma Press, 2000.

Brumfiel, Elizabeth M. "Meaning by Design: Ceramics, Feasting, and Figured Worlds in Postclassic Mexico." In *Mesoamerican Archaeology: Theory and Practice*, edited by Julia A. Hendon and Rosemary Joyce, 239–264. Oxford, UK: Wiley-Blackwell Publishing, 2003.

Burkhart, Louise M. "Meeting the Enemy: Moteuczoma and Cortés, Herod and the Magi." In *Invasion and Transformation: Interdisciplinary Perspectives on the Conquest of Mexico*, edited by Rebecca C. Brienen and Margaret A. Jackson, 11–24. Boulder: University Press of Colorado, 2008.

———. *The Slippery Earth: Nahua-Christian Moral Dialogue in Sixteenth-Century Mexico*. Tuscon: University of Arizona Press, 1989.

Campbell, R. Joe. *A Morphological Dictionary of Classical Nahuatl: A Morpheme Index to the* Vocabulario en Lengua Mexicana y Castellana *of Fray Alonso De Molina*. Madison: Hispanic Seminary of Medieval Studies, 1985.

Carrasco, Davíd. *City of Sacrifice: The Aztec Empire and the Role of Violence in Civilization*. Boston: Beacon Press, 1999.

———. *Quetzalcoatl and the Irony of Empire: Myths and Prophecies in the Aztec Tradition*. Chicago: University of Chicago Press, 1982.

———. *Religions of Mesoamerica: Cosmovision and Ceremonial Centers*. Edited by H. Byron Earhart. Religious Traditions of the World Series. San Francisco: Harper, 1990.

———. "Spaniards as Gods: The Return of Quetzalcoatl." In *The History of the Conquest of New Spain by Bernal Díaz del Castillo*, edited by Davíd Carrasco, 466–473. Albuquerque: University of New Mexico Press, 2008.

Cervantes, Fernando. *The Devil in the New World: The Impact of Diabolism in New Spain*. New Haven: Yale University Press, 1994.

Chávez Balderas, Ximena. *Rituales funerarios en el Templo Mayor de Tenochtitlan*. Mexico City: Instituto Nacional de Antropología e Historia, 2007.

Clavijero, Francisco Xavier. *Reglas de la lengua mexicana con un vocabulario*. Mexico City: Universidad Nacional Autónoma de México, 1974.

Clayton, Mary L. "A Trilingual Spanish-Latin-Nahuatl Manuscript Dictionary Sometimes Attributed to Fray Bernardino De Sahagún." *International Journal of American Linguistics* 55, no. 4 (1989): 391–416.

Clendinnen, Inga. *Aztecs: An Interpretation*. Cambridge: Cambridge University Press, 1991.

Cline, Howard F. "Missing and Variant Prologues and Dedications in Sahagun's *Historia General*: Texts and English Translations." *Estudios de Cultura Nahuatl* 9 (1971): 237–251.

Codex Azcatitlan/El Códice Azcatitlan. Facsimile edition with commentary by Robert Barlow. *Journal de la Société des Américanistes* 37 (1949): 101–135, Atlas.

Codex Boturini/Códice Boturini. In *Antigüedades de México, basadas en la recopilación de Lord Kingsborough*, edited by José Corona Núñez, 2, part 1. Mexico City: Secretaría de Hacienda y Crédito Público, 1964.

Codrington, Robert Henry. *The Melanesians: Studies in Their Anthropology and Folklore*. Oxford, Clarendon Press, 1891.

Cortés, Hernán. *Hernán Cortés: Letters from Mexico*. Translated by Anthony Pagden. New Haven: Yale University Press, 1986.

Couch, N. C. Christopher. *The Festival Cycle of the Aztec Codex Borbonicus*. Oxford, England: B. A. R., 1985.

Davis, Richard. *Lives of Indian Images*. 2nd ed. Delhi, India: Motilal Banarsidass Publishers, 1999.

Dean, Carolyn. *A Culture of Stone: Inka Perspectives on Rock*. Durham and London: Duke University Press, 2010.

Dehouve, Danièle. *L'imaginaire des nombres chez les anciens Mexicains*. Rennes, France: Presses Universitaires de Rennes, 2011.

Díaz del Castillo, Bernal. *The Discovery and Conquest of Mexico*. Translated by A. P. Maudsley. New York: Farrar, Straus and Giroux, 1956.

DiCesare, Catherine. "History and Time in the Aztec 'Codex Borbonicus.'" Paper presented at the College Art Association annual meeting, Los Angeles, 2012.

———. *Sweeping the Way: Divine Transformation in the Aztec Festival of Ochpaniztli*. Boulder: University Press of Colorado, 2009.

Diehl, Richard A. "Previous Investigations at Tula." In *Tula of the Toltecs: Excavations and Survey*, ed. Dan M. Healan, 13–29. Iowa City: University of Iowa Press, 1989.

Doniger, Wendy. *Other Peoples' Myths: The Cave of Echoes*. New York: Macmillan, 1988.

Durán, Diego. *Book of the Gods and Rites and the Ancient Calendar*. Translated by Fernando Horcasitas and Doris Heyden. Norman: University of Oklahoma Press, 1971.

———. *Historia de las Indias de Nueva España e islas de la Tierra Firme [1581]*. Edited by Ángel Ma. Garibay K. 2 vols. Mexico City: Editorial Porrúa, 1967.

———. *The History of the Indies of New Spain*. Translated by Doris Heyden. Norman: University of Oklahoma Press, 1994.

———. "Ritos y fiestas de los antiguos mexicanos." Edited by César Macazaga Ordoño. Mexico City: Editorial Innovación, 1980.

Durkheim, Émile. *The Elementary Forms of Religious Life*. Translated by Karen E. Fields. New York: The Free Press, 1995.

Eck, Diana. *Darśan: Seeing the Divine Image in India*. 3rd ed. New York: Columbia University Press, 1988.

Eliade, Mircea. *The Sacred and the Profane: The Nature of Religion*. Translated by Willard R. Trask. San Diego: Harcourt, 1959.

Escalante Gonzalbo, Pablo. "The Painters of Sahagún's Manuscripts: Mediators between Two Worlds." In *Sahagún at 500: Essays on the Quincentenary of the Birth of Fr. Bernardino De Sahagún*, edited by John Frederick Schwaller, 167–191. Berkeley: Academy of American Franciscan History, 2003.

Flueckiger, Joyce Burkhalter. "Writing with Fragments and Silences: An Ethnographer's Anxiety and Responsibility." *Practical Matters* 6 (Spring 2013). http://www.practicalmattersjournal.org/issue/6/centerpieces/writing-with-fragments-and-silences.

Furst, Jill Leslie. "Skeletonization in Mixtec Art: A Reevaluation." In *The Art and Iconography of the Late Post-Classic Central Mexico*, edited by Elizabeth Hill Boone, 207–225. Washington, D.C.: Dumbarton Oaks, 1982.

García Icazbalceta, Joaquín, ed. *Historia de los mexicanos por sus pinturas*. Vol. 3. Mexico City: Salvador Chávez Hayhoe, 1941.

García Márquez, Gabriel. "Nobel Lecture: The Solitude of Latin America." http://nobelprize.org/nobel_prizes/literature/laureates/1982/marquez-lecture-e.html.

Garibay Kintana, Ángel María de. *Historia de la literatura náhuatl*. 2 vols. Mexico City: Editorial Porrúa, 1953.

Gell, Alfred. *Art and Agency: An Anthropological Theory*. Oxford: Clarendon Press, 1998.

———. "The Technology of Enchantment and the Enchantment of Technology." In *Anthropology, Art, and Aesthetics*, edited by Jeremy Coote and Anthony Shelton, 40–63. Oxford: Clarendon Press, 1992.

Gillespie, Susan D. *The Aztec Kings: The Construction of Rulership in Mexica History*. Tuscon: University of Arizona Press, 1989.

———. "Blaming Moteuczoma: Anthropomorphizing the Aztec Conquest." In *Invasion and Transformation: Interdisciplinary Perspectives on the Conquest of Mexico*, edited by Rebecca C. Brienen and Margaret A. Jackson, 25–56. Boulder: University Press of Colorado, 2008.

Gómez Martínez, Arturo. *Tlaneltokilli: La espiritualidad de los nahuas chicontepecanos*. Mexico City: Ediciones del Programa de Desarrollo Cultural de la Huasteca, 2002.

González de Lesur, Yolotl. "El dios Huitzilopochtli en la peregrinación mexica, de Aztlán a Tula." *Anales del Museo Nacional de Antropología* 19, no. 6 (1967): 175–190.

Gruzinski, Serge. *Man-Gods in the Mexican Highlands: Indian Power and Colonial Society, 1520–1800*. Translated by Eileen Corrigan. Stanford, CA: Stanford University Press, 1989.

Gutiérrez Solana, Nelly. "Xiuhcóatl tallada en piedra del Museum of Mankind, Londres." *Anales del Instituo de Investigaciones Estéticas* 12, no. 48 (1978): 5–18.

Haly, Richard. "Bare Bones: Rethinking Mesoamerican Divinity." *History of Religions* 31, no. 3 (1992): 269–304.

Hamann, Byron. "Chronological Pollution: Potsherds, Mosques, and Broken Gods before and after the Conquest of Mexico." *Current Anthropology* 49, no. 5 (2008): 803–836.

———. "Seeing and the Mixtec Screenfolds." *Visible Language* 38, no. 1 (2004): 68–111.

Harbottle, Garman, and Phil C. Weigand. "Turquoise in Pre-Columbian America." *Scientific American* (February 1992): 78–85.

Hassig, Ross. *Time, History and Belief in Aztec and Colonial Mexico*. Austin: University of Texas Press, 2001.

Healan, Dan M. "Tula, Tollan, and the Toltecs in Mesoamerican Prehistory." In *Tula of the Toltecs: Excavations and Survey*, edited by Dan M. Healan, 3–6. Iowa City: University of Iowa Press, 1989.

Hosler, Dorothy. "Sound, Color and Meaning in the Metallurgy of Ancient West Mexico." *World Archaeology* 27, no. 1 (1995): 100–115.

Houston, Stephen, David Stuart, and Karl Taube. *The Memory of Bones: Body, Being, and Experience among the Classic Maya*. Joe R. and Teresa Lozano Long Series in

Latin American and Latino Art and Culture. Austin: University of Texas Press, 2006.

Hughes, Jennifer. "Cradling the Sacred: Image, Ritual, and Affect in Mexico Material Religion." *History of Religions* (under revision).

———. "Mysterium Materiae: Vital Matter and the Object as Evidence in the Study of Religion." *Bulletin for the Study of Religion* 41, no. 4 (2012): 16–24.

Hvidtfeldt, Arild. *Teotl and *Ixiptlatli: Some Central Conceptions in Ancient Mexican Religion, with a General Introduction on Cult and Myth*. Copenhagen: Munksgaard, 1958.

Izeki, Mutsumi. *Conceptualization of 'Xihuitl': History, Environment and Cultural Dynamics in Postclassic Mexica Cognition*. Bar International Series. Oxford, England: Archaeopress, 2008.

Johansson K., Patrick. "Teoxihuitl: Turquoise in Aztec Thought and Poetry." In *Turquoise in Mexico and North America: Science, Conservation, Culture and Collections*, edited by J. C. H. King, Max Carocci, Caroline Cartwright, Colin McEwan, and Rebecca Stacey, 135–144. London: Archetype Publications, 2012.

Karttunen, Frances. *An Analytical Dictionary of Nahuatl*. Norman: University of Oklahoma Press, 1983.

Katzew, Ilona. *Casta Painting: Images of Race in Eighteenth-Century Mexico*. New Haven: Yale University Press, 2004.

Keane, Webb. *Christian Moderns: Freedom and Fetish in the Mission Encounter*. Berkeley: University of California Press, 2007.

Keen, Benjamin. *The Aztec Image in Western Thought*. New Brunswick, NJ: Rutgers University Press, 1971. Reprint, 1990.

Keesing, Roger M. "Rethinking *Mana*." *Journal of Anthropological Research* 40, no. 1 (1984): 137–156.

Kidwell, Clara Sue. "Systems of Knowledge." In *America in 1492: The World of the Indian Peoples before the Arrival of Columbus*, edited by Alvin M. Josephy Jr., 369–403. New York: Knopf, 1992.

King, J. C. H., Max Carocci, Caroline Cartwright, Colin McEwan, and Rebecca Stacey, eds. *Turquoise in Mexico and North America: Science, Conservation, Culture and Collections*. London: Archetype Publications, 2012.

Kirchhoff, Paul. Review of *Teotl and *Ixiptlatli: Some Central Conceptions in Ancient Mexican Religion, with a General Introduction on Cult and Myth* by Arild Hvidtfeldt. *American Antiquity* 25, no. 3 (1960): 438–439.

Klein, Cecelia F. "The Devil and the Skirt: An Iconographic Inquiry into the Pre-Hispanic Nature of the *tzitzimime*." *Ancient Mesoamerica* 11, no. 1 (January 2000): 1–26.

———. "The Shield Women: Resolution of an Aztec Gender Paradox." In *Current Topics in Aztec Studies: Essays in Honor of Dr. H. B. Nicholson*, edited by Alana Cordy-Collins and Douglas Sharon, 39–64. San Diego, CA: San Diego Museum, 1993.

———. "Teocuitlatl, 'Divine Excrement': The Significance of 'Holy Shit' in Ancient Mexico." *Art Journal* (Fall 1993): 20–27.

Klor de Alva, J. Jorge. *Spiritual Warfare in Mexico: Christianity and the Aztecs.* Vol. 1. Santa Cruz: University of California Santa Cruz, 1980.

Kubler, George, and Charles Gibson. *The Tovar Calendar: An Illustrated Mexican Manuscript ca. 1585.* Vol. 11. New Haven: Connecticut Academy of Arts and Sciences and Yale University Press, 1951.

Lacadena, Alfonso. "Regional Scribal Traditions: Methodological Implications for the Decipherment of Nahuatl Writing." *The PARI Journal* 8, no. 4 (2008): 1–22.

Landa, Diego de. *Account of the Affairs of Yucatán.* Translated by A. R. Pagden. Chicago: J. Philip O'Hara, 1975.

Las Casas, Bartolomé de. *Apologética historia sumaria: Cuanto a las cualidades, dispusición, descripción, cielo y suelo destas tierras, y condiciones naturales, policías, repúblicas, manera de vivir e costumbres de las gentes destas Indias occidentales y meridionales cuyo imperio soberano pertenece a los reyes de Castilla.* Edited by Edmundo O'Gorman. 2 vols. Mexico City: Instituto de Investigaciones Históricas, UNAM, 1967.

Latour, Bruno. *On the Modern Cult of the Factish Gods.* Durham: Duke University Press, 2010.

León-Portilla, Miguel. *Bernardino de Sahagún: First Anthropologist.* Norman: University of Oklahoma Press, 2002.

———. "Bernardino de Sahagún: Pioneer of Anthropology." In *Sahagún at 500: Essays on the Quincentenary of the Birth of Fr. Bernardino de Sahagún,* edited by John Frederick Schwaller, 1–10. Berkeley, CA: Academy of American Franciscan History, 2003.

———. "Estudio preliminar." In *Vocabulario en lengua castellana y mexicana y mexicana y castellana.* Mexico City: Editorial Porrúa, 1970. 5th reprint.

———. "Have We Really Translated the Mesoamerican 'Ancient Word'?" In *On the Translation of Native American Literatures,* edited by Brian Swann, 313–338. Washington, D.C.: Smithsonian Institution Press, 1992.

Lockhart, James. *The Nahuas after the Conquest: A Social and Cultural History of the Indians of Central Mexico, Sixteenth through Eighteenth Centuries.* Stanford, CA: Stanford University Press, 1992.

———. *Nahuatl as Written: Lessons in Older Written Nahuatl, with Copious Examples and Texts.* Edited by James Lockhart and Rebecca Horn. Nahuatl Studies Series. Stanford, CA: Stanford University Press and UCLA Latin American Center Publications, 2001.

———, ed. *We People Here: Nahuatl Accounts of the Conquest of Mexico.* Edited by Geoffrey Symcox. Vol. 1, Repertorium Columbianum. Berkeley: University of California Press, 1993.

López Austin, Alfredo. *Hombre-Dios: Religión y política en el mundo náhuatl.* 3rd ed. Serie de Cultura Náhuatl. Mexico City: Universidad Nacional Autónoma de México, 1998. Originally published 1973.

———. *The Human Body and Ideology: Concepts of the Ancient Nahuas.* Vol. 1. Translated by Thelma Ortiz de Montellano and Bernard R. Ortiz de Montellano. Salt Lake City: University of Utah Press, 1988.

———. *Los mitos del tlacuache: Caminos de la mitología mesoamericana*. 5th ed. Mexico City: Universidad Nacional Autónoma de México and Instituto de Investigaciones Antropológicas, 2003.

———. *The Myths of the Opossum: Pathways of Mesoamerican Mythology*. Translated by Bernard R. Ortiz de Montellano and Thelma Ortiz de Montellano. Albuquerque: University of New Mexico Press, 1990.

———. *Tamoanchan, Tlalocan: Places of Mist*. Translated by Bernard R. Ortiz de Montellano and Thelma Ortiz de Montellano. Boulder: University Press of Colorado, 1997.

———. *Una vieja historia de la mierda*. Mexico City: Ediciones Toledo, 1988.

López Austin, Alfredo, and Leonardo López Luján. "Aztec Human Sacrifice." In *The Aztec World*, edited by Elizabeth M. Brumfiel and Gary F. Feinman, 137–152. New York and Chicago: Abrams and The Field Museum, 2008.

López de Gómara, Francisco. *La conquista de México*. Edited by José Luis de Rojas. Madrid: Historia 16, 1987.

López Luján, Leonardo. *The Offerings of the Templo Mayor of Tenochtitlan*. Translated by Bernard R. Ortiz de Montellano and Thelma Ortiz de Montellano. Albuquerque: University of New Mexico Press, 2005.

MacLaury, Robert E. *Color and Cognition in Mesoamerica: Constructing Categories as Vantages*. Austin: University of Texas Press, 1997.

Maffie, James. "The Centrality of Nepantla in Conquest-Era Nahua Philosophy." *The Nahua Newsletter 77* (2007): 11–31.

Magaloni Kerpel, Diana. "Painting a New Era: Conquest, Prophecy, and the World to Come." In *Invasion and Transformation: Interdisciplinary Perspectives on the Conquest of Mexico*, edited by Rebecca P. Brienen and Margaret A. Jackson, 125–149. Boulder: University Press of Colorado, 2008.

Martínez González, Roberto. *El nahualismo*. Mexico City: Universidad Nacional Autónoma de México, 2011.

Mason, Alden J. "Mirrors of Ancient America." *The Museum Journal* (Philadelphia) 18, no. 2 (1927): 201–209.

Mauss, Marcel. *The Gift: The Form and Reason for Exchange in Archaic Societies*. Translated by W. D. Halls. New York: W. W. Norton, 1990.

McEwan, Colin, Andrew Middleton, Caroline Cartwright, and Rebecca Stacey. *Turquoise Mosaics from Mexico*. Durham: Duke University Press, 2006.

Medina Hernández, Andrés. "La cosmovisión nahua actual." In *La religión de los pueblos nahuas*, edited by Silvia Limón Olvera, 193–218. Madrid: Editorial Trotta, 2008.

Meehan, Patricia, and Valerie Magar. "Conservation of a Turquoise Mosaic Disk from Tula, Mexico." In *Turquoise in Mexico and North America: Science, Conservation, Culture and Collections*, edited by J. C. H. King, Max Carocci, Caroline Cartwright, Colin McEwan, and Rebecca Stacey, 41–54. London: Archetype Publications, 2012.

Mendieta, Gerónimo de. *Historia eclesiástica indiana*. Edited by Joaquín García Icazbalceta. Mexico City: Porrúa, 1980.

Mengin, Ernst. "Commentaire du Codex Mexicanus nos. 23–24 de la Bibliothèque Nationale de Paris." *Journal de la Société des Américanistes* 41, no. 2 (1952): 367–498. (A
facsimile of the codex was also published as a supplement to the journal.)

Miller, Mary Ellen. *The Art of Mesoamerica: From Olmec to Aztec*. London: Thames
and Hudson, 1996.

Miller, Mary, and Karl Taube. *An Illustrated Dictionary of the Gods and Symbols of Ancient Mexico and the Maya*. London: Thames and Hudson, 1993.

Molina, Alonso de. *Vocabulario en lengua castellana y mexicana y mexicana y castellana* (1571). Mexico City: Editorial Porrúa, 2004. 5th reprint.

Muñoz Camargo, Diego. *Historia de Tlaxcala (Ms. 210 de la Biblioteca Nacional de
París)*. Edited by Luis Reyes García and Javier Lira Toledo. Tlaxcala: Gobierno del
Estado de Tlaxcala and the Centro de Investigaciones y Estudios Superiores en
Antropología Social, Universidad Autónoma de Tlaxcala, 1998.

Nagao, Debra. *Mexica Buried Offerings: A Historical and Contextual Analysis*. Vol. 235,
Bar International Series. Oxford: B.A.R., 1985.

"Nahuatl Dictionary." In *The Wired Humanities Project*, edited by Stephanie Wood.
University of Oregon, 2012. http://whp.uoregon.edu/dictionaries/nahuatl/.

Navarrete Linares, Federico. "Las fuentes indígenas más allá de la dicotomía entre historia y mito." *Estudios de Cultura Náhuatl* 30 (1999): 231–256.

———. *Los orígenes de los pueblos indígenas del Valle de México*. Mexico City: Universidad Nacional Autónoma de México, 2011.

Nicholson, H. B. "Preclassic Mesoamerican Iconography from the Perspective of the
Postclassic: Problems in Interpretational Analysis." In *Origins of Religious Art and
Iconography in Preclassic Mesoamerica*, edited by H. B. Nicholson, 158–175. Los An-
geles: UCLA Latin American Center Publications and Ethnic Arts Council of Los
Angeles, 1976.

———. "Religion in Pre-Hispanic Central Mexico." In *Handbook of Middle American
Indians: Archaeology of Northern Mesoamerica, Part One*, edited by Gordon F. Eck-
holm and Ignacio Bernal, 395–446. Austin: University of Texas Press, 1971.

———. *The "Return of Quetzalcoatl": Did It Play a Role in the Conquest of Mexico?* Lan-
caster, CA: Labyrinthos, 2001.

Nicholson, H. B., and Eloise Quiñones Keber. *Art of Aztec Mexico: Treasures of Tenochtitlan*. Washington, D.C.: National Gallery of Art, 1983.

Obeyesekere, Gananath. *The Apotheosis of Captain Cook: European Mythmaking in the
Pacific*. Princeton: Princeton University Press, 1997.

Olivier, Guilhem. *Mockeries and Metamorphoses of an Aztec God: Tezcatlipoca, "Lord
of the Smoking Mirror."* Translated by Michel Besson. Edited by Davíd Carrasco and
Eduardo Matos Moctezuma. Boulder: University Press of Colorado, 2003.

———. "Sacred Bundles and the Coronation of the Aztec King in Mexico-Tenochtit-
lan." In *Sacred Bundles: Ritual Acts of Wrapping and Binding in Mesoamerica*, edited

by Julia Guernsey and F. Kent Reilly, 199–225. Barnardsville, N.C.: Boundary End Archaeology Research Center, 2006.

———. *Tezcatlipoca: Burlas y metamorfosis de un dios azteca*. Mexico City: Fondo de Cultura Económica, 2004.

Olivier, Guilhem, and Leonardo López Luján. "Images of Moctezuma and His Symbols of Power." In *Moctezuma: Aztec Ruler*, edited by Colin McEwan and Leonardo López Luján, 78–91. London: British Museum, 2009.

Olko, Justyna. *Turquoise Diadems and Staffs of Office: Elite Costume and Insignia of Power in Aztec and Early Colonial Mexico*. Warsaw: Polish Society for Latin American Studies and Centre for Studies on the Classical Tradition, University of Warsaw, 2005.

Pagden, Anthony. "Introduction." In *Hernán Cortés: Letters from Mexico*, xxxix–lxxi. New Haven: Yale University Press, 2001.

Paso y Troncoso, Francisco del. *Descripción, historia y exposición del Códice Pictórico de los antiguos nahuas que se conserva en la Biblioteca de la Cámara de Diputados de Paris (Antiguo Palais Bourbon)*. Florence, Italy: Tip de Salvador Landi, 1898.

Pasztory, Esther. *Aztec Art*. Norman: University of Oklahoma Press, 1983.

Patton, Kimberley C. *Religion of the Gods: Ritual, Paradox, and Reflexivity*. London: Oxford University Press, 2009.

Peirce, Charles S. *The Writings of Charles S. Peirce: A Chronological Edition*. Vol. 2 of 8 vols. Edited by Peirce Edition Project. Bloomington: Indiana University Press, 1984.

Pereira, Grégory. "The Utilization of Grooved Human Bones: A Reanalysis of Artificially Modified Human Bones Excavated by Carl Lumholtz at Zacapu, Michoacán, Mexico." *Latin American Antiquity* 16, no. 3 (2005): 293–312.

Peterson, Jeanette F. "Perceiving Blackness, Envisioning Power: Chalma and Black Christs in Colonial Mexico." In *Seeing Across Cultures in the Early Modern World*, edited by Dana Leibsohn and Jeanette F. Peterson, 49–72. New York: Ashgate, 2012.

Pohl, John M. D. *The Politics of Symbolism in the Mixtec Codices*. Nashville, TN: Vanderbilt University Publications in Anthropology, 1994.

Pohl, John M. D., and Claire L. Lyons, eds. *The Aztec Pantheon and the Art of Empire*. Los Angeles: J. Paul Getty Museum, 2010.

Pomar, Juan Bautista de. "Relación de Tezcoco." In *Relaciones geográficas del siglo XVI: México*, edited by Réne Acuña, 23–113. Mexico City: Instituto de Investigaciones Antropológicas, UNAM, 1986.

Pratt, Mary Louise. *Imperial Eyes: Travel Writing and Transculturation*. London: Routledge, 1992.

Prem, Hanns J. "Aztec Hieroglyphic Writing System—Possibilities and Limits." *Proceedings of the 38th International Congress of Americanists* (Stutgart-Munich) 12–18 (August 1968), 2:159–165.

Ranere, Anthony J., Dolores R. Piperno, Irene Holst, Ruth Dickau, José Iriarte, and Jeremy A. Sabloff. "The Cultural and Chronological Context of Early Holocene Maize and Squash Domestication in the Central Balsas River Valley, Mexico." *Proceed-*

ings of the National Academy of Sciences of the United States of America 106, no. 13 (2009): 5014–5018.

Rao, Ida Giovanna. "Florentine Codex." In *Aztecs*, edited by Eduardo Matos Moctezuma and Felipe Solís Olguín, 487–488. London: Royal Academy of Arts, 2002.

Read, Kay. "Sacred Commoners: The Notion of Cosmic Powers in Mexica Rulership." *History of Religions* 34, no. 1 (1994): 39–69.

———. "Sun and Earth Rulers: What the Eye Cannot See in Mesoamerica." *History of Religions* 34, no. 4 (1995): 351–384.

———. *Time and Sacrifice in the Aztec Cosmos*. 2nd ed. Bloomington: Indiana University Press, 1998.

Ricoeur, Paul. *Hermeneutics and the Human Sciences: Essays on Language, Action, and Interpretation*. Translated by John B. Thompson. Cambridge: Maison des Sciences de l'Homme and Cambridge University Press, 1981.

Ruiz de Alarcón, Hernando. *Treatise on the Heathen Superstitions That Today Live among the Indians Native to This New Spain, 1629*. Translated by J. Richard Andrews and Ross Hassig. The Civilization of the American Indian Series. Norman: University of Oklahoma Press, 1984.

Russo, Alessandra. "Cortés's Objects and the Idea of New Spain." *Journal of the History of Collections* 23, no. 2 (2011): 229–252.

———. "Plumes of Sacrifice: Transformations in Sixteenth-Century Mexican Feather Art." *RES* 42 (Autumn 2002): 227–250.

Sahagún, Bernardino de. *Conquest of New Spain: 1585 Revision*. Translated by Howard F. Cline. Salt Lake City: University of Utah Press, 1989.

———. *Florentine Codex: General History of the Things of New Spain: Book 1: The Gods*. Translated by Arthur J. O. Anderson and Charles E. Dibble. Vol. 2 of 12 vols. Santa Fe, NM: The School of American Research and the University of Utah, 1970.

———. *Florentine Codex: General History of the Things of New Spain: Book 2: The Ceremonies*. Translated by Arthur J. O. Anderson and Charles E. Dibble. Vol. 3 of 12 vols. Santa Fe, NM: The School of American Research and the University of Utah, 1981.

———. *Florentine Codex: General History of the Things of New Spain: Book 3: The Origin of the Gods*. Translated by Arthur J. O. Anderson and Charles E. Dibble. Vol. 4 of 12 vols. Santa Fe, NM: The School of American Research and the University of Utah, 1978.

———. *Florentine Codex: General History of the Things of New Spain: Book 4: The Soothsayers and Book 5: The Omens*. Translated by Charles E. Dibble and Arthur J. O. Anderson. Vol. 5 of 12 vols. Santa Fe, NM: The School of American Research and the University of Utah, 1979.

———. *Florentine Codex: General History of the Things of New Spain: Book 6: Rhetoric and Moral Philosophy*. Translated by Charles E. Dibble and Arthur J. O. Anderson. Vol. 6 of 12 vols. Santa Fe, NM: The School of American Research and the University of Utah, 1969.

———. *Florentine Codex: General History of the Things of New Spain: Book 7: The Sun, Moon, and Stars, and the Binding of the Years*. Translated by Arthur J. O. Anderson and Charles E. Dibble. Vol. 7 of 12 vols. Santa Fe, NM: The School of American Research and the University of Utah, 1953.

———. *Florentine Codex: General History of the Things of New Spain: Book 8: Kings and Lords*. Translated by Arthur J. O. Anderson and Charles E. Dibble. Vol. 8 of 12 vols. Santa Fe, NM: The School of American Research and the University of Utah, 1979.

———. *Florentine Codex: General History of the Things of New Spain: Book 9: The Merchants*. Translated by Charles E. Dibble and Arthur J. O. Anderson. Vol. 9 of 12 vols. Santa Fe, NM: The School of American Research and the University of Utah, 1959.

———. *Florentine Codex: General History of the Things of New Spain: Book 10: The People*. Translated by Charles E. Dibble and Arthur J. O. Anderson. Vol. 10 of 12 vols. Santa Fe, NM: The School of American Research and the University of Utah, 1961.

———. *Florentine Codex: General History of the Things of New Spain: Book 11: Earthly Things*. Translated by Charles E. Dibble and Arthur J. O. Anderson. Vol. 11 of 12 vols. Santa Fe, NM: The School of American Research and the University of Utah, 1963.

———. *Florentine Codex: General History of the Things of New Spain: Book 12: The Conquest*. Translated by Arthur J. O. Anderson and Charles E. Dibble. Vol. 12 of 12 vols. Santa Fe, NM: The School of American Research and the University of Utah, 1975.

———. *Florentine Codex: General History of the Things of New Spain: Introductions and Indices*. Translated by Arthur J. O. Anderson and Charles E. Dibble. Vol. 1 of 12 vols. Santa Fe, NM: The School of American Research and the University of Utah, 1982.

———. *Historia general de las cosas de Nueva España*. Edited by Alfredo López Austin and Josefina García Quintana. 2 vols. Madrid: Alianza Editorial, 1988.

Sahagún, Bernardino de, Thelma Sullivan, and H. B. Nicholson. *Primeros memoriales*. The Civilization of the American Indian Series. Norman: University of Oklahoma Press, 1997.

Sahlins, Marshall David. *How "Natives" Think: About Captain Cook, For Example*. Chicago: University of Chicago Press, 1995.

Sandstrom, Alan R. *Corn Is Our Blood*. Norman: University of Oklahoma Press, 1992.

Saunders, Nicholas J. "Biographies of Brilliance: Pearls, Transformations of Matter and Being, c. AD 1492." *World Archaeology* 31, no. 2 (1999): 243–257.

———. "'Catching the Light': Technologies of Power and Enchantment in Pre-Columbian Goldworking." In *Gold and Power in Ancient Costa Rica, Panama, and Colombia*, edited by Jeffrey Quilter and John W. Hoopes. Washington, D.C.: Dumbarton Oaks Research Library and Collection, 2003.

———. "Chatoyer: Anthropological Reflections on Archaeological Materials." In *Recent Studies in Pre-Columbian Archaeology*, edited by Nicholas J. Saunders and Oliver de Montmollin, 1–40. Oxford, England: B.A.R. International Series, 1988.

———. "A Dark Light: Reflections on Obsidian in Mesoamerica." *World Archaeology* 33, no. 2 (2001): 220–236.

———. "Stealers of Light, Traders in Brilliance: Amerindian Metaphysics in the Mirror of the Conquest." *RES: Anthropology and Aesthetics* 33, no. 1 (1998): 225–252.

Schroeder, Susan. "The Truth about the *Crónica Mexicayotl*." *Colonial Latin American Review* 20, no. 2 (2011): 233–247.

Schroeder, Susan, Anne J. Cruz, Cristián Roa de la Carrera, and David E. Tavárez, eds. and trans. *Chimalpahin's Conquest: A Nahua Historian's Rewriting of Francisco López de Gómara's* La conquista de México. Stanford, CA: Stanford University Press, 2010.

Schwaller, John F. "The Expansion of Nahuatl as a Lingua Franca among Priests in Sixteenth-Century Mexico." *Ethnohistory* 59, no. 4 (2012): 675–690.

Seler, Eduard. "The Character of Aztec and Maya Manuscripts." In *Collected Works in Mesoamerican Linguistics and Archaeology*, edited by J. Eric S. Thompson and Frances B. Richardson, 113–118. Los Angeles: Labyrinthos, 1990.

———. *Gesammelte Abhandlungen zur Amerikanische Sprach- und Alterthumskunde.* Vol. 2 of 5 vols. Berlin: E. Asher, 1902–1923.

Sepúlveda y Herrera, María Teresa, ed. *Procesos por idolatría al cacique, gobernadores y sacerdotes de Yanhuitlán, 1544–1546.* Mexico City: Insituto Nacional de Antropología e Historia, 1999.

Silko, Leslie Marmon. *Ceremony.* New York: Penguin Books, 1986.

Siméon, Rémi. *Diccionario de la lengua náhuatl o mexicana.* Translated by Josefina Olivia de Coll. 1st Spanish ed. of *Dictionnaire de la langue nahuatl ou mexicaine.* Mexico City: Siglo Vientiuno Editores, 1977.

Smith, Jonathan Z. *Drudgery Divine: On the Comparison of Early Christianities of Late Antiquity.* Edited by William Scott Green. Chicago Studies in the History of Judaism. Chicago: University of Chicago Press, 1990.

Smith, Michael E. "The Archaeology of Tezcatlipoca." Version of 9/13/2007. http://www.public.asu.edu/~mesmith9/1-CompleteSet/0-Tez-MES-Full.pdf.

Solís, Felipe. "Head of Coyolxauhqui." In *Aztecs*, edited by Eduardo Matos Moctezuma and Felipe Solís Olguín, 304 and 464. London: Royal Academy of Arts, 2002.

Stone, Rebecca. *The Jaguar Within: Shamanic Trance in Ancient Central and South American Art.* Joe R. And Teresa Lozano Long Series in Latin American and Latino Art and Culture. Austin: University of Texas Press, 2011.

Stuart, David. "Kings of Stone: A Consideration of Stelae in Ancient Maya Ritual and Representation." *RES: Anthropology and Aesthetics*, no. 29/30 (1996): 148–171.

Taube, Karl A. "The Symbolism of Turquoise in Ancient Mesoamerica." In *Turquoise in Mexico and North America: Science, Conservation, Culture and Collections*, edited by J. C. H. King, Max Carocci, Caroline Cartwright, Colin McEwan, and Rebecca Stacey, 117–134. London: Archetype Publications, 2012.

Taussig, Michael. *Defacement: Public Secrecy and the Labor of the Negative.* Stanford, CA: Stanford University Press, 1999.

Tavárez, David. *The Invisible War: Indigenous Devotions, Discipline, and Dissent in Colonial Mexico.* Stanford, CA: Stanford University Press, 2011.

Taylor, Diana. *The Archive and the Repertoire: Performing Cultural Memory in the Americas.* Durham: Duke University Press, 2005.

Taylor, John H. *Death and the Afterlife in Ancient Egypt*. Chicago: University of Chicago Press, 2001.

Terraciano, Kevin. "Three Texts in One: Book XII of the Florentine Codex." *Ethnohistory* 57, no. 1 (2010): 51–72.

Thibodeau, Alyson M., John T. Chesley, Joaquín Ruiz, David J. Killick, and Arthur Vokes. "An Alternative Approach to the Prehispanic Turquoise Trade." In *Turquoise in Mexico and North America: Science, Conservation, Culture and Collections*, edited by J. C. H. King, Max Carocci, Caroline Cartwright, Colin McEwan, and Rebecca Stacey, 65–74. London: Archetype Publications, 2012.

Thouvenot, Marc. *Chalchihuitl: Le Jade chez les Aztèques*. Vol. XXI, Mémoires de l'Institut d'ethnologie. Paris: Institut d'ethnologie, 1982.

Todorov, Tzvetan. *The Conquest of America: The Question of the Other*. Translated by Richard Howard. Norman: University of Oklahoma Press, 1999.

Townsend, Camilla. "Burying the White Gods: New Perspectives on the Conquest of Mexico." *American Historical Review* 108, no. 3 (2003): 659–687.

———. "No One Said It Was Quetzalcoatl: Listening to the Indians in the Conquest of Mexico." *History Compass* 1, no. 1 (2003): 1–14.

Townsend, Richard F. *State and Cosmos in the Art of Tenochtitlan*. Studies in Pre-Columbian Art and Archaeology. Washington, D.C.: Dumbarton Oaks, Trustees for Harvard University, 1979.

Tregear, Edward. *The Maori Race*. Wanganui, NZ: A. D. Willis, 1904.

Trouillot, Michel-Rolph. *Silencing the Past: Power and the Production of History*. Boston: Beacon Press, 1997.

Tylor, Edward B. *Primitive Culture: Researches into the Development of Mythology, Philosophy, Religion, Art and Custom*. Vol. 2 of 2 vols. New York: Harper and Row, 1958.

Umberger, Emily. "Coyolxauhqui's Body." Paper presented at a meeting of the Society of American Anthropology, Vancouver, Canada, 2008.

Urton, Gary. *The History of a Myth*. Austin: University of Texas Press, 1990.

van der Loo, Peter L. "Codices, Customs, Continuity: A Study of Mesoamerican Religion." PhD diss., Universiteit Leiden, 2005.

Viveiros de Castro, Eduardo. "Cosmological Deixis and Amerindian Perspectivism." *The Journal of the Royal Anthropological Institute* 4, no. 3 (1998): 469–488.

———. "Exchanging Perspectives: The Transformation of Objects into Subjects in Amerindian Ontologies." *Common Knowledge* 10, no. 3 (2004): 463–484.

Vokes, Arthur W., and David A. Gregory. "Exchange Networks for Exotic Goods in the Southwest and Zuni's Place in Them." In *Zuni Origins: Toward a New Synthesis of Southwestern Archaeology*, edited by David A. Gregory and David R. Wilcox, 319–357. Tuscon: University of Arizona Press, 2007.

Wagoner, Roy. "Mana." In *Encyclopedia of Religion*, edited by Lindsay Jones, 5631–5633. Detroit: Macmillan Reference USA, 2005.

Wake, Eleanor. "Contact: Indo-Christian Art." In *Aztecs*, edited by Eduardo Matos Moctezuma and Felipe Solís Olguín, 343–358. London: Royal Academy of Arts, 2002.

Weigand, Phil C. "Observations on Ancient Mining within the Northwest Regions of the Mesoamerican Civilization, with Emphasis on Turquoise." In *In Quest of Mineral Wealth: Aboriginal and Colonial Mining and Metallurgy in Spanish America*, edited by Alan K. Craig and Robert C. West, 21–35. Baton Rouge: Louisiana State University Press, 1994.

Weigand, Phil C., and Garman Harbottle. "The Role of Turquoises in the Ancient Mesoamerican Trade Structure." In *The American Southwest and Mesoamerica: Systems of Prehistoric Exchange*, edited by Jonathon E. Ericson and Timothy G Baugh, 159–178. New York: Plenum Press, 1993.

Weigand, Phil C., Garman Harbottle, and Edward V. Sayre. "Turquoise Sources and Source Analysis: Mesoamerica and the Southwestern U.S.A." In *Exchange Systems in Prehistory*, edited by Timothy K. Earle and Jonathon E. Ericson, 15–34. New York: Academic Press, 1977.

West, Robert C. "Aboriginal Metallurgy and Metalworking in Spanish America: A Brief Overview." In *In Quest of Mineral Wealth: Aboriginal and Colonial Mining and Metallurgy in Spanish America*, edited by Alan K. Craig and Robert C. West, 5–20. Baton Rouge: Louisiana State University Press, 1994.

Yoon, Carol Kaesuk. *Naming Nature: The Clash between Instinct and Science*. New York: W. W. Norton, 2009.

Young, Otis E. "Black Legends and Silver Mountains: Spanish Mining in Colonial Spanish America Reconsidered." In *In Quest of Mineral Wealth: Aboriginal and Colonial Mining and Metallurgy in Spanish America*, edited by Alan K. Craig and Robert C. West, 109–118. Baton Rouge: Louisiana State University Press, 1994.

Zamora, Lois Parkinson. *The Inordinate Eye: New World Baroque and Latin American Fiction*. Chicago: University of Chicago Press, 2006.

Zedeño, María Neves. "Bundled Worlds: The Roles and Interactions of Complex Objects from the North American Plains." *Journal of Archaeological Method and Theory* 15 (2008): 362–378.

INDEX >>>

www.ingramcontent.com/pod-product-compliance
Lightning Source LLC
Chambersburg PA
CBHW070608270326
41926CB00013B/2456